A POPULAR SURVEY OF THE NEW TESTAMENT

A POPULAR SURVEY OF THE NEW TESTAMENT

NORMAN L. GEISLER

BakerBooks
Grand Rapids, Michigan

Published by Baker Books
a division of Baker Publishing Group
P.O. Box 6287, Grand Rapids, MI 49516-6287
www.bakerbooks.com

Design copyright © 2007 Lion Hudson/
Tim Dowley Associates

All photographs by kind permission of Scott
Matscherz, Joseph M. Holden (WhenTheyAsk.
com), and Tim Dowley Associates Ltd.

Library of Congress Cataloging-in-
Publication Data is on file at the Library of
Congress, Washington, DC.

ISBN 10: 0-8010-1299-6 (cloth)
ISBN: 978-0-8010-1299-0 (cloth)

Worldwide co-edition produced by
Lion Hudson plc,
Wilkinson House,
Jordan Hill Road,
Oxford OX2 8DR, England
Tel: +44 (0) 1865 302750
Fax: +44 (0) 1865 302757
Email: coed@lionhudson.com
www.lionhudson.com

Printed in Singapore

1 2 3 4 5 6 7 8 9

Contents

Illustrations

Maps

1
A Christ-Centered Introduction to the Bible

Introduction

Jesus said five times that he was the theme of the entire Bible. Once is enough to draw our attention to the fact, and five times makes it an important teaching of our Lord.

> Matthew 5:17—"Do not think that I came to destroy the Law or the Prophets. I did not come to destroy but to fulfill."
>
> Luke 24:27—"And beginning at Moses and all the Prophets, He expounded to them in all the Scriptures the things concerning Himself."
>
> Luke 24:44—"All things must be fulfilled which were written in the Law of Moses and the Prophets and the Psalms concerning me."
>
> John 5:39—"You search the Scriptures, for in them you think you have eternal life; and these are they which testify of me."
>
> Hebrews 10:7—"Behold, I have come—in the volume of the book it is written of Me—to do Your will, O God."

Of course the New Testament was not yet written when Jesus uttered these words. However, most people have no problem understanding that Jesus is the theme of the New Testament.

> In the *Gospels*—Jesus is the *prophet* to his people.
>
> In *Acts* and *the Epistles*—Jesus is the *priest* for his people.
>
> In the *book of Revelation*—Jesus is the *King* over his people.

But what about the Old Testament? It is not clear to all that the entire Old Testament is about Christ. This will become more evident as the next

Jesus Is the Theme of Both Testaments

In the Old Testament	In the New Testament
Anticipation of Christ	Realization of Christ
He is coming	He has arrived
He is prophesied	He is present
He is contained	He is explained
He is enfolded	He is unfolded
He is in shadow	He is in substance
He is found in type	He is found in truth

three points unfold. First of all, Jesus is the theme of both Testaments (see box above).

St. Augustine put it succinctly: "The New is in the Old concealed; the Old is in the New revealed."[1] Christ is *implicit* in the Old and *explicit* in the New. In the Old Testament the Rose of Sharon is just budding, but in the New Testament it is in full bloom. The whole Bible is all about Jesus.

Jesus in Every Section of the Bible

The Bible is divided into eight major sections: four in the Old and four in the New. In each Old Testament section there is a different direction.

1. Law—Downward Look

There are five books of the Law (Genesis, Exodus, Leviticus, Numbers, and Deuteronomy). In these books God moves down into human history by choosing a nation (Genesis), redeeming them (Exodus), sanctifying them (Leviticus), guiding them (Numbers), and instructing them (Deuteronomy).

2. History—Outward Look

In the next twelve books of the Old Testament there is an outward look. Moses brought Israel out of bondage, but Joshua took them into the blessing of the Promised Land. God had to get the Holy Nation into the Holy Land so they could bring forth the Holy Son of God (the Savior) and the Holy Word of God (the Scriptures). In Joshua they *possessed* the land; in Judges they were *oppressed* by the people of the land. Ruth is a *lily* in contrast to the mud pond of Judges. It is a story of faithfulness in a day of unfaithfulness. In 1 Samuel the nation is *established* under Saul (the people's choice). In 2 Samuel the nation is *expanded* under David (God's choice). In 1 Kings the nation is *declining* because of polygamy, idolatry, and disunity. In 2 Kings the nation is *deported*, the northern ten tribes going into Assyria in 722 BC and the southern two tribes (Judah and Benjamin) going into captivity under Babylon in 605 BC. In Ezra the remnant of the nation is *returned*, in Nehemiah they are *rebuilt*, and in

Figure 1.1
Biblical Bookshelf

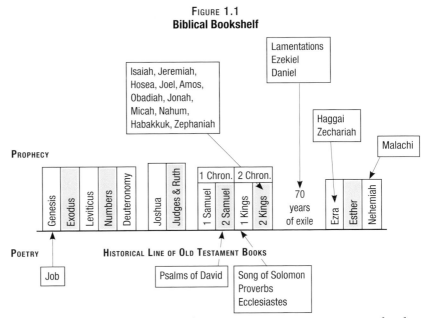

Esther they are *protected*. Thus the messianic nation returns to its land and begins to rebuild, preparing for the coming Messiah.

3. Poetry—Upward Look

By the end of the historical books (Nehemiah) we are at the end of the Old Testament at about 400 BC. So all the poetic and prophetic books fit back into this historical structure. This can be illustrated by a biblical bookshelf (see above).

The poetic books show the aspiration of the nation for Christ in spiritual and moral matters. In Job the aspiration is for *mediation* (see 9:33), of which Christ is the ultimate fulfillment (1 Tim. 2:5). In Psalms the aspiration is for *communion* with God, which is also fulfilled in Christ who taught us to pray (Matt. 6:5–15). Proverbs manifests the aspiration for *wisdom*, which Christ personified for "in [Him] are hidden all the treasures of wisdom and knowledge" (Col. 2:3). In Ecclesiastes the aspiration is for ultimate *satisfaction* (1:8) found only in the "one Shepherd" (see 12:11–13). And in the Song of Solomon the aspiration is for intimate *union* with the Lover of our souls. Hence, all the poetic books find their ultimate focus in Christ.

4. Prophecy—Forward Look

The last seventeen books of the Old Testament look forward to Christ. These prophetic books are divided into two sections: the five Major prophets (Isaiah, Jeremiah, Lamentations, Ezekiel, and Daniel) and the Minor prophets (Hosea, Joel, Amos, Obadiah, Jonah, Micah, Nahum, Habakkuk, Zephaniah, Haggai, Zechariah, and Malachi).

The prophets all looked forward in anticipation of Christ. Before the seventy-year captivity (the exile), the prophets, including Isaiah, Jeremiah, Hosea, Joel, Amos, Obadiah, Jonah, Micah, Nahum, Habakkuk, and Zephaniah, stressed *exhortation*.

The prophetic books, written during the captivity, were Lamentations (which looked back in *lamentation* on the destruction of Jerusalem and the temple), Ezekiel (which looked forward to Israel's *spiritual restoration*), and Daniel (which anticipated their *political restoration*).

After the captivity, three books were written. Haggai exhorted the people to build the temple of the *present* (under Zerubbabel), and Zechariah urged them to behold the temple of the *future* (under Christ). While these writers spoke of the nation's *spiritual restoration*, Malachi wrote of their *moral restoration*.

After Malachi, four hundred "silent years" passed before "the fullness of the time had come" (Gal. 4:4) and the next Jewish prophet declared: "Behold! The Lamb of God who takes away the sin of the world!" (John 1:29). In Christ the anticipation of the Old became the realization of the New. The prophetic expectation became a historical manifestation.

5. Gospels—Downward Look

In the New Testament there is an exact four-directional parallel with the four sections of the Old Testament. In the Gospels there is a downward move. God does not simply act in history as he did in he law, but he entered history in the life of his Son. He does not merely manifest himself in laws for his people (as through Moses), but he manifests himself in the life of his people (through Christ). Christ is manifest as King to the Jews in Matthew, as Servant to the Romans in Mark, as the Perfect Man to the Greeks in Luke, and as God to the world in John.

6. Acts—Outward Look

At the end of the Gospels Jesus died, rose again, and ascended into heaven (Luke 24:51; Mark 16:19). In Acts he promised the Holy Spirit would come and empower the apostles to be witnesses in Jerusalem and Judea (Acts 1–7), Samaria (chap. 8), and to the uttermost parts of the earth (chaps. 9–28). Herein is the outward movement of the church.

7. Epistles—Upward Look

Once Jesus ascended to heaven and took his place at the right hand of the Father (Heb. 1:2–3), he became head over all things to his body, the church (Eph. 1:22–23). Hence, the church looks upward to its Head in the Epistles. It is he who through his Spirit gave instructions to the churches through the apostles. Thus they were to build up one another (internally—Eph. 4:7–16) and reach out (externally—Matt. 28:18–20) to disciple believers in all nations, awaiting his blessed return (1 Thess. 4:13–18; Titus 2:11–14).

8. Revelation—Forward Look

The last section of the Bible, like the last section of the Old Testament, is prophetic. It looks forward to the consummation of all things in Christ. Not only was the world created by him (John 1:3; Col. 1:16), but it "consists" (is held together) by him (Col. 1:17; Heb. 1:3), and it will find its consummation in him (Rev. 11:15). He is the Alpha and the Omega, the Beginning and the End of all things.

So each of these eight sections of the Bible unfolds in a Christocentric way.

1. Law—*Foundation for Christ*
2. History—*Preparation for Christ*
3. Poetry—*Aspiration for Christ*
4. Prophecy—*Expectation of Christ*
5. Gospels—*Manifestation of Christ*
6. Acts—*Propagation of Christ*
7. Epistles—*Interpretation of Christ and Application*
8. Revelation—*Consummation in Christ*

Christ in Every Book of the Bible

Christ is the theme of each book in the Bible. Indeed, in most books Christ is presented in many ways, but there is one significant way he is presented in connection with the theme of each book:

Genesis—*the Seed of the woman*

Exodus—*the Passover Lamb*

Leviticus—*the Atoning Sacrifice*

Numbers—*the Smitten Rock*

Deuteronomy—*the Prophet*

Joshua—*our Leader*

Judges—*our Deliverer*

Ruth—*our Kinsman Redeemer*

1 Samuel—*the Anointed One*

2 Samuel—*the Son of David*

1 and 2 Kings—*the Glorious King*

1 and 2 Chronicles—*the Priestly King*

Ezra—*the Restorer of the temple*

Nehemiah—*the Restorer of the nation*

Esther—*our Protector*

Job—*our Mediator*

Psalms—*our All in All*

Proverbs—*the Wisdom of God*

Ecclesiastes—*the Chief Good*

Song of Solomon—*the Lover of our soul*

Isaiah—*the Messiah*

Jeremiah—*a Man of Sorrows*

Lamentations—*the weeping Prophet*

Ezekiel—*the Restorer of God's glory*

Daniel—*the Great Rock*

Hosea—*the Healer of the backslider*

Joel—*the Hope of his people*

Amos—*the Husbandman*

Obadiah—*the Savior*

Jonah—*the Resurrected One*

Micah—*the Witness*

Nahum—*the Avenger*

Habakkuk—*the Holy God*

Zephaniah—*the Judge*

Haggai—*the Restorer of the temple's glory*

Zechariah—*the Righteous Branch*

Malachi—*the Sun of Righteousness*

Matthew—*the King of the Jews*

Mark—*the Servant of the Lord*

Luke—*the Son of Man*

John—*the Son of God*

Acts—*our risen Lord*

Romans—*our Righteousness*

1 Corinthians—*our Sanctification*

2 Corinthians—*our Sufficiency*

Galatians—*our Liberty*

Ephesians—*the Head of the church*

Philippians—*our Joy*

Colossians—*the Preeminent One*

1 Thessalonians—*the Coming One*

2 Thessalonians—*the Glorified One*

1 Timothy—*our Teacher*

The Garden Tomb, Jerusalem, believed by some to be Jesus's tomb.

2 Timothy—*our Helper*

Titus—*the Great God and Savior*

Philemon—*our Substitute*

Hebrews—*our Great High Priest*

James—*our Wisdom*

1 Peter—*our Rock*

2 Peter—*our Hope*

1 John—*the Life*

2 John—*the Truth*

3 John—*the Way*

Jude—*our Advocate*

Revelation—*King of Kings and Lord of Lords*

The Bloodline of the Messiah

The Old Testament reveals the progressive narrowing down of the bloodline of the Messiah.

> Genesis 3:15—the Seed of the woman
>
> Genesis 4:25—the line of Seth
>
> Genesis 9:27—the son of Shem
>
> Genesis 12:3—the seed of Abraham
>
> Genesis 21:12—the offspring of Isaac
>
> Genesis 25:23—a descendant of Jacob
>
> Genesis 49:10—the tribe of Judah
>
> 2 Samuel 7:12–16—the Son of David (see Matthew 1; Luke 3:23–39)

This bloodline is further narrowed to the Son of a virgin (Isa. 7:14), who would be born in Bethlehem (Micah 5:2); the suffering Servant (Isaiah 53); the dying Messiah who would be cut off about AD 33 (Dan. 9:24–27). One and only one person in history fulfilled all those predictions—Jesus of Nazareth. He claimed to be the Messiah (John 4:25–26; Mark 14:61–62), and he proved to be the Messiah by fulfilling nearly one hundred predictions at his first coming.

A Poetic Picture of Christ in Scripture

An anonymous author put the Christ-centered structure of the Bible in this poetic form:

> I find my Lord in the Bible
> Wherever I chance to look,
> He is the theme of the Bible
> The center and heart of the Book;
> He is the Rose of Sharon,
> He is the Lily fair,
> Wherever I open my Bible
> The Lord of the Book is there.
>
> He, at the Book's beginning,
> Gave to the earth its form,
> He is the Ark of shelter
> Bearing the brunt of the storm,
> The Burning Bush of the desert,
> The budding of Aaron's Rod,
> Wherever I look in the Bible
> I see the Son of God.

The Sinai desert.

The Ram upon Mt. Moriah,
The Ladder from earth to sky,
The Scarlet Cord in the window,
And the Serpent lifted high,
The Smitten Rock in the desert,
The Shepherd with staff and crook,
The face of my Lord I discover
Wherever I open the Book.

He is the Seed of the Woman,
The Savior Virgin-born;
He is the Son of David,
Whom men rejected with scorn,
His garments of grace and of beauty
The stately Aaron deck,
Yet he is a priest forever,
For He is Melchizedek.

Lord of eternal glory
Whom John, the Apostle saw;
Light of the golden city,
Lamb without spot or flaw,
Bridegroom coming at midnight,
For whom the virgins look.
Wherever I open my Bible,
I find my Lord in the Book.

STUDY QUESTIONS

1. What does Jesus claim about the Scriptures?

2. What is the relation of Jesus in the Old Testament to Jesus in the New Testament?

3. What are the eight sections of the Bible?
   How do these sections reveal Christ?

4. How is Christ revealed in each book of the Bible?

5. What does the Old Testament predict about the Messiah?
   Does Jesus fit the requirements?

SELECTED SOURCES

Geisler, Norman. *A Popular Survey of the Old Testament.* 1977. Grand Rapids: Baker, 2007.

————. *To Understand the Bible, Look for Jesus.* Eugene, OR: Wipf and Stock, 2005.

Hodgkin, A. M. *Christ in All the Scripture.* London: Pickering & Inglis, 1922.

Payne, J. Barton. *Encyclopedia of Biblical Prophecy.* Grand Rapids: Baker, 1980.

Scroggie, William Graham. *Christ the Key to Scripture.* Chicago: Bible Institute Colportage Assn., 1924.

————. *A Guide to the Gospels.* London: Pickering & Inglis, 1948. Reprint, Grand Rapids: Kregel, 1995.

2

The Gospel Record— History or Mythology?

The reliability of the New Testament depends on the answer to two questions: Have the documents been copied accurately? Were the words and events recorded accurately?

As we shall see, the answer to the first question is that we have more manuscripts, earlier manuscripts, and more accurately copied manuscripts of the New Testament than for any other book from the ancient world. And the answer to the second is that we have more books written by more authors who were closer to the events and whose record has been confirmed in more ways than for any other book from the ancient world.

The Reliability of New Testament Manuscripts

As figure 2.1 on page 20 illustrates, the manuscripts of the New Testament are earlier, more abundant, and more accurately copied than any book from antiquity.

More New Testament Manuscripts

There are over 5,700 Greek manuscripts of the New Testament. Most other books from the ancient world survive based on about 10 to 20 manuscripts. The most manuscripts for any book besides the Bible are for Homer's *Iliad* with 643. Thus the New Testament has an overwhelming advantage in the number of manuscripts to support the integrity of the text it is transmitting.

Earlier New Testament Manuscripts

The New Testament manuscripts are much earlier than those for other books from antiquity. Most other books survive on the basis of manuscripts created one thousand years after the time the book was composed, there being no known original manuscripts. The New Testament, by contrast, has manuscripts that date from within

FIGURE 2.1
Reliability of the New Testament Documents

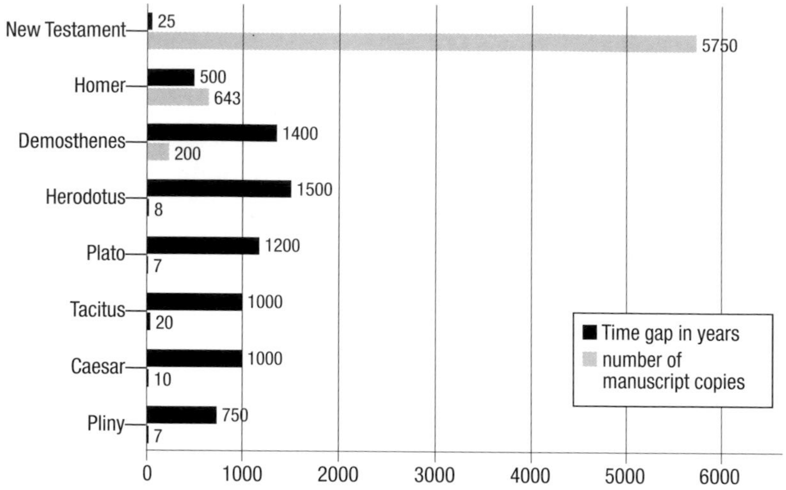

about twenty-five years from the time the book was written!

John Ryland fragment—ca. AD 115ff.
—five verses from John 18:31–33; 37–38
Bodmer Papyri—AD 200
—most of John, 1 and 2 Peter, and Jude
Chester Beaty Papyri—AD 250
—nearly all the New Testament books
Vaticanus Manuscript—AD 325–350
—most of Old Testament and New Testament

Noted manuscript expert Sir Frederic Kenyon wrote:

The interval between the dates of original composition and the earliest extant evidence becomes so small as to be in fact negligible, and the last foundation for any doubt that the Scriptures have come down substantially as they were written has now been removed. Both the authenticity and the general integrity of the books of the New Testament may be regarded as finally established.[1]

Better Copied Manuscripts
The New Testament manuscripts are copied with greater accuracy than other books from the ancient world. Dr. Bruce Metzger of Princeton University and A. T. Robertson compared the accuracy of three great books from antiquity and found the following:

The Marabharata	90 percent accuracy
Iliad of Homer	95 percent accuracy
The New Testament	99.9 percent accuracy[2]

Sir Frederic Kenyon's testimony is to the point:

> The number of mss. of the New Testament, of early translations from it, and of quotations from it in the oldest writers of the Church, is so large that it is practically certain that the true reading of every doubtful passage is preserved in some one or the other of these ancient authorities. *This can be said of no other book in the world.*[3]

The Testimony of the Fathers

In addition to all of this, if all Greek and ancient translations of the Bible were destroyed, almost the entire New Testament could be reconstructed from the quotations of the Church Fathers from the first few centuries! They cited the New Testament more than thirty-six thousand times! In fact they provide every verse of the New Testament except for eleven verses. This too can be said of no other book from the ancient world. (See figure 2.2 below.)

The New Testament has more manuscripts, earlier manuscripts, and more accurately copied manuscripts than any other book from the ancient world. In other words, if we cannot trust the transmission of its text, then we cannot trust any other book that has come to us from antiquity.

FIGURE 2.2
Early Citations of the New Testament

Writer	Gospels	Acts	Pauline Epistles	General Epistles	Revelation	Totals
Justin Martyr	268	10	43	6	3*	330
Irenaeus	1,038	194	499	23	65	1,819
Clement of Alexandria	1,017	44	1,127	207	11	2,406
Origen	9,231	349	7,778	399	165	17,922
Tertullian	3,822	502	2,609	120	205	7,258
Hippolytus	734	42	387	27	188	1,378
Eusebius	3,258	211	1,592	88	27	5,176
Grand Totals	**19,368**	**1,352**	**14,035**	**870**	**664**	**36,289**

*266 allusions

The Reliability of the New Testament Writers

There are two links in the chain of New Testament reliability. First, have the documents been copied accurately? Second, were the words and events recorded accurately? Now that we have seen that there is very strong evidence for an affirmative answer to the first question, let's turn our attention to the second. The answer to this question depends on several factors: the number of the writings, the date of the writings, and the accuracy of the writings. In brief, we can say that the New Testament has more writers, earlier writers, and more accurate writers than any other book from the ancient world!

More Writers

Most events from the ancient world are known on the basis of one or two writers from the time period or some time after it. By contrast the New Testament has nine writers (Matthew, Mark, Luke, John, Paul, Peter, James, Jude, and the writer of Hebrews[4]). For the life, works, and words of Christ alone, there were four writers, and as the ancient principle states, "In the mouth of two or three witnesses every word shall be established,"[5] nine witnesses is certainly sufficient. In addition, as will be shown below, all the essential elements of Jesus's life and teaching are preserved in the almost universally accepted Epistles of the apostle Paul.

Earlier Writers

The New Testament writers were closer to the events than most other writers from the ancient world were to the events about which they wrote. Indeed, many of the New Testament writers were eyewitnesses or contemporaries of the eyewitnesses, and some of them wrote within twenty to twenty-five years of the events of which they spoke. Jesus died by AD 33, and both Paul and Luke wrote books by about AD 55 to 60.

Of the nine New Testament writers:

1. Matthew was an apostle and eyewitness of Christ (Matt. 10:3).[6]
2. Mark was an associate of the apostle Peter (1 Peter 5:13).
3. Luke was an associate of the apostle Paul (2 Tim. 4:11).
4. John was an apostle and eyewitness (John 21:24; 1 John 1:1–4).
5. Paul was an apostle and contemporary of Jesus (Acts 9; 1 Cor. 15:8).
6. James was the "brother" of Jesus and an eyewitness (1 Cor. 15:7).
7. Peter was an apostle and eyewitness (Matt. 10:2; 2 Peter 1:16–17).
8. Jude was the brother of James (Jude 1).
9. The writer of Hebrews was a contemporary of the twelve apostles (2:3; 13:23).

Church of the Holy Sepulchre, Jerusalem, traditional site of Jesus's death and burial.

John, an eyewitness

John writes the following: "And he who has seen has testified [to the crucifixion], and his testimony is true" (John 19:35). "This is the disciple who testifies of these things, and wrote these things; and we know that his testimony is true" (21:24). "That which was from the beginning, which we have heard, which we have seen with our eyes, which we have looked upon, and our hands have handled, concerning the Word of life" (1 John 1:1).

Eyewitnesses in Acts

In Acts we read the testimony of eyewitnesses: "This Jesus God has raised up [to life], of which we are all witnesses" (2:32). "But Peter and John answered . . . 'For we cannot but speak the things which we have seen and heard'" (4:19–20). "And we are witnesses of all things which He did both in the land of the Jews and in Jerusalem, whom they killed by hanging on a tree. Him God raised up [from the dead] on the third day, and showed Him openly" (10:39–40).

Five hundred eyewitnesses of the resurrection
The following was written in AD 55 to 56, when most of the eyewitnesses of the resurrection were still alive:

> He [Jesus] was buried, and . . . He rose again the third day according to the Scriptures, and . . . He was seen by Cephas [Peter], then by the twelve. After that He was seen by over five hundred brethren at once, of whom the greater part remain to the present, but some have fallen asleep. After that He was seen by James, then by all the apostles. Then last of all He was seen by me also.
>
> 1 Corinthians 15:4–8

Luke based on eyewitness accounts
Luke states at the beginning of his Gospel that what he wrote is based on eyewitness accounts:

> Inasmuch as many have undertaken to compile an account of the things accomplished among us, just as they were handed down to us by those who from the beginning were eyewitnesses and servants of the word, it seemed fitting for me as well, having investigated everything carefully from the beginning, to write it out for you in consecutive order, most excellent Theophilus; so that you might know the exact truth about the things you have been taught.
>
> Luke 1:1–4 NASB

Hebrews confirmed by apostles
The truth of the gospel is confirmed to the writer of Hebrews by the apostles: "How shall we escape if we neglect so great a salvation, which at the first began to be spoken by the Lord, and was confirmed to us by those who heard Him, God also bearing witness both with signs and wonders, with various miracles, and gifts of the Holy Spirit, according to His own will?" (Heb. 2:3–4).

Peter an eyewitness
Peter affirms that he was an eyewitness to Jesus's life and death. "For we did not follow cunningly devised fables [myths] when we made known to you the power and coming of our Lord Jesus Christ, but were eyewitnesses of His majesty" (2 Peter 1:16). "The elders who are among you I exhort, I who am a fellow elder and a witness of the sufferings of Christ, and also a partaker of the glory that will be revealed" (1 Peter 5:1).

Early Dates for New Testament Books
Not only were the Gospels written by eyewitnesses and contemporaries, but they were written early. Noted Roman historian Colin Hemer

Titus's Arch, Rome, commemorates the Roman sack of Jerusalem and destruction of Herod's temple.

has offered numerous lines of evidence that the book of Acts was written by AD 62. Only five of them are sufficient to make the point. Acts must have been written before the following dates, since these are very important events that no Christian historian writing about the period would have failed to mention if they had already occurred:

- There is no mention of the fall of Jerusalem—AD 70.
- There is no reference to the Jewish War—AD 66.
- There is no hint of Nero's persecutions—ca. AD 65.
- There is no mention of the death of the apostle Paul —ca. AD 65. Indeed, he is still alive in the last chapter of the book of Acts (chap. 28).
- Finally, the apostle James is still alive —ca. AD 62. But the first-century Jewish historian Josephus recorded James's death at AD 62.[7]

Not mentioning these events in a history of these times would be like writing the life of President Kennedy without mentioning his assassination (in 1963). The reader would know that the book was written before 1963.

The person who wrote Acts also wrote the Gospel of Luke.[8] Both books are addressed to the same person, Theophilus (Luke 1:3; Acts 1:1). The later book mentions the "former account" (Acts 1:1). Acts was written by an accurate historian by AD 62 and has been confirmed in nearly a hundred details, which could be known only by someone familiar with the facts. Further, Luke (1:1) refers to "many" (Gk. "two or more") narratives on the life of Jesus before him (possibly Matthew and Mark) and claims (as well as proves) to be an accurate account of the matter based on "eyewitness" testimony (v. 2). This means we have a good historical account from within twenty-seven to thirty years of the time of the events.

Evidence from the Early Fathers

Overlapping with the time of the apostles and shortly thereafter, there were a number of books that cite the New Testament, thus proving it was in existence at that time. These include *The Epistle of Barnabas* (70–90), *The Epistles of Clement* (94–95), *The Epistles of Polycarp* (ca. 90–155), the Didache (ca. 80–120?), *The Shepherd of Hermas* (90–100), *The Epistles of Ignatius* (by 117), *An Ancient Homily* [?] (120–40), and *Fragments of Papias* (130–40).

Early Dates for Other New Testament Books

Even critical scholars agree that 1 Corinthians was written by ca. AD 55 to 56, and 2 Corinthians, Romans, and Galatians were written shortly thereafter. Yet these books provide the same basic information about the life, teaching, death, and resurrection of Christ found in the Gospels (see below).

Historical Crosshairs

One of the strongest signs of authenticity and reliability found in Luke is the provision of historical crosshairs for the events he records. Not only does he point to the very year Jesus began his ministry (AD 29), but he provides eight persons known to history to have existed at the same time whose lives intersected with Jesus's life. Luke wrote:

> Now in the fifteenth year of the reign of Tiberius Caesar, Pontius Pilate being governor of Judea, Herod being tetrarch of Galilee, his brother Philip tetrarch of Iturea and of the region of Trachonitis, and Lysanias tetrarch of Abilene, Annas and Caiaphas being high priests, the word of God came to John the son of Zacharias in the wilderness.
>
> Luke 3:1–2

We should note the following:

1. An exact date is given ("the fifteenth year of the reign of Tiberius" [i.e., AD 29]).
2. All eight people are known from history.
3. All were known to live at this exact time.
4. This is not a "once upon a time" story (myth).

Are the New Testament Books Myths?

The time between the events of Jesus's life (by AD 33) and the earliest records (AD 55 to 60) is way too short for any significant myths to develop. Indeed, any dates in the first century are too early to allow mythological development, and even radical New Testament critics, like many in the Jesus Seminar, accept that most New Testament books, if not all, were written between AD 70 and 100. As one scholar pointed out: "The writings of the Greek historian Herodotus enable us to test the rate at which a legend accumulates; the tests show that even the span of two generations is too short to allow legendary tendencies to wipe out the hard core of historical fact."[9]

It should be noted that there are mythological accounts of Jesus, and they appeared at the very time myths *should* appear—more than two generations after the events. *The Gospel of Thomas* (mid–second century) and the other apocryphal gospels of the second and third centuries following are cases in point. A comparison of the New Testament Gospels and these apocryphal books nearly a hundred years later reveals the authentic nature of the former and the embellished, apocryphal nature of the latter. The words of the early Christian expert Edwin Yamauchi serve to summarize the contrast:

> The apocryphal [pseudopigraphal] gospels, even the earliest and soberest among them, can hardly be compared with the canonical gospels. The former are all patently secondary and legendary or obviously slanted. Commenting on the infancy gospels, Morton Enslin concludes: "Their total effect is to send us back to the canonical gospels with fresh approval of their chaste restraint in failing to fill in the intriguing hidden years."[10]

The former atheist and famous myth writer of the Narnia series concluded that the New Testament was not myth. C. S. Lewis declared:

> All I am in private life is a literary critic and historian, that's my job. And I am prepared to say on that basis if anyone thinks the Gospels are either legend or novels, then that person is simply showing his incompetence as a literary critic. I've read a great many novels and I know a fair amount about the legends that grew up among early people, and I know perfectly well the Gospels are not that kind of stuff.[11]

A helpful comparison is that of the records of Christ's life with those of Alexander the Great. In Alexander's case we have no contemporary eyewitness documents—none. Even one hundred years later there are only fragments. It is not until three to five hundred years after Alexander's time that we have several biographies of this great military leader. By contrast the essential elements of the life, teaching, death, and resurrection of Christ were written by contemporaries of Jesus and eyewitnesses to the events of his life and were begun as early as about twenty years after his ministry.

Dean of Biblical Archaeology Speaks Out
William F. Albright began his scholarly career with serious doubts about the authenticity of much of the Bible. After a generation of studying the archaeological evidence, he declared: "In my opinion, every book of the New Testament was written by a baptized Jew between the forties and the eighties of the first century AD (very probably sometime between about 50 and AD 75)."[12] AD 50 is only seventeen years after Jesus died!

The Confessions of a Liberal Critic
One of the men credited with the beginning of the "Death of God" movement several decades ago, liberal theologian Bishop John Robinson, later took a serious second look at the dates for the New Testament in his book *Redating the New Testament*. His conclusion was nearly as radical in a conservative direction as his theology had been in a liberal direction. He concluded that the dates for the Gospels should be as follows:

> Matthew—AD 40–60+
> Mark—AD 45–60+
> Luke—AD 57–60+
> John—AD 40–65+[13]

The date AD 40 would be only seven years after Jesus died! This is indeed a radical redating of the New Testament. Even considering Robinson's later figures of AD 60, if the Gospels were written less than thirty years after Jesus's death, this is much too early for them not to be accurate.

The Accuracy of New Testament Writers

Not only were there more numerous and earlier writers of the New Testament than other books from its time, but they are known to be more accurate for many reasons.

The Early Date of the Writings
As has been shown, the basic New Testament documents on Christ's life were possibly written as early as AD 40 to 60. They were probably penned by AD 55 to 60, and they were most certainly recorded during the lifetimes of the eyewitnesses. Even these later dates are too early for mythological development, much earlier than for other ancient books (like those on Alexander the Great), and certainly early enough to be considered reliable witnesses to the events.

The "Erastus inscription," Corinth, archaeological evidence for the city treasurer Paul mentions in Romans 16:23.

Confirmation by Other Early Writings

Not only were the Gospels early enough to be reliable, but the basic information in them is confirmed by the early writings of Paul that are generally accepted, even by most critics, to be written between AD 50 and 61. In these books Paul confirmed at least thirty-one facts recorded in the Gospels:

1. the Jewish ancestry of Jesus (Gal. 3:16)
2. his Davidic descent (Rom. 1:3)
3. his virgin birth (Gal. 4:4)
4. his life under Jewish law (Gal. 4:4)
5. he had brothers (1 Cor. 9:5)
6. he had twelve disciples (1 Cor. 15:7)
7. one disciple was named James (1 Cor. 15:7)
8. some disciples had wives (1 Cor. 9:5)
9. Paul knew Peter and James (Gal. 1:18–2:16)
10. Jesus's poverty (2 Cor. 8:9)
11. his humility (Phil. 2:5–7)
12. his meekness and gentleness (2 Cor. 10:1)
13. his abuse by others (Rom. 15:3)
14. his teachings on divorce and remarriage (1 Cor. 7:10–11)
15. his view on paying wages to ministers (1 Cor. 9:14)
16. his view on paying taxes (Rom. 13:6–7)
17. his command to love one's neighbors (Rom. 13:9)

18. Jewish ceremonial uncleanness (Rom. 14:14)

19. Jesus's titles of deity (Rom. 1:3–4; 10:9)

20. the need for vigilance in view of Jesus's second coming (1 Thess. 4:15)

21. his second coming like a thief in the night (1 Thess. 5:2–11)

22. his institution of the Lord's Supper (1 Cor. 11:23–25)

23. his sinless life (2 Cor. 5:21)

24. his death on the cross (Gal. 3:13; see Rom. 4:25; 5:8; 1 Cor. 15:3)

25. his death by crucifixion (Rom. 6:6; Gal. 2:20)

26. his death by Jewish instigation (1 Thess. 2:14–15)

27. his burial (1 Cor. 15:4)

28. his resurrection on the "third day" (1 Cor. 15:4)

29. his post-resurrection appearance to the apostles (1 Cor. 15:5–8)

30. his post-resurrection appearances to others (1 Cor. 15:6)

31. his present position at God's right hand (Rom. 8:34)[14]

The Authentic Nature of the Writings

The Gospels show every sign of authenticity. They are vivid, fresh, unembellished, detailed, self-incriminating, diverse, but mutually confirming (that is, historical and not mythological). The following points make all of this clear.

- The writers made no attempt to harmonize their accounts, even though they are harmonizable.[15]
- They included material that put Jesus in a bad light.
- They left many difficult passages in their text.
- They retained many self-incriminating details.
- They included many demanding sayings of Jesus.
- They distinguished their words from Jesus's words.
- They did not deny their testimony under threat of death.
- They claimed their record was based on eyewitnesses.
- They had women witnessing the resurrection before men.
- They challenged readers to check out the facts.
- They discarded long-held Jewish beliefs overnight.
- They include more than thirty historical people.[16]

Thirty-one Historical Persons in the New Testament

Another sign of the historical reliability of the New Testament is its accurate presentation of some thirty-one historical persons. These include:

1. Herod Agrippa I—Acts 12
2. Agrippa II—Acts 25
3. Ananias—Acts 23–24
4. Annas—Luke 3; John 18; Acts 4
5. Aretas—2 Corinthians 11
6. Augustus—Luke 2
7. Bernice—Acts 25
8. Caiaphas—Matthew 26; Luke 3; John 11, 18; Acts 4
9. Claudius—Acts 11, 18
10. Drusilla—Acts 24
11. Egyptian—Acts 21 (a false prophet who started a revolt)
12. Erastus—Acts 19
13. Felix—Acts 23
14. Gallio—Acts 18
15. Gamaliel—Acts 5
16. Herod Antipas—Matthew 14; Mark 6; Luke 3, 23
17. Herod Archelaus—Matthew 2
18. Herod the Great—Matthew 2; Luke 1
19. Herod Philip I—Matthew 14; Mark 6
20. Herod Philip II—Luke 3
21. Herodias—Matthew 14; Mark 6
22. James—Acts 15; Galatians 1
23. John the Baptist—Matthew 3; Mark 1; Luke 3; John 1
24. Judas of Galilee—Acts 5
25. Lysanias—Luke 3
26. Pilate—Matthew 27; Mark 15; Luke 23; John 18
27. Porcius Festus—Acts 24–26
28. Quirinius—Luke 2
29. Salome—Matthew 14; Mark 6
30. Sergius Paulus—Acts 13
31. Tiberius Caesar—Luke 3

Confirmation by Noted Roman Historians

A. N. Sherwin-White, noted authority on Roman society and law, wrote:

> So it is astonishing that while Greco-Roman historians have been growing in confidence, the twentieth-century study of the gospel narratives, starting from no less promising material, have taken so gloomy a turn in the development of form-criticism . . . that the historical Christ is unknowable and the history of his mission cannot be written. This seems very curious.[17]

He calls the mythological view "unbelievable."

Another noted expert on the period confirmed nearly a hundred details in Acts from Roman sources. This evidence shows that the author of the third Gospel was a first-rate historian because of his knowledge of:

- minute geographical details known to the readers
- specialized details known only to special groups
- specifics of routes, places, and officials that were not widely known
- correlation of dates in Acts with general history
- details appropriate to that period but not others
- events that reflect a sense of "immediacy"
- idioms and culture that bespeak a firsthand awareness
- verification of numerous details of times, people, and events of that period best known by contemporaries[18]

Harvard Legal Expert Confirms Gospels

Simon Greenleaf (1783–1853), professor of law at Harvard University, was one of the greatest legal minds in American history. He wrote *A Treatise on the Law of Evidences* (1853), the standard book on legal evidence that was used to train lawyers in how to test evidence and witnesses. When challenged to apply the legal standards to the New Testament, he wrote *The Testimony of the Evangelists* (1846 ed.) in which he concluded that were the New Testament documents and witnesses so tested in a court of law they would prove to be reliable. He wrote:

> The narratives of the evangelists are now submitted to the reader's perusal and examination, upon the principles and by the rules already stated. . . . If they had thus testified on oath, in a court of justice, they would be entitled to credit; and whether their narratives,

as we now have them, would be received as ancient documents, coming from the proper custody. If so, then it is believed that every honest and impartial man will act consistently with that result, by receiving their testimony in all the extent of its import.[19]

Greenleaf added:

All that Christianity asks of men on this subject is that they would be consistent with themselves; that they would treat its evidences as they treat the evidence of other things; and that they would try and judge its actors and witnesses, as they deal with their fellow men, when testifying to human affairs and actions, in human tribunals. Let the witnesses be compared with themselves, with each other, and with surrounding facts and circumstances; and let their testimony be sifted, as if it were given in a court of justice, on the side of the adverse party, the witness being subjected to rigorous cross-examination. The result, it is confidently believed, will be an undoubting conviction of their integrity, ability, and truth.[20]

The *bema*, or speaker's platform, before which, according to Acts 18:12–17, Paul stood before the proconsul Gallio.

Non-Christian Sources for the New Testament

Another line of supporting evidence for the historical accuracy of the New Testament is found in non-Christian sources outside the New Testament. The two best sources for this information are F. F. Bruce, *Jesus and Christian Origins Outside the New Testament* and Gary Habermas, *The Historical Jesus*. Summarizing the non-Christian writers of the times, such as Josephus, Tacitus, Suetonius, Thallus, the Jewish Talmud, and others, we get the following confirmation of the basic historicity of the New Testament:

- Jesus was from Nazareth.
- He lived a virtuous life.
- He performed unusual feats.
- He introduced new teaching contrary to Judaism.
- He was crucified under Pontius Pilate.
- His disciples believed he rose from the dead.
- His disciples denied polytheism.
- His disciples worshiped him.
- His teachings spread rapidly, and the number of his disciples quickly grew.
- His followers believed they were immortal.
- His followers had contempt for death.
- His followers renounced material goods.

Archaeological Confirmation of the New Testament

The archaeological evidence for the New Testament's general historicity can be summarized in two points: (1) No archaeological evidence has ever refuted the Bible. (2) Abundant archaeological evidence supports the historical reliability of the New Testament. As to the first point, noted biblical scholar Nelson Glueck wrote: "As a matter of fact, however, it may be stated categorically that no archaeological discovery has ever controverted a biblical reference. Scores of archaeological findings have been made which confirm in clear outline or exact detail historical statements in the Bible."[21]

On the second point, Donald J. Wiseman wrote: "The geography of Bible lands and visible remains of antiquity were gradually recorded until today more than 25,000 sites within this region and dating to Old Testament times, in their broadest sense, have been located. . . ."[22]

Summarizing the evidence for *US News and World Report*, Jeffery Sheler wrote: "In extraordinary ways, modern archaeology has affirmed the historical core of the Old and New Testaments—corroborating key portions of the stories of Israel's patriarchs, the Exodus, the Davidic monarchy, and the life and times of Jesus."[23]

Some archaeological evidence relating directly to Jesus includes the excavation of his hometown of Nazareth; Pilate's name inscribed in stone; an inscription of Caiaphas the high priest who tried Jesus; the discovery of Yohanan—a crucifixion victim from ca. AD 70 (found in 1968)—which verifies the method of crucifixion; and the Nazareth Decree of Emperor Claudius (AD 41–54), which forbade removal of bodies from graves under pain of death—this seems to hint at the story that circulated in the wake of Jesus's resurrection (Matt. 28:11–15).

Of course there are numerous other finds in and around Jerusalem that intersect with Jesus's life, including Bethlehem, Bethany, Jericho, the Sea of Galilee, and a multitude of geographical and topological details in the Gospels. On top of this there is all the evidence, detailed above, for Luke's historicity through the many persons known to history whom he included in his book and whose lives intersected with that of Jesus.

A Summary of the Evidence

The evidence for the historical reliability of the New Testament is overwhelming. It can be summarized as follows:

- There are nine different authors.
- There are twenty-seven different books.
- They are based on eyewitness testimony.
- Early, accepted Pauline letters confirm them.
- There was not enough time for myths to develop.
- The nature of the records is authentic.
- Non-Christian sources support them.
- Noted Roman historians have confirmed them.
- Noted legal experts have vouched for them.
- Many archaeological finds have supported them.

Nothing like this evidence exists for any other book from the ancient world! In short, if a person does not accept the authenticity of the New Testament, then logically he or she must reject the evidence for any other event from the ancient world, since all such events are believed to have happened on much less evidence than that available for the New Testament. Hence, when the Gospels say Jesus said it, then Jesus actually said it. And when they say Jesus did it, then Jesus actually did it.[24]

STUDY QUESTIONS

1. What is the evidence that the New Testament documents are historically reliable? Why is their reliability important?

2. What are some reasons to trust the New Testament authors?

3. When was the book of Acts written? Why is this date important?

4. Why are the lists of historical persons in the New Testament significant?

5. What can be known about Jesus outside the New Testament?

SELECTED SOURCES

Albright, William F. "Toward a More Conservative View." *Christianity Today*, January 18, 1963, 3–5.

Blomberg, Craig. *The Historical Reliability of John's Gospel*. Downers Grove, IL: InterVarsity, 1998.

———. *The Historical Reliability of the Gospels*. Downers Grove, IL: InterVarsity, 1987.

Bruce, F. F. *Jesus and Christian Origins Outside the New Testament*. Grand Rapids: Eerdmans, 1974.

———. *The New Testament Documents: Are They Reliable?* Grand Rapids: Eerdmans, 2003.

Craig, William Lane. *The Son Rises*. Eugene, OR: Wipf & Stock, 2001.

Geisler, Norman L., and Thomas Howe. *When Critics Ask: A Popular Handbook on Bible Difficulties*. Grand Rapids: Baker, 1997.

Geisler, Norman L., and William E. Nix. *A General Introduction to the Bible*. Rev. ed. Chicago: Moody, 1986.

Geisler, Norman L., and Frank Turek. *I Don't Have Enough Faith to Be an Atheist*. Wheaton: Crossway, 2004.

Glueck, Nelson. *Rivers in the Desert*. New York: Farrar, Straus and Cudahy, 1959.

Greenleaf, Simon. *The Testimony of the Evangelists*. Grand Rapids: Kregel, 1995.

Habermas, Gary. *The Historical Jesus: Ancient Evidence for the Life of Christ*. Joplin, MO: College Press, 1996.

Hemer, Colin. *The Book of Acts in the Setting of Hellenic History*. Winona Lake, MN: Eisenbrauns, 1990.

Kenyon, Frederic. *The Bible and Archaeology*. New York: Harper & Brothers, 1940.

———. *Our Bible and the Ancient Manuscripts*. London: Eyre & Spottiswoode, 1958.

Lewis, C. S. *Christian Reflections*. Grand Rapids: Eerdmans, 1967.

Metzger, Bruce. *The Text of the New Testament*. New York: Oxford University Press, 1990.

Robertson, A. T. *Introduction to the Textual Criticism of the New Testament*. Nashville: Broadman, 1925.

Robinson, John A. T. *Redating the New Testament*. Eugene, OR: Wipf & Stock, 2000.

Sheler, Jeffrey. "Is the Bible True?" *US News and World Report*, October 25, 1999, 50.

Sherwin-White, A. N. *Roman Society and Roman Law in the New Testament*. Oxford: Clarendon Press, 1963.

Wiseman, Donald J. "Archaeological Confirmation of the Old Testament." Quoted in Carl F. H. Henry, *Revelation and the Bible* (Grand Rapids: Baker, 1958), 301–16.

Yamauchi, Edwin. "The Word from Nag Hammadi" *Christianity Today*, January 13, 1978, 19–22.

3
Introduction
to the Gospels

Before we begin our study of the Gospels, it will be helpful to discuss several introductory matters. First, we will look at the overall chronology of the life of Jesus.

Chronological Indicators in the New Testament

There are certain chronological indicators in the New Testament from which we can begin to build an overall time line. Some of the evidence is internal and some is external.

On the Birth of Jesus

The New Testament does not state the year, month, or day of Christ's birth. It simply says it was during the reigns of Caesar Augustus (31 BC–AD 14) (Luke 2:1) and Herod the Great of Palestine (4 BC–AD 34) (Matt. 2:1).

We know from external sources that Herod reigned from 8 to 4 BC. We also know that the census of Quirinius, which Luke mentioned in 2:2, would have been about 6 BC.[1] Thus it would appear that Jesus was born between 4 and 6 BC. Being more specific would require speculation and inference. The traditional date of December 25 was probably chosen to correspond with the winter solstice on the Roman calendar, though one cannot say for sure that Jesus was not born at this time.

On Jesus's Baptism

The Bible places more emphasis on Jesus's baptism and entrance into his ministry than on his birth. This date is fixed firmly by eight historical crosshairs in Luke 3:1–2, which name eight historical persons who are known to have lived at that time (Tiberius Caesar, Pontius Pilate, Herod, Philip, Lysanias, Annas,

Caiaphas, and John the Baptist). Indeed it says specifically that it was in "the fifteenth year of the reign of Tiberius Caesar," which is known to be AD 29.

On Jesus's Age at His Baptism

According to Luke, Jesus was "about thirty years of age" (Luke 3:23) when he was baptized. Luke may be assuming this general age from the Old Testament, which states that this is the minimum age at which a priest could enter his ministry (Num. 4:3). However, since Jesus was born during Herod's reign, which ended in 4 BC, it follows that he must have been at least thirty-three at his baptism.

On Jesus's Death

We know the time of year but not the exact year of Jesus's death. It was Passover time (Matt. 26:2; John 13:1). There was also an eclipse of the sun (Mark 15:33), but according to astronomy, there was an eclipse at Passover during this time only in AD 29 and 33. But AD 29 is too early, since Jesus was baptized that year and he ministered for at least two or three years (see below). Thus AD 33 seems to be the time of his death. This also fits with the prediction of Daniel that there would be 483 lunar years between 444 BC and the time of Christ's death.[2]

One of the time indicators for Jesus's death is found in John 8:57 in which Jesus's enemies say to him: "You are not yet fifty years old." Even taken literally, this means they thought he was still in his forties, and no doubt they added some time for good measure. With a three-year ministry (see below), this would fit with a midthirties age at the time of his death.

The Length of Jesus's Ministry

Given that Jesus was baptized in AD 29, the date of his death will be determined by the length of his ministry. The answer to this revolves around how many Passovers are mentioned in the Gospels, and there seem to be either three or four Passovers during Jesus's ministry. Three are mentioned explicitly (John 2:13; 6:4; 18:28; and some believe Luke 6:1 alludes to another Passover). Another may be implied in John 5:1, which, though not a Passover, may indicate that another year had gone by in which there was a Passover. If there were four Passovers (with three years between them), it would fit perfectly with the traditional view that Jesus ministered for three and one-half years (adding the extra one-half year for a ministry beginning in the fall and going to the spring Passover.

The Jordan River, where Jesus was baptized.

The Chronological Timetable

Building on the indicators given above, a likely timetable of important dates can be proposed as follows:

- Christ's birth—5/4 BC
- Herod the Great's death—4 BC
- Christ in the temple at age twelve—AD 9 (Luke 2:41–50)
- John the Baptist begins ministry—AD 29 (Luke 3)
- Jesus was baptized—AD 29 (Luke 3:21–22)
- Christ's first Passover after the beginning of his ministry—AD 30 (John 2:13)
- Christ's second Passover after the beginning of his ministry—AD 31 (John 5:1)
- Christ's third Passover after the beginning of his ministry—AD 32 (John 6:4)
- Christ's last Passover and Lord's Supper—AD 33 (John 13)
- Christ's death—April 3, AD 33 (John 19)
- Christ's ascension—May 14, AD 33 (Acts 1)
- Day of Pentecost—May 24, AD 33 (Acts 2)[3]

The Geographical Background of the Gospels

The geographical setting for the Gospels is depicted by maps of the area at the time. The Holy Land itself consisted of Galilee in the north, Judea in the south, and Samaria in between them. Jesus was born in Bethlehem in Judea, raised in Nazareth in Galilee, and crucified near Jerusalem in Judea. His ministry in the first three Gospels was largely in Galilee and in John it was mainly in Judea.

The Literary Background of the Gospels

There are two main questions concerning the literary background of the Gospels: Why are there four Gospels? Why are three of them so similar (Matthew, Mark, and Luke) and one (John) so different? Before this is answered in more detail, it will be helpful to look at the differences between the Synoptic Gospels and the autoptic Gospel.[4] The following contrast will help generalize and summarize the differences:

Synoptic Gospels (Matthew, Mark, Luke)	Autoptic Gospel (John)
public ministry	private ministry
Galilean ministry	Judean ministry
parables	no parables
human side	divine side
earthly aspect	heavenly aspect
synoptical	supplementary
official	personal

The Synoptic Problem

Let's deal with the synoptic problem. Why do the first three Gospels view the ministry of Christ from the same general perspective? To be more specific: Why are they so similar in content? And why are there marked differences between them? A whole host of subsidiary questions are involved here: Who wrote first? Who is depending on whom? What sources did each writer have?

The Basic Data of the Gospels

Book	Peculiarities	Coincidences
Matthew	42%	58%
Mark	7%	93%
Luke	59%	41%
John	92%	8%

This chart is attributed to Bishop Westcott. Reprinted from William Graham Scroggie, *Guide to the Gospels* (Grand Rapids: Kregel, 1995), 189.

Galilee in the Time of
Jesus.

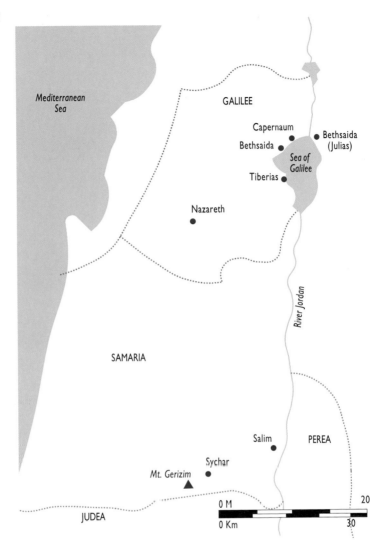

Only 50–55 verses are unique to Mark. Matthew has 1,068 verses; 500 are common with Mark. Luke has 1,149 verses; 320 are common with Mark. Mark has 661 verses; 50–55 are not in Matthew or Luke. Matthew and Luke have 250 verses in common that are not in Mark. Luke has 580 verses peculiar to itself (which have a Gentile tone). Matthew has 300 verses peculiar to itself (which have a Jewish tone).[5]

Some Proposed Solutions
Numerous theories have been put forth to solve the synoptic problem. Some are held by liberal scholars, some by evangelicals, and some by both (at least in part).

The One-Source Theory (Urevangelium)
This theory proposes one primitive Gospel from which all three Synoptics drew information. Accordingly, the similarities are due to one common source, and the differences result from the individual author's theme, interests, and style.

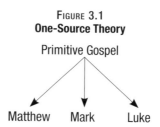

FIGURE 3.1
One-Source Theory

Primitive Gospel

Matthew   Mark   Luke

Problems: (1) The disappearance of the original source is difficult to explain. (2) The differences between the three Gospels are difficult to understand. (3) There is no record or manuscripts of any such primitive Gospel.

Two-Document Theory
The two-document theory claims that the similarities between the three Gospels are due to Matthew and Luke following Mark in order and wording. And the differences are explained by positing a hypothetical common source called Q (from the German: *quelle*, meaning "source") from which Matthew and Luke's common material comes.

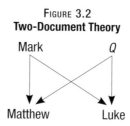

FIGURE 3.2
Two-Document Theory

Mark   Q

Matthew   Luke

Problems: (1) Q is a purely hypothetical source. There are no manuscripts of it or citations from it. (2) It is inconceivable that Q does not have a Passion and a resurrection narrative! This is the heart of the gospel (see 1 Cor. 15:1–19). (3) The absence of Jesus's many miracles betrays an anti-supernatural bias.

Mutual-Use Theory

According to mutual-use theory, the similarities among the three Gospels are due to two Gospels using the form of the third (for example, Matthew and Luke using Mark). The differences result from their own purpose and way of presentation.

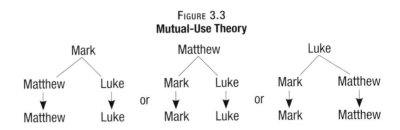

FIGURE 3.3
Mutual-Use Theory

Problems: (1) All possible combinations have been held of who used whom, and this weakens the view. (2) This theory does not explain verses that are common to two but not in the third. (3) While stressing "literary identity," it neglects each writer's individuality.

Four-Document Theory

The four-document theory contends that the similarities among the three Gospels result from the other two using Mark (from Rome AD 60) and Q (from Antioch AD 50). And the differences are due to L—Proto Luke (from Caesarea), which accounts for material unique to Luke (AD 60) and M—from Jerusalem (AD 65), to account for material unique to Matthew.

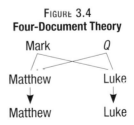

FIGURE 3.4
Four-Document Theory

Problems: (1) The theory is too complicated. (2) Mark is reduced to a literary enigma. (3) It is contrary to the claim and early confirmation of the Gospel writers as eyewitnesses. (4) Q is a purely hypothetical document.

Fragment Theory

The fragment theory holds that various people wrote down certain episodes of the teachings and acts of Jesus, resulting in one teacher having a collection of sayings, another having a collection of miracles, and another the Passion narrative. The various Gospels are accounted for as these collections were compiled into their current form. Luke's prologue is used as a support of this theory (Luke 1:1–4).

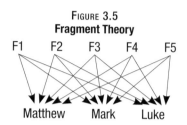

FIGURE 3.5
Fragment Theory

Problems: This theory fails to account for the similarities of the Gospels. Further, it is difficult to explain away the disappearance of these "collections." This theory fares no better than theories involving a Q document (see the form criticism theory below).

Oral Tradition Theory

The oral tradition theory proposes that the similarities in the Gospels result from all the writers using a common core of fixed oral tradition, and the differences are due to individual writers' choices to fit their different themes.

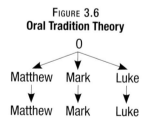

FIGURE 3.6
Oral Tradition Theory

Problems: (1) This theory does not account for the differences in the Gospels. (2) It neglects the role of the Gospel writers as eyewitnesses (Luke 1:1–4; John 19:35; 21:24; Acts 2:32; 4:19–20; 10:39; 1 Cor. 15:3–8; Heb. 2:3–4), supposing a later date.

Form Criticism Theory

According to this theory, the similarities in the Gospels result from all the writers using an original Q document from which they all copied. Meanwhile, the differences are due to the many different forms this information took in the early church. The information needs to be stripped of its mythological form to get at the original core of truth.

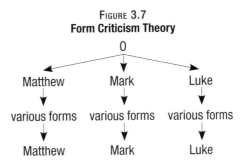

FIGURE **3.7**
Form Criticism Theory

Problems: (1) Q is a purely hypothetical source. (2) The theory wrongly assumes late dates for the Gospels (AD 70–100). (3) It neglects the role of eyewitnesses. (4) It is contrary to information in the accepted books of Paul (1 and 2 Corinthians, Romans, Galatians), which were written early (AD 55–60) and provide the same basic facts about Christ as the Gospels.

Independent Eyewitness Records Theory

The independent eyewitness records view contends that the similarities in the Gospels result from a natural overlap of eyewitness testimony of the same events, and the differences are due to individual writers' different choices to fit their respective themes.

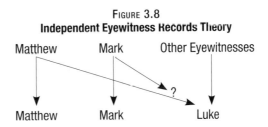

FIGURE **3.8**
Independent Eyewitness Records Theory

Problems: This theory has difficulty accounting for the apparent literary identity, but (1) impact events result in vivid memories; (2) very little is really literarily identical—only about 8 percent, which

45

Machaerus, where, according to Josephus, Herod Antipas put John the Baptist to death.

is easily memorized;[6] (3) the writers had supernaturally activated memories (John 14:26; 16:13); (4) the Gospel writers make a clear distinction between their words and Jesus's words, as is evident in the editions of the Bible in which Jesus's words are printed in red; and (5) the verified historicity of Acts[7] demonstrates the historical reliability of Dr. Luke and, thereby, the accuracy of the Gospel of Luke, which he also wrote (see Acts. 1:1 and Luke 1:3).

The Rational Background for the Gospels

Often the question of why there are four Gospels is asked. There are at least three basic reasons—veracity, doxology, and universality. The first reason is clearly apologetic.

Veracity

Multiple testimony confirms veracity. The Bible declares, "By the mouth of two or three witnesses every word may be established" (Matt. 18:16, from Deut. 19:15). Something as important as the entrance of God's Son into the world demanded multiple witnesses. Ordinarily two (or at the most three) would suffice, and four is more than sufficient to confirm the incarnation.

Doxology

But the reason for four Gospels is not only theological, it is also doxological (having to do with God's glory). They present a fourfold manifestation of God's glory. "And the Word became flesh and dwelt among us, and we beheld His glory" (John 1:14),

The Gospels:
A Fourfold Manifestation of Christ

	Matthew	Mark	Luke	John
Theme	King	Servant	Man	God
Presented to	Jews	Romans	Greeks	World
Ancestry	Abraham	(none)	Adam	God
Traced to	royalty	(none)	humanity	eternity
Symbol	Lion	Ox	Man	Eagle
Emphasis	taught	wrought	sought	thought
Provision	righteous	service	redemption	life
Key Verse	21:5	10:45	19:10	10:10
Key Word	sovereignty	ministry	humanity	deity
Savior	promised	powerful	perfect	personal

which in Ezekiel was manifested as a lion, ox, man, and eagle (Ezek. 1:10). Each of these images corresponds to the theme of one of the Gospels: Matthew the Lion (the king of beasts), Mark the Ox (the servant of man), Luke the Man, and John the Eagle (the heavenly one).

Universality

The four Gospels are targeted to everyone so that Christ is manifest to all. Matthew presents Christ as King to the Jews, Mark presents him as Servant to the Romans; Luke as Man to the Greeks, and John as God to the whole world. In short, the four Gospels manifest that the message of Christ is universal. The chart above illustrates this point.

There are many reasons for four Gospels, not the least of which are veracity, doxology, and universality. By multiple testimony and universal appeal—to the Jews, Romans, Greeks, and the entire world—the Son of God was manifested in human flesh. Deity entered the bloodstream of humanity; the Creator was born in a cowshed; the Master lay in a manger. As Paul put it, "Great is the mystery of godliness: God was manifested in the flesh" (1 Tim. 3:16).

STUDY QUESTIONS

1. About when was Jesus born? When did he die? How long did his public ministry last? Give reasons for your answers.

2. Where did Jesus spend the majority of his public ministry?

3. What is the synoptic problem? Why is it significant?

4. What are some possible solutions to the synoptic problem? Which one do you think best solves the problem? Give reasons for your answer.

5. What would be some reasons for having four Gospels?

SELECTED SOURCES

Blomberg, Craig. *The Historical Reliability of the Gospels*. Downers Grove, IL: InterVarsity, 1987.

Carson, D.A., Douglas Moo, and Leon Morris. *An Introduction to the New Testament*. Grand Rapids: Zondervan, 1992.

Geisler, Norman L., and Thomas Howe. *When Critics Ask: A Popular Handbook on Bible Difficulties*. Grand Rapids: Baker, 1997.

Gromacki, Robert G. *New Testament Survey*. Grand Rapids: Baker, 1974.

Guthrie, Donald. *New Testament Introduction*. Downers Grove, IL: InterVarsity, 1990.

Hemer, Colin. *The Book of Acts in the Setting of Hellenic History*. Winona Lake, MN: Eisenbrauns, 1990.

Hoehner, Harold. *Chronological Aspects of the Life of Christ*. Grand Rapids: Zondervan, 1977.

Linnemann, Eta. *Historical Criticism of the Bible*. Translated by Robert Yarborough. Grand Rapids: Kregel, 2001.

———. "Is There a Q?" *Biblical Review*, October 1995, 18–23, 42–43.

———. *Is There a Synoptic Problem?* Grand Rapids: Baker, 1992.

Radmacher, Earl, Ronald Allen, and H. Wayne House, eds. *Nelson's New Illustrated Bible Commentary*. Nashville: Thomas Nelson, 1999.

Robertson, A.T. *A Harmony of the Gospels*. New York: HarperCollins, 1922.

Scroggie, William Graham. *A Guide to the Gospels*. London: Pickering & Inglis, 1948. Reprint, Grand Rapids: Kregel, 1995.

Thomas, Robert, and Stan Gundry. *The New Harmony of the Gospels*. New York: HarperSanFrancisco, 1991.

Walvoord, John F., and Roy B. Zuck, eds. *The Bible Knowledge Commentary*. 2 vols. Wheaton: Victor, 1983.

4
The Gospel of Matthew

Who Wrote It? The traditional author of this book is revealed by its title: Matthew. He was one of the twelve apostles chosen by Christ (Matt. 10:1–3) and was a tax collector by profession (v. 3), which was considered one of the lower levels of the social strata, listed along with "heathen" (18:17).

Internal Evidence
Internal evidence is what is found inside a book and external evidence is what is discovered outside a book. The internal evidence for Matthew's authorship includes the following: (1) there are numerous references to money in this Gospel, which fits Matthew's role as a tax collector (see 17:24, 27; 18:24); (2) the many self-references to "Matthew the tax collector" fit his Christian humility; (3) his invitation of friends to a mere "dinner" (9:9–10) as opposed to a "great banquet" (Luke 5:29, where Matthew is called Levi) fits his humility; (4) perhaps in deference to his profession, he omits the parable of the tax collector (Luke 18:9–14) and the story of Zacchaeus, a tax collector (19:1–10); (5) in accord with his experience at keeping records, he recorded the long discourses of Jesus (Matthew 5–7, 10, 13, 20, 23–25); and (6) as an apostle, he had direct access to words, events, and supernatural guidance (John 14:26; 16:13).

External Evidence
There are many lines of external evidence: (1) The church has accepted that Matthew is the author of this book from the earliest known times. (2) The early Father Papias,[1] who was a disciple of Polycarp, the disciple of the apostle John, ascribed it to Matthew.

Papias wrote: "So then, Matthew, indeed, in the Hebrew language put together the Logia in writing; but as to their interpretation, each man dealt with it as he was able."[2] (3) Later Fathers of the church are virtually unanimous in ascribing it to Matthew. These include Clement of Rome, Polycarp, Justin Martyr, Clement of Alexandria, Tertullian, and Origen, who left little doubt about what the early church taught: "As I have learned by tradition concerning the Four Gospels, which alone are received without dispute by the Church of God under heaven: the first was written by St. Matthew, once a tax-gatherer, afterwards an Apostle of Jesus Christ, who published it for the benefit of the Jewish converts, composed in the Hebrew language."[3]

When Was It Written?

Matthew was written between 50 and 55 AD. The date of the book is supported by many factors: (1) it was some time after the events Matthew wrote about (ca. AD 29–33), as indicated by the phrase "to this day" (27:8; 28:15); (2) it was before the destruction of Jerusalem in AD 70, since he presented this event as yet future (24:1–2) and Jerusalem was still standing (24:15; 27:53); (3) the early and ancient church said Matthew wrote before Mark, and they were in a better position to know, being closer to the sources; (4) since Luke was written by ca. AD 60 (see chapter 6), and he refers to "many" (i.e., two or more) Gospels before that (1:1), of which Matthew and Mark are the only known candidates, it is likely that Matthew wrote between AD 50 and 55; (5) putting Mark first, as many contemporary critics do, is unnecessary literarily, questionable philosophically, and unjustified historically; (6) some liberal (for example, William R. Farmer) and some conservative (for example, Harold Hoehner) scholars support an early Matthew; and (7) since the literary evidence can be read either way and the earliest records attribute it to Matthew, Mark can be viewed as a more abbreviated version (basically Matthew minus the long discourses), since his theme was to stress what Jesus did more than what he said; this is appropriate to Mark's theme of Jesus as a servant (Mark 10:45).

To Whom Was It Written?

Since Matthew is presenting Christ as the King of the Jews, it is understandable that his audience would be primarily Jewish Christians. This is supported by several lines of evidence: (1) it may have been written originally in Aramaic (or Hebrew), as Papias affirmed; (2) it stresses the King and "kingdom of heaven" (see below), a phrase that would resonate with Jews familiar with Daniel's prophecy of the Messiah who would bring in the kingdom for the "God of heaven" (Dan. 2:44); (3) Matthew has

Some of the caves at Qumran where biblical scrolls were discovered.

numerous Old Testament references—129 citations from 25 Old Testament books; and (4) some have suggested that he wrote to Christians who were witnessing to Jews, which may be implied by the Gentile references, such as: the visit of Magi (2:1 NIV), the command to "preach to all nations" (28:18–20), Jesus's genealogy (1:1–17) with Gentile women (Ruth and Rahab) in it, the Roman Centurion story (8:5–10), and the reference of the kingdom being given to Gentiles (21:43).

Where Were Its Readers Located?

The immediate destination of Matthew's Gospel is not certain. Early Fathers said the people of Judea were the audience. The Qumran *Manual of Discipline* (1, 4, 10) has the Matthew quote about hating your enemy (from Matt. 5:43), which Jesus rebuked, and Qumran is in Judea.

Others suggest Antioch was the intended audience, since that city boasted a significant Jewish population, was a missionary center for early Christianity, and some early Syro-Jewish quotes came from Matthew. Whether directly to Jewish Christians or to Gentile Christians working with them, it seems clear that Matthew has an apologetic purpose to confirm that Jesus was the Jewish Messiah.

Why Was It Written?

The purposes of the book of Matthew are manifest in several factors: (1) it aimed to present Christ as the fulfillment of Old Testament prophecy as an apologetic to unbelieving Jews; (2) it was geared to provide the teaching content of Christ's ministry for use in the church, as evidenced by the long discourses of Jesus; and (3) it also provided hope in view of the impending judgment that the King would soon return and set up his kingdom (19:28; 24:30; 25:31).

What Is It About?

The Theme: Christ is the King of the Jews.

The Key Verse: "Behold, your King is coming to you" (21:5).

Key Words and Phrases: *end of the age* (5x), *Father* (of God) (44x), *kingdom* (23x), *kingdom of heaven* (32x), *righteous* (17x), *righteousness* (7x), *Son of David* (10x), *that it might be fulfilled* (15x), *which was spoken* (in the Old Testament) (20x), and *worship* (14x). See appendix 3 for a more complete word study.

Ancestry of Christ: The ancestry of Christ is traced to Abraham, the first ancestor of the Jews, and to David, the king of the Jews through whom the Messiah would come (1:1).

Old Testament References: Matthew has 129 references to the Old Testament (from 25 books). Some of the more popular books referenced are Psalms (29x), Deuteronomy (27x), Isaiah (26x), Jeremiah (13x), Leviticus (12x), Genesis (10x), Zechariah (10x), and Daniel (9x).[4]

Matthew's Use of *Church*: Matthew is the only Gospel to call the "church" by name (Matt. 16:18; 18:17).

Matthew's Use of *Fulfill*: *Fulfill* means "to fill completely, to accomplish, to make full, to complete, to end." Matthew used the term *fulfilled* (*fulfill*) fifteen times of Christ:

1. "Now all this was done that it might be *fulfilled* which was spoken by the Lord through the prophet, saying, 'Behold, a virgin shall be with child, and bear a Son, and they shall call His name Immanuel,' which is translated, 'God with us'" (1:22–23).

2. "And [Jesus] was there until the death of Herod, that it might be *fulfilled* which was spoken by the Lord through the prophet, saying, 'Out of Egypt I called My Son'" (2:15).

3. "Then was *fulfilled* what was spoken by Jeremiah the prophet, saying: 'A voice was heard in Ramah, lamentation, weeping, and great mourning, Rachel weeping for her children, refusing to be comforted, because they were no more'" (2:17–18).

4. "And he came and dwelt in a city called Nazareth, that it might be *fulfilled* which was spoken by the prophets, 'He shall be called a Nazarene'" (2:23).

The town of Nazareth is today dominated by the Church of the Annunciation.

5. "That it might be *fulfilled* which was spoken by Isaiah the prophet, saying: 'The land of Zebulun and the land of Naphtali, the way of the sea, beyond the Jordan, Galilee of the Gentiles: the people who sat in darkness saw a great light'" (4:14–16).

6. "Do not think that I came to destroy the Law or the Prophets. I did not come to destroy but to *fulfill*" (5:17).

7. "That it might be *fulfilled* which was spoken by Isaiah the prophet, saying, 'He Himself took our infirmities and bore our sicknesses'" (8:17).

8. "That it might be *fulfilled* which was spoken by Isaiah the prophet, saying: 'Behold! My Servant whom I have chosen, My Beloved in whom My soul is well pleased; I will put My Spirit upon Him, and He will declare justice to the Gentiles'" (12:17–18).

9. "And in them the prophecy of Isaiah is *fulfilled*, which says: 'Hearing you will hear and shall not understand, and seeing you will see and not perceive'" (13:14).

10. "That it might be *fulfilled* which was spoken by the prophet, saying: 'I will open My mouth in parables; I will utter things which have been kept secret from the foundation of the world'" (13:35).

11. "All this was done that it might be *fulfilled* which was spoken by the prophet, saying: 'Tell the daughter of Zion, "Behold, your King is coming to you, lowly, and sitting on a donkey, a colt, the foal of a donkey"'" (21:4–5).

12. "How then could the Scriptures be *fulfilled*, that it must happen thus?" (26:54).

13. "'But all this was done that the Scriptures of the prophets might be *fulfilled*.' Then all the disciples forsook Him and fled" (26:56).

14. "Then was *fulfilled* what was spoken by Jeremiah the prophet, saying, 'And they took the thirty pieces of silver, the value of Him who was priced, whom they of the children of Israel priced, and gave them for the potter's field, as the Lord directed me'" (27:9–10).

15. "Then they crucified Him, and divided His garments, casting lots, that it might be *fulfilled* which was spoken by the prophet: 'They divided My garments among them'"(27:35).

Key Sayings: There are nine Beatitudes (5:1–12) and thirteen more often-quoted sayings (6:21, 24, 33; 7:1, 7, 12, 20; 10:39; 11:19, 28, 29; 12:30, 37).

Discourses: Matthew has many long discourses (chaps. 5–7, 10, 11, 13, 18, 20, 23, 24–25).

Parables: There are forty-five parables in the book of Matthew.[5] Thirteen parables are unique to Matthew (most of which are in chapter 13).

Trinitarian Formula: Matthew alone records the "Trinitarian" baptismal formula (28:18–20). All three members of the Trinity are present at Jesus's baptism (3:16–17).

THE OUTLINE:

    I. The Person of the King (1:1–3:12)
        A. Ancestry—Abraham (1:1–17)
        B. Advent—Mary (1:18–2:23)
        C. Ambassador—John (3:1–12)
    II. The Preparation of the King (3:13–4:11)
        A. Baptism (3:13–17)
        B. Temptation (4:1–11)
    III. The Proclamation of the King (4:12–9:38)
        A. His message (4:12–25)
        B. His manifesto (5:1–7:29)
        C. His methods (8:1–9:38)
    IV. The Propagation of the King (10:1–25:46)
        A. The messengers (10:1–15)
        B. The mission (vv. 16–42)
        C. The message (11:1–30)

THE CONTENTS: Matthew is the Gospel of the King and his kingdom. The summary of the content of Matthew follows the main points of the outline: the Person of the King is presented (1:1–3:12); the preparation of the King is made (3:13–4:11), then the proclamation of the King is declared (4:12–9:38); the propagation of the King is carried out (chaps. 10–25), the Passion of the King is recorded (chaps. 26–27); and the power of the King is demonstrated in his resurrection (chap. 28).

First, we have the Person of the King presented. His ancestry is traced back to King David, the descendent of Abraham, the father of the Jewish nation (1:1–17). His advent features his mother, the Virgin Mary (vv. 18–25), and the Magi who come to worship the King (2:1–12). Then his ambassador, John the Baptist, heralds the King (3:1–12). Next we see the preparation of the King by his baptism (3:13–17) and temptation (4:1–11).

Once the King is anointed and announced, he is proclaimed. First, he announces his mission: "Repent, for the kingdom of heaven is at hand" (4:17). Then he sets forth the manifesto of his kingdom—the Sermon on the Mount (chaps. 5–7). Following this we see the methods of the King. Succinctly put, he provides miracles to confirm his message, signs to verify his sermon (chaps. 8–9).

Then the King chooses messengers (apostles) for the propagation of his kingdom (10:1–15). Their mission is to "the lost sheep of the house of Israel" (10:6). The message is to preach the gospel of the kingdom, which John had proclaimed (chap. 11). The King, however, was rejected by his people (chap. 12). He proclaimed parables of the mystery of his spiritual kingdom through which he would reign until he returned to restore the messianic kingdom to Israel (chap. 13). Nonetheless, he continued to provide his messianic credentials by miracles (14:1–16:12), and elicited from his messengers that he was indeed the Messiah and that he would build his church during this interregnum period (16:13–28), giving them a foretaste of his coming kingdom glory on the mount of transfiguration (17:1–13).

After this he announces his death and final rejection by his people, presenting both the paradigm (model) for his disciples (chaps. 18–20) and a parable of his rejection (chaps. 21–23). Looking beyond his death and resurrection, he predicts the events leading up to his coming again in power and great glory (chaps. 24–25). Finally, Matthew presents the Passion of the King as he prepares for it by eating the Passover lamb (26:1–46) and then being the Passover Lamb (1 Cor. 5:7) in his death on the cross (chap. 27), only to triumph over death in his powerful resurrection and great commission to his disciples (chap. 28).

How to Respond to Critics

Matthew 1:17—*Were there fourteen or thirteen generations listed between the captivity and Christ?*[6]
Problem: Matthew says the generations "from the captivity in Babylon until the Christ are fourteen generations." However, he lists only thirteen names after the captivity. So, which is correct, thirteen or fourteen?
Solution: Both are correct. Jeconiah is counted in both lists, since he lived both before and after the captivity. So there are literally fourteen names listed "from the captivity in Babylon until the Christ," just as Matthew says. There are also literally fourteen names listed between David and the captivity, just as Matthew claims (vv. 6–12). There is no error in the text at all.

Matthew 4:14–16—*Why does Matthew seem to incorrectly quote Isaiah?*
Problem: It appears that Matthew does not quote Isaiah 9:1–2 accurately. Rather, he seems to have changed it.
Solution: It is not necessary to quote a passage *verbatim* to cite it *accurately*. Matthew does not distort the meaning of this passage. He simply condenses or summarizes it. To *paraphrase* accurately is not to *distort*. Otherwise, no news report or historical account was ever accurate, since summary is essential to history.

The Mount of
Beatitudes, Galilee.

Matthew 8:20 (see also 20:18; 24:30)—*If Jesus was the Son of God,
why did he call himself the Son of Man?*

Problem: Jesus referred to himself most often as the Son of Man.
This seems to point to his humanity more than his deity. If he
was really the Messiah, the Son of God, why did he use the self-
description "Son of Man"?

Solution: First of all, even if the phrase "Son of Man" is a reference
to Jesus's humanity, it is not a denial of his deity. By becoming
man, Jesus did not cease being God. The incarnation of Christ did
not involve the subtraction of deity but the addition of humanity.
Clearly Jesus claimed to be God on many occasions (see Matt.
16:16–17; John 8:58; 10:30). But in addition to being divine, he
was also human. He had two natures conjoined in one person.

Furthermore, Jesus was not denying his deity by referring
to himself as the Son of Man. The term *Son of Man* is used to
describe Christ's deity as well. The Bible says that only God can
forgive sins (Isa. 43:25; Mark 2:7), but as the Son of Man, Jesus
had the power to forgive sins (Mark 2:10). Likewise, Christ will
return to earth as the Son of Man in clouds of glory to reign on
earth (Matt. 26:63–64). In this passage Jesus is citing Daniel 7:13
where the Messiah is described as the "Ancient of Days," a phrase
used to indicate his deity (see v. 9).

When Jesus was asked by the high priest whether he was the Son of God (Matt. 26:63), he responded affirmatively, declaring that he was the Son of Man who would come on the clouds of heaven (v. 64). This indicated that Jesus used the term *Son of Man* to indicate his deity as the Son of God.

Finally, the phrase *Son of Man* emphasizes who Jesus is in relation to his incarnation and his work of salvation. In the Old Testament the kinsman redeemer was a close relative of someone who was in need of redemption (see Lev. 25:25–26, 48–49; Ruth 2:20). So Jesus, as our Kinsman Redeemer, was identifying himself with humankind as its Savior and Redeemer. Those who knew the Old Testament truth about Messiah being the Son of Man understood Jesus's implicit claims to deity. Those who did not know, would not recognize this. Jesus often said things in this way to test his audience and separate believers from unbelievers (see Matt. 13:10–17).

Matthew 8:28–34 NIV (see also Mark 5:1–20 NIV; Luke 8:26–39 NIV)—*Where were the demoniacs healed?*
Problem: The first three Gospels (Matthew, Mark, and Luke) each give an account of Jesus healing demoniacs. Matthew states that the place where the healing took place was the country of the Gadarenes. However, Mark and Luke say it was in the country of the Gerasenes.
Solution: There is a textual problem here. The critical text of the Greek New Testament[7] renders Mark and Luke the same as Matthew, namely, in the country of the Gadarenes. However, some manuscripts give the name of the country as the Gerasenes. It is possible to account for the variant reading in these manuscripts as a scribal error. Gadara may have been the capital of the region, and Matthew therefore referred to the area as the "country of the Gadarenes" because the people of that region, whether they lived in Gadara or not, were identified as Gadarenes. Mark and Luke were perhaps giving a more general reference to the country of the Gerasenes, which was the wider area in which the incident occurred. However, a scribe, confusing the reference in Matthew as a reference to the town instead of the people of the region, may have attempted to correct the manuscripts and altered the references to make those in Matthew uniform. It seems that the best textual evidence is in favor of Gadara, although there are varying opinions among commentators. There is no contradiction or error here, because the problem developed as a result of transcription, and there is no evidence to demonstrate that there was a conflict in the original manuscripts.

Matthew 8:28–34 (see also Mark 5:1–20; Luke 8:26–39)—*How many demoniacs were healed?*

Problem: Matthew reports that two demoniacs came to Jesus, while Mark and Luke say that only one demoniac approached him. This appears to be a contradiction.

Solution: There is a very fundamental mathematical law that reconciles this apparent contradiction—wherever there are two, there is always one. There are no exceptions! There were actually two demoniacs that came to Jesus. Perhaps Mark and Luke mentioned the one because he was more noticeable or prominent for some reason. However, the fact that Mark and Luke mention only one does not negate the fact that there were two, as Matthew said, for wherever there are two, there is always one. It never fails. If Mark or Luke had said there was *only* one, then that would be a contradiction. But, the word *only* is not in the text. The critic has to change the text to make it a contradiction, in which case the problem is not with the Bible but with the critic.

Matthew 12:40 (see also John 19:14)—*If Jesus was crucified on Friday, how could he have been in the grave three days and nights?*

Problem: Christ rose on Sunday (Matt. 28:1), but he stated that he would be "three days and three nights in the heart of the earth." If Christ was crucified on Friday, how could he have been three days and three nights in the earth and rise on Sunday only two days later?

Solution 1: Some scholars believe Jesus was in the grave for three full days and nights (seventy-two hours), being crucified on Wednesday. They offer the following in support of this contention. (1) They insist that this is the literal meaning of the phrase "three days and nights." (2) They point out that, on the view that Jesus was crucified on Friday, there is no explanation for what he did on Wednesday. All other days are accounted for. (3) They argue that the Passover was not on a fixed day (Friday) but floated.

Solution 2: Most biblical scholars believe that Jesus was crucified on Friday. They take the phrase "three days and nights" to be a Hebrew figure of speech referring to any part of three days and nights. They offer the following in support of their position.

1. The phrase "day and night" does not necessarily mean a complete twenty-four-hour period. The psalmist's reference to meditating "day and night" on God's Word (Ps. 1:2) does not mean one has to read the Bible all day and all night.

2. It is clear from the use of the phrase "three days and three nights" in the book of Esther (4:16) that it does not mean

seventy-two hours. For, although they fasted three days and nights between the time they started and the time she appeared before the king, the passage states that Esther appeared before the king "on the third day" (5:1). If they began on Friday, the third day would be Sunday. Hence, "three days and nights" must mean any part of three days and nights.

3. Jesus used the phrase "on the third day" to describe the time of his resurrection after his crucifixion (Matt 16:21 NIV; 17:23 NIV; 20:19 NIV; see also 26:61). But "*on the third day*" cannot mean "*after* three days," which seventy-two hours demands. On the other hand, the phrase "the third day" or "three days and nights" can be understood to mean within three days and nights.

4. This view fits best with the chronological order of events as given by Mark (see 14:1), as well as the fact that Jesus died on Passover day (Friday) to fulfill the conditions of being our Passover Lamb (1 Cor. 5:7; see Lev. 23:1–7).

Matthew 16:16 (see Mark 8:29; Luke 9:20)—*Why does Peter's confession here differ from that recorded in Mark and Luke?*
Problem: Peter's confession of Christ in Caesarea Philippi is stated differently in the three Gospels:

Matthew: "You are the Christ, the Son of the living God."

Mark: "You are the Christ."

Luke: "The Christ of God."

If the Bible is the inspired Word of God, why are there three different reports of what Peter said? What did he really say?

Solution: There are several reasons why the Gospel accounts of Peter's statements differ. (1) Peter probably spoke Aramaic, while the Gospels are written in Greek. So some changes come naturally as a result of translating the words differently. (2) The Gospel writers sometimes paraphrased the essence of what people said, much like the way journalists do today. (3) Other writers selected and abbreviated what was said to fit the theme of their book or the emphasis they wished to make.

What is important to notice is that the Gospel writers never *created* these sayings, rather, they *reported* them. Further, their reports were in accordance with journalistic standards of the day (and even today for that matter). Also, whenever there are multiple

Caesarea Philippi.

reports, they all give the essence of what was said. For example, all three reports note that Peter confessed that Jesus is "the Christ of God." Sometimes, all the reports can be put together as a whole, giving what may have been the word-for-word original statement of Peter. For example, Peter may have said exactly what Matthew reported, and the others may have reported the important parts of Peter's confession, as illustrated in the following:

> Matthew: "You are the Christ, the Son of the living God."
> Mark: "You are the Christ [the Son of the living God]."
> Luke: "[You are] the Christ [the Son] of [the living] God."

Matthew 20:29–34 (see Mark 10:46–52; Luke 18:35–43)—*Did Jesus heal two blind men or just one?*
Problem: Matthew says that Christ healed two men, but Mark and Luke refer to only one man being healed. This appears to be a clear contradiction.
Solution: Although Mark and Luke record one individual getting healed, this does not mean that there were not two, as Matthew

says there were. First of all, Mark does not declare that there was *only* one blind man healed. Matthew says there were two, and, as we saw earlier, where there are two, there is always one, every time! The fact that Mark mentions the name of one blind man, Bartimaeus, and his father (Timaeus, 10:46), indicates that Mark is centering on the one who was personally known to him. If two men were to receive a medal of honor from the president of the United States and one was your friend, it is understandable that, when you relate the story, you might speak only of the one you know who received the medal.

Matthew 20:29–34 (see also Mark 10:46–52; Luke 18:35–43)—
Did Jesus heal the blind man coming into or going out of Jericho?
Problem: According to Luke, a blind man was healed as Jesus entered the city of Jericho, but Matthew and Mark declare that the healing took place as Jesus left the city of Jericho. Again, the accounts do not seem to be harmonious.
Solution: Some believe that the healing in Luke may have actually taken place as Jesus left Jericho, claiming that it was only the initial contact that took place as "He was coming near Jericho" (v. 35). The blind man may have followed him through the city, since he was continually begging Jesus to heal him (vv. 38–39). But this seems unlikely, since even after the healing (v. 43), the very next verse (19:1) says, "Then Jesus entered and passed through Jericho."

Others respond by noting there were two Jerichos, the old and the new, so that as he went out of one, he came into the other.

Still others suggest that these are two different events. Matthew and Mark clearly affirm the healing occurred as Jesus left the city (Matt. 20:29; Mark 10:46). But Luke speaks of healing one blind man as he entered the city. The suggestion that this is a different healing is supported by the fact that Luke refers to only a "multitude" of people being present as Jesus entered the city (v. 36), but both Matthew (v. 29) and Mark (v. 46) make a point to say there was a "great multitude" of people by the time Jesus left the city. If the word spread of the miraculous healing on the way into the city, this would account for the swelling of the crowd. It might also explain why two blind men were waiting on the other side of the city to plead for Jesus to heal them. Perhaps the first blind man who was healed went quickly to tell his blind friends what had happened to him. Or maybe the other blind men were already stationed at the other end of the city in their customary begging position. At any rate, there is no irresolvable difficulty in the passage. The two accounts can be understood in a completely compatible way.

The Kidron Valley, Jerusalem.

Matthew 21:2 (see also Mark 11:2; Luke 19:30)—*Were there two donkeys involved in the triumphal entry or just one?*

Problem: Matthew's account records Jesus's request of two disciples to go into a village and get two donkeys. But in Mark and Luke, he requests that the two disciples get just the colt.

Solution: Both animals were involved in Jesus's triumphal entry into Jerusalem. There is no mistake in the accounts, because Mark and Luke mention just the colt (*pōlos*), and Matthew refers to the colt (*pōlos*, 21:2, 5) and its mother. The passage in Matthew is pointing out the literal fulfillment of the prophecy of Zechariah 9:9, which states, "Behold, your King is coming to you; . . . lowly and riding on a donkey, a colt, the foal of a donkey." The Greek version of the Old Testament uses the same word for colt (*pōlos*) as do the New Testament passages. Matthew states literally that once the disciples placed their garments on the donkeys, Jesus sat on them, that is, on their garments. Matthew does not say that Jesus rode on both the mother and the colt. It merely states that Jesus sat on the garments that the disciples had placed on the donkeys. Perhaps they placed some garments on the mother and others on the colt, and Jesus sat on those garments that were placed on the colt. The fact is the text of Matthew simply does not say on which donkey Jesus sat.

Mark and Luke focus on the colt on which Jesus rode, while Matthew mentions the presence of the colt's mother. Her presence may have been necessary because the colt was so young. Mark states that no one had ridden on the colt (v. 2) and that the colt would be taking a passenger through a noisy crowd (v. 9). Perhaps the mother was brought along to be a calming influence on her young.

Matthew 27:5 (see also Acts 1:18)—*Did Judas die by hanging or by falling on rocks?*
Problem: Matthew declares that Judas hanged himself. However, the book of Acts says that he fell and his body burst open.
Solution: These accounts are not contradictory but complementary. Judas hanged himself exactly as Matthew affirms that he did. The account in Acts simply adds that Judas fell, and his body opened up at the middle and his intestines gushed out. This is the very thing one would expect of someone who hanged himself from a tree over a cliff and fell on sharp rocks below.

Matthew 27:37 (see also Mark 15:26; Luke 23:38; John 19:19)—*Why are all the Gospel accounts of the inscription on the cross different?*
Problem: The wording of the accusation above Christ's head on the cross is rendered differently in each Gospel account.

Matthew:	"This is Jesus the king of the Jews."
Mark:	"The king of the Jews."
Luke:	"This is the king of the Jews."
John:	"Jesus of Nazareth, the king of the Jews."

Solution: While there is a difference in what is omitted, the important phrase, "the king of the Jews," is identical in all four Gospels. The differences can be accounted for in different ways.

First, John 19:20 says, "Then many of the Jews read this title, for the place where Jesus was crucified was near the city; and it was written in Hebrew, Greek, and Latin." So there are at least three different languages in which the sign above Christ's head was written. Some of the differences may come from it being rendered in different languages.

Further, it is possible that each Gospel gives only part of the complete statement as follows:

Matthew:	"This is Jesus [of Nazareth] the king of the Jews."
Mark:	"[This is Jesus of Nazareth] the king of the Jews."
Luke:	"This is [Jesus of Nazareth] the king of the Jews."
John:	"[This is] Jesus of Nazareth, the king of the Jews."

Thus the whole statement may have read "This is Jesus of Nazareth, the king of the Jews." In this case, each Gospel is giving the essential part ("the king of the Jews"), but no Gospel is giving the whole inscription. But neither is any Gospel contradicting what the other Gospels say. The accounts are divergent and mutually complementary, not contradictory.

Matthew 27:44—*Did both robbers revile Christ, or did only one do this?*

Problem: Matthew says here: "Even the robbers who were crucified with Him reviled Him." However, according to Luke, only one reviled him (Luke 23:39), while the other one believed in him, asking, "Lord, remember me when You come into Your kingdom" (v. 42).

Solution: This difficulty is easily resolved on the supposition that at first both reviled the Lord, but that later one repented. Perhaps he was so impressed with hearing Jesus forgive those who crucified him (v. 34) that he was convinced that Jesus was the Savior and asked to be part of his coming kingdom (v. 42).

Matthew 28:5 (see also John 20:12)—*Why does Matthew say there was only one angel at the tomb when John says there were two?*

Problem: Matthew 28:5 refers to the "angel" at the tomb after Jesus's resurrection, and yet John says there were "two angels" there.

Solution: Matthew does not say there was only *one* angel. John says there were two, and wherever there are two, there is always one; it never fails! The critic has to add the word "only" to Matthew's account to make it contradictory. But then the problem would not be with what the Bible actually says, but with what the critic adds to it.

Matthew probably focuses on the one who *spoke* and "said to the women, 'Do not be afraid'" (Matt. 28:5). John referred to the number of angels they *saw*; "and she saw two angels."

Matthew 28:18–20—*How can three persons be God when there is only one God?*

Problem: Matthew speaks of the Father, Son, and Holy Spirit, all being part of one "name." But these are three distinct persons. How can there be three persons in the Godhead when there is only "one God" (Deut. 6:4; 1 Cor. 8:6)?

Solution: God is one in *essence*, but three in *persons*. God has one *nature*, but three *centers of consciousness*. That is, there is only one *What* in God, but there are three *Whos*. There is one *It* but three *Is*. This is a mystery but not a contradiction. It would be contradictory to say God is only one person but also three persons. Or that God is only one nature, but that he also has three natures. But to declare, as orthodox Christians do, that God is one essence, eternally revealed in three distinct persons is not a contradiction.

STUDY QUESTIONS

1. What is the evidence, internal and external, that Matthew is the author of this Gospel?

2. When was Matthew written?
   List your reasons for the date chosen.

3. To whom was Matthew writing?

4. What were possible destinations of Matthew's Gospel?

5. What was Matthew's theme and purpose in writing the Gospel?

6. Given Matthew's presentation of Christ as the King of the Jews, why is it appropriate that Matthew is the first Gospel in the New Testament?

7. Why is it that the promise to Israel in the Old Testament of a literal kingdom is not fulfilled in the New Testament?
   What evidence did Matthew give that it will be fulfilled some day?

SELECTED SOURCES

Blomberg, Craig. *The Historical Reliability of the Gospels*. Downers Grove, IL: InterVarsity, 1987.

———. Matthew. *New American Commentary*. Nashville: Broadman, 1992.

Carson, D.A. Matthew. *Expositor's Bible Commentary*. 2 vols. Grand Rapids: Zondervan, 1984.

Carson, D.A., Douglas Moo, and Leon Morris. *An Introduction to the New Testament*. Grand Rapids: Zondervan, 1992.

Geisler, Norman L., and Thomas Howe. *When Critics Ask: A Popular Handbook on Bible Difficulties*. Grand Rapids: Baker, 1997.

Glasscock, Lawrence E. *Matthew*. Moody Gospel Commentary. Chicago: Moody, 1997.

Guthrie, Donald. *New Testament Introduction*. Downers Grove, IL: InterVarsity, 1990.

Harrison, Everett F. *An Introduction to the New Testament*. Grand Rapids: Eerdmans, 1971.

Hemer, Colin. *The Book of Acts in the Setting of Hellenic History*. Winona Lake, MN: Eisenbrauns, 1990.

Linnemann, Eta. *Is There a Synoptic Problem?* Grand Rapids: Baker, 1992.

MacArthur, John. *Matthew*. MacArthur New Testament Commentary. 4 vols. Chicago: Moody, 1985–89.

Morris, Leon. *Matthew*. Pillar New Testament Commentary. Grand Rapids: Eerdmans, 1992.

Radmacher, Earl, Ronald Allen, and H. Wayne House, eds. *Nelson's New Illustrated Bible Commentary*. Nashville: Thomas Nelson, 1999.

Robertson, A.T. *A Harmony of the Gospels*. New York: HarperCollins, 1922.

Scroggie, William Graham. *A Guide to the Gospels*. London: Pickering & Inglis, 1948. Reprint, Grand Rapids: Kregel, 1995.

Thomas, Robert, and Stan Gundry. *The New Harmony of the Gospels*. New York: HarperSanFrancisco, 1991.

Walvoord, John F., and Roy B. Zuck, eds. *The Bible Knowledge Commentary*. 2 vols. Wheaton: Victor, 1983.

5
The Gospel of Mark

Who Wrote It? The book was written by John Mark, a companion of Peter. John was his Hebrew name and Mark his Latin name.

We know this about Mark. He was: (1) an associate of Peter (1 Peter 5:13), (2) once a missionary companion of Paul (Acts 13:5), (3) the son of one Mary (12:12), (4) a nephew (or cousin) of Barnabas (Col. 4:10), (5) the subject of dispute between Paul and Barnabas (Acts 15:37–40), (6) later reconciled to Paul (2 Tim. 4:11), (7) perhaps the person whose home was the "upper room" (see Mark 14:12–16; Acts. 12:12, 14),[1] (8) possibly well-to-do (owned a big home) and his cousin owned land (4:36–37), and (9) may have been the unclad lad who fled the Garden (Mark 14:51–52).

Internal Evidence

The internal evidence for Mark's authorship is supported by many lines of evidence: (1) he was familiar with the geography of the land and Jerusalem (5:1; 6:53; 8:10; 11:1; 13:3); (2) he knew Aramaic, the common language of the day (5:41; 7:11, 34; 14:36); (3) he understood Jewish institutions and customs (1:21; 2:14, 16, 18; 7:2–4); (4) the account is vivid and detailed, revealing contact with Jesus's "inner circle"—James, Peter, and John (1:16–20, 29–31, 35–38; 5:21–24, 35–43; 6:39, 53–54; 9:14–15; 10:32, 46; 14:32–34); (5) he used Peter's words and deeds (8:29, 32–33; 9:5–6; 10:28–30; 14:29–31, 66–72); (6) he alone added "and Peter" in the resurrection account (16:7; see 1 Cor. 15:5); (7) there is a striking similarity between his broad outline and Peter's sermon in Acts 10:34–43.

The External Evidence

The external evidence for Mark being the author of this Gospel is good. First, the earliest manuscripts have his name on them, and one of the earliest Church Fathers, Papias (AD 110), attributed it to Mark. Papias wrote:

> And the Presbyter used to say this, "Mark became Peter's interpreter and wrote accurately all that he remembered, not, indeed, in order, of the things said or done by the Lord. He had not heard the Lord, nor had he followed him, but later on, as I said, followed Peter, who used to give teaching as necessity demanded but not making, as it were, an arrangement of the Lord's oracles, so that Mark did nothing wrong in thus writing down single points as he remembered them."[2]

What is more, other early Fathers unanimously agreed that Mark was the author. These include Irenaeus, Clement of Alexander, Justin Martyr, Tatian, Tertullian, Origen, Jerome, and Eusebius.

When Was It Written?

The ancient church favored the primacy of Matthew, but most modern scholars believe Mark wrote first. On balance of external and internal evidence, it would appear that the ancient church was right. (1) The book must have been written before AD 70, since the temple was still standing (13:2, 14–23). (2) Luke, who wrote ca. AD 60, may have alluded to Mark (Luke 1:1) when he spoke of others who had written a Gospel before him. (3) Papias, who was the closest Father to the events, said Matthew wrote first and Mark later. If so, then Mark probably wrote ca. AD 55–60.

Irenaeus said Mark wrote after Peter's "departure." If this means his death, then Mark wrote between 68 and 70, but this is unlikely since the internal evidence favors an early date for Mark. This is because: (1) Luke may refer to Mark by ca. AD 60 (Luke 1:1); (2) Irenaeus may have been wrong or misinterpreted; (3) "departure" may be understood geographically; and (4) Papias said Matthew was first, then Mark before Luke (who wrote in AD 60). Hence, Mark would have been written ca. AD 55–60.

To Whom Was It Written?

Mark was written to Roman Christians. This is supported by: (1) the Latinisms (*modios* means "bushel" or "basket"—4:21; *kēnsos* means "census"—12:14; *kenturiōn* means "centurion"—15:39); (2) the Servant theme (see 10:45), which fits the Roman culture, since about half of its people were slaves; (3) his explaining the Jewish customs to his non-Jewish audience (see 7:3); (4) fewer Old Testament references (only 63) than Matthew (128) and Luke (90–100); (5) the

Roman tone; (6) the fact that Mark was probably in Rome with Peter (see 1 Peter 5:13); (7) the long discourses found in Matthew that are missing in Mark. Romans were not interested in what a servant *taught* but what he *wrought*.

Where Were Its Readers Located?

The readers of Mark were located in Rome and the Roman world.

Why Was It Written?

Several purposes for the writing of Mark may be derived from the text. (1) The basic reason was to depict Christ as a servant to Romans (10:45). (2) It aimed to give a historical explanation of "the gospel" (1:1). (3) Mark wanted to provide an apologetic to the Romans for Jewish unbelief in their own Messiah (see 3:5; 7:6). After all, the question would have been asked: why should Romans accept Jesus if the Jews had rejected him as their Messiah?

What Is It About?

The Theme: Christ the Servant of the Lord.

The Key Verse: "For even the Son of Man did not come to be served, but to serve, and to give His life a ransom for many" (10:45).

Key Words and Phrases: *authority* (10x), *straightway, immediately* (Gk. *eutheōs*; this word is used 40x, which is more than it's used in the rest of the New Testament), and *spirit* (23x). See appendix 3 for a more complete word study.

Ancestry of Christ: Mark does not give Christ's ancestry, since the theme is a Servant, and a servant needs none.

The Pattern: The basic outline of Mark is patterned after Peter's sermon (Acts 10:36–42):

> The word which God sent to the children of Israel, preaching peace through Jesus Christ—He is Lord of all—that word you know, which was proclaimed throughout all Judea, and began from Galilee after the baptism which John preached: how God anointed Jesus of Nazareth with the Holy Spirit and with power [Mark 1:1–20], who went about doing good and healing all who were oppressed by the devil, for God was with Him [1:21–10:52]. And we are witnesses of all things which He did both in the land of the Jews and in Jerusalem [chaps. 11–14], whom they killed by hanging on a tree [chap. 15]. Him God raised up on the third day, and showed Him openly, not to all the people, but to witnesses chosen before by God, even to us who ate and drank with Him after he arose from the dead. And He commanded us to preach to the people, and to testify that it is He who was ordained by God to be Judge of the living and the dead [chap. 16].

Miracles: Mark has eighteen miracles, only four parables (4:2–20, 26–29, 30–32; 12:1–9), and only one major discourse (13:3–37). **Other Characteristics:** Jesus is depicted as Servant of the Lord (see Isa. 42:1). Mark is more biographical than theological. It stresses the works not words of Jesus. Matthew emphasizes what Jesus *said* and Mark what Jesus *did*. It does not have the long didactic (teaching) passages (see Matthew 5–7; 10; 13; 18; 20; 23; 24–25). It is the Gospel of activity and power (both were desired by the Romans). Mark uses "Jesus," "Jesus Christ," "Lord," not "Christ" (Messiah). There are more questions (thirteen) asked of Jesus in Mark (only nine in Matthew and Luke). Mark is the most chronological of the Gospels. It alone mentions Simon's sons, Alexander and Rufus (15:21). It is the only Gospel calling Jesus a carpenter (6:3). It says Jesus had no leisure time (v. 31), and Jesus retires from the crowds eleven times. Mark presents Christ as an ideal Levite, Servant of man and God, before the altar and on the altar.

THE OUTLINE:

> I. **The Service of the Servant** (1:1–8:26)
>   A. His ministry (chaps. 1–2)
>   B. His message (3:1–6:29)
>   C. His miracles (6:30–8:26)
> II. **The Sacrifice of the Servant** (8:27–15:47)
>   A. Foretold—coming Passion (8:27–13:37)
>   B. Focused—crises present (chap. 14)
>   C. Fulfilled—culmination pressed (chap. 15)
> III **The Sovereignty of the Servant** (chap. 16)
>   A. In arising—resurrection (vv. 1–8)
>   B. In appearing—reappearances (vv. 9–14)[3]
>   C. In ascending—reception (vv. 15–20)

THE CONTENTS: *The service of the Servant* (1:1–8:26). First, we are introduced to the preparation of the Servant for his ministry (chaps. 1–3), which includes foretelling in the Old Testament (1:1–3), his forerunner John the Baptist (vv. 4–7), his approval by God the Father (vv. 9–11), and the fulfillment of Old Testament prophecies when Jesus began to preach: "the kingdom of God is at hand. Repent, and believe in the gospel" (vv. 12–15; see Dan. 2:44), and he called to himself followers who would be "fishers of men" (Mark 1:16–20). Then Jesus began his ministry of miracles by casting out a demon (vv. 21–28), healing Peter's mother-in-law (vv. 29–31) and many who were sick and demon possessed (vv. 32–39), cleansing a leper (vv. 40–45), and healing a paralytic (2:1–12).

After calling Levi (Matthew) (vv. 13–17), Jesus began offering his message against legalism (vv. 18–28). Jesus deliberately healed on the Sabbath to challenge the Jewish establishment (3:1–6) and drew a great crowd by his many miracles (vv. 1–12). He appointed the twelve apostles (vv. 13–19).

Then Jesus began facing opposition from his menaces, the Scribes, who rejected him with blasphemy of the Holy Spirit (saying he cast out demons by the power of the Devil) (vv. 20–29) and from his own family, who thought he was insane (vv. 31–35).

Having been officially rejected by his people, Jesus began to speak in parables, like that of the sower (4:1–9), which unveiled the mystery of the interim spiritual kingdom he was setting up in view of their rejecting his offer of the literal kingdom based on Old Testament promises (vv. 10–25). He told the parable of the growing seed (vv. 26–29) and of the mustard seed (vv. 30–34), both of which spoke of the spiritual kingdom he was establishing, which would grow until he returned. This ministry section is concluded by miracles of stilling the tempestuous sea (vv. 35–41), which is followed by a whole section on miraculous works (chaps. 5–8), including healing a demoniac (5:1–20), raising to life a girl, and healing a woman who touched his garment (vv. 22–43).

Returning to his own country, Jesus was faced by amazing unbelief (6:1–6) but sent out his disciples to heal the sick and call the people to repentance (vv. 7–13). After John the Baptist is beheaded (vv. 14–29), Jesus retired to a quiet place to get away from the crowd (vv. 30–32), only to be followed by the crowds and occasioning the feeding of the five thousand with five loaves and two fish (vv. 33–44). Jesus then walked on water (vv. 45–52) and healed as many as touched him (vv. 53–56). Again he faced opposition by the Pharisees, whom he rebuked (7:1–23), turning to heal the daughter of a Greek woman (vv. 25–30) and to heal a deaf mute (vv. 31–37) and to feed the four thousand (8:1–10).

The sacrifice of the Servant (8:27–15:47). The sacrifice of the Servant is foretold (8:27–13:37), focused (chap. 14), and fulfilled (chap. 15) in this section. First, Jesus turned his face as a flint toward Jerusalem, rebuking the Pharisees for seeking a sign when many signs had already been given (8:11–13) and warning of their leavening (evil) influence on others (vv. 14–21). To illustrate Israel's blindness, he healed a blind man in two stages, predicting the two stages of Israel's progressive enlightenment (vv. 22–26). Meanwhile, Peter's confession of Christ's messiahship (vv. 27–30) would become the basis of the church Christ would build in the interim (see also Matt. 16:16–18), based on his predicted death and resurrection (Mark 8:31–33), in spite of the denial of his disciple.

He revealed to them his coming glory on the mount of transfiguration (9:1–13). Rebuking his disciples for their unbelief (vv. 14–29), he again predicts his coming death and resurrection (vv. 30–32), instructs them in humility (vv. 33–37), forbids provincialism in his service (vv. 38–41), warns them of hell (vv. 42–50), instructs them on marriage (10:1–12), sets up little children as examples of how to enter his spiritual kingdom (vv. 13–16), and warns them about riches (vv. 17–22) and how hard it is to enter the kingdom of God (vv. 23–31). Again Jesus predicts his coming death and resurrection (vv. 32–34) and instructs them in humility in service (vv. 35–45). Passing through Jericho on the way to Jerusalem, Jesus healed blind Bartimaeus (vv. 46–52).

In fulfillment of prophecy, Jesus rode into Jerusalem on a donkey to cheers of hosanna (11:1–11). But his nation was soon to reject him by crucifying him, and Jesus symbolized this by cursing the fig tree, which had not produced the fruit of repentance (vv. 12–24). After cleansing the temple for the second time, his authority was questioned by the chief priests (vv. 27–33). In response Jesus told the parable of the owner of a vineyard (God) whose "beloved son" (Christ) was killed by vine keepers but whose vineyard would be given to others (Gentiles). Thus the rejected stone (Christ) would become the head cornerstone (12:1–12).

Looking beyond the cross, Jesus predicts the coming destruction of Jerusalem and his eventual second coming "with great power and glory" (13:1–37). Meanwhile the Jews were plotting to kill Jesus while he, the Passover Lamb (1 Cor. 5:7), ate the Passover with his disciples (14:1–21), instituted the Lord's Supper (vv. 22–26), predicted Peter's denial (vv. 27–31), and prayed his agonizing prayer in Gethsemane (vv. 32–42).

Jesus was arrested while his disciples fled (vv. 43–52). He was tried by the Jewish Sanhedrin, where he confessed that he was the Messiah (vv. 53–65). Peter repented of his denial (vv. 66–72). Jesus was taken to Pilate (15:1–15), released to be crucified (vv. 16–41), and buried in a borrowed tomb (vv. 42–47).

The sovereignty of the Servant (chap. 16). But, as predicted, on the third day the Servant showed his sovereignty in arising—his resurrection (vv. 1–8), in appearing to his disciples—reappearances (vv. 9–14), and in ascending to heaven—his reception by the Father (vv. 15–20).[4] The fresh, vivid, simple, unembellished account of the resurrection has the ring of authenticity. And if the short version (without verses 9–20) is correct, it fits with Mark's abrupt style as well.

Discourses of Jesus

	Matthew	Mark	Luke	John
1. Sermon on the Mount	5:2–7:27		6:20–49	
2. Commissioning the Twelve	10:5–42	6:7–13	9:1–6	
3. John the Baptist	11:4–19		7:18–35	
4. Unrepentant Cities	11:20–24			
5. Knowing the Father via Jesus	11:25–30			
6. Blasphemy and Signs	12:25–45	3:23–29	11:15–36	
7. Religious Traditions	15:1–20	7:1–23		
8. Christ Foresees His Church	16:13–18			
9. Humility, Sin, and Forgiveness	18:1–35	9:38–50		
10. Divorce	19:1–12	10:1–12		
11. Gaining Eternal Life	19:16–30	10:17–31	18:18–30	
12. The Mother's Request	20:20–28	10:35–45		
13. Cursing the Fig Tree	21:18–22	11:12–14, 20–26		
14. Resurrection	22:23–33	12:18–27	20:27–40	
15. Renunciation of Scribes	23:1–39	12:38–40	20:45–47	
16. Jerusalem's Destruction	24–25	13:1–37	21:5–36	
17. Take up Cross		8:34–38	9:23–37	
18. Greatest Commandment		12:28–34		
19. Forgiveness and Thankfulness			7:36–50	
20. Sending the Seventy-Two			10:1–20	
21. Woes to Pharisees and Lawyers			11:37–52	
22. Leaven, Fear, and Witnessing			12:1–12	
23. Anxiety			12:22–34	
24. Be Ready			12:35–48	
25. Divisions			12:49–53	
26. Discernment			12:54–59	
27. Narrow Door			13:22–30	
28. Temptation, Faith, Service			17:1–10	
29. Coming Kingdom			17:22–37	
30. Greatness			22:24–30	
31. Being Born Again				3:1–21
32. The Water of Life				4:4–26
33. Sowing and Reaping				4:31–38
34. Authority of the Son				5:19–47
35. Bread of Life				6:26–59

	Matthew	Mark	Luke	John
36. Who Sends the Christ				7:14–29
37. Light of the World				8:12–19
38. Object of Faith				8:21–30
39. The Truth Sets You Free				8:31–59
40. The Good Shepherd				10:1–18
41. Oneness with the Father				10:22–38
42. Savior of the World				12:23–36
43. Last Teachings				13:31–14:31
44. True Vine and Union				15:1–27
45. The Holy Spirit and Future				16:1–33

How to Respond to Critics

Mark 1:1—*Why does Mark not give any genealogy of Jesus, as Matthew and Luke do?*

Problem: Both Matthew (chap. 1) and Luke (chap. 3) give an ancestry of Jesus (see Matt. 1:1). However, Mark provides no genealogy whatsoever. Why the omission?

Solution: Mark presents Christ as a servant, and servants need no genealogy. The Roman audience to whom Mark directed his Gospel was not interested in *where* a servant came from but in *what* he could do. Unlike Mark's Roman audience, Matthew's Jewish audience looked for the Messiah, the King. Thus Matthew traces Jesus back to his Jewish roots as the Son of David the king (Matt. 1:1). Likewise, Luke presents Christ as the perfect man. Hence, Christ's ancestry is traced back to the first man, Adam (Luke 3:38). John, on the other hand, presents Christ as the Son of God. Therefore, he traces Christ back to his eternal source with the Father (John 1:1–2).

Mark 2:26—*Was Jesus wrong when he mentioned Abiathar as high priest instead of Ahimelech?*

Problem: Jesus says that at the time David ate the consecrated bread, Abiathar was high priest. Yet 1 Samuel 21:1–6 says that the high priest at that time was Ahimelech.

Solution: First Samuel is correct in stating that the high priest was Ahimelech. On the other hand Jesus was not wrong. When we take a closer look at Christ's words, we notice that he used the phrase "in the *days* of Abiathar" (v. 26), which does not necessarily mean that Abiathar was high priest at the time David ate the bread. After David met Ahimelech and ate the bread, King Saul had Ahimelech killed (1 Sam. 22:17–19). Abiathar escaped and went to David (v. 20) and later took the place of the high priest. So even though Abiathar was made high priest after David ate the bread, it is still correct to speak in this manner. After all,

Abiathar was alive when David did this, and soon following he became the high priest after his father's death. Thus it was during the *time* of Abiathar but not during his *tenure* in office when David ate the bread.

Mark 6:5—*If Jesus is God, why couldn't he do mighty works here?*
Problem: First of all, the Bible describes Jesus as God (John 1:1) who has, with the Father, "all authority in heaven and on earth" (Matt. 28:18 NIV). However, on this occasion Jesus "could do no mighty work there" (v. 5). Why couldn't he, if he is all-powerful?
Solution: Jesus is almighty as God but not almighty as man. As the God-man, Jesus has both a divine nature and a human nature. What he can do in one nature, he cannot necessarily do in the other. For example, as God, Jesus never got tired (Ps. 121:4), but as man he did (John 4:6).

Furthermore, just because Jesus *possessed* all power does not mean that he always chose to *exercise* it. The "could not" in Mark 6:5 is moral not actual. That is, he chose not to perform miracles "because of their unbelief" (v. 6). Jesus was not an entertainer, nor did he cast pearls before swine. So the necessity here is moral not metaphysical. He had the ability to do miracles there and in fact did some (v. 5), but he refused to do more because he deemed it a wasted effort.

Mark 10:17–31 (see also Matthew 19:16–30; Luke 18:18–30)—*If Jesus was God, why did he seem to rebuke the rich young ruler for calling him good?*
Problem: The rich young ruler called Jesus "Good Teacher," and Jesus rebuked him, saying, "Why do you call Me good? No one is good but One, that is, God." Yet on other occasions Jesus not only claimed to be God (Mark 2:8–12; John 8:58; 10:30), but he accepted the claim of others that he was God (John 20:28–29). Why did Jesus appear to deny that he was God to the young ruler?
Solution: Jesus did not deny he was God to the young ruler. He simply asked him to examine the implications of what he was saying. In effect, Jesus was saying to him, "Do you realize what you are saying when you call Me good? Are you saying I am God?"

The young man did not realize the implications of what he was saying. Thus Jesus was forcing him to a very uncomfortable dilemma. Either Jesus was good and God, or else he was bad and man—good God or a bad man, but not merely a good man. Those are the real alternatives with regard to Christ. For no good man would claim to be God when he was not. The liberal Christ, who was only a good moral teacher but not God, is a figment of human imagination.

Mark 10:35 (see Matthew 20:20)—*Who came to talk with Jesus,
the mother of James and John or James and John?*

Problem: In Matthew the mother of James and John made a request
of Jesus. However, Mark states that it was James and John who
came to Jesus to make their request.

Solution: It is clear that both the mother and her sons came to
Jesus to make the request, since the text declares "the mother
. . . came to Him with her sons" (Matt. 20:20). It is possible that
the mother spoke first, with the two sons closely following to
reiterate the request. This is supported by Matthew's account
because when Jesus responds, "Are you able to drink the cup that
I am about to drink?" the Bible says, "*They* said to him, 'We are
able'" (v. 22). So there is no unsolvable conflict here. The two
accounts are harmonious.

Mark 11:12–14, 20–24 (see Matthew 21:12–19)—*When did Jesus
curse the fig tree, before or after he cleansed the temple?*

Problem: Matthew places the cursing of the fig tree after the
cleansing of the temple. But Mark places the cursing before the
temple was cleansed. It cannot be both. Did one Gospel writer
make a mistake?

Solution: Jesus actually cursed the fig tree on his way to the temple
as Mark said, but this does not mean that Matthew's account is

77

mistaken. Christ made two trips to the temple, and he cursed the fig tree on his second trip.

Mark 11:11 says that Christ entered the temple the day of his triumphal entry. When Christ enters the temple, Mark does not mention Christ's making any proclamations against any wrongdoing. Verse 12 says, "Now the next day," referring to the trip to the fig tree on the way to the temple on the second day. On this day, Christ threw out those buying and selling in the temple. Matthew, however, addresses the two trips of Christ to the temple as though they were one event. This gives the impression that the first day, when Christ entered the temple, he drove out the buyers and sellers as well. Mark's account, however, gives more detail to the events, revealing that there were actually two trips to the temple. In view of this, we have no reason to believe that there is a discrepancy in the accounts.

Mark 13:32—*Was Jesus ignorant of the time of his second coming?*
Problem: The Bible teaches that Jesus is God (John 1:1) and that he knows all things (John 2:24; Col. 2:3). On the other hand, he "increased in wisdom" (Luke 2:52) and sometimes did not seem to know certain things (see, for example, John 11:34). Indeed, he denied knowing the time of his own second coming here, saying, "But of that day and hour no one knows, neither the angels in heaven, nor the Son, but only the Father."
Solution: We must distinguish between what Jesus knew as God (everything) and what he knew *as man*. As God, Jesus was omniscient (all-knowing), but as man, he was limited in his knowledge. This can be schematized as follows:

Jesus as God	**Jesus as Man**
unlimited in knowledge	limited in knowledge
no growth in knowledge	growth in knowledge
knew time of his coming	did not know time of his coming

Mark 14:30 (see Matthew 26:34; John 13:38)—*When Peter denied Christ, did the rooster crow once or twice?*
Problem: Matthew and John say before the rooster crows once, Peter will have denied the Lord three times. But Mark affirms that before the rooster crows *twice* Peter will deny Christ three times. Which account is right?
Solution: There is no contradiction between the two accounts because, given the correctness of the text, Matthew and John do not expressly state how many times the rooster will crow. They simply say Peter will deny Christ three times "before the rooster crows," but they do not

say how many times it will crow. Mark may simply be more specific, affirming exactly how many times the rooster will crow.

It is also possible that different accounts are due to an early copyist error in Mark, which resulted in the insertion of "two" in early manuscripts (at Mark 14:30 and 72). This would explain why some important manuscripts of Mark mention only one crowing, just like Matthew and John, and why "two" appears at different places in some manuscripts.

Mark 15:25 (see John 19:14)—*Was Jesus crucified in the third hour or the sixth hour?*

Problem: Mark's Gospel account says that it was the third hour (9 a.m. Jewish time) when Christ was crucified. John's Gospel says that it was about the sixth hour (12 noon Jewish time) when

A model of Herod's Temple.

Jesus was still on trial. This would make his crucifixion much later than specified by Mark. Which Gospel is correct?

Solution: Both Gospel writers are correct in their assertions. The difficulty is answered when we realize that the Gospel writers used a different time system. John, writing after the destruction of Jerusalem (see chapter 7), follows the *Roman* time system, while Mark follows the Jewish time system.

According to Roman time, the day ran from midnight to midnight. The Jewish twenty-four hour period began in the evening at 6 p.m. and the morning of that day began at 6 a.m. Therefore, when Mark asserts that at the third hour, Jewish time, Christ was crucified, this was about 9 a.m. And John stated that Christ's trial was about the sixth hour, Roman time, which would be 6 a.m. This would place the trial *before* the crucifixion and this would not negate any testimony of the Gospel writers. This fits with John's other references to time in the Roman context. For example, he speaks about Jesus being weary after his trip from Judea to Samaria at the "sixth hour" and asking for water from the woman at the well. Considering the length of his trip, his weariness, and the normal evening time when people come to the well to drink and to water their animals, this fits better with 6 p.m., which is "the sixth hour" of the night by Roman time reckoning. The same is true of John's reference to the tenth hour in John 1:39, which would be 10 a.m., a more likely time to be out preaching than 4 a.m. or even 4 p.m.

Mark 16:1–2 (see John 20:1)—*Was Mary at the tomb before sunrise or after?*

Problem: Mark states that Mary was there "very early in the morning . . . when the sun had risen" (v. 2), but John says it was "early, while it was still dark."

Solution: There are two general possibilities here. One possibility suggests that the phrase "when the sun had risen" (Mark 16:2) merely denotes early dawn (see Ps. 104:22), when it was "still dark" (John 20:1), relatively speaking.

Another view holds that Mary came alone at first when it was still dark before sunrise (John 20:1), and then again later after sunrise, she returned with the other women (Mark 16:1). In support of this is the fact that only Mary is mentioned in John, but Mary and the other women are named in Mark. Also Luke 24:1 says it was "very early in the morning," implying after sunrise, when the "women" (not just Mary) had come. Likewise, Matthew 28:1 speaks of it being "after the Sabbath, as the first day of the week began to dawn" that "Mary Magdalene and the other Mary

Order of Events Surrounding Jesus's Crucifixion

1. Jesus arrived at Golgotha (Calvary) (Matt. 27:33; Mark 15:22; Luke 23:33; John 19:17).
2. He refused to drink a mixture of wine and myrrh offered to him (Matt. 27:34; Mark 15:23).
3. The soldiers gambled for his garment (Matt. 27:35; Mark 15:24; Luke 23:34; John 19:23).
4. At 9 a.m. he was nailed to the cross between two thieves (Matt. 27:35; Mark 15:24–28).
5. They placed the accusation "King of the Jews" over his head (Matt. 27:37; Mark 15:26; Luke 23:38; John 19:19).
6. Both thieves railed at Jesus (Matt. 27:44; Mark 15:32).
7. First word from the cross: "Father, forgive them, for they do not know what they do" (Luke 23:34).
8. Second word from the cross, to the repentant thief: "Today you will be with Me in Paradise" (Luke 23:43).
9. Third word from the cross: "Woman, behold your son!" (John 19:26).*
10. Fourth word from the cross: "Behold your mother!" (John 19:27).*
11. At noon darkness began to fall and continued until 3 p.m. (Matt. 27:45; Mark 15:33; Luke 23:44).
12. Fifth word from the cross: "My God, My God, why have you forsaken Me?" (Matt. 27:46; Mark 15:34).
13. Sixth word from the cross: "I thirst" (John 19:28).
14. He drank sour wine from a sponge (Matt. 27:48; Mark 15:36; John 19:29).
15. Seventh word from the cross: "It is finished!" (John 19:30).
16. Eighth word from the cross: "Father, into Your hands I commend My spirit" (Luke 23:46).
17. At 3 p.m. he dismissed his spirit and died (Matt. 27:50; Mark 15:37; Luke 23:46; John 19:30).
18. The earth quaked and the temple curtain was torn in two (Matt. 27:51; Mark 15:38; Luke 23:45).
19. Some graves were opened, and later after Jesus's resurrection, these people were raised from the dead (Matt. 27:52–53).
20. The Roman soldiers confessed he was the Son of God (Matt. 27:54; Mark 15:39).
21. He was buried before sunset by Joseph of Arimathea (Matt. 27:57; Mark 15:42–46; Luke 23:50–53; John 19:38) with the assistance of Nicodemus (John 19:39–42).

*These two are usually combined to make seven words from the cross.

came to see the tomb." Only John mentions Mary being there alone "while it was still dark" (20:1).

Mark 16:9–20—*Why is this passage of Scripture omitted in some Bibles?*
Problem: Most modern Bibles contain this ending of the Gospel of Mark, including the King James Version (KJV), American Standard Version (ASV), New American Standard Bible (NASB), and the New King James Version (NKJV). However, both the Revised Standard Version (RSV) and the New International Version (NIV) set it off from the rest of the text. A note in the NIV says, "The earliest manuscripts and some other ancient witnesses do not have Mark 16:9–20." Were these verses in the original Gospel of Mark?
Solution: Scholars are divided over the authenticity of these verses. Those who follow the received text tradition point to the fact that this text is found in the majority of biblical manuscripts down through the centuries. Thus they believe it was in the original manuscript of Mark.

On the other hand, those who follow the critical text tradition insist that we should not *add* evidence but *weigh* it. Truth is not determined, they say, by majority vote but by the most qualified

The Order of the Twelve Appearances of Christ

Persons	Saw	Heard	Touched	Other Evidence
1. Mary (John 20:11–18)	X	X	X	empty tomb
2. Mary and women (Matt. 28:1–10)	X	X	X	empty tomb
3. Peter (1 Cor. 15:5)	X	X*		empty tomb, clothes
4. Two disciples (Luke 24:13–35)	X	X		ate with him
5. Ten apostles (Luke 24:36–49; John 20:19–23)	X	X	X**	saw wounds; he ate food
6. Eleven apostles (John 20:24–	X	X	X**	saw wounds
7. Seven apostles (John 21)	X	X		ate with him
8. All apostles (Matt. 28:16–20; Mark 16:14–18)	X	X		
9. 500 brethren (1 Cor. 15:6)	X	X*		
10. James (1 Cor. 15:7)	X	X*		
11. All apostles (Acts 1:4–8 NIV)	X	X		ate with him
12. Paul (Acts 9:1–9; 1 Cor. 15:8)	X	X		

*Implied
**Offered himself to be touched

witnesses. They point to the following arguments for rejecting these verses: (1) These verses are lacking in many of the oldest and most reliable Greek manuscripts, as well as in important Old Latin, Syriac, Armenian, and Ethiopic manuscripts. (2) Many of the ancient Church Fathers reveal no knowledge of these verses, including Clement, Origen, and Eusebius. Jerome admitted that almost all Greek copies do not have it. (3) Many manuscripts that do have this section place a mark by it indicating it is a spurious addition to the text. (4) There is another (shorter) ending to Mark that is found in some manuscripts. (5) Others point to the fact that the style and vocabulary are not the same as the rest of the Gospel of Mark.

Whether or not this piece of *text* belongs in the original, the *truth* it contains certainly accords with it. So the bottom line is that it does not make any difference, since, if it does belong here, there is nothing in it contrary to the rest of Scripture. And if it does not belong, there is no truth missing in the Bible, since everything taught here is found elsewhere in Scripture. This includes tongues (see Acts 2:1–21), baptism (v. 38), and God's first-century supernatural protection of his messengers unwittingly bitten by poisonous snakes (see 28:3–5). So in the final analysis, it is simply a debate about whether this particular *text* belongs in the Bible, not about whether any *truth* is missing.

STUDY QUESTIONS

1. What is the evidence, internal and external, that Mark is the author of this Gospel?
2. When was Mark written? List your reasons for the date chosen.
3. To whom was Mark writing?
4. What were possible destinations of Mark's Gospel?
5. What was Mark's theme and purpose in writing the Gospel?

SELECTED SOURCES

Baxter, Sidlow. *Explore the Book*. Grand Rapids: Zondervan, 1987.

Blomberg, Craig. *The Historical Reliability of the Gospels*. Downers Grove, IL: InterVarsity, 1987.

Brooks, James. *Mark*. New American Commentary. Nashville: Broadman & Holman, 1991.

Carson, D.A., Douglas Moo, and Leon Morris. *An Introduction to the New Testament*. Grand Rapids: Zondervan, 1992.

Earle, Ralph. *Mark: Gospel of Action*. Everyman's Bible Commentary Series. Chicago: Moody, 1987.

Garland, David. *Mark*. NIV Application Commentary. Grand Rapids: Zondervan, 1996.

Geisler, Norman L., and Thomas Howe. *When Critics Ask: A Popular Handbook on Bible Difficulties*. Grand Rapids: Baker, 1997.

Guthrie, Donald. *New Testament Introduction*. Downers Grove, IL: InterVarsity, 1990.

Harrison, Everett F. *An Introduction to the New Testament*. Grand Rapids: Eerdmans, 1971.

Hemer, Colin. *The Book of Acts in the Setting of Hellenic History*. Winona Lake, MN: Eisenbrauns, 1990.

Hughes, R. Kent. *Mark: Jesus, Servant and Savior. Preaching the Word*. 2 vols. Wheaton: Crossway, 1989.

Lane, William. *The Gospel of Mark*. New International Commentary on the New Testament. Grand Rapids: Eerdmans, 1993.

Linnemann, Eta. *Is There a Synoptic Problem?* Grand Rapids: Baker, 1992.

Radmacher, Earl, Ronald Allen, and H. Wayne House, eds. *Nelson's New Illustrated Bible Commentary*. Nashville: Thomas Nelson, 1999.

Robertson, A.T. *A Harmony of the Gospels*. New York: HarperCollins, 1922.

Scroggie, William Graham. *A Guide to the Gospels*. London: Pickering & Inglis, 1948. Reprint, Grand Rapids: Kregel, 1995.

Thomas, Robert, and Stan Gundry. *The New Harmony of the Gospels*. New York: HarperSanFrancisco, 1991.

Walvoord, John F., and Roy B. Zuck, eds. *The Bible Knowledge Commentary*. 2 vols. Wheaton: Victor, 1983.

6
The Gospel of Luke

Who Wrote It?

Luke the physician (Col. 4:14), companion of Paul (2 Tim. 4:11; Philem. 24), and possibly a Gentile, since he is not listed with the circumcised (Col. 4:10–14), is the author of this Gospel. Since Luke was an associate of Paul and his writings reflect Paul's teaching, it has been called the Gospel of Paul.[1]

Internal Evidence

The author was often a companion of Paul, since he uses the first person in certain sections of Acts (16:10, 17; 20:6; 27:1). Timothy and Mark are both referred to in the third person (20:5), so neither of them is the author. Luke is the only remaining possibility. What is more, his theological emphasis was like Paul's.[2] Also, Luke fits the known character of the author by his use of medical terms,[3] his Greek interest, and his literary ability.[4] Finally, Luke was the author of Acts[5] because he referred to his "former treatise" (Acts 1:1); both Acts and Luke are addressed to the same person, "Theophilus" (Luke 1:3; Acts 1:1); language and style in both are the same; and both show medical and Gentile interest.

External Evidence

The external evidence for Luke's authorship is also very strong. First of all, it bears Luke's name in the earliest manuscripts. Likewise, it was accepted as Luke's by the early Fathers (for example, Irenaeus, Tertullian, Clement, Origen, Gregory of Nasianzus, Jerome, and Eusebius). In addition, Sir William Ramsay supported Luke's authorship archaeologically. Even a liberal scholar like Adolph Harnack agreed that Luke wrote it. Finally, a noted Roman historian, Colin Hemer, agrees with the Lucan authorship.[6]

When Was It Written?

The evidence for the date of the writing points to ca. AD 60, during Paul's imprisonment at Caesarea (Acts 23:31–35). The reasons for this are straightforward. First, it was before AD 70, since the destruction of Jerusalem is yet a future event (Luke 21:5–38). And it was written before Acts, which refers to a "former" treatise to the same person, Theophilus (Acts 1:1), and it is known that Acts (see below) was written by 61 or 62 AD. Yet Luke was written after Gentiles were attracted to Christianity (Acts 18:1–4) in about AD 54. Further, it was written after other Gospels were written (see 1:1), which could mean Matthew and Mark who wrote between AD 50 and 60. What is more, Luke 10:7 is cited in 1 Timothy 5:18, which was written about 64–66 AD. So the Gospel of Luke must have been composed before then. Finally, since it was apparently recorded just before Luke wrote Acts (being a two-part series to Theophilus), a date of ca. AD 60 is likely.

To Whom Was It Written?

The Gospel of Luke was addressed to Theophilus, which means "lover of God" (1:3). He was a cultured Greek convert.

Where Were Its Readers Located?

The readers of Luke may have been in Caesarea (see Acts 23:23–24).

Why Was It Written?

There are several reasons for the composition of the Gospel of Luke. First of all, it was written to set forth Christ as the "ideal Man" to the Greeks. More particularly, it aimed to confirm the Christian faith to a Greek convert, Theophilus (1:3–4). And more broadly, it served as an apologetic for Christianity to the Greek world in general. Some even think it was used as part (with Acts) of a legal defense of Paul to the Roman authorities (see chaps. 21–28).

What Is It About?

The Theme: Christ is the Savior for the Gentiles.
The Key Verse: "For the Son of Man has come to seek and to save that which was lost" (19:10).
Key Words and Phrases: *announce glad tidings, preach good news* (10x), *grace* (8x), *salvation* (6x), *save* (19x), *Savior* (2x), and (*to*) *sin, sin, sinner, sinful* (*sinner* 18x, which is more than Matthew [5x], Mark [6x], or John [4x]; all forms 33x). See appendix 3 for a more complete word study.
Gentile Emphasis: This is shown by: (1) tracing Jesus's genealogy to Adam (3:23–38); (2) explaining Jewish customs and locations (4:31; 8:2; 21:37; 23:51; 24:13); (3) references to the Roman emperor (2:1) and government officials (3:1); (4) the use of the word *teacher* (rather than *rabbi*); (5) almost exclusive use of the Greek translation of the Old Testament (LXX or Septuagint) for

Sea of Galilee at dawn.

Old Testament citations; (6) the story of the non-Jewish good Samaritan (10:29–37); (7) the story of the thankful Samaritan leper (17:15–16); and (8) the reference to "their language" (referring to the Jews) (Acts 1:19).

Ancestry of Christ: It is traced (through Mary) to Adam, the first man (3:23–38), as is fitting to his theme of the ideal Man.

Jesus's Childhood: Luke alone narrates Jesus's childhood: before his birth (1:41), his birth (2:6–7), his circumcision on the eighth day (v. 21), his dedication at forty days (vv. 22–24), and his early youth (vv. 41–50).

Old Testament References: In his Gospel, Luke has 90 to 100 direct citations of or allusions to the Old Testament; only the book of Matthew has more Old Testament references (129).[7]

Miracles: Luke has twenty miracles, six of which are unique to Luke (5:4–7; 7:11–16; 13:10–17; 14:1–4; 17:11–19; 22:50–51).

Parables: Luke has thirty-five parables, nineteen of which are unique to this book (7:41–43; 10:30–37; 11:5–8; 12:16–21; 12:35–40; 12:42–48; 13:6–9; 14:7–11; 14:16–24; 14:28–30; 14:31–33; 15:8–10; 15:11–32; 16:1–13; 16:19–31; 17:7–10; 18:1–5; 18:9–14; 19:11–27).

Women: The Gospel of Luke has more emphasis on women, mentioning women forty-three times and naming Elizabeth, Mary, Martha and Mary, Mary Magdalene, Anna, Joanna, and Susanna (8:2–3).

Roman Emperors in New Testament Times

Augustus (27 BC–AD 14)	He ordered the census that brought Joseph and Mary to Bethlehem (Luke 2:1).
Tiberius (AD 14–37)	He reigned during the ministry and death of Christ (Luke 3:1; 20:22, 25; 23:2; John 19:12, 15).
Caligula (AD 37–41)	
Claudius (AD 41–54)	A severe famine occurred during his reign (Acts 11:28). He expelled Jews from Rome, including Aquila and Priscilla (Acts 18:2).
Nero (AD 54–68)	He persecuted Christians and martyred Paul and Peter (Acts 25:8, 10–12, 21; 26:32; 27:24; 28:19).
Galba (AD 58–69)	Reigned during
Otho (AD 69)	the time of
Vitellius (AD 69)	the Jewish revolt.
Vespasian (AD 69–79)	He crushed the Jewish revolt, and his son Titus destroyed Jerusalem in AD 70.

Money: This book has a stronger emphasis on money than the other Gospels (see chap. 16), stressing Jesus's mercy to the poor (2:22–24; 6:20–25, 30; 14:12–15; 16:13, 19–25, among others) and his warning to the rich (12:13–34).

Individuals: Luke stresses individuals more than other Gospels—Zacharias, Elizabeth, Mary, Simeon, Anna, Martha and Mary, Levi, the centurion, the widow of Nain, John the Baptist, the Gadarene, Jairus, the woman with an infirmity, the would-be disciples, Zacchaeus, Mary Magdalene, Cleopas, Simon, and Joseph of Arimathea. He paints personal portraits of many of them (for example, Mary, Zacharias, Elizabeth, Simeon, Anna, Zacchaeus, and Cleopas).

The Poor: Jesus is champion of the poor. Seven or eight of his parables in this book contain references to them.

Prayer: Prayer is mentioned multiple times: at Jesus's baptism (3:21), for Peter (22:32), in the Garden (v. 42), on the cross (23:34), and many other times (including 5:16; 6:12; 9:18, 29; 22:40–41).

The Holy Spirit: Luke stresses the doctrine of the Holy Spirit, who empowered John, Jesus, Mary, Elizabeth, Zacharias, and Simeon.

Forgiveness: Luke stresses God's forgiveness (3:3; 5:18–26; 6:37; 7:36–50; 11:4; 12:10; 17:3–4; 23:34; 24:47) and his love for

The town of
Bethlehem.

sinners (7:12–13; 7:37–50; 11:5–8; 14:21–24; 18:1–8; 19:5–10; 23:42–43). See also chapters 15, 18, 23, and 24:46–47.

Luke also uses the word *justified* in 18:14 (see Romans 3–4).

Music: Luke is the most musical of all Gospels, containing the song of the angel to Mary (1:28–33), *Ave Maria*; the song of Mary (1:68–79), the *Magnificat*; the song of the angels (2:14), *Gloria in Excelsis*; the song of Simeon (2:29–32), *Nunc Dimittis* ("now you are letting").

The Glory of God: Luke stresses praise and glory to God: praise to God (2:13, 20; 19:37); glory to God (2:20; 5:25; 7:16; 13:13; 17:15; 18:43); blessing God (1:64; 2:28; 24:53).

Rejoicing: This book highlights joy and rejoicing (1:14, 44, 47; 6:21, 23; 10:21; 15:23, 32).

Children: It focuses on children: John, Jesus (chaps.1–2), babies (18:15), an only son (7:11–15), an only child (9:38).

Angels: There is more about angels in Luke than in the other Gospels. They are mentioned twenty-three times. They appeared to Zacharias (1:11–20), to Mary (vv. 26–38), to the shepherds (2:8–15), to Christ in Gethsemane (22:43), and to the women at the tomb (24:4–5, 23) The devil misuses the text on angels (4:10). Angels will accompany Christ at his second coming (9:26). They rejoice when a sinner repents (15:10). They carry believers to heaven (16:22). We will be like angels when we die (20:35–36).

Unique Features: Only Luke records the birth of John the Baptist (1:5–25), Jesus's birth and childhood (chaps. 1–2), Mary's *Magnificat* (1:46–55), Jesus's preaching at Nazareth (4:16), the story of the good Samaritan (10:29–37), the story of the prodigal son (15:11–32), the story of Zacchaeus (19:1–10), Herod's mocking of Jesus (23:8–11), and the experience of two disciples on the road to Emmaus (24:13–32). It is the most comprehensive Gospel, beginning earlier (except John) with the birth of John and ending later with the ascension.[8]

Jesus's Parables

Parable Name	Matthew	Mark	Luke
1. The Two Foundations	7:24–27		6:48–49
2. The New Cloth and New Wineskins	9:16–17		
3. The Sower	13:3–8	4:3–8	8:5–8
4. The Weeds	13:24–30		
5. The Mustard Seed	13:31–32	4:30–32	13:18–19
6. The Yeast	13:33		13:20–21
7. The Hidden Treasure	13:44		
8. The Pearl of Great Price	13:45–46		
9. The Fishing Net	13:47–50		
10. The House Owner	13:51–52		
11. The Unforgiving Servant	18:23–35		
12. The Vineyard Workers	20:1–16		
13. The Two Sons	21:28–31		
14. The Wicked Vinedressers	21:33–44	12:1–11	20:9–19
15. The Wedding Banquet	22:1–14		
16. The Two Servants	24:45–51		12:42–48
17. The Ten Virgins	25:1–13		
18. The Talents	25:14–30		
19. The Growing Seed		4:26–29	
20. The Doorkeeper		13:34–37	
21. The Rude Children			7:31–35
22. The Two Debtors			7:41–43
23. The Good Samaritan			10:30–37
24. The Friend at Midnight			11:5–8
25. The Rich Fool			12:16–21
26. The Barren Fig Tree			13:6–9
27. The Great Banquet			14:15–24
28. The Unfinished Tower			14:28–30
29. The King's Unwise War			14:31–33
30. The Lost Sheep	18:12–14		15:4–7
31. The Lost Coin			15:8–10
32. The Prodigal Son			15:11–32
33. The Shrewd Steward			16:1–9
34. The Servant's Reward			17:7–10
35. The Unjust Judge			18:1–8
36. The Pharisee and the Tax Collector			18:9–14
37. The Ten Minas			19:11–27

THE OUTLINE:

I. The Manhood of the Son of Man—His Advent (1–4:13)
   A. Introduction of Son of Man (chap. 1)
   B. Infancy of Son of Man (2:1–7)
   C. Identification of Son of Man (2:8–4:13)
      1. Adored by angels (chap. 2)
      2. Announced by man (3:1–20)
      3. Attested by God (3:21–38)
      4. Attacked by Satan (4:1–13)
II. The Ministry of the Son of Man—His Activity (4:14–23:56)
   A. Service in light of the cross—primary ministry—Galilee (Jewish) (4:14–9:62)
   B. Service on the way to the cross—passing ministry—Judea, Perea (Gentile) (chaps. 10–21)
      1. Principles of service defined (10:1–13:5)
      2. People of the servant described (13:6–19:27)
      3. Program of service declared (19:28–21:38)
         a. Passion over Jerusalem (19:28–48)
         b. Prophet in Jerusalem (chap. 20)
         c. Prediction about Jerusalem (chap. 21)
   C. Sacrifice on the cross (chaps. 22–23)
      1. Last Supper—Into your hands I commend my body (to the disciples) (22:19)
      2. Last submission—Into your hands I commend my life (to the world) (23:34, 39)
      3. Last saying—"Into your hands I commend my spirit" (to God) (23:46)
III. The Majesty of the Son of Man—His Ascension (chap. 24)
   A. The opened grave (vv. 1–12)
   B. The opened Scriptures (vv. 13–35)
   C. The opened understanding (vv. 36–48)
   D. The opened heavens (vv. 49–53)

THE CONTENTS: The overall content fits the theme of Luke and its outline. First, we have the manhood of the Son of Man (1–4:13), then his ministry (4:14–23:56), and finally his majesty (chap. 24). In the first part, the Son of Man is introduced by the angel to Mary (chap. 1) and his birth and infancy are described. He is adored by angels (chap. 2), announced by man (3:1–20), attested by God at his baptism (3:21–38), and attacked by Satan in his temptation (4:1–13).

Next is the ministry of the Son of Man (4:14–23:56), which can be divided into three parts: First was his service in light of the cross, which was his primary ministry in Galilee (to Jews) (4:14–9:62). Next was his service on the way to the cross, that is, his passing ministry in Judea and Perea to Gentiles (chaps. 10–21). Here the principles of service were defined (10:1–13:5), the people of the servant were described (13:6–19:27), and the program of service was declared (19:28–21:38). This included his passion over Jerusalem (19:28–48), his presence as a prophet in Jerusalem (chap. 20), and his prediction about Jerusalem (chap. 21). This is followed by his sacrifice on the cross (chaps. 22–23), which was introduced by the Last Supper (chap. 22), followed by his last submission to the cross (23:34, 39), and his last saying from the cross (v. 46).

Six Trials of Jesus

Jewish Trials

by Annas	John 18:12–14
by Caiaphas	Matthew 26:57–68
by the Sanhedrin	Matthew 27:1–2

Roman Trials

by Pilate	John 18:28–38
by Herod	Luke 23:6–12
by Pilate again	John 18:39–19:6

Finally, we have the majesty of the Son of Man (chap. 24). Jesus was delivered for our salvation and raised again for our justification (Rom. 4:25). First, the grave was opened for Jesus (Luke 24:1–12), then the Scriptures were opened by Jesus (vv. 13–35), the understanding of the disciples was opened by God (vv. 36–48), and finally the heavens were opened for Jesus (vv. 49–53).

How to Respond to Critics

Luke 1:26–33 (see Matt. 1:20)—*Was the announcement of the birth of Christ made to Mary or to Joseph?*
Problem: Matthew says the announcement of Jesus's birth was made to Joseph, but Luke asserts that it was made to Mary. Who is correct?
Solution: The announcement was made to Mary first and then to Joseph. Mary had to know first, since she would have been the first to know she was going to have the baby. Joseph needed to know next, since his future wife was going to have a baby that was not his! This kind of pairing of visions on important matters is found elsewhere in Scripture. Compare the visions of Cornelius and Peter (Acts 10:3–7, 9–16) and Saul and Ananias (9:3–7, 10–16).

Luke 2:1—*Did Luke make a mistake when he mentioned a worldwide census under Caesar Augustus?*

Problem: Luke refers to a worldwide census under Caesar Augustus when Quirinius was governor of Syria. However, according to the annals of ancient history, no such census took place.

Solution: It has been widely held by many critics that Luke made an error in his assertion about a registration under Caesar Augustus and that the census actually took place in AD 6 or 7 (this is mentioned by Luke in Gamaliel's speech in Acts 5:37). The lack of any extrabiblical support has led some to claim this is an error. However, recent scholarship has reversed this trend, and it is now widely admitted that there was in fact an earlier registration, as Luke records. This has been asserted on the basis of several factors.

1. Since the people of a subjugated land were compelled to take an oath of allegiance to the emperor, it was not unusual for the emperor to require an imperial census as an expression of this allegiance and as a means of enlisting men for military service, or, as was probably true in this case, in preparation to levy taxes. Because of the strained relations between Herod and Augustus in the later years of Herod's reign, as the Jewish historian Josephus reports, it is understandable that Augustus would begin to treat Herod's domain as a subject land and consequently would impose such a census to maintain control of Herod and the people.

2. Periodic registrations of this sort took place on a regular basis every fourteen years. According to the very papers that recorded the censuses, there was in fact a census taken in about 8 or 7 BC.[9] Because of this regular pattern of census taking, any such action would naturally be regarded as a result of the general policy of Augustus, even though a local census may have been instigated by a local governor. Therefore, Luke recognizes the census as stemming from the decree of Augustus.

3. A census was a massive project, which probably took several years to complete. Such a census for the purpose of taxation was begun in Gaul between 10 and 9 BC and took a period of forty years to complete. It is quite likely that the decree to begin the census, in about 8 or 7 BC, may not have actually begun in the land of Israel until some time later. Problems of organization and preparation may have delayed the actual census until 5 BC or even later.

4. It was not an unusual requirement that people return to the place of their origin, or to the place where they owned property. A decree of C. Vibius Maximus in AD 104 required all those who were away from their hometowns to return there for the purpose of the census. For the Jews, such travel would not have been unusual at all since they were quite used to the annual pilgrimage to Jerusalem.

There is simply no reason to suspect Luke's statement regarding the census at the time of Jesus's birth. Luke's account fits the regular pattern of census taking, and its date would not be an unreasonable one. Also this may have been simply a local census that was taken as a result of the general policy of Augustus. Luke simply provides us with a reliable historical record of an event not otherwise recorded. Since Dr. Luke has proven himself to be a reliable historian in other matters,[10] there is no reason to doubt him here (see also comments on Luke 2:2).

Luke 2:2—*Why does Luke say the census was during Quirinius's governorship since Quirinius was not governor until AD 6?*
Problem: Luke states that the census decreed by Augustus was the first one taken while Quirinius was governor of Syria. However, Quirinius did not become governor of Syria until after the death of Herod in about AD 6. Is this an error in Luke's historical record?
Solution: Luke has not made an error. There are reasonable solutions to this difficulty.

First, Quintilius Varus was governor of Syria from about 7 BC to about 4 BC. Varus was not a trustworthy leader, a fact that was disastrously demonstrated in AD 9 when he lost three legions of soldiers in the Teutoburger forest in Germany. In contrast, Quirinius was a notable military leader who was responsible for squelching the rebellion of the Homonadensians in Asia Minor. When it came time to begin the census, in about 8 or 7 BC, Augustus entrusted Quirinius with the delicate problem in the volatile area of Judea, effectively superseding the authority and governorship of Varus by appointing Quirinius to a place of special authority in this matter.

It has also been proposed that Quirinius was governor of Syria on two separate occasions, once while prosecuting the military action against the Homonadensians between 12 and 2 BC, and later beginning about AD 6. A Latin inscription discovered in 1764 has been interpreted to refer to Quirinius as having served as governor of Syria on two occasions.

It is possible that Luke 2:2 reads: "This census took place *before*

Tiberius Caesar.

Quirinius was governing Syria." In this case, the Greek word translated "first" (*prōtos*) is translated as a comparative, "before." Because of the awkward construction of the sentence, this is not an unlikely reading.

Regardless of which solution is accepted, it is not necessary to conclude that Luke has made an error in recording the historical events surrounding the birth of Jesus. Luke has proven himself to be a reliable historian even in the details. Sir William Ramsay has shown that, in making reference to thirty-two countries, fifty-four cities, and nine islands, Luke made no mistakes![11]

Luke 3:23–38—*Why does Luke present a different ancestral tree for Jesus than the one in Matthew?*

Problem: Jesus has a different grandfather in Luke 3:23 (Heli) than he does in Matthew 1:16 (Jacob). Which one is the right one?

Solution: These differences could result from two separate lines of ancestors, one traced through his *legal* father, Joseph, and the other through his *actual* mother, Mary. Matthew gives the *official* line, since he addresses Jesus's genealogy to Jewish concerns for the Jewish Messiah's credentials, which required that the Messiah come from the seed of Abraham and the line of David (Matt. 1:1). Luke, with a broader *Greek* audience in view, addresses himself to their interest in Jesus as the perfect Man (which was the quest of Greek thought). Thus he traces Jesus back to the first man, Adam (Luke 3:38).

That Matthew gives Jesus's paternal genealogy and Luke his maternal genealogy is further supported by several facts. First of all, while both lines trace Christ to David, each is through a different son of David. Matthew traces Jesus through Joseph (his *legal father*) to David's son, *Solomon* the king, by whom Christ rightfully inherited the throne of David (see 2 Sam. 7:12–17). Luke's purpose, on the other hand, is to show Christ as an actual human. So he traces Christ to David's son, *Nathan*, through his *actual mother*, Mary, through whom he can rightfully claim to be fully human, the redeemer of humanity.

Further, Luke does not say that he is giving Jesus's genealogy through Joseph. Rather, he notes that Jesus was "as was supposed" (Luke 3:23) the son of Joseph, while he was actually the son of Mary. Also Luke's recording of Mary's genealogy fits with his interest as a doctor in mothers and birth and with his emphasis on women in his Gospel, which has been called "the Gospel for women."

Finally, the fact that the two genealogies have some names in common (such as Shealtiel and Zerubbabel, Matt. 1:12; Luke 3:27) does not prove they are the same genealogy for two reasons. One, these are not uncommon names. Further, even the same genealogy (Luke's) names appear more than once (see Joseph and Judah in vv. 26, 30).

> Luke was tracing the actual line of Joseph. This view maintains that the legal line and the actual line of David through which Jesus came met at Joseph, the supposed father of Jesus. In this view Jacob, Joseph's uncle, would have died childless and therefore Joseph would have been the closest living heir. Thus Joseph and then Jesus would have been brought into the royal line.[12]

The two genealogies can be summarized as follows:

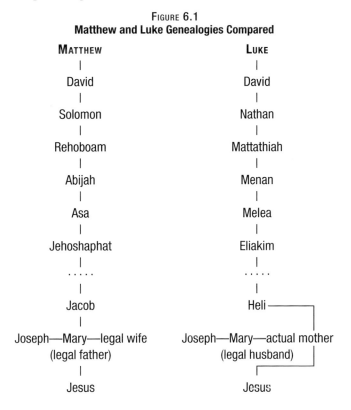

FIGURE 6.1
Matthew and Luke Genealogies Compared

MATTHEW	LUKE
David	David
Solomon	Nathan
Rehoboam	Mattathiah
Abijah	Menan
Asa	Melea
Jehoshaphat	Eliakim
.....	.....
Jacob	Heli
Joseph—Mary—legal wife (legal father)	Joseph—Mary—actual mother (legal husband)
Jesus	Jesus

Luke 4:3–12 (see Matthew 4:3–10)—*Is there a mistake in recording the wilderness temptation of Christ by Matthew or Luke?*

Problem: According to both Matthew and Luke, the first temptation was to turn stones into bread to satisfy Jesus's hunger. The second temptation listed by Matthew took place at the pinnacle of the temple. The third temptation listed by Matthew involved all the kingdoms of the world. However, although Luke mentions these same two events, he lists them in reverse order—the kingdoms of the world are mentioned second and the pinnacle of the temple is mentioned third. Which is the correct order?

Solution: It may be that Matthew describes these temptations *chronologically* while Luke lists them *climactically*, that is, topically. This may be to express the climax he desired to emphasize. Matthew 4:5 begins with the word "then" while verse 8 begins with the word "again." In Greek these words suggest a more sequential order of the events. In Luke's account, however, verses 5 and 9 both begin with a simple "and" (see NASB). The Greek in the case of Luke's account does not necessarily indicate a sequential order of events. Furthermore, there is no reason to doubt that all these temptations actually happened.

Luke 6:17 (see Matt. 5:1)—*Why does Luke say Jesus gave this sermon on a level place when Matthew declares it was given on the mountain?*
Problem: Luke affirms that Jesus "stood on a level place" when he gave this famous sermon, but Matthew says, "He went up on a mountain" to deliver it. How can this discrepancy be resolved?
Solution: The two accounts are referring to the same event (see comments on Luke 6:20 below), and the discrepancy can be reconciled by noting that Matthew's reference to the mountain indicates only the *general area* where everyone was, while the level place denotes the *particular spot* from which Jesus spoke. Luke says he "*stood* on a level place." It does not say all the people were *seated* in a level place. A level place from which to preach to a multitude on a mountainside would make a natural amphitheater.

Luke 6:17 (see Matt. 5:1–2)—*Why does Luke say Jesus stood to teach them when Matthew declares that he sat to teach them?*
Problem: Luke says that Jesus "stood on a level place" to preach. But Matthew recorded that "when He was seated . . . He opened His mouth and taught them."
Solution: These references may be of slightly different times during the same event. One possibility is that Matthew's reference is to the beginning of the event when "His disciples came to Him. . . . and [He] taught them" (Matt. 5:1–2). Then when the "great multitude" that followed him gathered to listen in, Jesus would naturally want to stand (as Luke records) to project his voice so that all could hear.

Another possibility is that Luke's reference to Jesus's standing is before he gave the sermon, while he is still healing people (vv. 17–19). Then, since "the whole multitude sought to touch Him," Jesus may have found a place to sit where "He lifted up His eyes toward His disciples, and said . . . [His message]" (v. 20). This fits the order given in Luke and would also explain why Matthew declares that Jesus was sitting when he spoke to his disciples. In any event, there is no irreconcilable difference in the two accounts, even assuming they both refer to the same occasion.

Luke 6:20–23 (see Matthew 5:3–12)—*Why does Luke's version of the Beatitudes differ from that in Matthew?*
Problem: Luke's version of the first beatitude states, "Blessed are you poor" (v. 20), while Matthew's account says, "Blessed are the poor in spirit" (v. 3). Luke appears to be speaking about poverty in a financial sense and Matthew about poverty in a spiritual sense.
Solution: Some believe that the difference in renditions could be because these are two different occasions. They point to the fact that Matthew says the message was given to a multitude *including*

Excavated ancient buildings at Capernaum.

his disciples (5:1), while Luke's version was given to his disciples (Luke 6:20). Also, in Matthew, Jesus spoke on a hill, while in Luke he spoke on level ground (v. 17). Then too Luke's account is much more brief than Matthew's. (But see "Solution" under the first Luke 6:17 above.)

Others note that both sermons were given at the same time, in the same geographical area, to the same group of people, with many of the exact same sayings. In both accounts his sermon was preceded by special healings and followed by his going to Capernaum. Furthermore, although Luke introduces the sermon by saying Jesus "lifted up His eyes toward His disciples," like Matthew, he notes that Jesus gave "all His sayings in the hearing of the people" (Luke 7:1; see Matt. 5:2). All of this makes it unlikely that two different events are represented.

The difference in the accounts can be accounted for in several ways. (1) Luke's account is much more brief than Matthew's. (2) Jesus may have said much more on this occasion than either writer recorded. So each writer selected from a larger body of material that which suited his theme. (3) Luke places a different emphasis on Jesus's words, stressing the significance for those who were poor. Matthew does not exclude financial poverty but speaks of that poverty of spirit that the poor often have, as opposed to the rich (see Luke 16:14–17; 1 Tim. 6:17).

Luke 7:2–10 (see Matthew 8:5–13)—*Is there a mistake in the accounts concerning Jesus and the centurion?*

Problem: Matthew seems to present the centurion as the one who seeks the help of Jesus (Matt. 8:5), but Luke seems to say that the centurion sent elders to see Jesus (Luke 7:3). Also Matthew appears to say that the centurion himself comes to talk with Jesus. However, in Luke, the Bible says only the centurion's representatives saw Jesus.

Solution: Both Matthew and Luke are correct. In the first century, it was understood that when a representative was sent to speak for his master, it was as if the master were speaking himself. Even in our day this is still the case. When the secretary of state meets individuals from other countries, he or she goes out in the name of the president of the United States. In other words, what the secretary of state says, the president says. Therefore, Matthew states that a centurion came entreating Jesus about his sick slave, when in fact the centurion sent others on his behalf. So, when Matthew declares that the centurion was speaking, this was true, even though he was (as Luke indicated) speaking through his official representative.

Luke 23:47 (see Matthew 27:54; Mark 15:39)—*What did the centurion really say about Christ on the cross?*

Problem: Matthew records the centurion saying, "Truly this was the Son of God!" while Mark says substantially the same thing, adding only the word "Man," rendering it, "Truly this Man was the Son of God!" Luke records the words of the centurion as follows: "Certainly this was a righteous Man!" What did he really say?

Solution: The centurion may have said both things. The centurion's words need not be limited to one phrase or sentence. In accordance with his own emphasis on Christ as the perfect Man, Luke may have chosen to use this phrase from what the centurion said, rather than the ones used by Matthew and Mark. There is no major difference between Matthew and Mark, for in Greek the word *man* is implied by the masculine singular use of the word *this*. It is also possible that Luke may have been paraphrasing or drawing an implication from what was actually said.

Christian scholars do not claim to have the exact words of the speakers in every case, but only an accurate rendering of what they really said. First of all, it is generally agreed that they spoke in Aramaic, but the Gospels were written in Greek. So the words we have in the Greek text on which the English is based are already a translation. Second, the Gospel writers, like writers today, sometimes summarized or paraphrased what was said. In this way, it is understandable that the renderings are slightly different. But in this case, as in all other cases, the essence of what was originally said is faithfully produced in the original text. While we do not have the *exact words*, we do have the *same meaning*. Finally, when the sentences are totally different (but not contradictory), then we may reasonably assume that both things were said on that occasion and that one writer uses one and another writer the other. This is a common literary practice even today.

Luke 24:31—*If Jesus had the same physical body after his resurrection, why did his disciples not recognize him?*
Problem: Two disciples walked with Jesus on the road to Emmaus. They talked with him and ate with him and still did not recognize him. Other disciples had the same experience (see verses below). If he was raised from the dead in the same physical body (see Luke 24:39; John 20:27), why didn't they recognize him?
Solution: Jesus did rise in the numerically same body of flesh and bones in which he died (see comments on 1 Cor. 15:35–38). There were many reasons for his not being immediately recognized by his disciples: dullness—Luke 24:25–26; disbelief—John 20:24–25; disappointment—verses 11–15; dread—Luke 24:36–37; dimness— John 20:1, 14–15; distance—21:4–7; different clothes—19:23–24; see 20:6–8.

Notice, however, two important things: the problem was only *temporary*, and before the appearance was over, they were absolutely convinced that it was the same Jesus in the same physical body of flesh, bones, and scars that he had before the resurrection! And they went out of his presence to turn the world upside down, fearlessly facing death, because they had not the slightest doubt that he had conquered death in the same physical body in which he had experienced it.

Luke 24:49 (see Matthew 28:10, 16)—*Why did the disciples go to Galilee when Jesus commanded them to stay in Jerusalem?*
Problem: According to Luke, the apostles were told to "tarry in the city of Jerusalem" until Pentecost. But Matthew tells us that they went into Galilee.
Solution: First, it is possible that the command was not given until after they had been in Galilee. In this event there would be no conflict whatsoever. Furthermore, the command to "tarry" simply meant to make Jerusalem their headquarters. It did not preclude taking short trips elsewhere. Jerusalem was the place they were to receive the Holy Spirit (Luke 24:49) and to begin their work.

STUDY QUESTIONS

1. What is the evidence, internal and external, that Luke is the author of this Gospel?

2. When was Luke written? List your reasons for the date chosen.

3. To whom was Luke writing?

4. What were possible destinations of Luke's Gospel?

5. What was Luke's theme and purpose in writing the Gospel?

SELECTED SOURCES

Baxter, Sidlow. *Explore the Book*. Grand Rapids: Zondervan, 1987.

Blomberg, Craig. *The Historical Reliability of the Gospels*. Downers Grove, IL: InterVarsity, 1987.

Bock, Darrell L. *Luke*. Baker Exegetical Commentary on the New Testament. 2 vols. Grand Rapids: Baker, 1994, 1996.

Carson, D. A., Douglas Moo, and Leon Morris. *An Introduction to the New Testament*. Grand Rapids: Zondervan, 1992.

Geisler, Norman L., and Thomas Howe. *When Critics Ask: A Popular Handbook on Bible Difficulties*. Grand Rapids: Baker, 1997.

Guthrie, Donald. *New Testament Introduction*. Downers Grove, IL: InterVarsity, 1990.

Harrison, Everett F. *An Introduction to the New Testament*. Grand Rapids: Eerdmans, 1971.

Hemer, Colin. *The Book of Acts in the Setting of Hellenic History*. Winona Lake, MN: Eisenbrauns, 1990.

Liefeld, Walter. *Luke*. Expositor's Bible Commentary. Grand Rapids: Zondervan, 1995.

Linnemann, Eta. *Is There a Synoptic Problem?* Grand Rapids: Baker, 1992.

Marshall, I. Howard. *The Gospel of Luke*. The New International Greek Testament Commentary. Grand Rapids: Eerdmans, 1983.

Morris, Leon. *The Gospel According to St. Luke*. Tyndale New Testament Commentary. Rev. ed. Grand Rapids: Eerdmans, 1988.

Radmacher, Earl, Ronald Allen, and H. Wayne House, eds. *Nelson's New Illustrated Bible Commentary*. Nashville: Thomas Nelson, 1999.

Robertson, A. T. *A Harmony of the Gospels*. New York: HarperCollins, 1922.

Scroggie, William Graham. *A Guide to the Gospels*. London: Pickering & Inglis, 1948. Reprint, Grand Rapids: Kregel, 1995.

Thomas, Robert, and Stan Gundry. *The New Harmony of the Gospels*. New York: HarperSanFrancisco, 1991.

Walvoord, John F., and Roy B. Zuck, eds. *The Bible Knowledge Commentary*. 2 vols. Wheaton: Victor, 1983.

7
The Gospel of John

Who Wrote It?   There are three views on the authorship of the Gospel of John. Traditionally, it is assigned to John the apostle, "the beloved disciple" (21:20–24). Some more recent scholars have proposed that it is another John known as John "the elder" (see 2 John 1). Others have suggested that it was a disciple of the apostle John who got his information from John. However, there is no real evidence for the last two views and very strong evidence for John the apostle, as follows:

(1) He was the son of Salome and Zebedee, a fisherman (Matt. 4:21). (2) He had a brother named James (4:21; 10:2) (3) Some say John was Jesus's cousin, conjecturing that his mother, Salome, was the Virgin Mary's sister. (4) John's family had servants and official connections in high places (27:55–56; Mark 1:20; Luke 8:3; John 18:15–16; 19:26–27). (5) John was one of the twelve apostles (Matt. 10:2). (6) He was first a follower of John the Baptist (John 1:35 40) and one of the first to follow Jesus (v. 40). (7) He was the beloved disciple of Jesus (21:7). (8) He outran Peter to the tomb and was the first disciple to believe in Jesus's resurrection (20:1–4, 8). (9) He was probably the youngest disciple (see points 7 and 8—the term "beloved" often refers to a young person, and a young person, as a general rule, can run faster than an older person). (10) He was one of the inner circle of apostles, along with James and Peter (Matt. 17:1). (11) He was the one to whom Jesus committed his mother at his death (John 19:25–27). (12) He appeared three times in Acts by name (3:1; 4:13; 8:14) and in one chapter is unnamed (15:2, 22–23). (13) He escaped the Neronian persecutions of the late 60s but was later banished by the Roman Emperor Domitian

to the Isle of Patmos (Rev. 1:9). (14) He is the author of four other books in the New Testament—1, 2, 3 John, and Revelation.

Internal Evidence

The internal evidence pointing to John the apostle as the author of the Gospel is as follows: (1) First of all, the author was a Jew (in thought, word, symbols, customs, and knowledge of the Old Testament). (2) Further, he was a Jew living in Israel (knowing well the customs, language, geography, and topography of the land). (3) Also he was an eyewitness of persons, time, numbers, places, manners, and other details (John 21:24). (4) He was one of the twelve apostles (13:23). (5) What is more, he was one of the disciples referred to but unnamed in John 21:2, 7 (along with Peter, Thomas, Nathanael, and James; see Matt. 4:21). (6) Also he was one of the "inner circle," along with Peter and James (John 20:2–10; Mark 5:37; 9:2–3; 14:33), who saw Jesus's glory (John 1:14). (7) He was not Peter (1:41), Thomas (14:5), Philip (v. 8), or Andrew (6:8) who are mentioned by name. (8) And he was not James who died in AD 44 (Acts 12:2). (9) Thus, by the process of elimination, the author of the Gospel must have been the apostle John, who leaned on Jesus's bosom at the Last Supper (13:23–25); he was the unnamed disciple who appears several times in the text (in 13:23; 19:26; 20:2; 21:7, 20); he was the one Jesus loved (21:7); he was given responsibility for Jesus's mother (19:26–27). John wrote the Gospel of John (21:24), as well as the Epistles of John (see chapters 26–27 of this book) and the book of Revelation (see chapter 28).

External Evidence

Other evidence for John the apostle is strong as well. First, the *John Ryland Fragment* (opposite; including John 18:31–33, 37–38), early second century (AD 117–38), confirms it was written in the first century. Further, the early testimony of Irenaeus, who knew John's disciple Polycarp, confirms that it was John the apostle. What is more, other early sources (including Tatian and the Muratorian canon, Clement of Alexandria, Tertullian, and Eusebius) confirm that John wrote it.

The first to challenge John's authorship was a late second-century group, the Alogoi sect (who denied the deity of Christ and the Holy Spirit).

When Was It Written?

(1) John wrote well after AD 70, since he doesn't refer to this important date at all. (2) Likewise, it was well before Irenaeus who cites the Gospel in the early second century and who knew John's disciple Polycarp. (3) It must have been written in the

late first century since it was written in Asia Minor and yet the *John Ryland Fragment* manuscript of it was found in a small town in Egypt, dated ca. AD 117–38. (4) Of course it must have been written before John died (in AD 98, according to Irenaeus). This would place the writing during the reign of Domitian (AD 81–96) (see chapter 28 on Revelation).

To Whom Was It Written?

The Gospel was written to the Christians of Asia Minor (perhaps centered around Ephesus).

Where Were Its Readers Located?

They were in Asia Minor (modern Turkey).

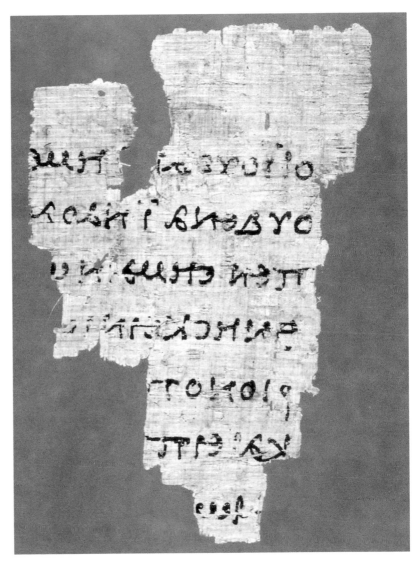

John Ryland fragment.

Why Was It Written?

The purposes of the book of John fall into several categories: (1) The *christological* purpose is stated in John 20:30–31: "that you may believe that Jesus is the Christ, the Son of God, and that believing you may have life in His name." (2) The *biographical* purpose is supplementary, namely, to provide additional material, not in the other three Gospels, on the life and teaching of Jesus. This is confirmed by Papias, Irenaeus, Jerome, Gregory of Nasianzus, and St. Augustine. (3) There is also an *apologetical* aim, evidenced by the seven miracles (see below), chosen to verify Jesus's claims; the use of the word *sign*, and the use of the words *witness* and *testimony*. (4) A *polemical* goal is also discernable, namely, to counter an early form of Gnosticism, which denied the deity and full humanity of Christ. (5) Finally, there may be a *spiritual* design, as reflected by Clement of Alexandria, who called it "a spiritual gospel," to show how one may have eternal life by knowing the eternal God (John 17:3).

What Is It About?

The Theme: Eternal life comes through belief in Christ (1:1; 3:16; 8:58; 10:30; 20:31).

The Key Verse: "I have come that they may have life, and that they may have it more abundantly" (10:10).

Key Words and Phrases: *abide* (41x), *ask* (37x), *believe* (100x), *eternal, eternity* (29x), *Father* (of God) (122x), *glorify, glory* (42x), *heaven* (19x), *hour* (26x), *the Jews* (71x), *judge, judgment* (30x), *know* (*ginōskō*, 54x) *know* (*oida*, 83x), *life* (36x), *light* (23x), (*to*) *love, love* (44x), *receive, take* (48x), *see, behold* (61x), *send* (28x), *sign, miracle* (17x), *sin, sinner* (25x), *truth, truly, true* (46x), *verily* (*truly*) (50x in KJV; *I tell you the truth* in NIV), *testify, testimony* (47x), and *world* (78x). See appendix 3 for a more complete word study.

Miracles: John lists seven miracles during Jesus's life, all of which are unique except the feeding of the five thousand and walking on water (see appendix 4 for a complete list of miracles in the Gospels). The seven miracles (before the resurrection) are:

1. Changing water to wine (2:1–11)
2. Healing an official's son (4:46–54)
3. Healing an invalid man (5:1–16)
4. Feeding five thousand (6:5–14)
5. Walking on water (6:16–21)
6. Healing a man born blind (9:1–7)
7. Raising of Lazarus (11:1–44)

There was also the resurrection (the eighth miracle) and the ninth miracle occurred after the resurrection—the large catch of fish (21:1–14).

The Power of the Logos (Word) over Cosmos (World): Jesus's power over the cosmos was seen by the fact that he manifested control over every category of the cosmos as listed by the famous Greek philosopher Aristotle in his *Categories*. Note Jesus's power over:

- substance (what?)—turning water into wine (2:1–10)
- quantity (how much?)—feeding the five thousand (6:1–14)
- quality (what kind?)—the blind man gets quality of sight (9:1–11)
- relation (to what?)—raising Lazarus to his new relationship with the living (11:1–44)
- space (where?)—healing the nobleman's son from a distance (4:46–54)
- time (when?)—healing a man who had been an invalid for thirty-eight years (5:1–9)
- position (on what?)—walking on water, an unnatural position (6:16–21)
- action (from what?)—his victorious death (19)
- passion (on what?)—his triumphant resurrection (20)
- state or habit (under what condition?)—catching a multitude of fish (21:1–6)

Parables: There are no parables in John (10:1–5 is an illustration or figure of speech).

Old Testament Citations: There are only 19 Old Testament quotations in this Gospel, but there are some 120 possible references or allusions.[1]

The Words of Jesus: The Gospel stresses Jesus's words. Of the 866 verses, 419 are Jesus's words (nearly 50 percent).

Jesus's Discourses: There are fourteen discourses of Jesus in John: new birth (3:1–21), water of life (4:1–26), source of life (chap. 5), bread of life (6:22–58), source of truth (7:14–24), light of the world (8:12–19), true object of faith (vv. 21–29), liberation by truth (vv. 31–58), Good Shepherd (10:1–18), oneness with the Father (vv. 22–38), Redeemer of the world (12:23–36), return to the Father (13:31–14:31), abiding in Christ (chap. 15), the Holy Spirit and future ministry (chap. 16).

The Feasts in John's Gospel

Feast	Date	Reference	Description
Passover	AD 27	2:13, 23	"the Jews' Passover"
Purim?	AD 28	5:1	"a feast of the Jews"
Passover	AD 29	6:4	"the Passover, a feast of the Jews was near"
Tabernacles	AD 29	7:2, 8	"the Jews' Feast of Tabernacles"; "this feast"
Dedication	AD 29	10:22	"the Feast of Dedication"
Passover	AD 30	11:55; 12:1	"the Passover of the Jews"

The Seven "I Ams":

1. "I am the bread of life" (6:35).
2. "I am the light of the world" (8:12).
3. "I am the door for the sheep" (10:7, 9).
4. "I am the good shepherd" (10:11, 14).
5. "I am the resurrection and the life" (11:25).
6. "I am the way, the truth, and the life" (14:6).
7. "Before Abraham was, I am!" (8:58; see Exod. 3:14).

Private Conversations of Jesus: There are several extended private conversations of Jesus, including one with Nicodemus (3:1–21), the Samaritan woman at the well (4:6–38), the Upper Room Discourse (chaps. 13–15), his High Priestly prayer (chap. 17), plus shorter ones (see chaps. 7, 8, 9, 10, 11, 12), totaling more than two dozen in all.

Character Sketches: We see portraits of many persons, including Nicodemus, Philip, Thomas, Mary, Martha, Peter, and Judas.

Supplemental Nature: The supplemental nature of the book of John is indicated by the fact that the author omitted (assumed) many important events in Christ's life, such as his birth, baptism, temptation, transfiguration, institution of the Lord's Supper, agony in Gethsemane, and ascension.

Other Characteristics: John has the only record of Jesus's early Judean ministry (chaps. 2–4). It has more details on the last days of Jesus than the other Gospels (chaps. 13–21). Ninety percent of

Political Division of
the Holy Land in the
Time of Jesus.

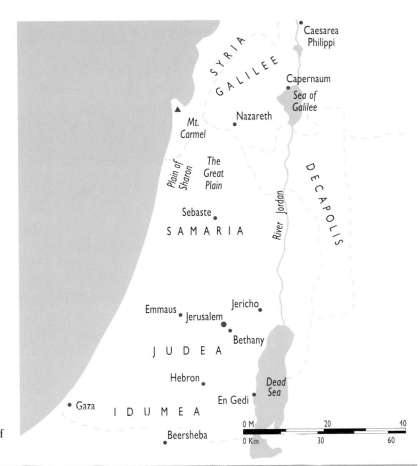

SYRIA

GALILEE

Caesarea
Philippi

Capernaum

Sea of
Galilee

Mt.
Carmel

Nazareth

DECAPOLIS

Plain of
Sharon

The
Great
Plain

River Jordan

Sebaste

SAMARIA

Emmaus

Jericho

Jerusalem

Bethany

JUDEA

Hebron

Dead
Sea

En Gedi

Gaza

IDUMEA

0 M   20   40

Temple of Hercules,
Philadelphia, a city of
the Decapolis.

Beersheba

0 Km   30   60

Tomb of Lazarus, Bethany.

John's Gospel is unique (as compared to the Synoptics). The name "Jesus" is used almost exclusively (239 of the 542 times in the Gospels are in John). This Gospel also stresses Jesus's humanity in that he got tired (4:6), wept (11:35), thirsted (19:28), suffered (v. 18), and died (v. 30). There are twenty-six parallels to the Synoptics.[2] Of the forty-six names given Christ in the Gospels, John gives thirty-three.

Two Classes of Gospels

Synoptic (Matthew, Mark, Luke)	Autoptic (John)
public ministry	private ministry
Galilean ministry	Judean ministry
parables	no parables
human side	divine side
earthly aspect	heavenly aspect
synoptical	supplementary
official	personal

Four Movements of Christ in John (see 16:28):

1. I came from the Father.
2. I have come into the world.
3. I leave the world.
4. I go to the Father.

The Message of All Four Gospels Compared:
Following the idea of Sidlow Baxter, the message of each Gospel can be summarized:

Matthew: The promised King is here; see his credentials.

Mark: This is how he worked as a Servant; see his power.

Luke: This is what he was like as the Son of Man; see his humanity.

John: This is who he really was; see his deity.[3]

THE OUTLINE:

I. **Revelation of Christ to the World** (chaps. 1–4)
　　A. The pedigree of Christ in the world (1:1–18)
　　B. The presentation of Christ to the world (1:19–51)
　　C. The preview of Christ by the world (chaps. 2–4)
　　　　1. By the wedding guests (2:1–12)
　　　　2. By the Jews (2:13–25)
　　　　3. By a teacher of the Jews (3:1–21)
　　　　4. By John's disciples (3:22–36)
　　　　5. By the Samaritans (4:1–42)
　　　　6. By the Galileans (4:43–54)
II. **Rejection of Christ by the World** (chaps. 5–12)
　　A. The principles of unbelief (chaps. 5–6)
　　B. The parties of unbelief (chap. 7)
　　C. The progress of unbelief (chaps. 8–9)
　　D. The persistence of unbelief (chaps. 10–12)
III. **Revelation of Christ to His Disciples** (13:1–16:24)
　　A. The pattern for the disciples' lives (13:1–30)
　　B. The preparation of the disciples' hearts (13:31–14:31)
　　C. The prospect for the disciples' future (chap. 15)
　　D. The promise for the disciples' comfort (16:1–24)
IV. **Reception of Christ by His Disciples** (16:25–21:25)
　　A. The pronouncement of the disciples' conviction (16:25–33)
　　B. The prayer for the disciples' consecration (chap. 17)

THE CONTENTS: First, we have the revelation of Christ to the world (chaps. 1–4), which contains the pedigree of Christ in the world (1:1–18), the presentation of Christ to the world by John the Baptist (1:19–51), and the preview of Christ by the world (chaps. 2–4), including the wedding guests (2:1–12), the Jews (vv. 13–25), a teacher of the Jews (3:1–21), John's disciples (vv. 22–36), the Samaritans (4:1–42), and the Galileans (vv. 43–54).

Next, there is the rejection of Christ by the world (chaps. 5–12), which includes the principles of unbelief (chaps. 5–6), the parties of unbelief (chap. 7), the progress of unbelief (chaps. 8–9), and the persistence of unbelief (chaps. 10–12), highlighted by the response of those who didn't believe the healing of the blind man (chap. 9), their attempt to stone Jesus (10:31), their response to the resurrection of Lazarus (11:46–57), and their rejection of the light (12:37–43). John's sad conclusion says it all: "But although He [Jesus] had done so many signs before them, they did not believe in Him" (12:37).

There follows the revelation of Christ to his disciples (13:1–16:24) in which he gives the pattern of humility for the disciples' lives (13:1–30), the preparation of the disciples' hearts (13:31–14:31), the prospect for the disciples' future (chap. 15), and the promise for the disciples' comfort in the Person of the Holy Spirit (16:1–24).

In the final section, John records the reception of Christ by his disciples (16:25–21:25), which begins with the pronouncement of the disciples' conviction that he is the Son of God (16:25–33), Jesus's high priestly prayer for the disciples' consecration (chap. 17), the plight of the disciples' courage (chaps. 18–19), the peak of the disciples' certainty (chap. 20), and the perfecting of the disciples' confidence through his resurrection and appearances to them (chap. 21).

How to Respond to Critics

John 1:1—*Is Jesus God or just a god?*

Problem: Orthodox Christians believe Jesus is God and often appeal to this passage to prove it. However, Jehovah's Witnesses translate this verse "and the Word (Christ) was a god," because there is no definite article (*the*) in the Greek of this verse.

Solution: In Greek, when the definite article is used, it often stresses the *individual*, and, when it is not present, it refers to the *nature* of the one denoted. Thus the verse can be rendered, "and the Word was of the nature of God." The full deity of Christ is supported not only by general usage of the same construction, but by other references

Jerusalem in the Time of Jesus.

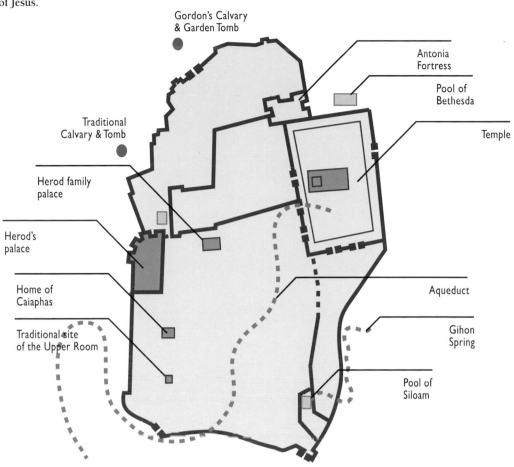

Gordon's Calvary & Garden Tomb

Antonia Fortress

Pool of Bethesda

Temple

Traditional Calvary & Tomb

Herod family palace

Herod's palace

Home of Caiaphas

Aqueduct

Gihon Spring

Traditional site of the Upper Room

Pool of Siloam

Artist's impression of Herod's Temple and the Antonia Fortress in the time of Jesus.

in John to Jesus being God (see 8:58; 10:30; 20:28) and in the rest of the New Testament (see, for example, Col. 1:15–16; 2:9; Titus 2:13).

Furthermore, some New Testament texts use the definite article and speak of Christ as "the God." So it does not matter whether John did or did not use the definite article here—the Bible clearly teaches that Jesus is God, not just a god (see Heb. 1:8). That Jesus is Jehovah (Yahweh) is clear from the fact that the New Testament attributes to Jesus characteristics that in the Old Testament apply only to God (see, for example, John 19:37 and Zech. 12:10).

John 1:33 (see Matthew 3:13–14)—*Did John the Baptist know Jesus before his baptism or not?*
Problem: Before his baptism John said categorically, "I did not know Him," yet in Matthew 3:13–14 John recognized Jesus before he baptized him and said, "I have need to be baptized by You."
Solution: John may have known Jesus before his baptism only by *reputation*, not by *recognition*. Or he may have known Jesus only by *personal acquaintance*, but not by *divine manifestation*. After all, Jesus and John were relatives (Luke 1:36), even though they were reared in different places (1:80; 2:51). However, even though John may have had some previous family contact with Jesus, he had never known Jesus as he was revealed at his baptism when the Spirit descended on him and the Father spoke from heaven (Matt. 3:16–17). The context indicates that, up to his baptism, no one really knew Jesus as he would then "be revealed to Israel" (John 1:31).

John 2:13–17 (see Matt. 21:12–13; Mark 11:15–17; Luke 19:45–46)—*When did Jesus cleanse the temple?*
Problem: John 2:13–17 declares that Jesus cleansed the temple in his early ministry, but Mark 11:15–17 says he cleansed the temple later in his ministry after the transfiguration and before the crucifixion. This is clearly not the same time. How can we resolve this contradiction?
Solution: When one examines the two texts more carefully, it becomes apparent that these were two different circumstances. This is evident from the two different responses Jesus gave. In John 2:16 he said, "Take these things away! Do not make My Father's house a house of merchandise!" And his disciples remembered that it was written: "Zeal for Your house will consume me" (v. 17 NASB). Later, when he cleansed the temple again, he said something very different. He said, "Is it not written, 'My house shall be called a house of prayer for all nations'? But you have made it a 'den of thieves'" (Mark 11:17). These are different things said on different occasions, one in his early ministry and one several years later.

The Temple Mount, Jerusalem.

John 3:13—*How could Christ say no one has ascended to heaven when Elijah had?*

Problem: Jesus declared in this text: "No one has ascended to heaven. . . ." However, the Old Testament records Elijah's ascension into heaven in a chariot (2 Kings 2:11).

Solution: In this context, Jesus is setting forth his superior knowledge of heavenly things. In essence he is saying, "No other human being can speak from firsthand knowledge about these things, as I can, since I came down from heaven." He is claiming that no one has ascended to heaven to bring down the message that he brought. In no way is he denying that anyone else is *in* heaven, such as Elijah and Enoch (Gen. 5:24). Rather, Jesus is simply claiming that no one on earth has gone *to* heaven and *returned* with a message such as he offered to them.

John 4:26—*Why did Jesus confess he was the Messiah here but avoid doing it elsewhere?*

Problem: In the Synoptic Gospels (Matthew, Mark, and Luke), Jesus seemed to go out of his way to avoid claiming he was the Jewish Messiah. He would ask his disciples in private (Matt 16:13) and would sometimes exhort people who discovered it "to tell no man." Yet here in John the woman of Samaria said, "I know that

115

Messiah is coming (who is called Christ)" (4:25). Forthrightly Jesus volunteered: "I who speak to you am He."

Solution: Here Jesus was in Samaria not Judea. The Jews of Jesus's day had a distorted concept of the Messiah, namely, as one who would deliver them from the political oppression of Rome. In this context Jesus was careful to make his claims more covert, so as to elicit from his disciples a more spiritual concept of the one who came to redeem his people (see Luke 19:10; John 10:10).

Indeed, this is the reason Jesus spoke so often in parables, so that those who were truly seeking would understand, but those who had a false concept would be confused (see Matt. 13:13). This is the reason, when Jesus performed miracles, he would sometimes exhort the person to tell no one, since he did not want to be thronged by the curious. Indeed, Jesus rebuked those who, having seen him multiply the loaves, wanted to make him king (John 6:15), declaring that they followed him "because you ate of the loaves and were filled" (v. 26). However, in Samaria, where this false Jewish concept of a political deliverer from Rome who could feed the masses did not prevail, Jesus did not hesitate to claim that he indeed was the true Messiah. Jesus said this to only one Samaritan woman in private, not to the masses of Jews in Judea.

Nonetheless, Jesus did claim to be the Messiah in public, in Judea, and to the Jews. Usually, however, his claim was more covert, trying to get them to discover for themselves who he was. When it became necessary to declare himself before the high priest, Jesus didn't hesitate to give an explicit answer to the question "Are You the Christ, the Son of the Blessed?" by declaring, "I am [the Christ]" (Mark 14:61–62; see Matt. 26:64 and Luke 22:70).

John 5:28–29—*Is Jesus advocating salvation by works?*

Problem: Jesus says in John's Gospel that the time is coming when people in the graves will hear his voice "and come forth—those who have done good, to the resurrection of life, and those who have done evil, to the resurrection of condemnation" (5:29). This seems to be a clear contradiction to salvation by grace (see Eph. 2:8–9).

Solution: First, Jesus does not believe in salvation by works. In the beginning of his Gospel, John writes, "But as many as received Him, to them He gave the right to become children of God, to those who believe in His name: who were born, not of blood, nor of the will of the flesh, nor of the will of man, but of God" (1:12–13). Jesus says in John 3:16–18:

> For God so loved the world that He gave His only begotten Son, that whoever *believes* in Him should not perish but have

everlasting life. For God did not send His Son into the world to condemn the world, but that the world through Him might be saved. He who *believes* in Him is not condemned; but he who does not believe is condemned already, because he has not *believed* in the name of the only begotten Son of God.

Furthermore, in John 5:24 Jesus says, "Truly, truly, I say to you, he who hears My word, and *believes* Him who sent Me, has eternal life" (NASB). From these passages it is clear that Jesus did not believe in salvation through works.

Second, Jesus's reference to good works in John 5:28–29 is to works that are done after saving faith. To be saved, one needs the grace of God (Eph. 2:8–9), but authentic faith expresses itself in good works (v. 10). The apostle Paul in the book of Romans says something very similar to what Jesus says in John 5:28–29. In Romans Paul says that God "will render to each person according to his deeds: to those who by perseverance in doing good seek for glory and honor and immortality, eternal life; but to those who are selfishly ambitious and do not obey the truth, but obey unrighteousness, wrath and indignation" (Rom. 2:6–8 NASB). But Paul also wrote, "For by grace you have been saved through faith, and that *not of yourselves*; it is the gift of God" (Eph. 2:8). In the passage in Romans, Paul is not talking about the one who obtains eternal life by faith, but the individual who shows this life in his good works. In Ephesians Paul is saying that none can save himself or herself by works *prior* to salvation. (See also comments on James 2:21 in chapter 23.)

So Jesus does not contradict himself or the rest of Scripture concerning the matter of salvation. Those who receive the resurrection of life have shown their saving faith by their works.

John 6:53–54—*What did Jesus mean when he said we should eat his flesh?*
Problem: Evangelical Christians believe in taking the Bible literally. But Jesus said, "Unless you eat the flesh of the Son of Man and drink His blood, you have no life in you." Should this be taken literally too?
Solution: The literal (i.e., actual) meaning of a text is the correct one, but the literal meaning does not mean that everything should be taken literally. For example, the literal meaning of Jesus's statement, "I am the true vine" (John 15:1) is that he is the real source of our spiritual life. But it does not mean that Jesus is a literal vine with leaves growing out of his arms and ears! Literal meaning can be communicated by means of figures of speech. Christ is the actual

foundation of the church (1 Cor. 3:11; Eph. 2:20), but he is not literally a granite cornerstone with engraving on it.

There are many indications in John 6 that Jesus meant literally that the command to eat his flesh should be taken in a figurative way. (1) Jesus indicated that his statement should not be taken in a materialistic sense when he said, "The words that I speak to you are spirit, and they are life" (v. 63). (2) It is absurd and cannibalistic to take his statement in a physical sense. (3) He was not speaking of physical life but "eternal life" (v. 54). (4) He called himself the "bread of life" (v. 48) and contrasted this with the physical bread the Jews ate in the wilderness (v. 58). (5) He used the figure of "eating" his flesh in parallel with the idea of "abiding" in him (see 15:4–5), which is another figure of speech. Neither figure is to be taken literally. (6) If the directive to eat his flesh and drink his blood is to be taken in a literal way, it would contradict other commands of Scripture not to eat human flesh and blood (see, for example, Acts 15:20). (7) In view of the figurative meaning here, this verse cannot be used to support the Roman Catholic concept of transubstantiation, that is, eating Jesus's actual body in the communion.

John 7:53–8:11—*Why do some scholars question whether this story should be in the Bible?*
Problem: This story of the woman taken in adultery is found in the King James, the American Standard, the New American Standard, and the New International versions of the Bible. The New English Bible places it at the end of the Gospel under the caption "An incident in the temple." And since 1971 the Revised Standard Version places it in special print set off from the rest of the text, as does the New Revised Standard Version. The standard Greek New Testament (Nestle-Aland Text, United Bible Societies) places brackets around it, indicating that it is not part of the text of John. Why do many scholars believe this story is not part of the original manuscript of the Gospel of John?
Solution: There are several reasons that many scholars question whether this passage belongs here in John's Gospel: (1) The passage does not appear in the oldest and most reliable Greek manuscripts. (2) It is not found in the best manuscripts of the earliest translations of the Bible into Old Syriac, Coptic, Gothic, and Old Latin. (3) No Greek writer commented on this passage for the first eleven centuries of Christianity. (4) It is not cited by most of the great early Church Fathers, including Clement, Tertullian, Origen, Cyprian, Cyril, and others. (5) Its style does not fit that of the rest of the Gospel of John. (6) It interrupts the flow of thought

The Western Wall, Jerusalem, contains some Herodian masonry.

in John. John reads better if one goes right from John 7:52 to 8:12. (7) The story has been found in several different places in Bible manuscripts—after John 7:36; after John 7:44; after John 21:24; and after Luke 21:38. (8) Many manuscripts that include it in John 7:53–8:11 have marked it with an obelus, indicating they believe it is doubtful that it belongs there.

In spite of this, many Bible scholars believe this story is authentic. It certainly contains no doctrinal error and fits with the character of Jesus and his teaching, but there is no certainty that it was in the original text of John.

John 10:11—*Did Jesus die just for his friends or for his enemies too?*
Problem: John quotes Jesus as claiming that he lays down his "life for the sheep" (see also 15:13). But Paul claims "Christ died for the ungodly," while they were still "enemies" (Rom. 5:6, 10). How can both be true?
Solution: Jesus died for both his friends (disciples) and his enemies. In fact his "friends" were enemies when he died for them. There is no contradiction here, since the text does not say that Christ died *only* for his friends. He did die for those who would become his

friends, but he also died for those who would remain his enemies. Peter refers to the apostates who were "denying the Lord who bought them" (2 Peter 2:1).

John 10:30—*Was Christ one with the Father?*

Problem: Jesus said here, "I and My Father are one." But on other occasions he distinguished himself from the Father, saying, "I came forth from the Father and . . . I leave the world and go to the Father" (16:28). Further, he prayed to the Father as one person to another (chap.17), and even said, "My Father is greater than I" (14:28).

Solution: Jesus was one with the Father in *nature* but distinct from him in *person*. The triune Godhead has one *essence* but three distinct *persons* (see comments on John 14:28). So Jesus was the same in substance as the Father and yet was a different individual from the Father.

John 11:26—*How could Jesus say we will never die when the Bible declares all will eventually die?*

Problem: God said to Adam, "In the day that you eat of it you shall surely die" (Gen. 2:17). Paul reaffirmed this, declaring that "through one man sin entered the world, and death through sin, and thus death spread to all men, because all sinned" (Rom. 5:12). But Jesus seems to contradict this when he affirmed, "Whoever lives and believes in Me shall never die" (John 11:26).

Solution: First of all, even taken literally, Jesus was not denying that believers would die. In fact he affirmed it in the previous verse, saying, "Though he may die, he shall live." In other words, Jesus claimed that because he was "the resurrection and the life" (v. 25), he would resurrect to eternal life those who believe in him (see 5:28–29).

Further, Jesus may have been speaking about spiritual life and spiritual death. In this sense, those who believe in him will have spiritual life (3:16, 36), even though they will experience physical death. For those who are born only once will die twice, once physically and once again at the "second death" (Rev. 20:14) or final separation from God. But those who are born twice (John 3:3, 7) will die only once (physically), and will live with God forever.

John 14:28—*Did Jesus think of himself as less than God?*

Problem: Orthodox Christianity confesses Jesus is both fully man and fully God. Yet Jesus said in John 14:28: "My Father is greater than I." How can the Father be greater if Jesus is equal to God?

Solution: The Father is greater than the Son by *office*, but not by *nature*, since both are God (see John 1:1; 8:58; 10:30). Just as an earthly father is equally human with, but holds a higher office than, his son, even so the Father and the Son in the Trinity are equal in *essence* but different in *function*. In like manner, we speak of the president of our country as being a greater man, not by virtue of his *character* but by virtue of his *position*. Therefore, no one can say that Jesus considered himself anything less than God by nature. The following summary helps to crystallize the differences:

Jesus is equal to the Father	The Father is greater than Jesus
In essence	In function
In nature	In office
In character	In position

John 20:17—*If Jesus had not yet ascended to the Father, how could he have committed his Spirit to the Father?*
Problem: Jesus said here, "I have not yet ascended to My Father." But earlier, on the cross, he said, "Father, into Your hands I commend My spirit" (Luke 23:46). If he was already with the Father, then why did he say that he had not yet ascended to him?
Solution: The day he died, Jesus's spirit went to be with the Father (as Luke 23:43, 46 records). So his *spirit* had been with the Father, but his *body* had not yet ascended into heaven when he spoke to Mary. The bodily ascension took place some forty days later (see Acts 1:3, 9–10).

STUDY QUESTIONS

1. Who wrote this Gospel?
2. What is its central theme?
3. What evidence does John give for Christ's deity?
4. According to John, what is the only condition for receiving salvation?
5. Why did Jesus perform miracles?
6. List several key words in John.
7. How does John differ from the Synoptic Gospels?

SELECTED SOURCES

Baxter, Sidlow. *Explore the Book*. Grand Rapids: Zondervan, 1987.

Blomberg, Craig. *The Historical Reliability of the Gospels*. Downers Grove, IL: InterVarsity, 1987.

Bruce, F. F. *The Gospel According to John*. New International Commentary on the New Testament. Grand Rapids: Eerdmans, 1994.

Burge, Gary. *John*. NIV Application Commentary. Grand Rapids: Zondervan, 2000.

Carson, D.A. *The Gospel According to John*. Pillar New Testament Commentary. Grand Rapids: Eerdmans, 1992.

Carson, D.A., Douglas Moo, and Leon Morris. *An Introduction to the New Testament*. Grand Rapids: Zondervan, 1992.

Geisler, Norman L., and Thomas Howe. *When Critics Ask: A Popular Handbook on Bible Difficulties*. Grand Rapids: Baker, 1997.

Guthrie, Donald. *New Testament Introduction*. Downers Grove, IL: InterVarsity, 1990.

Harrison, Everett F. *An Introduction to the New Testament*. Grand Rapids: Eerdmans, 1971.

Hemer, Colin. *The Book of Acts in the Setting of Hellenic History*. Winona Lake, MN: Eisenbrauns, 1990.

Linnemann, Eta. *Is There a Synoptic Problem?* Grand Rapids: Baker, 1992.

MacArthur, John. *John 1–11*. MacArthur New Testament Commentary. Chicago: Moody, 2006.

Morris, Leon. *The Gospel According to John*. New International Commentary on the New Testament. Rev. ed. Grand Rapids: Eerdmans, 1995.

Radmacher, Earl, Ronald Allen, and H. Wayne House, eds. *Nelson's New Illustrated Bible Commentary*. Nashville: Thomas Nelson, 1999.

Robertson, A.T. *A Harmony of the Gospels*. New York: HarperCollins, 1922.

Scroggie, William Graham. *A Guide to the Gospels*. London: Pickering & Inglis, 1948. Reprint, Grand Rapids: Kregel, 1995.

Thomas, Robert, and Stan Gundry. *The New Harmony of the Gospels*. New York: HarperSanFrancisco, 1991.

Walvoord, John F., and Roy B. Zuck, eds. *The Bible Knowledge Commentary*. 2 vols. Wheaton: Victor, 1983.

8
The Book of Acts

Who Wrote It? The author of the book of Acts is Luke, a companion of the apostle Paul (Philem. 24; Acts 16:9–10; 20:1, 4–5). By profession he was a physician (Col. 4:14). Many believe he was a Gentile because he was not listed with those "of the circumcision" in Colossians 4:11, but is mentioned in verse 14. However, this may be a more technical term for Jews, and Luke may have been a Gentile proselyte to Judaism. Luke may have been a native of Antioch of Syria, given the number of times he refers to it (Acts 6:5; 11:19 27; 13:1–3; 14:26–28; 15:1–2, 22, 30–40; 18:22). He lived at Philippi for a while (16:11–17, 40; 20.5) and was with Paul when Colossians and Philemon were written (Col. 4:14; Philem. 24). He was faithful to Paul to the end (2 Tim. 4:11). He was also the author of the Gospel of Luke, as is evident from a comparison of Luke 1:3 and Acts 1:1, which are addressed to the same person, and Acts 1:1 refers to his "former account" (or treatise). Also the same polished Greek, the same style, and the same Pauline content are used in both.

Internal Evidence
The internal evidence for Luke's authorship of this Gospel is strong: (1) The "we" sections (Acts 16:10–17; 20:5–21:18; 27:1–28:16) indicate he was on those occasions a companion and fellow traveler of Paul. (2) The rest of the book is by the same author, as is evidenced by the same style and unity. (3) Alleged differences in style (for example, his use of shorter words) can be explained by his use of sources that differed from his own style and the influence of the Greek translation of the Old Testament (the LXX) used in his work. (4) Alleged differences in theology

overlook the important similarities (for example, Paul preaching justification in Acts 13:39) and neglect to note that differences are due to Luke's interest being more ecclesiastical (see Acts 15) and Paul's more theological (see Galatians). (5) Medical language suggests that a physician was the author (see Col. 4:14).[1] (6) It must have been Luke by the process of elimination. It was not Timothy (16:1), not Silas (v. 25), not Titus (who wasn't on Paul's third journey), not many others (20:4), since the author of Acts writes of these people in the third person. Hence, by the process of elimination, the only one left who fits the evidence is Luke.

External Evidence

The evidence outside Acts is also strong for Luke's authorship. As noted, it was written by the same author as the Gospel of Luke (Acts 1:1). For another thing, the early Fathers of the church attribute it to Luke. It was cited numerous times by them, including Clement of Rome, Ignatius, Polycarp, the Didache, Irenaeus, Justin Martyr, Tertullian, Clement of Alexandria, and Origen. Even the Gnostic heretic Marcion accepted Luke. Further, the Gospel of Luke, written by Luke, is cited by Paul in a canonical book of the New Testament (1 Tim. 5:18 cites Luke 10:7).[2] Finally, there is overwhelming archaeological confirmation of it being written by a knowledgeable companion of Paul and a contemporary of the events, as Luke was.[3]

When Was It Written?

Acts ends with Jerusalem and the temple still standing and Paul alive and well in a Roman prison. This indicates that Acts was written before Jerusalem fell in AD 70 and before Paul was martyred by AD 68. Further, there is no indication the Jewish War had begun (in AD 66). Nor had Nero's persecutions commenced (in AD 64). What is more, the apostle James is still alive, and he died, according to Josephus, in AD 62. On the other hand, the book of Acts must have been written after AD 54 when Gentiles were attracted to Christianity (Acts 18:2, AD 54), since Luke gears his message to them. Most likely it was written when Luke had time while Paul was in jail (Acts 23). Since Paul came to Rome in AD 50 and was there two years (28:30), about AD 61 to 62 is the likely date.

To Whom Was It Written?

The book of Acts is addressed to Theophilus (lover of God). Certain things are known about the person to whom Luke wrote. He was Greek and a person of rank who was addressed as "most excellent" (see 23:26; 24:3; 26:25). Theophilus was a common name among Jews and Gentiles (like John). It is possible he was a young Christian—needing confirmation of his faith (see Luke 1:4). Maybe

Acts was intended for the wider Greek public (i.e., any lover of God), but a specific person seems to be addressed in the first verse. Some argue that Acts was a legal brief in defense of Paul to the Roman court, and no doubt the book had a wider audience in view as well. It was not uncommon to address a book to a noble individual and also intend it for a wider audience.

Where Were Its Readers Located?

The readers of Acts were located in Antioch of Syria and they were generally Gentiles.

Why Was It Written?

The reasons for writing Acts may be divided into several categories. Historically, it provided an accurate record of early Christianity. Spiritually, it was written to confirm the faith of Theophilus (Acts 1:1; Luke 1:4), who was probably a young Greek convert. Legally, it explained Paul's journeys in the right light, showing that he wasn't a traitor to Rome, thus vindicating him of the charges against him. Polemically, it showed that Paul was not an apostate from Judaism or the law. Ecclesiastically, it aimed to show the unity of the Christian movement in the doctrine of the apostles (Acts 1:2; 2:42). Missiologically, it provided the Christian reader with an accurate account of the spread of early Christianity. And finally, apologetically it showed how God authenticated early Christianity by miracles through the apostles (1:3).

What Is It About?

The Theme: The theme is the propagation of the gospel of Christ (1:8). It is the acts of the apostles in the foundation and spread of early Christianity. Or more properly, it is the acts of the Holy Spirit through the apostles.

The Key Verse: "But you shall receive power when the Holy Spirit has come upon you; and you shall be witnesses to Me in Jerusalem, and in all Judea and Samaria, and to the end of the earth" (1:8).

Key Words and Phrases: *announce good news, bring good news, gospel* (17x), *apostle* (30x), *baptize, baptism* (27x), *be written, scriptures* (19x), *believe* (38x), *church* (24x), *grow, increase* (4x), *Holy Spirit* (42x), *name (in reference to Jesus)* (33x), *people* (22x), *persecute, suffer, persecution, affliction* (21x), *pray (beseech), prayer* (32x), *raise, raise up* (19x), *raise, stand up* (44x), *repent, repentance* (11x), *resurrection* (11x), *save* (13x), *spirit (in reference to things other than the Holy Spirit)* (19x), *(to) witness, witness* (27x), *word* (32x), *word (in connection with the Lord)* (20x), *word of God* (12x). See appendix 3 for a more complete word study.

A Comparison of the Gospels and Acts

Gospels	Acts
What Jesus began to do and teach	What Jesus continued to do and teach (Acts 1:1)
Foundation of church (Matt. 16:18; Eph. 2:19–22)	Origin and growth of the church (Acts 2; 1 Cor. 12:13)

A Fulfillment of John 14:12: "Greater works than these he will do, because I go to My Father." The works of the apostles, while not greater in kind, were certainly greater in extent since they carried the message of the gospel to the ends of the earth (see Col. 1:23).

A Fulfillment of Matthew 16:18: Acts is the initial fulfillment of Jesus's statement: "I will build My church, and the gates of Hades shall not prevail against it." Israel did reject their Messiah, but God had plans to set them aside "until the fullness of the Gentiles has come in" (Rom. 11:25) at which time "all Israel will be saved" (v. 26) when the "natural branches [will] be grafted into their own olive tree" (v. 24).

Titles Given to Acts: Acts has been called the Gospel of the Holy Spirit, the Book of Act(ion), the Gospel of Resurrection, the Fifth Gospel, and the Acts of the Holy Spirit.

The Work of the Holy Spirit: He is the source of effective witness (4:8), miraculous power (13:9–11), wisdom in the church (15:28), administrative authority (5:3; 13:2), and spiritual guidance (10:19; 16:6–10).

A Book with No Conclusion: In one noncanonical sense the book of Acts never ends; the work of the church continues until Jesus comes.

Prominence of Persons: God's plan features persons, 110 of which are named in Acts.

It Is a Book of History: Acts is an accurate account of the times. It provides an invaluable intersection with the non-Christian history of the period, revealing ten major Roman and Jewish dates with numerous Roman rulers. It contains nearly a hundred historical facts that have been verified by secular sources.[4]

The Values of Acts: There are many values to the book of Acts. Historically, it is a factually accurate account of the times.[5] Doctrinally, it provides important teaching about the Messiah, the Holy Spirit, and the resurrection. Biographically, it is a crowded platform of 110 characters, both Christian and non-Christian. Evangelistically, it provides a pattern for missions in the journeys

Ruins of ancient Philippi.

of Paul. Dispensationally, it shows the crucial transition from Judaism to Christianity. Spiritually, it provides a vivid account of a Spirit-directed church.

Acts Is a Book of Growth: There is the growth of the church (2:47; 5:14; 6:7; 9:31); of the Word of God (12:24; 19:20); and of faith (16:5).

Acts Gives Various Names for Christianity: First, it was called "the Way" (9:2); next, "the sect of the Nazarenes" (24:5); and its followers were called "Christians" (11:26) in Antioch (see 26:28; 1 Peter 4:16).

It Is a Book of Great Sermons:

Sermons by Peter and Others
Peter to Jewish proselytes—2:14–41
Peter to Jewish people—3:12–26
Stephen to Jewish leaders—7:1–53
Peter to Gentiles—10:23–43

Sermons by Paul
To Jews in Antioch—13:14–49
To pagans in Lystra—14:14–18
To Gentiles in Athens—17:16–31
To Christians in Ephesus—20:7

Various Ways to Outline Acts:

Geographically
    I. From Jerusalem to Antioch (chaps. 1–12)
    II. From Antioch to Rome (chaps. 13–28)
Ethnically
    I. To the Jews (chaps. 1–7)—neapolitan
    II. To the Samaritans (chap. 8)—metropolitan
    III. To the World (chaps. 9–28)—cosmopolitan
Biographically
    I. Ministry of Peter and Others (chaps. 1–12)
    II. Ministry of Paul and Others (chaps. 13–28)
Theologically
    I. The Ascension of Christ (chap. 1)
    II. The Descension of the Spirit (chap. 2)
    III. The Extension of the Gospel (chaps. 3–28)
Dispensationally
    I. Formation of Christianity (chaps. 1–7)
    II. Transition to Christianity (chaps. 8–12)
    III. Expansion of Christianity (chaps. 13–28)

The Reason for the Dispensational Nature:

    I. *Its Nature Is Transitional*
        A. Acts is a bridge from the Gospels to the Epistles
        B. Acts should be interpreted by the Epistles (not the reverse)
            1. They did not receive the Holy Spirit when they believed (Acts 19:2)
            2. Later they received the Holy Spirit when they believed (Rom. 8:9)
    II. *Its Conditions Are Temporary*
        A. Because the apostolic office was temporary (Acts 1:21–22)
        B. Because the apostolic gifts were temporary (2 Cor. 12:12)

THE OUTLINE:

    I. The Formation of the Church—Jews (chaps. 1–7)
        A. First days (chaps. 1–3)
            1. Ascension of the Christ (chap. 1)
            2. Descension of the Spirit (chap. 2)

Paul's First Missionary
Journey.

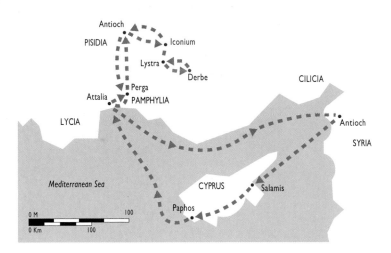

3. Expansion of the church (2:43–4:4)
   B. First deliverance of the church (chap. 4)
   C. First discipline in the church (5:1–11)
   D. First deacons in the church (6:1–6)
   E. First death (or martyr) in the church (7:54–60)
II. The Transition of the Church—Greeks (chaps. 8–12)
   A. The three conversions (8:1–11:18)
      1. Eunuch, an Ethiopian (8:26–39)—a son of Ham
      2. Saul, a Tarsian (9:1–19)—a son of Shem
      3. Cornelius, an Italian (chap. 10)—a son
         of Japheth
   B. The two persecutions (11:19–12:25)
      1. Because of Stephen (11:19–30)
      2. Because of Peter (chap. 12)
III. The Expansion of the Church—Romans (chaps. 13–28)
   A. First missionary journey—to distribute the church's
      ministry (chaps. 13–14)
   B. First church summit—to defend the church's
      catholicity (chap. 15)
   C. Second missionary journey—to deepen the
      church's charity (16:1–18:17)
   D. Third missionary journey—to disseminate the
      church's ministry (18:18–28:16)
   E. First imprisonment—to define the church's mystery
      (28:17–31)
   F. Second imprisonment—to describe the church's
      polity (in 1 Timothy, Titus, 2 Timothy).[6]

THE CONTENTS: The book of Acts can be divided into three basic sections. First, there is the formation of the church (chaps. 1–7). Next is the transition of the church (chaps. 8–12). Finally, there is the expansion of the church (chaps. 13–29). In the formation of the church, the first days record the ascension of the Christ (chap. 1), who is the head of the church, and the descension of the Spirit (chap. 2), by whom the church is born on the day of Pentecost. Then we see the expansion of the church (chap. 3). Under persecution, we observe the first deliverance of the church (chap. 4) and the first discipline in the church (chap. 5). Out of dissension, the first deacons of the church are chosen (chap. 6). This section ends with the first death (of a martyr) in the church (chap. 7).

In the second major section, the transition of the church occurs (chaps. 8–12). Three conversions signal the future ministry of the church (8:1–11:18). First, an Ethiopian (the eunuch) was converted. Of Noah's three sons, he was a son of Ham (chap. 8). Next, a Tarsian was converted (Saul), who was a son of Shem (chap. 9). Finally, an Italian (Cornelius) was converted to Christianity. He was a son of Japheth (chap. 10). Thus the universality of the Gospel was symbolized—embracing the whole race.

After the three conversions there were two persecutions (chaps. 11–12). The first was because of Stephen (chap. 11) and the second because of Peter (chap. 12). The adage of church history was proven: "The blood of the martyrs is the seed of the church," for this leads to the great expansion of the church in the final section.

While the church was established with Jews (chaps. 1–7) and made its transition to the Greeks (chaps. 8–12), it made its greatest expansion to the Romans in the last chapters of Acts (chaps. 13–28). This began with the first missionary journey of Paul (chaps. 13–14), which spread the ministry of the church into Asia. As more Gentiles were saved, this gave rise to the first apostolic counsel (chap. 15), which defended the catholicity (universality) of the gospel. Paul's second missionary journey (16:1–18:17) not only deepened the church's charity toward their poorer brethren, but disseminated the church's mission into Europe as Paul responded to the call of the man of Macedonia. This led to the third missionary journey (18:18–28:16), which further disseminated the church's ministry all the way to Rome. In an unlikely missionary condition of Roman imprisonment, Paul defined the church's mystery of how Jew and Gentile could be brought together in one body, unforeseen in the Old Testament (see Ephesians 3; Colossians 1).

Apparently Paul was released for a time, and in the interim he wrote 1 Timothy and Titus. In his second imprisonment he

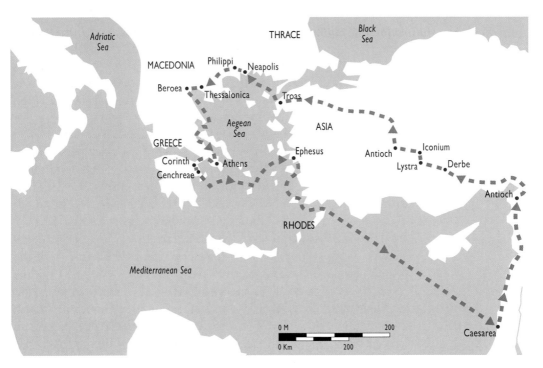

Paul's Second Missionary Journey.

wrote 2 Timothy, his last book. These three books are known as the Pastoral Epistles.

How to Respond to Critics

Acts 2:16–21 (see Joel 2:28–32)—*Did Peter make a mistake in quoting Joel?*

Problem: In Acts 2 Pentecost arrives, and the disciples are filled with the Holy Spirit. In response to criticism, Peter says that what they hear and see was "spoken by the prophet Joel." Yet in the passage that Peter quotes, there are events mentioned that did not happen at Pentecost, like the moon turning to blood. Does Peter err on this occasion?

Solution: First, Peter was simply showing that Pentecost involved a partial or initial fulfillment of Joel 2:28–32. This partial fulfillment was in regard to the indwelling Holy Spirit for believers. And this is exactly what happened on the day of Pentecost. In Joel God says, "I will pour out My spirit on all flesh. . . . I will pour out My Spirit in those days" (Joel 2:28–29). And God did pour forth his Spirit on the day of Pentecost.

Second, Peter's reference was to indicate that the last days had been inaugurated (see Heb. 1:1–2; 2:4). The wonders of the sky above and the signs on the earth beneath (Acts 1:19–21) are to take place later on in earth's history at the time of Christ's second coming. Notice that these things will happen "before the . . . great and notable day of the Lord" (v. 20), which is yet future (see Matt. 24:1–51).

Acts 2:38—*Did Peter declare that baptism was necessary for salvation?*

Problem: Peter seems to be saying that those who responded to his message had to repent and be baptized before they could receive the Holy Spirit. But this is contrary to the teaching of Paul that baptism is not part of the gospel (1 Cor. 1:17) and that we are saved by faith alone (Rom. 4:4; Eph. 2:8–9).

Solution: This is resolved when we consider the possible meaning of being baptized "for" the remission of sins in the light of its usage, the whole context, and the rest of Scripture. Consider the following: (1) The word *for* (*eis*) can mean "with a view to" or even "because of." In this case, water baptism would be *because* they had been saved, not *in order* to be saved. (2) People are saved by receiving God's word, and Peter's audience "gladly received his word" before they were baptized (Acts 2:41). (3) Verse 44 speaks of "all who believed" as constituting the early church, not all who were baptized. (4) Later those who believed Peter's message clearly received the Holy Spirit *before* they were baptized. Peter said, "Can anyone forbid water, that these should not be baptized who have received the Holy Spirit just as we have?" (10:47). (5) Paul separates baptism from the gospel, saying, "Christ did not send me to baptize, but to preach the gospel" (1 Cor. 1:17). It is the gospel that saves us (Rom. 1:16). Therefore, baptism is not part of what saves us. (6) Jesus referred to baptism as a work of righteousness (Matt. 3:15), and the Bible declares clearly that it is "not by works of righteousness which we have done, but according to His mercy He saved us" (Titus 3:5). (7) Not once in the entire Gospel of John, written explicitly so that people could believe and be saved (20:31), does it give baptism as part of the condition of salvation. It simply says over and over that people should "believe" and be saved (see 3:16, 18, 36). (8) Some have noted that their response was not determining their salvation (those present were already saved). It was only to determine whether they would receive the gift of the Holy Spirit, who would empower them to serve (Acts 1:8).

In view of all these factors, it seems best to understand Peter's statement like this: "Repent and be baptized with a view to the forgiveness of sins." That this view looked backward (to their sins being forgiven after they were saved) is made clear by the context and the rest of Scripture. Believing (or repenting) and being baptized are placed together, since baptism should follow belief. But nowhere does it say, "He who is not *baptized* will be condemned" (see Mark 16:16). Yet Jesus said emphatically: "He who does not believe is condemned already" (John 3:18). So neither Peter nor the rest of Scripture makes baptism a condition of salvation.

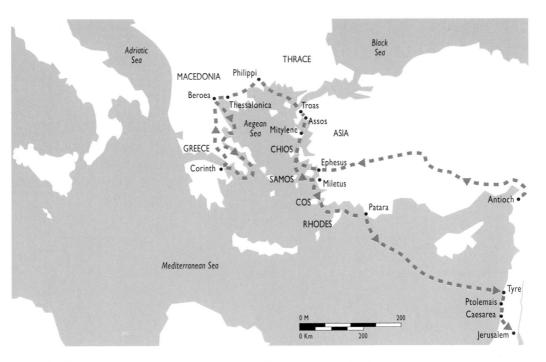

Paul's Third Missionary Journey.

Acts 4:12—*Is Christ the only way of salvation?*

Problem: Peter declares, "There is no other name under heaven given among men by which we must be saved." But isn't this a narrow exclusivism? What about the sincere pagan or Buddhist? Is God going to send them to hell?

Solution: Several observations are relevant to this question.

1. Sincerity is not a good test of truth. Many people can and have been sincerely wrong about many things (Prov. 14:12).

2. All *truth* is exclusive. The truth that "two plus three equals five" is very exclusive too. It does not allow for any other conclusion. The same is true of value statements, such as "Racism is wrong" and "People should not be cruel." These views do not tolerate any alternatives.

3. All truth *claims* are exclusive. For example, if humanism is true, then all nonhumanisms are false. If atheism is true, then all who believe in God are wrong. Every truth claim excludes its opposite. Hence, if Jesus is the only way to God, then there are no other ways. This is no more exclusive than any other truth claim. The question is whether the claim is true.

4. Jesus and the New Testament clearly and repeatedly emphasize that Jesus is the only way of salvation: Jesus said, "I am the way, the truth, and the life. No one comes to the Father except

through Me" (John 14:6). Jesus also claimed he was the door (10:9), insisting that "he who does not enter the sheepfold by the door . . . the same is a thief and a robber" (v. 1). The apostle Peter added, "Nor is there salvation in any other, for there is no other name under heaven given among men by which we must be saved" (Acts 4:12). And Paul contended: "There is one God and one Mediator between God and men, the Man Christ Jesus" (1 Tim. 2:5).

Acts 9:7 (see 22:9)—*Did Paul's companions hear the voice?*
Problem: According to Acts 9:7: "The men which journeyed with him stood speechless, hearing a voice, but seeing no man" (KJV). But Acts 22:9 declares, "Those who were with me indeed saw the light and were afraid, but they did not hear the voice of Him who spoke to me." This appears to be an outright contradiction.
Solution: The contradiction is only verbal not real. The word *hear* (*akouō*) can have different meanings in Greek, just as it does in English. It can mean "hear a voice" (as in Acts 9:7), or it can mean "understand the meaning of what was said." Thus the NIV correctly translates the two passages:

> Acts 9:7: "The men traveling with Saul stood there speechless; they heard the sound but did not see anyone."

> Acts 22:9: "My companions saw the light, but they did not understand the voice of him who was speaking to me."

This resolves the apparent contradiction. A number of considerations support these translations:

1. The same word *hear* (*akouō*) can mean different things. It can mean hear a voice without understanding the words. It can also mean hear a voice with understanding of the words. It can also mean to hear in the sense of to obey (see Matt. 17:5).

2. Though the usual meaning of *hear* (*akouō*) is simply audio without understanding (*suniēmi*), there are examples in the New Testament where *hear* (*akouō*) means "understand." For example, 1 Corinthians 14:2 (NIV) reads: "For anyone who speaks in a tongue does not speak to men but to God. Indeed, no one understands [*akouō*] him; he utters mysteries with his spirit."

3. There are even times when "hear" (*akouō*) and "understand" (*suniēmi*) are used interchangeably. In Matthew 13:13 (NIV), Jesus said, "This is why I speak to them in parables: 'Though

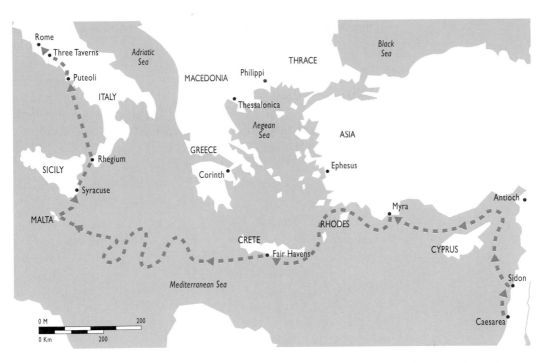

Paul's Journey to
Rome.

seeing, they do not see; though hearing [*akouō*], they do not hear [*akouō*] or understand [*suniēmi*].'"

4. The word voice (*phōnē*) is used in a different form in Acts 9:7 (*phōnēs*, the genitive) from that in 22:9 (*phōnēn*, the accusative). This may signal a different sense of the word in each context. Since the basic significance of the genitive is to stress quality, its use here may indicate that, even though they heard the voice, its quality was such that they did not understand it. This would reconcile it with Acts 22:9, which says they did not "hear" (understand) the voice.

5. Voice (*phōnē*) is sometimes translated "sound" or "noise" that is not in intelligible words (see Rev. 4:5; 6:1; 8:5). In John 12:28 it is even used of the voice of God, which some heard only as thunder. In 1 Corinthians 14:11, Paul refers to not knowing the meaning of the voice (*phōnē*) that is being heard.

6. There is another example in Scripture of the same voice of God being heard only by some audibly, but also understood by others. The voice of God spoke from heaven (John 12:28) about glorifying the Father's name, declaring, "I have both glorified it and will glorify it again." When this happened, some heard only the noise but did not understand the meaning, affirming that it had merely thundered (v. 29), but others heard the message (vv. 28, 30).

135

Acts 16:1–3—*Why did Paul have Timothy circumcised when he spoke so strongly against it?*

Problem: Paul's main point in Galatians can be summarized in his words: "If you become circumcised, Christ will profit you nothing" (Gal. 5:2). Yet Paul admits that he had Timothy circumcised "because of the Jews who were in that region" (Acts 16:3). Didn't this contradict his own teaching?

Solution: Even if Paul were wrong here in his action, it would not prove that the Bible erred in its teaching, but simply that Paul erred. Paul, like any other human being, was capable of error. Since the Bible is the Word of God, it is not capable of erring in anything it teaches.

Furthermore, Paul's action in having Timothy circumcised is not necessarily inconsistent with what he taught in Galatians, since the two cases are different. Paul was violently opposed to any who made circumcision *necessary for salvation*. But he never opposed it as *helpful for evangelism*. Indeed, Paul said elsewhere: "To the Jews I became as a Jew, that I might win Jews" (1 Cor. 9:20). However, when Judaizers insisted, "Unless you are circumcised according to the custom of Moses, you cannot be saved" (Acts 15:1), Paul took an intractable stand against circumcision.

Acts 23:5—*Did Paul lie when he said he didn't know the high priest?*

Problem: The high priest Ananias commanded that Paul be struck on the mouth. Paul rebuked him for doing so, and those who stood by condemned Paul for reviling the high priest. Paul responded by claiming, "I did not know . . . that he was the high priest" (Acts 23:5). But this is highly unlikely, since Paul himself had been a member of the Jewish Sanhedrin and worked closely with him before his conversion (9:1–3).

Solution: There are several views taken on this passage. Some suggest that Paul may have not known the high priest personally, even though he was previously a member of the Jewish Council. Others claim that Paul may have had poor vision (perhaps his "thorn in the flesh") and was not able to see him clearly. Still others believe that Paul could have been lying to get himself out of a bad situation. Apostles sinned too (see Gal. 2:11–13), and in this case, Acts is simply giving us a true record of Paul's sin. It seems more plausible, however, to take Paul's statement as sarcastic but not false. In this case, his statement, "I did not know . . . he was the high priest," could be translated something like this: "This is the high priest of God's law? I would never have known it by his unlawful command to strike me!"

The Parthenon, on the Acropolis, Athens.

STUDY QUESTIONS

1. What is the evidence, internal and external, that Luke is the author of Acts?

2. When was Acts written? List your reasons for the date chosen.

3. How does the date for Acts affect the date for and authenticity of the Gospel record?

4. To whom was Luke writing?

5. What is the theme and purpose of Acts?

6. Explain the transitional nature of the book of Acts.

7. When did the church begin? Give your reasons.

SELECTED SOURCES

Baxter, Sidlow. *Explore the Book*. Grand Rapids: Zondervan, 1987.

Blomberg, Craig. *The Historical Reliability of the Gospels*. Downers Grove, IL: InterVarsity, 1987.

Bruce, F. F. *Acts*. New International Commentary on the New Testament. Grand Rapids: Eerdmans, 1968.

Carson, D. A., Douglas Moo, and Leon Morris. *An Introduction to the New Testament*. Grand Rapids: Zondervan, 1992.

Fernando, Ajith. *Acts*. NIV Application Commentary. Grand Rapids: Zondervan, 1998.

Geisler, Norman L., and Thomas Howe. *When Critics Ask: A Popular Handbook on Bible Difficulties*. Grand Rapids: Baker, 1997.

Guthrie, Donald. *New Testament Introduction*. Downers Grove, IL: InterVarsity, 1990.

Harrison, Everett F. *An Introduction to the New Testament*. Grand Rapids: Eerdmans, 1971.

Hemer, Colin. *The Book of Acts in the Setting of Hellenic History*. Winona Lake, MN: Eisenbrauns, 1990.

Longenecker, Richard N. *Acts*. Expositor's Bible Commentary. Grand Rapids: Zondervan, 1996.

MacArthur, John. *Acts*. MacArthur New Testament Commentary. 2 vols. Chicago: Moody, 1994, 1996.

Marshall, I. Howard. *Acts*. Tyndale New Testament Commentary. Grand Rapids: Eerdmans, 1980.

Mounce, Robert. *Luke–Acts*. Grand Rapids: Zondervan, 2007.

Radmacher, Earl, Ronald Allen, and H. Wayne House, eds. *Nelson's New Illustrated Bible Commentary*. Nashville: Thomas Nelson, 1999.

Ramsay, Sir William. *Luke the Physician and Other Stories*. Grand Rapids: Baker, 1979.

———. *St. Paul the Traveller and the Roman Citizen*. New York: G. P. Putnam's Sons, 1896.

Ryrie, Charles. *Acts of the Apostles*. Everyman's Bible Commentary Series. Chicago: Moody, 1961.

Walvoord, John F., and Roy B. Zuck, eds. *The Bible Knowledge Commentary*. 2 vols. Wheaton: Victor, 1983.

9
Introduction to the Epistles

The Epistles are the most doctrinally definitive section of the Bible. In the Old Testament we have the *anticipation* of Christ, and in the New Testament the *realization* of Christ. The New is in the Old *concealed*, but the Old is in the New *revealed*. And in the Gospels we have the historic *manifestation* of Christ; Acts provides the worldwide *propagation* of the gospel of Christ; but the Epistles give us the *interpretation* and *application* of the gospel of Christ. And, of course, in Revelation we see the *consummation* in Christ.

While there is both exposition and exhortation in the Pauline and General Epistles, nonetheless, in Paul's epistles there is stress on the former, and in the General Epistles the emphasis is on the latter. The Pauline Epistles (Romans–Philemon) give the most important and doctrinally definitive *exposition* found anywhere in the Bible of what we have in Christ. The General Epistles (Hebrews–Jude) provide *exhortation* of what we should do for Christ.

A Comparison of the Gospels and Epistles

Gospels	Epistles
deeds	doctrine
information	interpretation
evangelization	edification
pattern of the church	policy for the church

The Nature of an Epistle

What is an epistle? In the New Testament, it is a letter written by an apostle or associate of an apostle, and it has a number of characteristics, including the following: missiological character, literary character, canonical character, doctrinal or practical character, and geographical character.

Missiological Character

The New Testament Epistles were missionary letters. They were written to encourage church growth. Since the church was built "on the foundation of the apostles" (Eph. 2:20) and was established in the doctrine of the apostles (Acts 2:42), they were written by apostles and their associates to encourage the apostolic church to continue in the faith "once for all delivered to the saints" (Jude 3). As such, the letters were designed for publication. Though some were addressed to individuals, they were intended for a wider reading and circulation in the church in general (James 1:1; 1 Peter 1:1; see also Col. 4:16; Rev. 1:4).

Literary Character

As a piece of literature the New Testament Epistles had their own genre. They were a letter with an author, which in the New Testament was an apostle or an associate (Jude, James). Often the author used a secretary (1 Peter 5:12; Rom. 16:22). A messenger carried the letter to its destination (see, for example, Rom. 16:1–2). A recipient—individual, local church, or group of churches—received it. Usually there was a salutation and greeting attached.

Canonical Character

The Epistles are unique in the Bible. There are none in the Old Testament, but there are twenty-one in the New Testament. Not counting Revelation (which is categorized as prophecy[1]), there are thirteen epistles of Paul (or fourteen, if he wrote Hebrews) and seven General Epistles. All the Epistles share the same canonical characteristic: they were inspired of God and intended by God for the church of God as a whole (see 2 Tim. 3:16–17). This is evident not only from their divine character but from the fact that they were read (1 Thess. 5:27), circulated (Col. 4:16), and collected into a canon from the earliest time. Peter had a collection of Paul's letters, which he placed alongside the Old Testament "Scriptures" (2 Peter 3:15–16). Paul considered all "Scripture" as inspired of God (2 Tim. 3:16). And from the earliest times, the disciples of the apostles and their disciples, known as Fathers of the church (see appendix 1), cited and collected these Epistles into a canon of sacred Scripture, which we know as the New Testament.

Doctrinal/Practical Character

The New Testament Epistles usually addressed both doctrine and deed, belief and behavior. Depending on the condition of the audience, one is stressed more than the other. Usually in Paul's writings, he will state the truth and then apply it to life. His application is based in his exposition. At other times, as in the General Epistles, doctrine and deed are intertwined. Nonetheless, in the Epistles in general, it is clear that the aim is to establish believers in Christian teaching and living, changing both thought and life in the direction of Christ, the founder and head of the church.

Geographical Character

The geographical distribution of the Epistles follows the missionary activity of the early church. First, the gospel began in Judea and Samaria (Acts 1–8) (Fig. 9.1), and then it spread throughout the rest of the world (Acts 9–28) (Fig. 9.2). The Epistles followed in the wake of the apostles in their fulfillment of the Great Commission of Christ to make disciples of all nations (Matt. 28:18–20). The following maps show the geographical distribution of the Epistles.

The Theme of Paul's Epistles

The key to understanding the theme of Paul's epistles is the phrase "in Christ." As a general rule, the word or phrase connected with the first usage of the phrase "in Christ" is the theme of that Epistle.[2] Following this rule, the themes of Paul's epistles in their biblical order are as follows:

> Romans (3:24)—*Redemption* in Christ
>
> 1 Corinthians (1:2)—*Sanctification* in Christ
>
> 2 Corinthians (2:14)—*Jubilation* in Christ
>
> Galatians (2:4)—*Emancipation* in Christ
>
> Ephesians (1:3)—*Exaltation* in Christ
>
> Philippians (1:26)—*Exultation* in Christ
>
> Colossians (1:28)—*Completion* in Christ
>
> 1 Thessalonians (1:3)—*Expectation* in Christ
>
> 2 Thessalonians (1:12)—*Glorification* in Christ
>
> 1 Timothy (1:14)—*Faithfulness* in Christ
>
> 2 Timothy (1:13)—*Steadfastness* in Christ
>
> Titus (1:9)—*Soundness* in Christ
>
> Philemon (6)—*Benefaction* in Christ

The Classification of Paul's Epistles

Doctrinally, Paul's epistles fall into four broad categories. They begin with his stress on eschatology (last things), enter into the realm of soteriology (salvation), proceed to explain ecclesiology (the church), and end with a pastoral emphasis on the organization and order within the church.

Eschatological—1 and 2 Thessalonians (AD 50–51, written during Paul's second missionary journey)

Soteriological—Galatians,[3] 1 and 2 Corinthians, and Romans (AD 55–57, written during Paul's third missionary journey)

Ecclesiological—Ephesians, Colossians, Philemon, and Philippians (AD 60–62, written during Paul's first imprisonment)

Pastoral—1 Timothy, Titus (during his release), 2 Timothy (during second imprisonment, AD 64–67)

The Order and Dates of Paul's Epistles

With the exception of Galatians, the general order, date, and place of Paul's epistles are as follows:

Decade	Book	Place	Date
AD 40s	Galatians	Antioch	48 (or 55)
AD 50s	1 Thessalonians	Corinth	50–51
	2 Thessalonians	Corinth	50–51
	1 Corinthians	Ephesus	55–56
	Galatians	Ephesus	55 (or 48)
	2 Corinthians	Macedonia	55–56
	Romans	Corinth	57
AD 60s	Ephesians	Rome	60
	Colossians	Rome	60
	Philemon	Rome	60
	Philippians	Rome	61–62
	1 Timothy	Macedonia?	64–66
	Titus	Macedonia?	64–66
	2 Timothy	Macedonia?	67

With this general overview in mind, we will now take a closer look at each of Paul's epistles. This survey will go with the biblical order and begin with the greatest of Paul's epistles, the book of Romans.

STUDY QUESTIONS

1. How do the Epistles relate to the other sections of the New Testament?

2. Describe the character of the Epistles.

3. What is the key phrase in Paul's epistles for understanding the message of each one?

4. What are the four classifications into which Paul's epistles fall in their chronological order? Which Epistles fit in each category?

5. Why do you suppose Paul's early epistles of 1 and 2 Thessalonians stressed Christ's second coming?

6. What was Paul's last epistle, and why did he emphasize what he did in it?

SELECTED SOURCES

Baxter, Sidlow. *Explore the Book*. Grand Rapids: Zondervan, 1987.

Carson, D. A., Douglas Moo, and Leon Morris. *An Introduction to the New Testament*. Grand Rapids: Zondervan, 1992.

Geisler, Norman L., and Thomas Howe. *When Critics Ask: A Popular Handbook on Bible Difficulties*. Grand Rapids: Baker, 1997.

Guthrie, Donald. *New Testament Introduction*. Downers Grove, IL: InterVarsity, 1990.

Harrison, Everett F. *An Introduction to the New Testament*. Grand Rapids: Eerdmans, 1971.

Linnemann, Eta. *Historical Criticism of the Bible*. Translated by Robert Yarborough. Grand Rapids: Kregel, 2001.

Longenecker, Richard. *Paul: Apostle of Liberty*. New York: Harper & Row, 1964.

Radmacher, Earl, Ronald Allen, and H. Wayne House, eds. *Nelson's New Illustrated Bible Commentary*. Nashville: Thomas Nelson, 1999.

Ramsay, Sir William. *St. Paul the Traveller and the Roman Citizen*. New York: G. P. Putnam's Sons, 1896.

Walvoord, John F., and Roy B. Zuck, eds. *The Bible Knowledge Commentary*. 2 vols. Wheaton: Victor, 1983.

10
Romans

The book of Romans has been called the greatest doctrinal treatise in the New Testament.[1] It certainly is the best, most extensive, and most comprehensive exposition of the gospel anywhere in Scripture. As such, it is of eminent importance that every Christian understand the message of the book of Romans. This can best be done in the context of the basic questions asked of all biblical books.

Who Wrote It? The author is the apostle Paul (Rom. 1:1). From here and elsewhere in the New Testament we can put together a portrait of Paul. First of all, he identifies his ancestry in the tribe of Benjamin (Rom. 11:1; Phil. 3:5). He was also a Pharisee (Phil. 3:5; Acts 23:6), which was the orthodox party of Judaism that believed, among other things, in angels and the physical resurrection of the dead. Further, Paul, then called Saul, was trained by the great Jewish Rabbi Gamaliel (Acts 22:3; see 5:34).

Paul's native city was Tarsus (9:11) of Cilicia (22:3) in Asia Minor. He was a tentmaker by vocation (18:3) and a Roman citizen by birth (22:27–28). He was an ardent opponent of Christianity (9:1), having held the clothes of those who stoned Stephen, the first Christian martyr (7:58). Not too long after this, he was converted by a direct appearance of Christ to him on the road to Damascus (9:3–9). Being blinded by the experience, he was commanded to go to the house of Ananias, who baptized Paul (22:12–16).

After spending time in Arabia and making a private visit to Jerusalem to talk to Peter and other pillars of the church (Gal. 2:1–10), he was eventually commissioned by the church at Antioch to engage in missionary journeys (Acts 13). During these journeys and incarcerations he authored thirteen (or fourteen, if Hebrews is included) of the twenty-seven New Testament books. The Pauline authorship of this book is seldom questioned, even by critics. There is good internal and external evidence for this.

Internal Evidence

The internal evidence that Paul wrote Romans is as follows: (1) The author claims to be "Paul . . . an apostle" (1:1). (2) As in Philippians 3:5, the author of Romans claims to be of the tribe of Benjamin (Rom. 11:1). (3) He greets two of his companions, Priscilla and Aquila (16:3). (4) He speaks of his journey to deliver a love gift to the poor saints at Jerusalem (15:25–27) and of his intention to visit Rome (1:10–13, 15; 15:22–23), both of which are known to be activities of Paul (Acts 24:17; 28:11–31). (5) In addition, there were numerous people to whom he sent greetings (16:3–23). (6) The style and unity of the book are clearly that of Paul. In addition, the anti-Judaizer theme (see Galatians) is strictly Pauline. (7) Paul confirmed his authorship by the fact that he personally signed all his epistles (2 Thess. 3:17), so the earliest Christians would have recognized his handwriting (see Gal. 6:11).

The External Evidence

The evidence of Paul's authorship outside the book of Romans is as strong as the evidence inside it. (1) The oldest manuscripts of the book bear Paul's name. (2) The early Fathers of the church attribute it to Paul. (3) Citations from Romans are found in the writings of the early Church Fathers, including Clement of Rome, Ignatius, Polycarp, the Didache, Irenaeus, Justin Martyr, Clement of Alexandria, Tertullian, Origen, Cyril of Jerusalem, Eusebius, Jerome, and Augustine (4) In addition to this, even the truncated and heretical canon of Marcion the Gnostic contained Romans. (5) Add to this the nearly unanimous and continuous testimony of the Medieval, Reformation, and even modern critical scholars, and you get some idea of the overwhelming testimony in favor of Paul's authorship.

When Was It Written?

Romans was written about AD 55 to 56 (during the time of Acts 20:1–3) on Paul's third missionary journey. This is indicated by several factors. First, Paul hadn't yet visited Rome (1:13; 15:22–24), which is where he was later martyred under Nero in AD 67 to 68 (2 Timothy 4). Also he was still collecting gifts for Jerusalem (see 1 Cor. 16:1–3) when he wrote it, shortly after he wrote 2 Corinthians in AD 55 to 56 (during the time of Acts 20:3). The doctrinal similarity between Romans and Corinthians supports that he wrote the two letters about the same time.

To Whom Was It Written?

The recipients of this epistle were Roman Christians (Rom. 1:7), living in the capital of the Roman empire, which had a population of between one and four million people. More than half of the people were slaves. Many of the slave owners were wealthy.

Just how Christianity got its roots in Rome is not known for sure. It could have been through converts from the day of Pentecost (Acts 2:10) or through friends and converts of Paul (see Romans 16). The outreach from the church at Antioch (a trade center of the East) is also a possibility. The church at Antioch was mission-minded (Acts 11:26), and Paul himself was later sent out from that church (13:1–5).

Some of the Roman Christians met at the home of Aquila and Priscilla (Rom. 16:3–5), although there may have been many groups there, since no one "church of Rome" is mentioned, (as is true in other books; see, for example, 1 Cor. 1:2), and it was a very large city. There were both Jews (Rom. 2:17) and Gentiles (1:16) among the believers there. But at this time Peter was not there, since no greeting was sent to him in chapter 16, even though numerous others of lesser status were greeted.

Nero was emperor at the time (see Rom. 13:1–7, written when Nero was emperor), although he had not yet gone on his rampage against Christians. This occurred later, between AD 64 and 68.

Where Were the Readers Located?

The recipients of the letter to the Romans lived in Rome, the capital of the Roman world.

Why Was It Written?

A study of Romans reveals many possible reasons for Paul's writing this letter. The one stated up front was to explain the gospel (1:16–17). In addition, Paul desired to help establish in the faith Christians of this strategic city (vv. 11–15). What is more, he desired to resolve the tension between Jewish and Gentile believers by explaining God's plan for each (3:1–6; chaps. 9–11, esp. 11:24–26). Then, too, he wanted to announce his plans to visit Rome and enlist their help for his mission to Spain (15:23–24, 28–29, 32). And since special supernatural gifts were given only through the apostles (2 Cor. 12:12; Acts 8:18), he desired to impart spiritual gifts to them (Rom.1:11; see 2 Tim. 1:6).

What Is It About?

The content of Romans centers around the nature of redemption or salvation. The chief characteristics of the book manifest this central message.
The Theme: The central message is "*redemption* that is in Christ Jesus" (Rom. 3:24). As will be seen, *redemption* is a broader word for salvation than is *justification*, which is only the initial stage of salvation (see below).

A Key Verse: Habakkuk 2:4 is the background for three books in the New Testament. Each book emphasizes a different third of this important Old Testament text:

> "The just . . ." (Rom. 1:17)—positional
> ". . . shall live . . ." (Gal. 3:11)—practical
> ". . . by faith" (Heb. 10:38)—personal

Few verses in the Bible occur more than twice and very few four times or more. This tiny verse influenced not only three New Testament books but the Protestant Reformation under Luther and Methodism through John Wesley.

Key Words and Phrases: *all* (71x), *all* (whole, quantity) (12x), *announce good news, gospel* (10x), *believe* (21x), *brethren* (19x), *certainly not, may it never be, God forbid* (10x), *counted, impute, imputed, reckon* (21x), *die, put to death, death* (45x), *faith* (40x), *flesh* (27x), *Gentiles* (28x), *God* (71x), *grace* (25x), *in Christ* (11x), *Israel, Israelite* (13x), *Jesus Christ* (39x), *judge, judgment* (22x), *justified, righteous deed, righteous* (57x), *law* (75x), *be lord of, rule, Lord* (49x), *love, brotherly love* (18x), *make alive, life* (14x), *save, salvation* (13x), *sin* (48x), and *Spirit* (35x). See appendix 3 for a more complete word study.

New Testament Words for Redemption

Greek Words	English Meanings	References
agorazō (verb)	to purchase or buy in the marketplace	I Cor. 6.20; 7:23; 2 Peter 2:1; Rev. 5:9; 14:3–4, etc.
exagorazō (verb)	to purchase from or buy from the marketplace	Gal. 3:13; 4:5; Eph. 5:16; Col. 4:5
lytron (noun)	a means of release, means of redeeming	Matt. 20:28; Mark 10:45
lytroomai (verb)	to ransom for release by paying the ransom price	Luke 24:21; Titus 2:14; I Peter 1:18
lytrōsis (noun)	the act of freeing after ransom has been paid	Luke 1:68; 2:38; Heb. 9:12
apolytrōsis (noun)	an act of setting free, deliverance, release	Luke 21:28; Rom. 3:24; 8:23; I Cor. 1:30; Eph. 1:7, 14; 4:30; Col. 1:14; Heb. 9:15; 11:35

The Value of Romans: There are many values to the book of Romans. Intellectually, it has a very logical structure and has been used by both lawyers and logicians to teach logical thinking. Historically, it casts light on early Christianity and its doctrinal development. Theologically, it is the most comprehensive teaching on the gospel in the entire New Testament (chaps. 1–8). Spiritually, the scope and secret of the Christian life are revealed (chaps. 6–7). Biographically, Paul greets more than thirty people (chap. 16). Dispensationally, it explains the relation of Israel to the church (chaps. 9–11).

Old Testament Citations: Romans contains some seventy-four references to the Old Testament (mostly from Psalms and Isaiah). "It is written" occurs nineteen times in this book, more than half of all the times Paul uses the phrase.

A Comparison with Galatians

Romans	**Galatians**
what the gospel *is*	what the gospel *is not*
irenic in tone	polemic in tone
rhetorical opponent	actual opponent
victory is won	battle in progress

THE OUTLINE:

> I. Doctrinal—Theology of Redemption (chaps. 1–8)
>   A. Condemnation (1:1–3:20)
>   1. The charge against
>   a. The crude ones—Barbarians (chap. 1)
>   b. The cultured ones—Greeks (2:1–11)
>   c. The covenant ones—Jews (2:12–3:8)
>   2. The conclusion—3:9–20
>   B. Justification (3:21–5:21)
>   1. Interpretation (root)—by grace through faith (3:21–4:25)
>   2. Application (fruit)—actually (to believers) and potentially (to world) (chap. 5)
>   C. Sanctification (6:1–8:17)
>   1. Principles for—identification with Christ (chap. 6)
>   2. Power for—emancipation by Christ (chap. 7)
>   3. Provision for—direction by the Spirit (8:1–17)

Paul's prison in Rome.

D. Glorification (8:18–39)
  1. Pledge of glorification (vv. 18–25)
  2. Purpose for glorification (vv. 26–30)
  3. Permanence of glorification (vv. 31–39)
II. **Dispensational—Philosophy of Redemption** (chaps. 9–11)
  A. Israel's past privileges (chap. 9)
  B. Israel's present plight (chap. 10)
  C. Israel's future prospect (chap. 11)
III. **Exhortation—Ethic of Redemption** (chaps. 12–16)
  A. Duty to God (chap. 12)
  B. Duty to state (chap. 13)
  C. Duty to man (chaps. 14–16)

THE CONTENTS: The first section of Romans is doctrinal (chaps. 1–8). In it Paul speaks of our condemnation (1:1–3:20), justification (3:21–5:21), sanctification (6:1–8:17), and glorification (8:18–39). The charge of condemnation includes Barbarians (chap. 1), Greeks (2:1–11), and Jews (2:12–3:8). Paul's conclusion: the world is guilty before God (3:9–20). Once the judgment of condemnation is pronounced on all human beings (1:1–3:20), he turns to a discussion of their salvation (3:21–8:39). Salvation is divided into three stages: salvation from the past penalty of sin, called *justification* (3:21–5:21); salvation from the present power of sin, labeled *sanctification* (6:1–8:17), and salvation from the future presence of sin, referred to as *glorification* (8:31–39).

Justification is the act of declaring a sinner righteous in the eyes of God. The root of justification is that it comes from God but through faith (chaps. 3:21–4:25). The person "who does not work but believes on Him who justifies the ungodly, his faith is accounted for righteousness" (4:5). The fruit of justification is found in its potential application to all persons and its actual application to those who believe (chap. 5).

While justification *declares* a person righteous and free from the penalty of sin, sanctification actually *makes* a person righteous and delivers him or her from the power of sin (chaps. 6:1–8:17). The former is a once-for-all act and the latter is a continual process. The principles for sanctification are *knowing* we are dead with Christ, *reckoning* it to be so, and *yielding* to Christ (chap. 6). The power for sanctification (chap. 7) comes through our emancipation by Christ, and the provision for continual sanctification comes by the Holy Spirit who indwells us (8:1–17).

Glorification, the final state of salvation, is salvation from the very presence of sin (8:18–39). The pledge of glorification is present with us by the Holy Spirit (vv. 18–25). The purpose for glorification is that we be conformed to Christ's image (vv. 26–30), and the permanence of glorification is guaranteed because of our inseparability from Christ (vv. 31–39).

Once salvation in all of its stages has been discussed, Paul turns to discuss the matter of salvation for Jews, God's chosen people. He sets forth Israel's past privileges (chap. 9), their present plight of unbelief (chap. 10), and their future prospect of restoration (chap. 11). He explains that Israel as a nation was set aside for their unbelief, but in God's providence he was able to bring in "the fullness of the Gentiles" (v. 25) before Israel would be regrafted into their place of promised blessing.

The final section of Romans is not one of exposition of salvation but of exhortation to live out our salvation (chaps. 12–16). It begins, "I beseech you therefore, brethren, by the mercies of God, that you present your bodies a living sacrifice. . . ." First, Paul speaks of our duty to God (chap. 12), then our duty to the state (chap. 13), and finally our duty to others (chaps. 14–16).

How to Respond to Critics

Romans 2:14–15 (see Ephesians 2:3)—*How can those who are by nature sinners keep God's laws of nature?*
Problem: Ephesians 2:3 asserts that all humans are "by nature children of wrath," but Paul speaks in Romans of unbelieving Gentiles who "by nature do the things contained in the law." These two things seem mutually opposed.
Solution: Ephesians is speaking of the *cause* of sinful actions,

whereas Romans refers to the *rule* for our actions. The former relates to our *propensity* to sin and the latter to the *norm* for what is sin. There is a difference between what humans are *inclined* to do by nature and what they *ought* to do according to the natural law "written in their hearts" (Rom. 2:15).

Romans 5:12–21—*Does Paul teach in this passage that everyone will be saved?*

Problem: The Bible says that not everyone will go to heaven; there are some who will go to hell (Rev. 19:19–20). Indeed, Paul elsewhere says the wicked will not inherit God's kingdom (1 Cor. 6:9; Eph. 5:5). But these verses in Romans say that all will be made righteous by Christ. If all are made righteous, how can some people go to hell?

Solution: The following comparison will help to identify the parallels in this passage.

Adam	**Christ**
act of sin (vv. 12, 14, 16)	act of grace (v. 15)
offense (vv. 15–18)	act of righteousness (v. 18)
disobedience (v. 19)	obedience (v. 19)
Physical Results	
death on all (vv. 12, 14–15, 17)	life for all (vv. 17–18, 21)
Moral Results	
sin enters for all (v. 12)	grace enters for all (v. 15)
sin reigns on all (v. 21)	grace reigns for all (v. 21)
Legal Results	
all made sinners (v. 19)	all made righteous (v. 19)
judgment for all (v. 18)	gift for all (v. 18)
condemnation for all (vv. 16, 18)	justification for all (vv. 16, 18)

As this chart shows, Paul's use of "righteous" and "justification" cannot mean that all will actually be saved but only that they are potentially saved. This is because: (1) The Bible says not all will be saved (Matt. 25:41; Luke 16:19–31; Rev. 20:11–15). (2) Salvation is a "gift" (Rom. 5:15–16, 18), and gifts must be received (see John 1:12). (3) The phrase "those who receive" (Rom. 5:17) implies that it will be received. (4) The phrase "not like" (vv. 15–16) shows that the parallel is not perfect. (5) The same parallel is found with reconciliation, which is potential for all (2 Cor. 5:19) but only actual for some (v. 20).

Romans 5:14—*Is it fair to judge all people because of Adam's sin?*

Problem: Death came to all people because of the sin of Adam

(Rom. 5:12), but Romans 5:14 says, "Nevertheless death reigned from Adam to Moses, *even over those who had not sinned according to the likeness of the transgression of Adam*." But if they did not sin like Adam, why are they held accountable?

Solution: There are two types of people who may fall into this category: infants and those who do not deliberately disobey God's dictates.

First, many Bible scholars believe that infants and small children who die before the age of moral accountability will go to heaven. This is based on the following verses: In 2 Samuel 12:23, when David's baby died, he said, "I shall go to him, but he shall not return to me." This implies that the baby was with the Lord. In Psalm 139 David speaks of even an unborn baby as written in God's book in heaven (v. 16). Isaiah distinguishes between those who are not yet old enough to "know to refuse the evil and choose the good" (7:15), which implies they are not yet morally accountable. Jesus said, "If you were blind, you would have no sin" (John 9:41). And Paul speaks of Christ's sacrifice making all righteous (Rom. 5:19), which would cover even little children who are born in sin (Ps. 51:5).

Second, we "all sinned [in Adam]" as our representative (Rom. 5:12), and as a consequence, the guilt of Adam's sin was imputed to all of us. But Christ's death cancelled this and released the human race from this judicial guilt (vv. 18–19). Even so, those who attain the age of accountability are responsible for their personal sin and therefore are justly condemned.

So those who did not sin in the likeness of Adam, nevertheless still sinned in Adam (v. 12). That is why death still reigned from the time of Adam and Moses. Romans 2:14–15 affirms that the Gentiles, even if they have not the Mosaic Law, are still a law to themselves. They have the law written in their hearts and their conscience bears witness to their actions. After Adam, humans are sinful and responsible for their actions.

Just because people do not sin in the likeness of Adam does not mean that they are not sinful. In other words, it doesn't mean that God does not hold humans accountable for their actions. Man dies because man sins (6:23). God is just in condemning sin, and he is merciful in providing salvation for those who will receive it.

Romans 5:19—*If all are made righteous by Christ, why aren't all saved?*

Problem: Scholars agree that in Paul's contrast between the "one" and the "many" here, "many" means all. For the "many" were "made sinners" by the "one" (Adam's) sin, and Paul had already concluded that "all have sinned [in Adam]" a few verses earlier

The ancient forum, Rome.

(Rom. 5:12). But if all were "made sinners" means all actually became sinners, then why doesn't all "will be made righteous" in the same verse mean that all will be saved?

Solution: There are two broad responses to this question—universalism and particularism. That is, those who claim this verse as proof that all people will eventually be saved and those who believe only some will be saved. Since the Bible clearly rejects universalism (see comments on Col. 1:20), we will focus here on the two general responses of particularists.

The Potential View. Some scholars believe Paul is simply referring to being "made righteous" by Christ's death in a *potential* sense. That is to say, by the cross all people are made *savable*, but not all people will be saved. Those who hold this position point to the fact that the parallel is not perfect, for we were "made sinners" in Adam without our personal free choice. Nevertheless, we cannot be "made righteous" in Christ without freely receiving the "gift" (Rom. 5:16–17).

The Judicial View. According to this position, all persons were "made sinners" and "made righteous" in the same sense—*judicially*. That is, both Christ and Adam were our *legal* representatives. And while in Adam all his race were *officially* made sinners before God; nonetheless, in Christ all are officially made righteous, though not actually and personally. And just as every person, when they come to the age of accountability (see comments on Rom. 5:14), must personally sin to be personally guilty, even so everyone must personally accept Christ to be personally saved. Christ removed the official and judicial guilt that was imputed to the race because of Adam's sin. This does not mean that everyone is *actually* saved, but only that they are no longer *legally* condemned.

Romans 9—*Is this chapter contrary to God's desire for all persons to be saved?*
This text has several verses that seem to say that God wills only some to be saved and that he hardens others he does not will to save. But this is contrary to God's love for all persons (John 3:16; Rom. 5:18–19; 2 Cor. 5:19; Heb. 2:9; 2 Peter 2:1; 1 John 2:2) and his desire to save all (Matt. 23:37; 1 Tim. 2:3–6; 2 Peter 3:9). How can these verses be explained?

Romans 9:8—*Is God responsible for hardening Pharaoh's heart?*
Problem: Referring to God's dealings with Pharaoh, Paul wrote, "Therefore He has mercy on whom He wills, and whom He wills He hardens" (v. 18). If it is God who hardens the hearts of unbelievers, how can he hold unbelievers responsible?
Solution: First of all, God did not harden Pharaoh's heart against Pharaoh's will (see comments on Rom. 9:17). Other than the prediction in advance that this would happen, the text says seven times that Pharaoh hardened his own heart before God hardened it (see Exod. 7:13–14, 22; 8:15, 19, 32; 9:7). Only then does it say God hardened Pharaoh's heart (v. 12). So the sense in which God hardened Pharaoh's heart was not against his will but in accordance with Pharaoh's will. The same sun that melts wax hardens clay. If Pharaoh's heart had been receptive to God's desire to soften it, his heart would not have become hard. So God was not responsible for it becoming hard; Pharaoh was.

Romans 9:13—*This verse seems to teach that God does not love everybody.*
Problem: Paul, quoting Malachi, wrote, "Jacob have I loved, but Esau have I hated." But how can God hate someone if he is love (1 John 4:16)?
Solution: This is not speaking about an individual (Esau) but a country that came from him (Edom). It is not a quote from Genesis (before Esau the individual was born) but from Malachi (1:2–3), a thousand years later after the nation Edom had done such heinous evil against God's people. Further, this is not

154

Roman emperor Nero.

speaking of the salvation of individuals within Edom or any other nation. It is speaking about God's choosing a nation for a temporal purpose, namely, to be the channel of salvation for the whole world (Gen. 12:1–3). Even so, "hate" should not be taken literally. It is a figure of speech meaning "love less." This is clear from Genesis 29:30–31 when the fact that Leah was "loved less" by Jacob was also described as "hate." Jesus used the term "hate" in the same way when he said we should "hate" our parents (Luke 14:26), meaning our love for God should be so great that it would make our love for our parents, which is less, look like hate by comparison. Hence, there is nothing in this text that says God does not love every individual in a salvific (salvation) sense and desire him or her to be saved (see 1 Tim. 2:4; 2 Peter 3:9).

Romans 9:17—*How can Pharaoh be free if God hardened his heart?*
Problem: God said to Pharaoh, "For this very purpose I raised you up, to demonstrate My power in you, and that My name might be proclaimed throughout the whole earth" (Rom. 9:17 NASB). In fulfillment of this, it says that God hardened Pharaoh's heart (Exod. 4:21; 7:3). But if God raised up Pharaoh and even hardened his heart to accomplish his divine purposes, then isn't Pharaoh exempt from responsibility for his actions?
Solution: First, God in his omniscience foreknew exactly how Pharaoh would respond, and he used it to accomplish his purposes. God ordained the means of Pharaoh's free but stubborn action, as well as the end of Israel's deliverance. In Exodus 3:19 God told

Moses, "But I am sure that the king of Egypt will not let you go, no, not even by a mighty hand." Pharaoh rejected the request of Moses and only after ten plagues did Pharaoh finally let the people go.

Second, it is important to note that Pharaoh first hardened his own heart. When Moses initially approached Pharaoh concerning the release of the Israelites (Exod. 5:1), Pharaoh responded, "Who is the LORD, that I should obey His voice to let Israel go? I do not know the LORD, nor will I let Israel go" (v. 2). The passage Paul quoted (in Rom. 9:17) is Exodus 9:16, which in context comes after the plague of the boils, the sixth plague. But Pharaoh hardened his own heart before God made this statement. Just because God raised up Pharaoh does not mean that Pharaoh is not responsible for his actions.

Third, God uses the unrighteousness of humans to show his glory. God still holds Pharaoh accountable, but as Pharaoh hardened his heart, God used him to display God's greatness and glory. God sometimes uses evil acts to bring about good results. The story of Joseph is a good example of this point. Joseph is sold by his brothers and later becomes a ruler in Egypt. In Egypt Joseph saves many lives during a famine. When he later reveals himself to his brothers and forgives them, he says, "But as for you, you meant evil against me; but God meant it for good, in order to bring it about as it is this day, to save many people alive" (Gen. 50:20). God can use bad actions to reveal his glory.

Romans 9:22—*Does this verse teach that God creates some people specifically for destruction?*
Problem: Paul wrote, "What if God, wanting to show His wrath and to make His power known, endured with much longsuffering the vessels of wrath prepared for destruction?" (Rom. 9:22). Paul seems to indicate here that God has predestined certain persons as vessels of wrath. But if they are predestined as such, then they can never be saved. Hence, how can God be loving if he predestines people to be destroyed?
Solution: Again, they were not vessels of wrath because God had predestined them to be such against their will. Indeed, God does not desire that anyone should be lost (1 Tim. 2:4). The very phrase "endured with much longsuffering" reveals that God was waiting for them to repent. As Peter said, God is "longsuffering toward us, not willing that any should perish but that all should come to repentance" (2 Peter 3:9). So the unrepentant make themselves vessels of wrath. As Paul said earlier in this very book to unbelievers, it is by "your impenitent heart you are treasuring up for yourself wrath in the day of wrath" (Rom. 2:5).

Romans 11:26–27—*How can there be a future for the nation of Israel since they rejected the Messiah?*

Problem: The nation of Israel clearly rejected Christ as their Messiah (Romans 9–10; John 1:10–11), and the Bible says that the promises of Abraham go to his spiritual seed, not his descendants according to the flesh (Romans 4; Galatians 3). Why then does Romans 11 speak of a future for the nation of Israel?

Solution: Abraham has both a spiritual seed (descendants) and literal descendants. Anyone who believes in Christ can become a *spiritual* heir of the promise for justification (Romans 4; see Genesis 15), because Christ came of the seed of Abraham (Gal. 3:16).

However, there are also promises to Abraham's *literal* descendants, the Jews, that have never yet been completely fulfilled. For example, God promised unconditionally that Abraham's literal descendants would inherit the land of Israel forever (Gen. 12:1–3; 13:15–17; 15:7–21; 17:8). Only one short time in Israel's history did they inherit this land (Josh. 11:23), but God gave it to them by an unconditional oath (see Gen. 15:7–21) "forever" (13:15), as an "everlasting possession" (17:8). Since God cannot break an unconditional promise (Heb. 6:17–18; 2 Tim. 2:13), this promise is yet to be fulfilled for the nation of Israel.

In Romans 9–11 Paul is speaking of the literal descendants of Abraham, the children of Israel. He calls them "my kinsmen according to the flesh, who are Israelites" (9:3–4), and "Israel" (10:1). This same national group (Israel) that was temporarily cut off will be grafted in again into the tree, and "all Israel will be saved" (11:26). Jesus spoke of this time in Acts 1 when his disciples asked him: "Will You at this time restore the kingdom to Israel?" (v. 6). His answer was not a stern rebuke for misunderstanding the Scriptures, but an assurance that only the Father knows the "times or seasons" in which this will occur (v. 7). Earlier Jesus spoke of "the regeneration, when the Son of Man sits on the throne of His glory, [and] you who have followed Me will also sit on twelve thrones, judging the twelve tribes of Israel" (Matt. 19:28). Indeed, in the final book of the Bible, the apostle John spoke of God's redeeming out of the tribulation "one hundred and forty-four thousand of all the tribes of the children of Israel" (Rev. 7:4). So there is every reason to believe that God will honor his unconditional covenant to Israel to give them the land of Israel forever.

STUDY QUESTIONS

1. What is the internal and external evidence that Paul wrote Romans?

2. List the reasons Paul wrote Romans at the time assigned to it.

3. To whom was Romans written?

4. Why was it not addressed to the church in that city, as were other Epistles?

5. Since Paul did not start it, how did the church get started in Rome?

6. What were Paul's purposes for writing Romans?

7. What does "redemption" or "salvation" in the broad sense mean in Romans?

8. What arguments does Paul offer that salvation is not by works?

9. According to Romans 11, does God have a future for the nation of Israel?

SELECTED SOURCES

Baxter, Sidlow. *Explore the Book.* Grand Rapids: Zondervan, 1987.

Bruce, F. F. *Paul, Apostle of the Heart Set Free.* Grand Rapids: Eerdmans, 2000.

————. *Romans.* Tyndale New Testament Commentary. Grand Rapids: Eerdmans, 1989.

Carson, D. A., Douglas Moo, and Leon Morris. *An Introduction to the New Testament.* Grand Rapids: Zondervan, 1992.

Conybeare, William, and J. S. Howson. *The Life and Epistles of St. Paul.* Grand Rapids: Eerdmans, 1953.

Cranfield, C. E. B. *Romans:* Critical and Exegetical Commentary. 2 vols. New York: T & T Clark, 1975, 1979.

Dunn, James D. G. *Romans.* Word Biblical Commentary. Nashville: Thomas Nelson, 1988.

Forster, Roger, and Paul Marston. *God's Strategy in Human History.* Wheaton: Tyndale, 1974.

Geisler, Norman. *Chosen But Free.* Minneapolis: Bethany House, 1999.

Geisler, Norman L., and Thomas Howe. *When Critics Ask: A Popular Handbook on Bible Difficulties.* Grand Rapids: Baker, 1997.

Guthrie, Donald. *New Testament Introduction.* Downers Grove, IL: InterVarsity, 1990.

Harrison, Everett F. *An Introduction to the New Testament.* Grand Rapids: Eerdmans, 1971.

————. *Romans. Expositor's Bible Commentary.* Grand Rapids: Zondervan, 1995.

Hawthorne, Gerald F., Ralph P. Martin, and Daniel G. Reid, eds. *Dictionary of Paul and His Letters.* Downers Grove, IL: InterVarsity, 1993.

Johnson, Alan. *Romans.* Everyman's Bible Commentary Series. Chicago: Moody, 2000.

Linnemann, Eta. *Historical Criticism of the Bible.* Translated by Robert Yarborough. Grand Rapids: Kregel, 2001.

Longenecker, Richard. *Paul: Apostle of Liberty.* New York: Harper & Row, 1964.

MacArthur, John. *Romans.* MacArthur New Testament Commentary. 2 vols. Chicago: Moody, 1991, 1994.

Moo, Douglas J. *The Epistle to the Romans.* New International Commentary on the New Testament. Grand Rapids: Eerdmans, 1996.

———. *Romans.* NIV Application Commentary. Grand Rapids: Zondervan, 2000.

Murray, John. *Epistle to the Romans.* New International Commentary on the New Testament. Grand Rapids: Eerdmans, 1960.

Radmacher, Earl, Ronald Allen, and H. Wayne House, eds. *Nelson's New Illustrated Bible Commentary.* Nashville: Thomas Nelson, 1999.

Ramsay, Sir William. *St. Paul the Traveller and the Roman Citizen.* New York: G. P. Putnam's Sons, 1896.

Walvoord, John F., and Roy B. Zuck, eds. *The Bible Knowledge Commentary.* 2 vols. Wheaton: Victor, 1983.

11
1 Corinthians

First Corinthians is one of the least disputed books of Paul in the New Testament. Along with 2 Corinthians, Romans, and Galatians, it has Paul's fingerprints all over it. It is also one of the early books in the New Testament and provides an insightful portrait of a cosmopolitan, worldly, and struggling New Testament church.

Who Wrote It? The evidence that the apostle Paul wrote this book is beyond all reasonable doubt. This is clear from the book itself as well as from early and later sources outside 1 Corinthians that cite it.

Internal Evidence
The book begins with the claim that "Paul, called to be an apostle," wrote it (1:1). This claim is repeated throughout the book (1:12–14; 3:4–5, 22; 16:21). Further, the character of the book is Pauline. Not only is it in his writing style, but it manifests his doctrinal interest as well as his pastoral care for the church. Even the critics of the book are virtually unanimous in supporting the Pauline authorship. Typically, he signs off with a greeting in his "own hand" (16:21; see 2 Thess. 3:17).

External Evidence
The evidence from outside the book supports strongly the internal evidence. First of all, Paul's name is found on it in the earliest known manuscripts of the book. Further, the earliest Fathers, beginning in apostolic times (with Clement of Rome, ca. AD 95), attributed it to Paul. From the first century on, there is a continuous and nearly unanimous consent of Fathers and later scholars who cite it. This includes Ignatius, Polycarp, *Shepherd*

of *Hermas*, the Didache, Irenaeus, Justin Martyr, Clement of Alexandria, Tertullian, Origen, Cyril of Jerusalem, Eusebius, Jerome, and Augustine.

When Was It Written?

The book was written between AD 55 and 56, while Paul was at Ephesus (Acts 19:1). The evidence in support of this date comes from several internal and external facts combined. First of all, we know from secular sources that the proconsul Gallio began his term in AD 51 (18:12). Further, according to Acts 18, Paul ministered in Corinth there in AD 50 to 51. And Paul was in Ephesus for more than two years (19:10). It was during this time that he wrote 1 Corinthians. This would place it about AD 55 to 56.

To Whom Was It Written?

The book of 1 Corinthians was written to the pagan converts of Corinth called "the church of God, which is at Corinth, to those who are sanctified in Christ Jesus, called to be saints" (1:2).

There were some one-half million people in Corinth. It was known as the "vanity fair" of the Roman Empire. It was considered a city of vulgar materialism and immorality and a place of idolatry. The goddess Aphrodite was a favorite. Corinth was also a place of pleasure and sensuality, which had even penetrated the church and meant that one of its members should be excommunicated (5:1). The Christians were chiefly poor and pagan and not rich or Jewish.

Where Were They Located?

The recipients of the letter were located in the city of Corinth in the province of Achaia (Europe). Corinth was an important center of commerce. It was a place of athletic contests, second only to Olympia (see the athletic metaphor in 1 Cor. 9:24–27). It was also an international city with a mixed population. Although it was Greek, it boasted no great philosophers as Athens had. Indeed, Paul chided the church for the lack of many wise people in their number (see 1:20).

Why Was It Written?

There were many reasons for the writing of this Epistle. They can be divided according to corresponding chapters. (1) Paul was concerned about administering the church's affairs (chaps. 1–6). (2) He desired to answer the church's questions (chaps. 7–14). (3) Paul wanted to address the church's misgivings (chap. 15). (4) He wished to ask for the church's contribution to help the poor saints in Jerusalem (chap. 16).

What Is It About?

The Theme: Sanctification in Christ (1:2).
The Key Verse: The key verse is 2:14: "The natural man does not receive the things of the Spirit of God, for they are foolishness to him;

nor can he know them, because they are spiritually discerned."

Key Words and Phrases: *body* (44x), *brethren* (38x), *church* (22x), *cross* (2x), *crucify* (4x), *discern, examine, judge* (10x), *exercise authority, authority* (13x), *holy, saints* (13x), *know* (48x), *power* (15x), *raise, raise up, resurrection* (20x), *sanctify* (4x), *Spirit* (41x), *spiritual, spiritually* (15x), *unbelievers* (11x), *wisdom, wise* (26x), *world* (21x), *you, your* (150x). See appendix 3 for a more complete word study.

A Contrast with Romans

Romans	I Corinthians
justification	sanctification
interpretation of the cross	application of the cross
Paul the theologian	Paul the administrator
gospel is power of God	gospel is wisdom of God
basis of Christianity	behavior of Christians
sin's penalty removed for us	sin's power removed in us

Other Characteristics: First Corinthians shows the social implications of the "spiritual" gospel. It contains thirteen references to the cross (there are six direct references and seven allusions). There is a strong emphasis on the lordship of Christ (see 1:2–3, 7–10). Paul stressed that problems were solved by spiritual principles not psychological expedients (see 6:12; 10:23). It was a church full of charismatic gifts, including tongues and prophecies, the misuse of which was covered in three chapters of Paul's epistle (chaps. 12–14). The church was not free from Greek pride (see chaps. 1–2). And it was characterized by immaturity, immorality, and disunity (chaps. 2–5, 11).

Christ's Relationship to the Church: Christ is the head of the church, but in Corinth this relationship was dishonored in numerous ways: worldly wisdom despises it (chaps. 1–2), factions dishonor it (chaps. 3–4), impurity destroys it (chaps. 5–6), idols defile it (chaps. 8–9), disorder disgraces it (chaps. 12, 14), and heresy denies it (chap. 15). On the other hand, marriage depicts it (chap. 7), communion declares it (chaps. 10–11), and charity (love) demonstrates it (chap. 13).

Apologetic Value: This book is of great apologetic value for many reasons. (1) It is an early book, written only twenty-two years after the death of Christ. (2) The authorship by an apostle and eyewitness of the resurrection is virtually unquestioned, even by critics. (3) Paul refers to some five hundred witnesses of the resurrection, most of whom were still alive, challenging the readers, as it were, to check it out for themselves (15:6). (4) Among the eyewitnesses were two unbelievers before the resurrection: James, the brother of Jesus, and Paul, an ardent opponent of Christianity (15:7–8). Few events from antiquity survive in even one book with this kind of eyewitness contemporary testimony.

THE OUTLINE:

I. **Manifestations of Carnalities in the Church** (chaps. 1–11)
   A. Division in the church (chaps. 1–4)
      1. The folly of divisions (chaps. 1–2)
      2. The flesh in divisions (chap. 3)
      3. The fallacy of divisions (chap. 4)
   B. Disorder in the church (chaps. 5–6)
      1. Lawlessness (chap. 5)
      2. Lawsuits (chap. 6)
   C. Difficulties in the church (chaps. 7–11)
      1. Marriage (chap. 7)
      2. Meats (chap. 8)
      3. Ministry (chap. 9)
      4. Morality (chap. 10)
      5. Memorial feast (chap. 11)
II. **Spiritualities in the Church** (chaps. 12–16)
   A. The manifestation of gifts (chaps. 12–14)
   B. The definition of the gospel (chap. 15)
   C. The instructions about giving (chap. 16)

THE CONTENTS: The message of 1 Corinthians breaks down into two broad sections: the problem of carnality (worldliness) in the church (chaps. 1–11) and the problem of the exercise of spiritual gifts and graces (chaps. 12–16). In the first section, Paul speaks of division in the church at Corinth (chaps. 1–4). He warns them of the folly of divisions (chaps. 1–2), the manifestation of the flesh in divisions (chap. 3), and the fallacy of divisions (chap. 4). Then he turns to address disorders in the church (chaps. 5–6), which were manifest in lawlessness (chap. 5) and lawsuits (chap. 6). In addition, he addresses difficulties in the church (chaps. 7–11), such as marriage (chap. 7), meat offered to idols (chap. 8), the ministry (chap. 9), morality (chap. 10), and the problems at the memorial feast (chap. 11), known as communion or the Lord's Supper.

The second section deals with the exercise of spiritual gifts and graces (chaps. 12–16). The manifestation of the gifts of the Spirit, particularly tongues, is addressed first (chaps. 12–14), followed by a definition of the gospel (15:1–4) and the evidence for the resurrection of Christ (vv. 5–58). Paul concludes by giving instructions about the grace of giving (chap. 16).

1 Corinthians 3:11 (see also Ephesians 2:20)—*Who is the foundation of the church, Christ or the apostles?*
Problem: In this text Paul insists: "No other foundation can anyone lay than that which is laid, which is Jesus Christ." On the other hand, Paul told the Ephesians that the church is "built on the foundation of the apostles" (Eph. 2:20). Which is it?
Solution: The answer is in the very next phrase of Ephesians 2:20: "Jesus Christ Himself being the chief cornerstone" (Eph. 2:20). Christ is the foundation in a *primary sense*, and his chosen apostles are the foundation in a *secondary sense*. Christ is, as it were, the substructure, and the apostles are the foundation built on the substructure (see Matt. 16:16–18). Christ is the kingpin that holds the apostolic foundation of the church together. It was his *deeds* (death and resurrection) and their *doctrine* about him (see Acts 2:42) that formed the foundation of the Christian church.

1 Corinthians 5:9—*How can we explain the so-called "lost letter"?*
Problem: First Corinthians 5:9 refers to a former letter Paul allegedly "wrote" to the Corinthians in the past. If there were such a letter, it would be the real 1 Corinthians, and as an authoritative letter from an apostle, it would be inspired. Yet it is not in the canon of Scripture. How could an authoritative letter inspired of God and intended for his church not be included in Scripture? Would not God preserve all the letters he intended for his church?
Solution: Three solutions have been offered as a response to this problem.

First view. One view states that this is a real lost book by the apostle Paul who wrote to the Corinthians before the 1 Corinthians in the New Testament. However, God did not desire this former book to be in the canon of Scripture, since he did not preserve it by his providence. According to this view, God did not intend every such letter that an apostle wrote to a church to be preserved as Scripture. Thus being apostolic is only a *necessary* condition but not a *sufficient* condition of canonicity.

The difficulty with this is that it rejects the common view that apostolicity is the test of canonicity. Thus it leaves the possibility that there were divinely authoritative books written by apostles to churches that are not inspired of God. But it is difficult in this view to determine what it is that makes a book inspired if it is not its divine authority.

Second view. This position overcomes the difficulty of the

Part of the site of
ancient Corinth.

first view by claiming that God did preserve this first, divinely
authoritative, apostolic book, and it is what we know as chapters
10–13 of 2 Corinthians. These chapters differ in tone from chapters
1–9, which seem to indicate they were written at another time.

While this proposal solves the problem of canonicity, it creates
other problems of its own. Why is there no real manuscript
evidence that these chapters ever existed as a separate book? Also,
how did it get attached to 2 Corinthians? Why is 2 Corinthians
a unit with a beginning and end but not two beginnings and two
endings, indicating it was two books?

Third view. According to this position, 1 Corinthians 5:9 is
not speaking of a previous book. Rather, when it says "I wrote"
it is in the aorist tense, not the past tense in Greek. Indeed, it is
an "epistolary aorist," which does not refer to the past but is an
emphatic way to refer to itself. Thus it can be translated "I am
now emphatically saying to you." Such a use of the aorist tense
is not unknown elsewhere. Indeed, Paul uses another one in the
same book (see 9:15). Likewise, the statement of Paul's enemies
that his "epistles are weighty" (2 Cor. 10:10) need not mean there
were other epistles to the church at Corinth but was simply a
metaphorical way of saying his writings are weighty in substance
or content. This view seems to explain the evidence without having
the problems of the previous views.

1 Corinthians 6:9–10—*Was Paul's condemnation of homosexuality merely his private opinion?*

Problem: Paul told the Corinthians: "Neither fornicators . . . nor homosexuals . . . will inherit the kingdom of God." But in the same book, on another issue, he admitted that he was only giving his private "opinion" (1 Cor. 7:25 NASB). In fact Paul said, "I have no commandment from the Lord," (v. 25), and "I [say this], not the Lord" (v. 12). Was not this, by his own confession, merely Paul's own nonbinding opinion on this issue?

Solution: Paul's condemnation of homosexuality is divinely authoritative and not merely his private opinion. This is made plain once the evidence is fully examined.

1. Paul's clearest condemnation of homosexuality is in Romans 1:26–27, the divine authority of which is not challenged by anyone who accepts the inspiration of Scripture.

2. Paul's apostolic credentials are firmly established in Scripture. He declared in Galatians that his revelations were not something that man made up, but were "received . . . through the revelation of Jesus Christ" (Gal. 1:12).

3. Paul declared to the Corinthians that, "The things that mark an apostle—signs, wonders, and miracles—were done among you" (2 Cor. 12:12 NIV). In short, he had exercised apostolic authority in his ministry to the Corinthian Christians.

4. Even here in the book of 1 Corinthians, where Paul's authority is severely challenged by his critics, his divine authority is made evident in three ways. (a) He begins the book by claiming that he has "words taught by the Spirit" (1 Cor. 2:13 NIV). (b) He concludes the books claiming, "what I am writing to you is the Lord's command" (14:37 NIV). (c) Even in the disputed chapter 7, where Paul is alleged to be giving his own uninspired opinion, he declares "I too have the Spirit of God" (v. 40 NIV). Indeed, when he said "I, not the Lord" he does not mean his words are not from the Lord; this would contradict everything he says elsewhere. Rather, it means that Jesus did not speak directly to this matter while on earth. But Jesus promised his apostles that he would send the Holy Spirit to "guide you into all truth" (John 16:13). And Paul's teaching in 1 Corinthians was a fulfillment of that promise.

1 Corinthians 7:10–16—*Does Paul contradict what Jesus said about divorce?*

Problem: This passage from 1 Corinthians talks about a Christian who has an unbelieving mate. At one point, Paul says, "But if the unbeliever departs, let him depart; a brother or a sister is not under bondage in such cases" (v. 15). Jesus said in Matthew 5:32 and 19:8–9 that one can divorce a spouse only in the case of marital unfaithfulness. Does Paul advocate divorce or abandonment?

Solution: There is no discrepancy between what Paul says and the words of the Lord Jesus. Paul says that if one spouse is a Christian and the other isn't, and if the unbelieving spouse does not want to leave, the Christian should not insist that he or she leave (vv. 12–13). And Paul says that if the wife leaves her husband, she should remain unmarried (v. 11). This would also hold true for a husband who leaves his wife.

Also Paul does not tell the spouse to divorce or remarry if the unbelieving spouse leaves. Rather, he suggests that he or she remain unmarried (v. 11), undoubtedly in hope of reconciliation. God's ideal for marriage is one man and one woman united till death (Rom 7:1–2; 1 Cor. 7:2). Hence, as long as there is hope for reunion, both partners are obligated to work to that end. This accords completely with what Jesus said about the permanence of marriage (Matt. 5:32; 19:8–9).

1 Corinthians 9:24 (see Rom. 9:16)—*Does Paul encourage or discourage running to obtain a spiritual goal?*

Problem: In this text the apostle encourages the believer to "run in such a way that you may obtain it." However, in Romans 9:16 Paul informs us that "it is not of him who wills, nor of him who runs, but of God who shows mercy."

Solution: The first passage is speaking about rewards, which do depend on our works (see 1 Cor. 3:11–17; 2 Cor. 5:10), while the passage in Romans is speaking about salvation, which is by grace and not by works (Rom. 4:5; Eph. 2:8–9; Titus 3:5–7).

1 Corinthians 11:5—*Should women wear veils when they pray?*

Problem: Paul insisted here: "Every woman who prays or prophesies with her head uncovered dishonors her head." Does this mean that women should wear veils in church today, or is this purely cultural? And if it is cultural, then how do we know what is cultural and what is not?

Solution: Several considerations will cast light on this difficult problem. First, a distinction should be made between the *meaning* of the text and its *significance*. The meaning is *what* it says to people in that culture, and the significance is *how* it applies to our cultural situation today. There is little doubt about its meaning. It means exactly what it says. When the women of Corinth threw back their veils and prayed in church, they dishonored their head (husband,

11:3, 7, 9, 11). In that day the veil was a symbol of a woman's respect for her husband. In such a cultural context, it was imperative that a woman wear a veil in church while praying or prophesying.

Also there is a difference between *command* and *culture*. The commands of Scripture are absolute—culture is relative. For example, few believe that Jesus's command to his disciples not to have an extra pair of sandals with them while on an evangelistic tour applies today. And most Christians do not literally "greet all the brethren with a holy kiss" anymore (1 Thess. 5:26). Nor do they believe that "lifting up holy hands" in prayer is essential to public prayer (1 Tim. 2:8).

There is a *principle* behind all these commands that is absolute, but the *practice* is not. *What* Christians must do is absolute, but *how* they do it is culturally relative. For example, Christians must greet one another (the *what*), but *how* they greet each other will be relative to their respective cultures. In some cultures, as in New Testament times, it will be with a kiss, in others with a hug, and in still others with a handshake. Many Bible scholars believe that this principle is also true of the practice of wearing a veil. That is, women in all cultures at all times must show respect for their husbands (the *what*), but *how* this respect is manifest may not always be with a veil. For example, it might be with a wedding ring or some other cultural symbol.

1 Corinthians 15:5–8—*Did Jesus only appear to believers?*
Problem: Some critics have attempted to cast doubt on the validity of Christ's resurrection by insisting that he appeared only to believers but never to unbelievers. Is this so?
Solution: It is incorrect to claim that Jesus did not appear to unbelievers. This is clear for several reasons:

1. He appeared to the most hostile unbeliever of all, Saul of Tarsus (Acts 9:1–9). The Bible devotes much of several chapters to relate this story (chaps. 9; 22; 26).

2. Even Jesus's disciples were unbelievers in the resurrection when he first appeared to them. When Mary Magdalene and others reported that Jesus was resurrected, "their words seemed to them like idle tales, and they did not believe them" (Luke 24:11). Later Jesus had to chide the two disciples on the road to Emmaus about disbelief in his resurrection, "O foolish ones, and slow of heart to believe in all that the prophets have spoken!" (v. 25). Even after Jesus had appeared to the women, to Peter, to the two disciples, and to the ten apostles, still Thomas said, "Unless I see the nail

Temple of Apollo,
Corinth.

marks in his hands and put my finger where the nails were, and put my hand into his side, I will not believe it" (John 20:25 NIV). He was hardly a believer in the resurrection.

3. In addition to appearing to his unbelieving disciples, Jesus also appeared to some who were not his disciples at all. He appeared to his brother James (1 Cor. 15:7), who, with his other brothers, was not a believer before the resurrection (John 7:5). So it is simply false to claim that Jesus did not appear to unbelievers.

1 Corinthians 15:5–8—*Why did Jesus appear only to a select few?*
Problem: Some critics have suggested that the fact only a few saw Jesus after his resurrection indicates that he was essentially invisible to the human eye and only materialized to a few people on select occasions. But this is contrary to the orthodox contention that Jesus's resurrection was literal and physical.
Solution:

1. Jesus did not appear to only a few people. He appeared to more than five hundred people (1 Cor. 15:6), including many women, his own apostles, his brother James, and to Saul of Tarsus (the chief anti-Christian of the day).

2. Jesus did not simply appear on a few occasions. He appeared on at least twelve different occasions. These were spread over

a forty-day period of time (Acts 1:3) and in many different geographical locations.

3. Jesus did not allow just anyone to lay hands on him, even before his resurrection. On one occasion, an unbelieving crowd tried to take Jesus and "throw Him down over the cliff. Then passing through the midst of them, He went on his way" (Luke 4:28–30; John 8:59; 10:39).

4. Even before his resurrection, Jesus was selective about those for whom he performed miracles. He refused to perform miracles in his own home area "because of their unbelief" (Matt. 13:58). Jesus even disappointed Herod, who had hoped to see him perform a miracle (Luke 23:8). The truth is that Jesus refused to cast pearls before swine (Matt. 7:6). In submission to the Father's will (John 5:30), he was sovereign over his activity both before and after his resurrection. But in no way does this prove that he was essentially invisible and immaterial either before or after his resurrection.

1 Corinthians 15:20—*Was Jesus the first one ever to be resurrected from the dead?*

Problem: The Bible seems to claim here that Christ was the first one ever to rise from the dead, calling him "the firstfruits of those who have fallen asleep." However, there are many other resurrections recorded in the Bible before Jesus's resurrection, both in the Old Testament (see 1 Kings 17:22; 2 Kings 13:21) and in the New Testament (see John 11:43–44). How then could Jesus's resurrection be the first one?

Solution: When Jesus returned from the dead, it was the first real *resurrection*. Every other raising from the dead was merely a *resuscitation* or *revivification* of a dead body. There are some crucial differences between a true resurrection and a mere resuscitation.

A resurrection is to an immortal body, whereas a resuscitation is merely a mortal body coming back to life (see 1 Cor. 15:53). That is to say, before Christ, Lazarus and everyone else who was raised from the dead died again eventually. When Christ was raised, it was declared that he was "alive forevermore" (Rev. 1:18).

Further, resurrection bodies manifest some supernatural qualities, not inherent in mortal bodies, such as the ability to appear and disappear from sight immediately (Luke 24:31) or to get inside a closed room (John 20:19).

Finally, while a resurrection is more than a resuscitation, it was not less than one. Resuscitated corpses die again, but Jesus's resurrection body was immortal. He conquered death (1 Cor.

15:54–55; Heb. 2:14), whereas bodies that are merely resuscitated will eventually be conquered by death. However, the fact that Jesus was the first to be raised in an immortal body does not mean it was an immaterial body. It was more than a reanimation of a material corpse, but it was not less than that. It was his same body of "flesh and bones" (Luke 24:39).

1 Corinthians 15:35–38—*Is Paul teaching that the resurrection body is a different one from the one that is sown—a kind of reincarnation?*

Problem: According to verse 37, we "do not sow that body that shall be." Some take this to mean the resurrection body is a different one, a "spiritual" body (v. 44) that is not essentially material (see comments on 1 Cor. 15:44). Does this prove that we are not raised in the same physical body of flesh and bones in which we die?

Solution: There are real changes in the resurrection body, but it is not changed into a nonphysical body—one substantially different from the one we possess now. The seed that goes into the ground brings forth more seeds that are the same kind, not immaterial seeds. It is in this sense that Paul can say "you do not sow [cause to die] that body that shall be" (v. 37), since it is immortal and cannot die. The body that is raised is different in that it is immortal (1 Cor. 15:53) not in that it is immaterial. Of his resurrection body Jesus said, "It is I Myself. Handle Me and see, for a spirit does not have *flesh and bones* as you see I have" (Luke 24:39).

There are many reasons for holding that the resurrection body, though transformed and glorified, is the *numerically same body* of flesh and bones Jesus possessed before his resurrection. And since our resurrection bodies will be like his (Phil. 3:21), the same is true of the believer's resurrection body. Notice these characteristics of Jesus's resurrection body: (1) It was the same body with the crucifixion scars it had from before the resurrection (Luke 24:39; John 20:27). (2) It was the same body that left the empty tomb behind (Matt. 28:6; John 20:5–7; see John 2:18–22). (3) The physical body of Jesus did not corrupt in the tomb (Acts 2:31). (4) Jesus said the same body that is destroyed will be built up again (John 2:19–22). (5) The immortal body is "put on" over, but does not replace, the mortal body (1 Cor. 15:53). (6) The plant that springs forth from the seed is both genetically and physically connected with the seed. What is sown is what is reaped (1 Cor. 15:37–38). (7) It is the same body of "flesh and bones" (Luke 24:39) that could be touched (Matt. 28:9; John 20:27) and could eat physical food (Luke 24:41–42).

The "change" Paul referred to at the resurrection (1 Cor. 15:51) is a change *in* the body, not a change *of* the body. The changes in the resurrection are *accidental* not *substantial*. They are changes in *secondary* qualities not changes in *primary* qualities. It is changed from a corruptible physical body to an incorruptible physical body. It is not changed from a physical body into a nonphysical body. It is changed from a mortal to an immortal physical body, but it is not changed from a material to an immaterial body.

1 Corinthians 15:44—*Is the resurrection body material or immaterial?*

Problem: Paul declares that the resurrection body is a "spiritual body," but a spiritual body is an immaterial body. However, elsewhere the Bible says Jesus's resurrection body was made of "flesh and bones" (Luke 24:39).

Solution: A "spiritual" body denotes an immortal body not an immaterial body. A "spiritual" body is one dominated by the spirit not one devoid of matter. The Greek word *pneumatikos* (translated "spiritual" here) means a body directed by the spirit, as opposed to one under the dominion of the flesh. It is not ruled by flesh that perishes but by the spirit that endures (1 Cor. 15:50–58). So "spiritual body" does not mean immaterial and invisible, but immortal and imperishable. This is clear from several facts:

First, notice the parallelism mentioned by Paul:

	Pre-resurrection Body	Post-resurrection Body
I Cor. 15:40	earthly	heavenly
I Cor. 15:42	perishable	imperishable
I Cor. 15:43	weak	powerful
I Cor. 15:44	natural	spiritual (supernatural)
I Cor. 15:53	mortal	immortal

The complete context indicates that "spiritual" (*pneumatikos*) could be translated "supernatural" in contrast to "natural." This is made clear by the parallels of perishable and imperishable and corruptible and incorruptible. In fact this same Greek word (*pneumatikos*) is translated "supernatural" in 1 Corinthians 10:4 (RSV) when it speaks of the "supernatural rock which followed them [in the wilderness]."

Second, the word "spiritual" (*pneumatikos*) in 1 Corinthians refers to material objects. Paul spoke of the "spiritual Rock" that followed Israel in the wilderness from which they got "spiritual drink" (1 Cor. 10:4). But the Old Testament story reveals that it was a physical rock from which they got literal water to drink

(Exod. 17:1–7; Num. 20:2–13). The actual water they drank from that material rock was produced supernaturally. When Jesus supernaturally made bread for the five thousand (John 6:1–14), he made literal bread. However, this literal, material bread could have been called "spiritual" bread (because of its supernatural source) in the same way that the literal manna given to Israel is called "spiritual food" (1 Cor. 10:3).

Further, when Paul spoke about a spiritual man (2:15), obviously he did not mean an invisible, immaterial man with no corporeal body. He was, as a matter of fact, speaking of a flesh and blood human being whose life was lived by the supernatural power of God. He was referring to a literal person whose life was Spirit directed. A spiritual man is one who is taught by the Spirit and who receives the things that come from the Spirit of God (vv. 13–15). The resurrection body can be called a "spiritual body" in much the same way we speak of the Bible as a "spiritual book." Regardless of their spiritual source and power, both the resurrection body and the Bible are material objects.

1 Corinthians 15:50—*If flesh and blood cannot enter heaven, how can there be a physical resurrection?*
Problem: The Bible speaks of the resurrection of the physical body from the grave (John 5:28–29), which is composed of "flesh and bones" (Luke 24:39) and which leaves an empty tomb behind (Matt. 28:6). However, according to this verse, "flesh and blood cannot inherit the kingdom of God."
Solution: To conclude from this phrase that the resurrection body will not be a body of physical flesh is without biblical justification. First of all, the very next phrase omitted from the above quotation of verse 50 clearly indicates that Paul is speaking not of flesh as such, but of *corruptible* flesh. For he adds, "nor does corruption inherit incorruption." So Paul is not affirming that the resurrection body will not have flesh; he is saying that it will not have *perishable* flesh.

To convince the frightened disciples that he was not an immaterial spirit (Luke 24:37), Jesus emphatically told them: "Look at my hands and my feet. It is I myself! Touch me and see; a ghost does not have *flesh and bones*, as you see I have" (Luke 24:39 NIV). Peter declared that the resurrection body would be the same body of *flesh* that went into the tomb and never saw corruption (Acts 2:31). Paul also reaffirmed this truth in a parallel passage (13:35). And John implies that it is against Christ to deny that he remains "in the *flesh*" even after his resurrection (1 John 4:2; 2 John 7).

This conclusion cannot be avoided by claiming that Jesus's resurrection body had flesh and bones but not flesh and blood. For if it had flesh and bones, then it was a literal, material body, whether or not it had blood. "Flesh and bones" stresses the solidity of Jesus's physical post-resurrection body. They are more obvious signs of tangibility than blood, which cannot be as easily seen or touched.

The phrase "flesh and blood" in this context apparently means *mortal* flesh and blood, that is, a mere human being. This is supported by parallel uses in the New Testament. When Jesus said to Peter, "Flesh and blood has not revealed this to you" (Matt. 16:17), he could not have been referring to the mere substance of the body as such, which obviously could not reveal that he was the Son of God.

The most natural interpretation of 1 Corinthians 15:50 seems to be that *humans, as they now are, earthbound and perishable creatures,* cannot have a place in God's glorious, heavenly kingdom.

STUDY QUESTIONS

1. What is the internal and external evidence that Paul wrote 1 Corinthians?

2. List possible reasons Paul wrote 1 Corinthians at the time assigned to it.

3. Describe the people to whom Paul wrote this book.

4. What were Paul's purposes for writing 1 Corinthians?

5. Compare and contrast 1 Corinthians with Romans.

6. How is Christ related to the church in 1 Corinthians?

7. Why is 1 Corinthians of such great apologetic value?

SELECTED SOURCES

Barrett, C. K. *1 Corinthians.* Black's New Testament Commentary. 2nd ed.; Peabody, MA: Hendrickson, 1993.

Baxter, Sidlow. *Explore the Book.* Grand Rapids: Zondervan, 1987.

Blomberg, Craig. *1 Corinthians.* NIV Application Commentary. Grand Rapids: Zondervan, 1995.

Bruce, F. F. *Paul, Apostle of the Heart Set Free.* Grand Rapids: Eerdmans, 2000.

Carson, D. A., Douglas Moo, and Leon Morris. *An Introduction to the New Testament.* Grand Rapids: Zondervan, 1992.

Conybeare, William, and J. S. Howson. *The Life and Epistles of St. Paul.* Grand Rapids: Eerdmans, 1953.

Forster, Roger, and Paul Marston. *God's Strategy in Human History.* Wheaton: Tyndale, 1974.

Geisler, Norman. *Chosen But Free.* Minneapolis: Bethany House, 1999.

Geisler, Norman L., and Thomas Howe. *When Critics Ask: A Popular Handbook on Bible Difficulties*. Grand Rapids: Baker, 1997.

Guthrie, Donald. *New Testament Introduction*. Downers Grove, IL: InterVarsity, 1990.

Harrison, Everett F. *An Introduction to the New Testament*. Grand Rapids: Eerdmans, 1971.

Hawthorne, Gerald F., Ralph P. Martin, and Daniel G. Reid, eds. *Dictionary of Paul and His Letters*. Downers Grove, IL: InterVarsity, 1993.

Linnemann, Eta. *Historical Criticism of the Bible*. Translated by Robert Yarborough. Grand Rapids: Kregel, 2001.

Longenecker, Richard. *Paul: Apostle of Liberty*. New York: Harper & Row, 1964.

MacArthur, John. *First Corinthians*. MacArthur New Testament Commentary. Chicago: Moody, 1984.

Morris, Leon. *1 Corinthians*. Tyndale New Testament Commentary. Grand Rapids: Eerdmans, 1988.

Radmacher, Earl, Ronald Allen, and H. Wayne House, eds. *Nelson's New Illustrated Bible Commentary*. Nashville: Thomas Nelson, 1999.

Ramsay, Sir William. *St. Paul the Traveller and the Roman Citizen*. New York: G. P. Putnam's Sons, 1896.

Walvoord, John F., and Roy B. Zuck, eds. *The Bible Knowledge Commentary*. 2 vols. Wheaton: Victor, 1983.

12
2 Corinthians

Like 1 Corinthians, Romans, and Galatians, the evidence is very strong that 2 Corinthians was written by the apostle Paul. This is true both of internal and external evidence. We will consider the internal evidence first.

Internal Evidence
Paul claims in 1:1 to be the author when he writes, "Paul, an apostle of Jesus Christ" (1:1). Later, he says, "I, Paul" (10:1). Also the book has the typical "in Christ" key to its theme of the book (2:14). Indeed, the character of the book is Pauline from beginning to end. Finally, its connection with 1 Corinthians is clear, for the wayward member excommunicated in his first letter (1 Cor. 5:5) is restored after repenting in this book (2 Cor. 2:6–7). The style, vocabulary, and doctrinal content are also that of Paul.

External Evidence
From the earliest times the existing manuscripts have had Paul's name on them (1:1; 10:1). Further, the early Fathers, including Irenaeus and the Muratorian canon, attributed the book to Paul. It is cited by Polycarp (the disciple of the apostle John) and by the *Shepherd of Hermas*, Justin Martyr, Clement of Alexandria, Origen, Cyril of Jerusalem, Eusebius, Jerome, and Augustine. Even most critical scholars hold to Paul's authorship.

Second Corinthians was written between AD 55 and 56 (a month or so after 1 Corinthians) from Philippi.

To Whom Was It Written?

The letter was written to a church that Paul founded on his second missionary journey (Acts 18:1–17). In his letter Paul addresses two groups in the church at Corinth:

1. Majority (1–9)—"you all"—jubilant in tone (2:3 5; 3:1–2; 5:10; 7:13)
2. Minority (10–13)— "some"—sad and severe in tone (10:2, 12; 11:4; 12:21)

There were false teachers who had infiltrated the church. Precisely who they were is a subject of debate. There are three main views:

1. Hellenistic Jews claiming to be in the line of Moses
2. Gnostic or Docetic false teachers denying Christ's humanity
3. Jews from Israel claiming to be apostles of Christ (11:22)

Where Were the Readers Located?

The readers lived in Corinth and in Achaia (Europe).

Why Was It Written?

There were, no doubt, many reasons that Paul wrote 2 Corinthians: (1) to answer the false teachers who had entered the church at Corinth (11:13–15), (2) to defend his apostleship and message (12:12), (3) to reveal his trials and triumphs as an apostle of Christ (chaps. 4, 11), (4) to show the consolation provided in the service of Christ (1:3–7; 4:17), (5) to encourage their giving to the poor (chaps. 8–9). Of course, overall, it was written to encourage the Corinthians to be jubilant and triumphant in their Christian faith (2:14).

What Is It About?

The Theme: Jubilation in Christ.
The Key Verse: The key verse is 2:14: "Now thanks be to God who always leads us in triumph in Christ."
Key Words and Phrases: *afflict, affliction, suffering* (15x, 7x in chap. 1), *be weak, weakness* (12x), *boast, boasting, act boldly* (35x, 8x in chapter 10 and 8x in chap. 11), *(to) comfort, comfort* (27x, 9x in chap. 1), *death* (9x), *forgive* (5x), *glory* (19x, 11x in chap. 3), *grace* (18x), *heart* (11x), *know* (29x), *(to) love, love* (13x), *manifest* (9x), *one another, other, another* (8x), *rejoice, joy* (13x), *service* (13x), *(to) sorrow, sorrow* (18x, 8x in chap. 2), *sufficient, adequate* (5x), *veil* (4x, all in chap. 3). See appendix 3 for a more complete word study.

Contrast with 1 Corinthians

1 Corinthians	2 Corinthians
objective and practical	subjective and personal
systematic	sentimental
pagan influence	Judaistic influence
Paul's mind	Paul's heart
character of church	character of Paul

Doctrinal Value: There are many doctrines taught in this book. These include: old and new covenant (3:6–18), substitutionary atonement (5:21), reconciliation to God (5:18–20), separation from the world (6:14), life and death (5:1–10), the Trinity (13:14), the nature of an apostle (12:12; see also 1 Cor. 9:1; 15:5–7; Acts 1:21–22).
Paul's Life: There are details of Paul's life in this book not found elsewhere in his writings: he had visions (12:1–4); he suffered from a thorn in the flesh (12:7); he suffered many perils (11:23–27).

The Outline:

I. **Consolation of God** (chaps. 1–7)
   A. For the minister—explanation (chaps. 1–2)
   B. In the ministry—exposition (chaps. 3–5)
   C. To those who received ministry—exhortation (chaps. 6–7)
II. **Solicitation for God's People** (chaps. 8–9)
   A. Exhortation to giving (chap. 8)
   B. Explanation for giving (chap. 9)
III. **Vindication of God's Apostle** (chaps. 10–13)
   A. Authentication of his authority (chap. 10)
   B. Justification of his ministry (chap. 11)
   C. Confirmation of his apostleship (chap. 12)
   D. Execution of his office (chap. 13)

The Contents: The basic message of the book can be summarized as follows: In the first chapters (1–7) Paul offers the consolation of God, for the minister (chaps. 1–2), in the ministry (chaps. 3–5), and to those to whom he ministered (chaps. 6–7).

In the second section (chaps. 8–9) Paul discusses giving, making a solicitation for God's people to give (chap. 8), and giving an explanation for giving (chap. 9).

The final section provides a vindication of God's apostle (Paul) to the minority who questioned his credentials (chaps. 10–13). This defense of his apostleship includes an authentication of his authority (chap. 10), a justification of his ministry (chap. 11), and a confirmation of his apostleship by special "signs of an apostle" (chap. 12). Finally, he speaks of the execution of his office (chap. 13), concluding with a great trinitarian benediction (v. 14).

Diversity of tone in 2 Corinthians. Students of 2 Corinthians have noted that chapters 1–9 are more conciliatory in tone than chapters 10–13, which are more severe in tone. On this basis some contemporary scholars have supposed these two sections were originally two different books, one of which was the alleged former "epistle" Paul alluded to in 1 Corinthians 5:9. However, there are good reasons to believe that there was no such former letter.[1] There is really only one introduction and conclusion to 2 Corinthians 1–13, and no separate manuscripts have ever been found dividing this book in two. Finally, the differences between the two sections can be explained by the two different groups Paul is addressing in Corinth—the majority who accepted him and the minority who challenged him. Obviously, his tone and topic would differ with each audience.

How to Respond to Critics

2 Corinthians 5:21—*How could Jesus be made sin when he was sinless?*

Problem: Paul asserts here that Jesus was "made . . . to be sin," but many other Scriptures insist that Jesus was "without sin" (Heb. 4:15; see 1 Peter 3:18). But how could Jesus be without sin if he was made sin for us?

Solution: Jesus was always without sin *actually*, but he was made to be sin for us *judicially*. That is, by his death on the cross, he paid the penalty for our sins and thereby cancelled the debt of sin against us. So, while Jesus never committed a sin *personally*, he was made to be sin for us *substitutionally*. The issue can be summarized as follows:

Christ Was Not Sinful	Christ Was Made to Be Sin
in himself	for us
personally	substitutionally
actually	judicially

2 Corinthians 11:5 (see 1 Cor. 15:9)—*Was Paul the greatest or the least of apostles?*

Problem: In 2 Corinthians 11:5 Paul claims, "I am not at all inferior to the most eminent apostles." Elsewhere he would have us believe that he is "the least of the apostles" (1 Cor. 15:9). But it would seem that both could not be true.

Solution: Paul is speaking in different contexts. In the first passage he is speaking with respect to his *ability*, *training*, and *zeal*. However, unlike the other apostles, Paul had persecuted the church of Christ before his conversion and, therefore, considered himself unworthy even to be an apostle (see Acts 9:1; Gal. 1:13). So with respect to his *preconversion antagonism to Christ*, he rightly considered himself "the least of the apostles."

STUDY QUESTIONS

1. What is the internal and external evidence that Paul wrote 2 Corinthians?

2. List the reasons Paul wrote 2 Corinthians at the time assigned to it.

3. What were Paul's purposes for writing 2 Corinthians?

4. Why are the two parts of the book so diverse in tone?

5. Compare and contrast 1 and 2 Corinthians.

6. List some of the important doctrines taught in 2 Corinthians.

SELECTED SOURCES

Baxter, Sidlow. *Explore the Book*. Grand Rapids: Zondervan, 1987.

Belleville, Linda L. *2 Corinthians*. IVP New Testament Commentary. Downers Grove, IL: InterVarsity, 1996.

Bruce, F. F. *Paul, Apostle of the Heart Set Free*. Grand Rapids: Eerdmans, 2000.

Carson, D.A., Douglas Moo, and Leon Morris. *An Introduction to the New Testament*. Grand Rapids: Zondervan, 1992.

Conybeare, William, and J. S. Howson. *The Life and Epistles of St. Paul*. Grand Rapids: Eerdmans, 1953.

Geisler, Norman L., and Thomas Howe. *When Critics Ask: A Popular Handbook on Bible Difficulties*. Grand Rapids: Baker, 1997.

Guthrie, Donald. *New Testament Introduction*. Downers Grove, IL: InterVarsity, 1990.

Hafemann, Scot. *2 Corinthians*. NIV Application Commentary. Grand Rapids: Zondervan, 2000.

Harrison, Everett F. *An Introduction to the New Testament*. Grand Rapids: Eerdmans, 1971.

Hawthorne, Gerald F., Ralph P. Martin, and Daniel G. Reid, eds. *Dictionary of Paul and His Letters*. Downers Grove, IL: InterVarsity, 1993.

Hughes, Philip. *2 Corinthians*. New International Commentary on the New Testament. Grand Rapids: Eerdmans, 1992.

Linnemann, Eta. *Historical Criticism of the Bible*. Translated by Robert Yarborough. Grand Rapids: Kregel, 2001.

Longenecker, Richard. *Paul: Apostle of Liberty*. New York: Harper & Row, 1964.

MacArthur, John. *Second Corinthians*. MacArthur New Testament Commentary. Chicago: Moody, 2003.

Radmacher, Earl, Ronald Allen, and H. Wayne House, eds. *Nelson's New Illustrated Bible Commentary*. Nashville: Thomas Nelson, 1999.

Ramsay, Sir William. *St. Paul the Traveller and the Roman Citizen*. New York: G. P. Putnam's Sons, 1896.

Walvoord, John F., and Roy B. Zuck, eds. *The Bible Knowledge Commentary*. 2 vols. Wheaton: Victor, 1983.

13
Galatians

Paul, the apostle (see the information on Paul in chapter 10), wrote Galatians. Formerly, Paul had been a zealous Jewish rabbi who lived by and defended the law of Moses (see Acts 7:58; 8:1–3; Philippians 3). Once converted (Acts 9), he became an ardent defender of the grace of God and the believer's deliverance from the bondage of the Old Testament law (Acts 15; Galatians 1–2; Colossians 2).

Internal Evidence
The internal evidence for Paul's authorship of Galatians is impeccable. (1) There is the clear claim, both at the beginning (1:1) and the end (5:2) that Paul the apostle is the author. (2) The character of the book is Pauline, in both its polemical style and its theological vocabulary. (3) The content is Pauline, stressing the grace of God and deliverance from the law. (4) The connection of events discussed in Galatians with the history recorded in the book of Acts shows it is Pauline. These include Paul's visits to Jerusalem and to the apostles (see Acts 11–16 and Galatians 1–2).

External Evidence
In addition to the evidence inside the book of Galatians, there is strong evidence from the earliest times that Paul wrote it. For one thing, the earliest known manuscripts of Galatians have Paul's name on them. For another, the earliest Fathers cite it as from Paul. They include Polycarp, Irenaeus, Diognetius, Justin Martyr, Clement of Alexandria, Tertullian, Origen, Cyril of Jerusalem, Eusebius, Jerome, and Augustine. Even Marcion, the Gnostic heretic, considered it Pauline. Finally, modern critics who do not agree with its inspiration nevertheless concede that Paul the apostle wrote it.

To Whom Was It Written?

The destination of the letter was "the churches of Galatia" (1:2) and the Galatians (3:1).

The word *Galatia* comes from the Gauls, a Celtic people. The Christians there were converts of Paul (1:11; 4:13) and were later infected by Judaizers who insisted that Christians needed to be circumcised according to the law of Moses (2:4; 6:12). Thus Paul was convinced they were losing their grip on the gospel and were in danger of falling from grace as a means of living the Christian life (3:1; 4:11; 5:2). Many Galatians were convinced by the Judaizers that circumcision was necessary for salvation (5:2). Against this, Paul violently protested.

Where Were the Readers Located?

There are two views as to exactly where these Galatians lived: the political (early) view and the geographical (later) view.

The Political View

The political (early) view asserts that the recipients of the letter were in southern Galatia in cities like Derbe, Lystra, and Antioch of Pisidia. Sir William Ramsay was a strong proponent of this view. If true, this letter was written to the southern Galatians, on Paul's first missionary journey (Acts 13–14) about AD 48.

Ramsay and followers argue that: (1) There is no clear evidence Paul ever went to northern Galatia. There is no record of any such visit in Acts 14 or 16. (2) Northern Galatia is wild country, and it is assumed that Paul's enemies would not go there. Further, more Jews were located in the south, which would be a more natural place from which the Judaizers would have come. (3) Barnabas, an associate of Paul's, was well-known in the south (2:13; see Acts 13:2; 14:1). (4) Indeed, Paul lived closer to this area (in Tarsus) and would have traveled the main road from his town through it. (5) Elsewhere Paul speaks of provinces, such as Judea (2 Cor. 1:16; 1 Thess. 2:14) and Achaia (Rom. 15:26; 1 Thess. 1:7), so it would not be unusual to do the same here. (6) What is more, persons from south Galatia, not the north, went with Paul when he took the offering to Jerusalem (Acts 20:4). (7) It is more likely that Paul wrote to churches he had visited, which were in the south (like Derbe and Lystra—Acts 16:1). (8) What seems even more significant is that Galatians 2:1 makes no mention of the decision of the Jerusalem council (Acts 15), which would have been relevant to his very point in Galatians, if he were writing after the council.[1]

The Geographical View

The geographical (later) view that the recipients lived in northern Galatia was championed by Bishop Joseph Lightfoot and his followers. It claims Galatians was composed on Paul's second missionary journey (Acts 15:30–17:34) about AD 55.[2]

This position is supported by many arguments: (1) Luke uses territorial (not political) terms in describing Paul's visit to Galatia (Acts 13:14; 14:6; see Gal. 1:2). (2) Acts 16:6 says Paul preached in the "region of Galatia." (3) Luke's report of Paul in south Galatia does not mention Paul's sickness (see Acts 14:1–7 and Gal. 4:13). (4) Paul doesn't mention any stoning at Lystra (Acts 14:19) in Galatians. Thus it can be inferred that he wrote before this time. (5) Paul wouldn't call people in the south "Galatians," which to those not from the northern region, settled by the Gauls, would have been an offensive term like "barbarian." (6) In Galatians 2:1 Paul refers to visiting Jerusalem fourteen years before Acts 11 (AD 47). But this would be AD 33—too early for Paul's conversion, since Jesus died that year and Paul was not converted until well after this time (Acts 9). However, fourteen years before the later date (AD 55) would be 41, while Paul was in his silent years (AD 39–46), after his conversion when no visit to Jerusalem was made (see chronology chart in chapter 9 for the order and dates of books written by Paul). (7) The similarity of Galatians with Romans (written ca. AD 57) argues for the later date. (8) The concept of doctrinal development favors a late date when other soteriological (having to do with salvation) books were written. (9) The evidence favors Galatians 2:1 as referring to the Jerusalem council, which places Galatians after Acts 15 and supports the late date (see below). As Lightfoot noted, both references have the same geography, time period, persons, subject, character (a dispute), and result. The differences may be accounted for by Luke's interest in the official public pronouncement on Paul's message, whereas Paul (in Galatians) is interested in the private apostolic confirmation of his ministry.

When Was It Written?

There are two views on when Galatians was written: the early view is AD 48; the later view is AD 55.

The questions of when and where the book was written go together. The *geographical view* (northern Galatia) calls for a date around AD 55 and means the letter would have been written from Ephesus (during the time of Acts 19:1 or later). The *political view* (southern Galatia) calls for a date around AD 48 just before the Jerusalem council (in AD 49, referred to in Acts 15) and would have been written from Antioch.

The Problem of Galatians 2:1
Was this Jerusalem visit of Paul the one mentioned in Acts 11:30 or the one in Acts 15:1–29? Paul made three visits to Jerusalem. The first visit to Jerusalem is referred to in Galatians 1:18 and Acts

Attalia, a harbor
to which Paul and
Barnabas sailed.

9:26. The second visit was the so-called "famine visit" (Acts 11:30), when Paul delivered gifts from believers to the poor saints in Jerusalem. According to the early view for the writing of Galatians (AD 48), this would be the visit mentioned in Galatians 2:1. Many believe the third visit was for the Jerusalem council (Acts 15:2–29). This would fit the late view since the visit had the same purpose, participants, and result as mentioned in Galatians 2. Proponents of this view believe the differences can be accounted for by Paul stressing the personal private aspect and Luke the official public dimension of his visit.

Paul's First Visit to Jerusalem

Not many scholars have maintained the position that Galatians 2:1–10 refers to Paul's first visit to Jerusalem (Acts 9:26). This is because Paul says he went up to Jerusalem "again" (2:1), which implies a second or third trip—not a first. Hence, those who hold this position must hold that Acts 9:26 is really Paul's second visit to Jerusalem and not his first.

Paul's Second Visit to Jerusalem

The argument that Galatians 2:1–10 refers to Paul's second visit to Jerusalem (Acts 11:30) is a stronger argument. The main points of this view are: (1) When Paul uses the word "again" (2:1), it literally means his second visit. (2) This view alleviates the problem of the omission in Galatians of the council's decrees (Acts 15:23–29). (3) It holds that Peter would not be inconsistent after Acts 15, and thus blunts the charge of Peter's fickleness.

There are several difficulties with this view, however. (1) The apostles are not mentioned in Acts 11:30, as they are in Acts 15. (2) It is more likely that Titus was present in Acts 15 than in Acts 11. (3) It is difficult to explain why the problem of Gentile fellowship would precede Gentile circumcision, which this view requires. (4) This view requires that Paul did preaching work before his first missionary journey, about which Acts is silent.

Paul's Third Visit to Jerusalem

The view that Galatians 2:1–10 describes Paul's third visit to Jerusalem (Acts 15:1–29) is the traditional view. It is supported by the following lines of evidence: (1) Both Paul and Barnabas consult the Jerusalem church and face strong opposition. (2) As noted above, there are similarities of geography, time period, persons, subject, character (a dispute), and result.

The main arguments against this view include the following: (1) Paul's use of the term *again* generally means "second" and hence this would be a reference to Acts 11:30 (and the second visit to Jerusalem). (2) There are important differences between Galatians 2 and Acts 15: Galatians 2 describes a private visit, but Acts 15 describes a public visit; there is no mention of the council's decrees (Acts 15) in Galatians 2; and Galatians 2:6 seems to indicate that no decrees had been added to Paul's gospel, but Acts 15:23–29 gives the council's additional directives. Despite these arguments, it still seems more likely that Galatians 2:1–10 is referencing the events of Acts 15. Again, the differences may be accounted for by Luke's interest in the official public pronouncement on Paul's message, whereas Paul (in Galatians) is interested in the private apostolic confirmation of his ministry.

Why Was It Written?

Many purposes can be inferred from the content of Galatians. (1) Paul wanted to refute legalism and teach justification by faith alone (chap. 3). (2) He wished to establish Christian freedom from the law (chaps. 4–5). (3) He desired to defend his apostleship to the Gentiles (chaps. 1–2).

What Is It About? **The Theme:** In accord with Paul's custom of introducing the theme with the first use of the phrase "in Christ," the phrase "emancipation in Christ" (2:4) is the central theme of Galatians. Hence, it has been called the "Magna Charta of Christian liberty."

The Key Verse: Galatians 2:4 is the key verse: ". . . our liberty which we have in Christ Jesus. . . ."

Key Words and Phrases: *believe, faith* (26x), *Christ* (41x), *cirucumcise, circumcision* (13x), *grace* (7x), *freedom, free* (9x), *Jesus* (17x), *law* (33x), *preach good news, gospel* (13x), *promise* (9x), *spirit* (18x) and *uncircumcision* (3x). See appendix 3 for a more complete word study.

Short Introduction: The short introduction with no commendation (1:1–3) fits with Paul's sobriety and anger expressed in Galatians. Nevertheless, in spite of the unusually sharp and polemical tone, there is a fatherly concern behind it.

Comparison with Romans: Galatians is a "little Romans." However, it is more negative than Romans. In Romans Paul speaks about justification in the positional sense, whereas in Galatians he refers to justification (sanctification) in the practical sense. Galatians is more polemical, and Romans is more irenic.

Unique Ending: While Paul was in the habit of signing his own letters (see 2 Thess. 3:17), Galatians is unique in that Paul signed it in large letters (6:11). This may have been for emphasis or it may have been due to his poor vision, which some believed resulted from his blinding experience of seeing Christ (Acts 9).

Citation of Habakkuk 2:4: This short phrase from the Old Testament is quoted three times in the New Testament. Each time one third of the quote is emphasized by its context:

> "The just . . ." (Rom. 1:17)—positional
>
> ". . . shall live . . ." (Gal. 3:11)—practical
>
> ". . . by faith" (Heb. 10:38)—personal

Explaining the Chronology: If Acts 11 is Paul's second visit (which is AD 47), then fourteen years earlier for the first visit (Gal. 2:1) would be AD 33, which is too early. It is the year Jesus died and Paul was not converted until some years later (Acts 9). Of course, according to the Jewish calculation where any part of a year was counted as a whole year, this could be only twelve years plus two days, making Paul's conversion in AD 35, two years after Jesus's crucifixion. And it is possible Jesus died earlier (AD 29 or 30).[3]

The Outline:

I. Liberty Stated—Personal Vindication (chaps. 1–2)
    A. Gospel received independently of apostles (chap. 1)
    B. Gospel recognized by the apostles (2:1–9)
    C. Gospel rebuked a chief apostle (vv. 10–21)
II. Liberty Defended—Doctrinal Justification (chaps. 3–4)
    A. Threefold argument (3:1–4:7)
        1. What faith does (3:1–14)
        2. What law does (vv. 15–23)
        3. What law is (3:24–4:7)—teacher
    B. Threefold appeal (4:8–31)
        1. To pride—consider your *past* bondage
            (vv. 8–11)
        2. To affection—consider your *present* bonds
            (of love) to me (vv. 12–20)
        3. To intellect—consider your *future* bondage
            (vv. 21–31)
III. Liberty Applied—Practical Application (5–6)
    A. Greatest enemy to liberty—legalism (5:1–12)
    B. Greatest error in liberty—lawlessness (vv. 13–26)
    C. Greatest exercise of liberty—love (6:1–18)

The Contents: The message of Galatians can be summarized as follows: First, our liberty in Christ is stated (chaps. 1–2), then it is defended (chaps. 3–4), and finally, it is applied (chaps. 5–6).

After a brief introduction, Paul argues in the first section that the gospel he preached was received independently of apostles (chap. 1), but it was, nonetheless, recognized by the apostles (2:1–9). Indeed, it was used to rebuke a chief apostle, Peter (vv. 10–21).

Paul then launches into the heart of his message—the defense of the gospel (chaps. 3–4). First, he offers a threefold argument for justification by faith alone (3:1–4:7). He states what faith does (3:1–14), namely, brings justification before God. Then he affirms what the law does (vv. 15–23), namely, it brings the consciousness of sin. He follows this with what the law is—a teacher that was in effect until Christ came (3:24–4:7).

Then Paul gives a threefold appeal (4:8–31). He appeals to their pride (vv. 8–11), exhorting them to consider their *past* bondage. He appeals to their affection (vv. 12–20), asking them to consider their *present* bonds (of love) to him. And he concludes by an appeal to their intellect (vv. 21–31) to consider their *future* bondage if they do not return to grace, rather than law, as a means of obtaining God's favor.

After stating and defending our liberty in Christ, Paul applies this liberty to their lives (chaps. 5–6). He reminds them that the greatest enemy to liberty is legalism (5:1–12), the greatest error in liberty is lawlessness (vv. 13–26), and the greatest exercise of liberty is found in love (6:1–18). The book is a study in both sound logic and persuasive writing.

How to Respond to Critics

Galatians 3:13—*Is Christ blessed or cursed?*

Problem: Paul declares that Christ was cursed of God, "having become a curse for us." However, the Bible declares repeatedly that Christ was blessed of God (see Ps. 72:17; Rom. 9:5), the one worthy to receive "glory and blessing" forever (Rev. 5:12).

Solution: These passages view Christ from different aspects. He is blessed in heaven, but he became a curse for us on earth. He is blessed in himself, but was cursed for us on the cross. Actually, as the perfect Son of God, he is the most blessed of all persons. Yet, judicially, as he became our substitute, he was the most cursed of all. The difference is manifest in this contrast:

Christ Was Blessed of God	Christ Was Cursed of God
actually	judicially
for who he is	for what he did for us
in heaven	on the cross
for the kind of person he is	for the kind of death he died

Galatians 6:5 (see 6:2)—*Are we to bear others' burdens or our own?*

Problem: In Galatians 6:2 Paul exhorts us to "bear one another's burdens, and so fulfill the law of Christ." But only a few verses later he says "every man shall bear his own burden" (KJV).

Solution: The word for "burden" is different in each case. In the first passage Paul urges *sympathy for others*. In verse 5 he is speaking of taking *responsibility for ourselves*. There is no conflict between being accountable for our own lives and being helpful to others.

STUDY QUESTIONS

1. What is the internal and external evidence that Paul wrote Galatians?
2. What are the best arguments for the early view of Galatians?
3. Give the most important reasons for the late view of Galatians.
4. Why did Paul write Galatians?
5. How do the books of Galatians and Romans differ?
6. What arguments does Paul give for justification by faith alone?

SELECTED SOURCES

Baxter, Sidlow. *Explore the Book*. Grand Rapids: Zondervan, 1987.

Bruce, F. F. *Epistle to the Galatians*. New International Greek Testament Commentary. Grand Rapids: Eerdmans, 1982.

————. *Paul, Apostle of the Heart Set Free*. Grand Rapids: Eerdmans, 2000.

Carson, D. A., Douglas Moo, and Leon Morris. *An Introduction to the New Testament*. Grand Rapids: Zondervan, 1992.

Conybeare, William, and J. S. Howson. *The Life and Epistles of St. Paul*. Grand Rapids: Eerdmans, 1953.

Geisler, Norman. *Chosen But Free*. Minneapolis: Bethany House, 1999.

Geisler, Norman L., and Thomas Howe. *When Critics Ask: A Popular Handbook on Bible Difficulties*. Grand Rapids: Baker, 1997.

Guthrie, Donald. *Galatians*. New Century Bible Commentary. Grand Rapids: Eerdmans, 1989.

————. *New Testament Introduction*. Downers Grove, IL: InterVarsity Press, 1990.

Harrison, Everett F. *An Introduction to the New Testament*. Grand Rapids: Eerdmans, 1971.

Hawthorne, Gerald F., Ralph P. Martin, and Daniel G. Reid, eds. *Dictionary of Paul and His Letters*. Downers Grove, IL: InterVarsity, 1993.

Linnemann, Eta. *Historical Criticism of the Bible*. Translated by Robert Yarborough. Grand Rapids: Kregel, 2001.

Longenecker, Richard. *Paul: Apostle of Liberty*. New York: Harper & Row, 1964.

MacArthur, John. *Galatians*. MacArthur New Testament Commentary. Chicago: Moody, 1987.

McKnight, Scot. *Galatians*. NIV Application Commentary. Grand Rapids: Zondervan, 1995.

Morris, Leon. *Galatians*. Downers Grove, IL: InterVarsity, 1996.

Radmacher, Earl, Ronald Allen, and H. Wayne House, eds. *Nelson's New Illustrated Bible Commentary*. Nashville: Thomas Nelson, 1999.

Ramsay, Sir William. *St. Paul the Traveller and the Roman Citizen*. New York: G. P. Putnam's Sons, 1896.

Walvoord, John F., and Roy B. Zuck, eds. *The Bible Knowledge Commentary*. 2 vols. Wheaton: Victor, 1983.

14
Ephesians

Who Wrote It? Ephesians was written by Paul, the apostle to the Gentiles (see the information on Paul in chapter 10).

Internal Evidence
The internal evidence that the apostle Paul wrote this book is very strong. (1) There is the explicit claim in two places in the book that Paul is the author (1:1; 3:1). (2) The theology of the book is Pauline, stressing the exalted Christ, unity in the church, and the grace of God. (3) The vocabulary is Pauline, with minor deviations fitting the theme of the book. In fact the style is more Pauline than any imitators could have been. The use of a pseudonym was not practiced by early Christians. (4) Ephesians has close similarities to Colossians (see chapter 16), which also has strong evidence for Pauline authorship. Here again, the differences between the two books fits their respective themes.

External Evidence
The evidence from other sources also supports Paul's authorship. The earliest manuscripts of the book all bear Paul's name, indicating it was accepted into the canon of Scripture as a work of Paul. The early Fathers support Paul's authorship. Citations from this book with Paul's name on it are found in both Ignatius and Polycarp among the earliest Fathers and all the other main Fathers from Irenaeus to Augustine after them.

When Was It Written? The book of Ephesians was written around AD 60. This would be during Paul's first Roman imprisonment (see Acts. 28). At the same time Paul wrote Philemon and Colossians (see chapter 16). As the

191

text makes plain, he was in prison when he wrote Ephesians (3:1; 4:1; 6:20).

There are three views as to the place and time of the writing of Ephesians: during the Caesarea incarceration, during the Ephesian imprisonment, or while Paul was at Rome.

Caesarea Incarceration (Acts 24:23)

Problems: This view has several difficulties: (1) Paul was at liberty to preach during his later Roman imprisonment (Acts 28:30–31; see Eph. 6:19), but there is no such indication of this in Caesarea. (2) If it was Caesarea, he would have been likely to seek contact with some of his churches there, but he did not. (3) There was no promise of release in Caesarea, as there was in Rome (Philem. 22). (4) The slave Onesimus would not have had access to Paul in Caesarea, which was possible in the more informal setting in Rome (Acts 28:30–31).

Ephesian Imprisonment

In 1 Corinthians 15:32, written when Paul was in Ephesus, Paul speaks of fighting "wild beasts" there; 2 Corinthians 1:8–10 speaks of a "sentence of death"; 2 Corinthians 11:23 refers to being often in prison.

Problems: (1) There is no statement that specifically links Paul to prison in Ephesus. (2) His close companion Luke (in Acts) said nothing of an imprisonment in Ephesus. (3) "Wild beasts" is figurative of a spiritual struggle (see Acts 20:29). (4) Even if it could be established that Paul was in prison in Ephesus, there is no evidence he wrote Ephesians there. (5) The reference to "chains" (Eph. 6:20) suggests Rome as the place of origin.

At Rome

Paul's writing the letter to the Ephesians from Rome (Acts 28) fits the situation better than the other possibilities, because: (1) he speaks of a palace guard (Phil. 1:13); (2) he refers to Caesar's household (Phil. 1:13; see Phil. 4:22); (3) he has freedom to preach there (Acts 28:30–31; Eph. 6:20; Phil. 1:12–18); (4) the conditions of disunity in the church (Eph. 4:1–6) fit this period; (5) the ecclesiological emphasis fits with Colossians, which was written at the same time, and doesn't feature as prominently his earlier salvation emphasis in Romans and Galatians.

Since the same general material is in both Ephesians and Colossians (in half of the verses), both books were undoubtedly written at this time. Indeed, the same person (Tychicus) carried both Colossians (4:7) and Ephesians (6:21) to their destinations. And the same companions (Tychicus and Onesimus) are in Ephesians,

Artemis (Diana) of
Ephesus.

Colossians, and Philemon (Eph. 6:21; Col. 4:7, 9; Philem. 10), so
Philemon was probably written at this same time (see chapter 16).

Many scholars believe this imprisonment is to be distinguished
from his later (second) imprisonment in Rome, since he had the
hope of release here (Philem 22), but later he looked forward only
to martyrdom (2 Tim. 4:6–8).

To Whom Was It Written? Ephesians was written to the church at Ephesus, in Asia Minor
and possibly the surrounding area. Some say its original destiny
was only the church of Ephesus in Asia Minor because of the
statement "in Ephesus" (1:1). Others claim it was a circular letter
for churches in Asia Minor because the phrase "in Ephesus" is not
in some early manuscripts and there are no personal references to
the church he served for three years (see Acts 20:31, which refers to
the church at Ephesus). It was probably "the epistle [coming] from
Laodicea" mentioned in Colossians 4:16,[1] which was written at the
same time, along with Philemon.

Where Were the Readers Located? The recipients of this letter lived in Ephesus in Asia Minor.

Why Was It Written?

Several reasons for the writing of this epistle can be discerned from the text. (1) Paul wanted to inform believers of their exalted position of blessings in Christ (1:3). (2) He wished to urge them to maintain unity in Christ (4:1–6). (3) He hoped to encourage believers in the love of Christ (the verb *agapō* is used nine times in this book—out of twenty-three times in the New Testament). Later they lost this love, as the letter to Ephesus reveals in Revelation 2:4. (4) Paul desired to encourage believers to stand for Christ (6:11–14). (5) He wanted to set forth the divine purposes in Christ (1:9–10) of the mystery involving the Christ (3:1–7).

What Is It About?

The Theme: Exaltation in Christ.
The Key Verse: "Blessed be the God and Father of our Lord Jesus Christ, who has blessed us with every spiritual blessing in the heavenly places in Christ" (1:3).
Key Words and Phrases: *body, same body* (9x), *church* (9x), *formerly* (6x), *grace* (12x), *heavenly places* (5x), *in Christ, in him, in whom* (32x), *(to) love, love* (20x), *make alive together, join together, build together, bring together* (5x), *one* (12x), *power* (5x), *spirit* (15x), and *walk* (8x). See appendix 3 for a more complete word study.

Contrast with Colossians

Colossians	Ephesians
polemical	irenic (peaceful)
Christ over the cosmos	Christ over the church
about heresy	about unity
emphasis on the head	emphasis on the body

Contrast with the Gospels:

> Gospels—the physical body of Christ—his humiliation
> Ephesians—the mystical body of Christ (the church)
> —his glorification

Contrast with Corinthians:

> Corinthians—the local church (visible)
> Ephesians—the universal church (invisible)

The Faith: Ephesians teaches felicity, unity, equality, mystery, and eternity of the faith.

Four Bodily Positions of the Believer:

Seated in Christ (chaps. 1–2)—2:6
Kneeling before Christ (chap. 3)—3:14
Walking for Christ (chaps. 4–5)—4:1
Standing for Christ (chap. 6)—6:11, 13

Description: Ephesians has been called the "Mt. Everest of the Bible." It is the highest pinnacle of Christian truth.

The Universal Church and the Local Church

The Universal Church	The Local Church
one church	many churches
an organism	an organization
only saved members	saved and unsaved members
dead and living members	only living members
whole body of Christ	only part of the body of Christ
Christ is the visible head (in heaven)	Christ is the invisible head (on earth)
no elders or deacons	elders and deacons
no ordinances	two ordinances
no denominations	many denominations
indestructible	destructible

Understanding Terms:

Unanimity means absolute concord of opinion within a given group of people.

Uniformity is complete similarity of organization or of ritual.

Union implies political affiliation without necessarily including individual agreement.

Unity requires oneness of inner heart and essential purpose, through the possession of a common interest or a common life.[2]

THE OUTLINE:

I. Positional—Our Heavenly Calling (Doctrine) (chaps. 1–3)
   A. The source (God's foreordination)
      —the church is a body (chap. 1)
   B. The result (man's reconciliation)
      —the church is a temple (chap. 2)

    C. The mystery (Gentiles' dispensation)
      —the church is a family (chap. 3)
  II. **Practical—Our Earthly Conduct (Duty)** (chaps. 4–6)
    A. Walking in unity (4:1–16)
    B. Walking in holiness (vv. 17–32)
    C. Walking in love (5:1–6)
    D. Walking in light (vv. 7–14)
    E. Walking in wisdom (5:15–6:9)
    F. Standing in warfare (6:10–20)
    G. Conclusion (vv. 21–24)

THE CONTENTS: Ephesians is a model for ministering. The first half (chaps. 1–3) deals with our position in Christ; the second with our practice for Christ (chaps. 4–6). The practical is rooted in the doctrinal.

Our positional status (chaps. 1–3) is about our heavenly calling (doctrine). First, Paul deals with the source of our position in Christ—God's foreordination. Here the church is described as a body (chap. 1). Then he discusses the result of our position—man's reconciliation to God. Here the church is pictured as a temple (chap. 2). Finally, he treats the mystery of our position—the mystery involving the church, which is here depicted as a family (chap. 3).

In the last section of the book (chaps. 4–6), Paul turns from position to practice, from our heavenly calling to our earthly conduct, from doctrine to duty. It shifts the focus from being seated in Christ (2:6) to walking for Christ (4:1). He urges walking in unity (vv. 1–16), then walking in holiness (vv. 17–32), walking in love (5:1–6), walking in light (vv. 7–14), and walking in wisdom (5:15–6:9). Finally, he exhorts believers to stand for Christ with the whole armor of God (6:10–20), taking the sword of the Spirit, which is the Word of God. His salutation is short, informing the readers about his affairs (vv. 21–22) and praying God's peace and grace on them (vv. 23–24).

How to Respond to Critics

Ephesians 2:1—*How can a person believe if he or she is dead in sins?*

Problem: The Bible repeatedly calls on the unbeliever to "believe on the Lord Jesus Christ and . . . be saved" (Acts 16:31). However, this passage declares that unbelievers are dead in their sins, and dead people cannot do anything, including believe.

Solution: "Death" in the Bible is not to be understood as annihilation but as separation or without life. Isaiah said, "Your iniquities have separated you from your God" (Isa. 59:2). Spiritually, as well as physically, death is the lack of life. If death were annihilation, then

Ancient street, Ephesus.

the second death would be eternal annihilation, but the Bible declares that the lost will be consciously separated from God, as was the rich man who was in hell in Luke 16, as will be the beast and false prophet who will be "tormented day and night forever and ever" (Rev. 20:10). Indeed, they were cast "alive" into the lake of fire at the beginning of the one-thousand-year reign of Christ (19:20), and they were still alive at the end of the one thousand years (20:10). So the second "death" is eternal, conscious separation from Christ.

Furthermore, believers die physically, but their souls survive death and are consciously in the presence of God. Paul said, "Absent from the body and . . . present with the Lord" (2 Cor. 5:8). And he also said, "having a desire to depart and be with Christ, which is far better" (Phil. 1:23).

Likewise, spiritual death is also separation from God not annihilation. For example, Adam and Eve died spiritually the moment they ate the forbidden fruit (Gen. 3:6; see Rom. 5:12), yet they were still alive and could hear God's voice speaking to them (Gen. 3:10). So, whereas the image of God in fallen man is effaced, it is not erased. It is marred but not destroyed. Thus unsaved persons can hear, understand the gospel, believe it, and be regenerated or made alive in a spiritual sense (Eph. 2:8–9; Titus 3:5–7).

Ephesians 4:9—*Did Jesus descend into hell?*
Problem: Paul claims here that Jesus "descended into the lower parts of the earth." And the Apostles' Creed declares that after Jesus died, he "descended into hell." However, when Jesus was dying, he committed his spirit into his Father's hands (Luke 23:46) and told the thief that he would be with him in "Paradise" (v. 43), which is in the "third heaven" (2 Cor. 12:2, 4). Where did Jesus go—to heaven or to hell?
Solution: There are two views as to where Jesus went the three days his body was in the grave before his resurrection.

The Hades view. One position claims that Christ's spirit went to the spirit world, while his body was in the grave. Here, they believe, he spoke to the "spirits in prison" (1 Peter 3:18–19) who were in a temporary holding place until he came and "led captivity captive" (Eph. 4:8), that is, took them to heaven. According to this view, there were two compartments in Hades (or *sheol*), one for the saved and another for the unsaved. They were separated by a "great gulf" (Luke 16:26), which no person could pass. The section for the saved was called "Abraham's bosom" (v. 23). When Christ, as the "firstfruits" of the resurrection (1 Cor. 15:20), ascended, he led these Old Testament saints into heaven with him for the first time.

The Heaven view. This teaching holds that the souls of Old Testament believers went directly to heaven the moment they died. It offers the following arguments in support of its teaching.

1. Jesus affirmed that his spirit was going directly to heaven, declaring, "Father, into Your hands I commend My spirit" (Luke 23:46).

2. Jesus promised the thief on the cross, "Today you will be with Me in Paradise" (v. 43). "Paradise" is defined as "the third heaven" in 2 Corinthians 12:2, 4.

3. When Old Testament saints departed this life, they went directly to heaven. God took Enoch to be with himself (Gen. 5:24; see Heb. 11:5), and Elijah was caught up into heaven when he departed (2 Kings 2:1).

4. "Abraham's bosom" (Luke 16:23) is a description of heaven. At no time does it ever describe hell. It is the place where Abraham went, which is the "kingdom of heaven" (Matt. 8:11).

5. When Old Testament saints appear before the cross, they appear from heaven, as Moses and Elijah did on the mount of transfiguration (Matt. 17:3).

6. Old Testament saints had to await Christ's resurrection before their *bodies* could be resurrected (Matt. 27:52–53; 1 Cor. 15:20), but their *souls* went directly to heaven. Christ was "the Lamb slain from the foundation of the world" (Rev. 13:8), and they were there on the merits of what God knew Christ would accomplish.

7. "Descending into the lower parts of the earth" is not a reference to hell but to the grave. Even a woman's womb is described as "lowest parts of the earth" (Ps. 139:15). The phrase simply means caves, graves, or enclosures on the earth, as opposed to higher parts, like mountains. Besides this, hell is not in the lower parts of the earth—it is "under the earth" (Phil. 2:10).

8. The phrase "descended into hell" was not in the earliest Apostles' Creed. It was not added until the fourth century. And, as a creed, it is not inspired—it is only a human confession of faith.

9. The "spirits in prison" were unsaved beings. Indeed, this term may refer to angels, not to human beings (see 1 Peter 3:18–19).

10. When Christ "led captivity captive" (Eph. 4:8), he was not leading friends into heaven, but bringing foes into bondage. It is a reference to his conquering the forces of evil. Christians are not "captives" in heaven. We are not forced to go there against our own free choice (see Matt. 23:37; 2 Peter 3:9).

STUDY QUESTIONS

1. What is the evidence, internal and external, that Paul wrote Ephesians?

2. What were the reasons Paul wrote this epistle?

3. What is the difference between unity and uniformity?

4. How do the universal and local church differ?

5. What is the significance of the order of the four bodily positions of the believer pictured in Ephesians?

6. How do Colossians and Ephesians differ?

SELECTED SOURCES

Baxter, Sidlow. *Explore the Book*. Grand Rapids: Zondervan, 1987.

Bruce, F. F. *Paul, Apostle of the Heart Set Free*. Grand Rapids: Eerdmans, 2000.

Carson, D.A., Douglas Moo, and Leon Morris. *An Introduction to the New Testament*. Grand Rapids: Zondervan, 1992.

Conybeare, William, and J. S. Howson. *The Life and Epistles of St. Paul*. Grand Rapids: Eerdmans, 1953.

Geisler, Norman. *Chosen But Free*. Minneapolis: Bethany House, 1999.

Geisler, Norman L., and Thomas Howe. *When Critics Ask: A Popular Handbook on Bible Difficulties*. Grand Rapids: Baker, 1997.

Guthrie, Donald. *New Testament Introduction*. Downers Grove, IL: InterVarsity, 1990.

Harrison, Everett F. *An Introduction to the New Testament*. Grand Rapids: Eerdmans, 1971.

Hawthorne, Gerald F., Ralph P. Martin, and Daniel G. Reid, eds. *Dictionary of Paul and His Letters*. Downers Grove, IL: InterVarsity, 1993.

Hughes, R. Kent. *Ephesians: The Mystery of the Body of Christ*. Preaching the Word. Wheaton: Crossway, 1990.

Liefeld, Walter. *Ephesians*. IVP New Testament Commentary. Downers Grove, IL: InterVarsity, 1997.

Linnemann, Eta. *Historical Criticism of the Bible*. Translated by Robert Yarborough. Grand Rapids: Kregel, 2001.

Longenecker, Richard. *Paul: Apostle of Liberty*. New York: Harper & Row, 1964.

MacArthur, John. *Ephesians*. MacArthur New Testament Commentary. Chicago: Moody, 1986.

Radmacher, Earl, Ronald Allen, and H. Wayne House, eds. *Nelson's New Illustrated Bible Commentary*. Nashville: Thomas Nelson, 1999.

Ramsay, Sir William. *St. Paul the Traveller and the Roman Citizen*. New York: G. P. Putnam's Sons, 1896.

Snodgrass, Klyne. *Ephesians*. NIV Application Commentary. Grand Rapids: Zondervan, 1996.

Walvoord, John F., and Roy B. Zuck, eds. *The Bible Knowledge Commentary*. 2 vols. Wheaton: Victor, 1983.

15
Philippians

Who Wrote It? The apostle Paul wrote Philippians (1:1).

Internal Evidence
There is much internal evidence that Paul wrote this epistle. (1) Paul claims to have written it: "Paul and Timothy, servants of Jesus Christ, to all the saints in Christ Jesus who are in Philippi" (1:1). (2) The character of the book fits the claim, for Paul describes his background as a Hebrew of the tribe of Benjamin and a Pharisee who was zealous to keep the law (3:4–6). (3) His companion Timothy fits what is known from the book of Acts (16:1–3). (4) The style, too, is Pauline, beginning with the familiar grace and peace (1:2) and ending with "the grace of our Lord Jesus Christ be with you all" (4:23). (5) The standard key phrase "in Christ" is used with the theme (1:26). (6) And the doctrine is Pauline throughout, as may be seen from his assertion that Christ is our life (1:21; see Gal. 2:20), that Christ is head over all things (2:9–11; see Col. 2:9–10), and Paul's opposition to Judaizers (3:1–3; see Gal. 5:1–6).

External Evidence
The external evidence is also abundant. Paul's name is on the earliest known manuscripts. The earliest Church Fathers support Pauline authorship, including Clement of Rome, Ignatius, Polycarp (in his *Epistle to the Philippians* 3:2), the Muratorian canon, and even the heretic Marcion. In addition, almost all critics accept this letter as Pauline.

When Was It Written?

The letter to the Ephesians was written between AD 61 and 62, while Paul was in prison (see Acts 28). It is clear that Paul was in prison when he wrote, since he speaks of his "chains" (1:13), his hope to be released (v. 19; 2:24), and his witness to the palace guards (1:13). But his confinement in Caesarea (Acts 23–24) does not fit the conditions of this imprisonment because there is reference to a palace guard here (1:13) but not there; there is no reference to the freedom to preach in Caesarea, as there is here (v. 18); elsewhere Paul has more associates (see Col. 4:7–14; Philem. 23–24) than here, where only Timothy is with him (1:1; 2:19–21).

The circumstances described in Philippians fit better Paul's later imprisonment, recorded in Acts 28 (ca. AD 61–62), since here he hints of a release (Phil. 1:19; see Philem. 22), which he did not do in 2 Timothy 4:6–8 regarding a later confinement (AD 67), where he anticipates death.

To Whom Was It Written?

The letter was written to Philippian Christians, "with bishops [elders] and deacons" (1:1). They were mostly Gentile, as is indicated by the fact there was no synagogue there. A group of women met regularly to pray on the Sabbath by the riverside (Acts 16:11–13). Paul's visit to Philippi resulted from a vision of a man of Macedonia (vv. 9–10), which Paul received while in Asia. This vision called him to Europe—to Philippi, a city of Macedonia.

By the time Paul wrote to the Philippians, the church was well organized, with both "bishops and deacons" (Phil. 1:1). From the beginning, women were prominent in the church (Acts 16:14–15; Phil. 4:2). The Philippians were a wealthy and generous church. One indication of this is that Lydia was a businesswoman (Acts 16:14) and the church gave generously to others (Phil. 4:10–18).

The original church consisted of three types of people, who typified what the gospel of Christ did for society. They were Lydia's household (Acts 16:14–15), portraying the liberation of women; the demonized damsel (vv. 16–18), picturing the emancipation of slaves; and the converted jailor (vv. 27–33) exemplifying the conversion of families to Christ. These emphases foreshadowed the very things Christianity was to achieve as the gospel spread through Europe.

Where Were the Readers Located?

The recipients of the letter lived in Philippi of Macedonia (in Europe). The Philippian church was the first European church. It resulted from Paul's obedience to the vision of the man of Macedonia (a European province). The city was started by (and named after) Philip of Macedon, a Roman king. It was a leading city of the area (Acts 16:12) and a likely place for a beachhead for the gospel in Europe. The circumstances that prompted Paul to

The site of ancient Philippi.

go there have been called "the hinge of history," for his personal desires were to press further into the remote areas of Asia. The Holy Spirit resisted that plan, however (v. 6), and Paul responded to God's call to go to Europe (vv. 9–10).

Why Was It Written?

Philippians was written for several purposes: (1) to encourage the readers to rejoice always in the Lord (1:26; 3:1; 4:4, 10–13) in every circumstance; (2) to relate his circumstances to them (1:19; 4:10) so as to ease their anxiety about him; (3) to thank them for their many gifts to him and the most recent one by way of Epaphroditus (2:25, 28; 4:15); (4) to warn them of the Judaizers (3:1–3, 18–19); (5) to rebuke the perfectionists (vv. 13–14); (6) to rebuff the sensualist and materialist (vv. 18–19); (7) to exhort them to harmony in Christ (4:2).

What Is It About? The Theme: The central theme of this letter is exultation (joy) in Christ (1:26).

The Key Verse: "Rejoice in the Lord always. Again I will say, rejoice!" (4:4).

Key Words and Phrases: *abound* (5x), *affection* (2x), *think, adopt an attitude, have a mind* (11x), *Christ* (38x), *fellowship* (3x), *gospel* (9x), *imprisonment* (4x), *know, knowledge* (18x), and *rejoice, joy* (14x). See appendix 3 for a more complete word study.

Contrast with Ephesians

Ephesians	Philippians
in the heavenlies	back to earth
head in the clouds	feet on earth
exaltation on the mountain	exultation (joy) in the valley

Old Testament Citations: Since the letter was written to a largely Gentile constituency, there are no direct quotations from the Old Testament in Philippians. However, the teaching is dependent on an Old Testament background (see 3:1–11). One important allusion to the Old Testament is found in 2:10 where it affirms that every knee will one day bow to Christ as Lord. This is derived from Isaiah 45:23.

Christ-Centered Nature: Each chapter centers on the person of Christ, who is our life (1:21), example (2:5), goal (3:14), and strength (4:13). As such, it is a handbook on Christian experience.

Church Organization: The church at Philippi was an organized church of bishops and deacons (1:1). Bishops are the Greek equivalent of elders, who were ordained in every church (Acts 14:23). Deacons were assistants to the elders, taking the material tasks from their hands, so the elders (bishops) could concentrate on the Word of God and prayer (see 6:1–4).

Other Characteristics: The church at Philippi was the first church in Europe, the forefather of Western Christianity. It was largely a Gentile church, one in which women were prominent (Acts 16:13; Phil. 4:2) and generosity abounded (vv. 16–19; 2 Cor. 11:9). Some see an early Christological hymn and/or creed in Philippians 2:5–11. It was a warmly personal letter, as indicated by the use of "I" some sixty-four times.

THE OUTLINE:

> I. **Philosophy of Christian Living—Christ Our Life**
> —Manifestation of the Christian Life (chap. 1)

    A. Prayer of confidence (vv. 1–11)
    B. Pressing circumstances (vv. 12–14)
    C. Preaching Christ (vv. 15–18)
    D. Personal commitment (vv. 19–26)
    E. Praiseworthy conduct (vv. 27–30)

II. Pattern for Christian Living—Christ Our Mind
—Illustration of the Christian Life (chap. 2)
    A. Plea for humility (vv. 1–4)
    B. Picture of humility (vv. 5–11)
    C. Program for humility (vv. 12–16)
    D. Practice of humility (vv. 17–30)

III. Prize for Christian Living—Christ Our Goal
—Motivation of the Christian Life (chap. 3)
    A. Pattern for it (vv. 1–3)
    B. Price for it (vv. 4–11)
    C. Pressing toward it (vv. 12–16)
    D. Prospect of it (vv. 17–21)

IV. Power for Christian Living—Christ Our Strength
—Demonstration of the Christian Life (chap. 4)
    A. Personality conflicts (vv. 1–5)
    B. Pure contemplations (vv. 6–9)
    C. Pressing circumstances (vv. 10–13)
    D. Practical contributions (vv. 14–23)

THE CONTENTS: The structure of Philippians falls neatly within the boundaries of the four chapters. First, we have the philosophy of Christian living—Christ is our life (chap. 1). Then there is the pattern for Christian living—Christ is our example (chap. 2). Next we have the prize for Christian living—Christ is our goal (chap. 3). Finally, there is the power for Christian living—Christ is our strength (chap. 4).

In the first chapter Paul speaks of the manifestation of Christ's life in pressing circumstances (vv. 12–14), in preaching the gospel (vv. 15–18), in Paul's personal commitment (vv. 19–26), and in praiseworthy conduct for Christ (vv. 27–30). In the second chapter we have the illustration of the Christian life in Paul's plea for humility (vv. 1–4), the picture of humility (vv. 5–11), the program for humility (vv. 12–16), and the practice of humility (vv. 17–30). Chapter 3 provides the motivation of the Christian life. Christ is the pattern for it (vv. 1–3) and the price for it (vv. 4–11). Believers are urged to press toward it (vv. 12–16) and to live in the prospect of it in Christ's coming again (vv. 17–21). The fourth chapter deals with the demonstration of the Christian life in personality conflicts (vv. 1–5), pure contemplations (vv. 6–9), pressing circumstances (vv. 10–13), and in their practical contributions (vv. 14–23).

**How to Respond
to Critics**

Philippians 2:5–7—*If Christ emptied himself of deity while on earth, how could he be God?*

Problem: Paul seems to say that Jesus "emptied himself" of his deity or "equality with God" (vv. 6–7), becoming "a man" (v. 8). But elsewhere Jesus claimed to be God on earth (John 8:58; 20:28–29). How could Jesus be God while on earth if he laid his deity aside to become man?

Solution: Jesus did not cease being God while on earth. Rather, in addition to being God, he also became man. His incarnation was not the subtraction of deity but the addition of humanity. Several things in this text support this position. First, it does not say Christ gave up or emptied himself of his deity, but merely of his *rights* as deity, assuming the "form of a servant" (v. 7) as an example for us (v. 5). Second, verse 6 declares that he was in the "form of God" or "in very nature God" (NIV). Just as the "form of a servant" is a servant by nature, so the "form of God" (v. 6) is God by nature. Third, this very passage declares that one day every knee will bow and every tongue confess Jesus is "Lord," a citation from Isaiah 45:23 that refers to *Yahweh*, a name used exclusively for God.

Philippians 3:15—*Are Christians perfect or still on the way to perfection?*

Problem: In this verse, Paul speaks to "as many as be perfect" (KJV) to act as he did, but only three verses earlier he claimed that he was not "already perfect" (v. 12), that he was still pressing on to attain perfection. Which statement should we believe?

Solution: Here is a good example of how the same word can be used with different senses. This is not uncommon in languages, as the English word *board* illustrates. Take this sentence for example: "The *board* members took a stroll on the *board*walk and then stopped at the desk to inquire about room and *board*." It is obvious that the same word *board* is being used here in three different senses. Likewise, Paul uses the word *perfect* in different senses. Some believers are "perfect" in the sense of being "mature" or "complete," but no believer this side of death is perfect in the sense of having "fully arrived" or having "reached the ultimate goal." This comes, as Paul indicated, only at "the resurrection from the dead" (v. 11).

Philippians 4:5—*Is the Lord's coming at hand or far off?*

Problem: According to this passage, "the Lord is at hand" (see 1 Peter 4:7). However, other passages portray Christ's coming as not being immediate, coming only after some intervening events. "For that Day will not come," writes Paul, "unless the falling away comes first" (2 Thess. 2:3).

Solution: Bible scholars respond to this problem in two different ways, depending on their view of future things (eschatology).

Nonimminent view. Those who believe Christ's coming is not imminent take the verses that speak of it as "at hand" as only general descriptions and not specific timeframes. They note that the "last days" includes the whole period of time between Christ's first and second comings (see Heb. 1:1–2; 1 John 2:18). Thus they see no difficulty with passages (like 2 Thess. 2:3) that speak of some events that must occur before Christ can return. That is, they believe that it is true *in a general sense* that "the Lord is at hand" but deny that this means he could literally come at any moment. Some specific events, like the "falling away," must come first, before Christ will actually return.

Imminent view. Other Bible scholars, including the author, take the verses declaring that Christ's coming is "at hand" literally. They claim that otherwise it could not be "the blessed hope" spoken of by Paul in Titus 2:13 or the purifying hope that John described (1 John 3:2–3). Further, why should the believer be exhorted to "watch" for it so as not to be taken by surprise (see Matt. 24:42; 1 Thess. 5:1–2)? They believe that if there were discernable signs and events that must occur before Christ returns for believers, then we could know "the day and hour" (Matt. 24:36) or "times or seasons" (Acts 1:7), which Christ said we cannot know.

According to this view, then, when the Bible speaks of Christ's return as a sign-less, imminent event that could happen at any moment, it is speaking about Christ's coming in the air *for* his saints before the tribulation (this is the rapture of 1 Thess. 4:13–18). His coming is "at hand" (Phil. 4:5), and he is "at the door" (James 5:9). The references to his coming "quickly" (for example, Rev. 22:12) mean suddenly, not soon. And when the Scripture talks about signs and events that must occur before the coming of Christ, it is referring to his coming *with* his saints to earth after the tribulation (Matt. 24:29–30).

The following chart outlines the two aspects of Christ's return:

Coming for His Saints	**Coming with His Saints**
before the tribulation	after the tribulation
in the air	on earth
no signs	many signs
imminent	not imminent
at hand	yet to come
a "now" coming	a near coming
suddenly	not suddenly

STUDY QUESTIONS

1. What is the evidence, internally and externally, that Paul wrote Philippians?

2. What were his purposes for writing it?

3. What is the historic importance of the Philippian church?

4. Who were two original converts who served as the nucleus of the church? What did their conversion signify about the impact Christianity has on a culture?

5. Given the circumstances from which Paul wrote this book, what does the theme tell us about his spiritual life?

6. What are the key verses in each chapter and how do they develop the theme of the book?

SELECTED SOURCES

Baxter, Sidlow. *Explore the Book.* Grand Rapids: Zondervan, 1987.

Bruce, F. F. *Paul, Apostle of the Heart Set Free.* Grand Rapids: Eerdmans, 2000.

Carson, D. A., Douglas Moo, and Leon Morris. *An Introduction to the New Testament.* Grand Rapids: Zondervan, 1992.

Conybeare, William, and J. S. Howson. *The Life and Epistles of St. Paul.* Grand Rapids: Eerdmans, 1953.

Geisler, Norman L., and Thomas Howe. *When Critics Ask: A Popular Handbook on Bible Difficulties.* Grand Rapids: Baker, 1997.

Guthrie, Donald. *New Testament Introduction.* Downers Grove, IL: InterVarsity, 1990.

Harrison, Everett F. *An Introduction to the New Testament.* Grand Rapids: Eerdmans, 1971.

Hawthorne, Gerald F., Ralph P. Martin, and Daniel G. Reid, eds. *Dictionary of Paul and His Letters.* Downers Grove, IL: InterVarsity, 1993.

Linnemann, Eta. *Historical Criticism of the Bible.* Translated by Robert Yarborough. Grand Rapids: Kregel, 2001.

Longenecker, Richard. *Paul: Apostle of Liberty.* New York: Harper & Row, 1964.

MacArthur, John. *Philippians.* MacArthur New Testament Commentary. Chicago: Moody, 2001.

Marshall, I. Howard. *Epistle to the Philippians.* Norwich, UK: Epworth, 1997.

Radmacher, Earl, Ronald Allen, and H. Wayne House, eds. *Nelson's New Illustrated Bible Commentary.* Nashville: Thomas Nelson, 1999.

Ramsay, Sir William. *St. Paul the Traveller and the Roman Citizen.* New York: G. P. Putnam's Sons, 1896.

Silva, Moisés. *Philippians.* Baker Exegetical Commentary on the New Testament. 2nd ed. Grand Rapids: Baker, 2005.

Thielman, Frank. *Philippians.* NIV Application Commentary. Grand Rapids: Zondervan, 1995.

Walvoord, John F., and Roy B. Zuck, eds. *The Bible Knowledge Commentary.* 2 vols. Wheaton: Victor, 1983.

16

Colossians
and Philemon

Colossians

Colossians was written by Paul the apostle.

Internal Evidence

This epistle claims to be written by "Paul, an apostle of Jesus Christ" (1:1). The author repeats his name, saying "I, Paul" (v. 23). He repeats this claim at the end, saying, "This salutation by my own hand—Paul" (4:18). The companions mentioned support Paul's authorship, since many are known from elsewhere in the New Testament to be associates of Paul. They include Tychicus (4:7), Onesimus (v. 9), Aristarchus and Mark (v. 10), Justus (v. 11), Epaphras (v. 12), Luke and Demas (v. 14), and finally Archippus (v. 17). The character of the book is Pauline, as determined by the doctrinal emphasis, controversy, and approach to ministry. The style varies only as the content demands, since different opponents and topics demand some different words. The thirty-four new words, which do not appear in his other letters, fit the theme of the book and the thought of Paul. The content of the book is Pauline, manifesting his typical emphasis against heresy, disunity, and Judaistic influence in the Christian church.

External Evidence

The earliest manuscripts of the letter to the Colossians have Paul's name on them. Indeed, early Christian writers accepted it as Pauline, including Irenaeus, Clement of Alexandria, the Muratorian canon, and even the heretic Marcion. About half the verses are the same as in Ephesians (see chapter 14), which was written by Paul. There is also a close link to the book of Philemon, which is Paul's work. Both books have Timothy in the introduction (1:1); greetings are sent from the same people in both—Aristarchus, Mark, Epaphras,

Luke, and Demas (4:10–14; Philem. 23–24); Archippus's ministry is mentioned in both (Col. 4:17; Philem. 2); Onesimus is referred to in both (Col. 4:9; Philem. 10).

Answering Critics

Some critics claim that Colossians is not Paul's work, since the vocabulary differs (thirty-four new words). However, all of Paul's letters have unique words. Words change with the topic. Some words are borrowed from the opposition to refute them.

Others insist that the style of Colossians differs, being more passive than Galatians. But Paul did not know the Galatians personally as he did the Colossians. And he is addressing an error in this letter that is different from the error addressed in Galatians. Further, Paul is older here and is writing under different conditions, namely, from prison.

Still others insist that the thought in this book differs from that in some of Paul's other books, since it contains nothing about justification or the Holy Spirit in our lives. Paul also adds new topics, like the cosmic significance of Christ. However, these charges are unjustified since Paul does affirm elsewhere that Christ is over the cosmos (1 Cor. 8:6; see Heb. 1:3), and justification by faith is not the issue here as it was in Romans and Galatians. Furthermore, Paul does speak here of love in the Holy Spirit (1:8), as well as growth (v. 6). Also it is noteworthy that this book is tied to Philemon (see above), the authorship of which is not doubted.

When Was It Written?

Colossians was written around AD 60, from a Roman prison (see Acts 28) at the same time as Ephesians and Philemon, indicated by the following facts: Tychicus carried both the Ephesian and the Colossian letters (Eph. 6:21; Col. 4:7), and one-half of the content of Ephesians overlaps that of Colossians. Since Ephesians was written from prison (3:1; 4:1; 6:20), then Colossians must have been written from prison at the same time. The time of Paul's imprisonment (in Acts 28) was ca. AD 60–62. But there is no hint here in Colossians of a possible release, as there was later in Philippians (1:19). Hence, Colossians must have been written about AD 60 and Philippians later in AD 61–62.

To Whom Was It Written?

Paul was writing to the church at Colosse. Epaphras had founded the church (1:7; 4:12–13), not Paul (2:1). The church was made up mostly of Gentiles (1:27; 2:13) who were influenced by a "vain" philosophy (2:8), composed of an incipient form of Gnosticism (vv. 8–10), legalism (vv. 11–17), mysticism (vv. 18–19), and asceticism (vv. 20–23). In brief, the heresy was a form of Judeo-

Roman highway at Hierapolis, near Colosse.

philosophical and mystical asceticism, a forerunner of second-century Gnosticism.

Where Were the Readers Located?

The recipients of Paul's letter lived in Colosse, in Asia Minor, a populous city, twelve miles from Laodicea. It lay about one hundred miles east of Ephesus and had rich mineral deposits and good pastureland but was subject to earthquakes.

Why Was It Written?

The various purposes for which the letter was written can be inferred from the text. (1) Paul desired to show the Colossians their completeness in Christ (chap. 1); (2) he wanted to lead believers into spiritual maturity (2:1–17); (3) his design was to counter the Gnostic-like, legalistic, mystical heresy in the church (2:18–23); (4) he desired to teach about our new life in Christ (3:1–4:6); (5) he wanted to inform them about his state of affairs (4:7–18).

What Is It About?

The Theme: Completion in Christ. The emphasis is on the eminence and sufficiency of Christ as the believer's completeness in Christ.

The Key Verse: "that we may present every man perfect [complete] in Christ Jesus" (1:28).

Key Words and Phrases: *all* (40x), *complete, fill* (5x), *elements* (2x), *faith, faithful* (9x), *knowledge* (4x), *mystery* (4x), *through, on account of* (14x), and *wisdom* (6x). See appendix 3 for a more complete word study.

Previously Unknown "Mysteries" Revealed in the New Testament

Matthew 13:11	The kingdom of heaven
Luke 8:10	The kingdom of God
Romans 11:25	Israel's hardening
Romans 16:25–26	The gospel
1 Corinthians 4:1	God's revelation
Ephesians 1:9	God's will
Ephesians 3:2–3	God's grace
Ephesians 3:4	Christ
Ephesians 3:9–10	God's church
Ephesians 5:32	Christ and the church
Colossians 1:26	The church
Colossians 1:27	Enfolding of Gentiles
Colossians 2:2	Knowledge of Christ
Colossians 4:3	Proclamation of Christ
2 Thessalonians 2:7	Lawlessness
1 Timothy 3:9	The Christian faith
1 Timothy 3:16	Godliness
Revelation 1:20	Seven stars
Revelation 10:7	God's goal
Revelation 17:5	Babylon, the Great

Reprinted from John F. Walvoord and Roy B. Zuck, eds. *The Bible Knowledge Commentary* vol. 2 (Wheaton: Victor, 1983), 46.

Contrast with Ephesians

Ephesians	Colossians
emphasis on the body	emphasis on the head
about unity	about heresy
Christ over the church	Christ over the cosmos
irenic	polemical

Contrast with Philippians

Philippians	Colossians
kenoō (2:7)—"empty"	*plerōma* (2:9)—"fullness"
Christian living	Christian knowing

Christ's Headship:

1 Corinthians 11:3—Christ is head of the individual.

Ephesians 1:22—Christ is head of the church.

Colossians 2:10—Christ is head of the cosmos.

THE OUTLINE:

I. Doctrinal—Deeper Life (1:1–2:7)
    A. Preeminence belongs to Christ (1:1–19)
    B. Reconciliation made by Christ (vv. 20–23)
    C. Mystery revealed in Christ (vv. 24–29)
    D. All wisdom and knowledge are in Christ (2:1–5)
    E. Therefore, live in Christ (vv. 6–7)

II. Polemical—Higher Life (2:8–23)
    A. "Gnosticism" is heresy—deity is in Christ (vv. 8–10)
    B. Legalism is heresy—reality is in Christ (vv. 11–17)
    C. Mysticism is heresy—headship is in Christ (vv. 18–19)
    D. Asceticism is heresy—dead in Christ (vv. 20–23)

III. Spiritual—Inner Life (3:1–17)
    A. Seek new life above (vv. 1–4)
    B. Put off old life below (vv. 5–11)
    C. Put on new life below (vv. 12–17)

IV. Practical—Outer Life (3:18–4:18)
    A. Perfect your private life (3:18–4:1)
    B. Perfect your prayer life (4:2–4)
    C. Perfect your public life (vv. 5–6)
    D. Perfect your personal life (vv. 7–18)

THE CONTENTS: Paul begins by greeting the brethren (1:1–2) and giving thanks to God for their faith and love (vv. 3–8). He asks God to fill them with the knowledge of his will and prays that they will be fruitful for Christ who has redeemed them (vv. 9–14), reminding them that all preeminence belongs to Christ (vv. 15–19) and that we were aliens and enemies of God (vv. 20–23) and that he suffered for the church so that God's fullness can be known to the Gentiles (vv. 24–27). To this end Paul labored that everyone may be perfect in Christ (vv. 28–29)—the theme of the book—for all true wisdom and knowledge is found in Christ (2:1–5). Therefore, just as they began in Christ, they should continue in him (vv. 6–7), not being deceived by vain human philosophy, for God's fullness dwells in Christ alone (vv. 8–10). Paul exhorts them that, since they have been identified with Christ in their baptism, they have no need to live under Jewish laws (vv. 11–17). Nor should they let anyone rob them of their prize by forsaking Christ their Head (vv. 18–19). For we died with Christ, so we need not submit to worldly (legalistic) rules (vv. 20–23).

And since we were raised with Christ, we should set our hearts on heavenly things above (3:1–4), putting to death our sinful worldly practices (vv. 5–11) and clothing ourselves with Christ's virtues (vv. 15–17). In view of their new exalted identity with Christ, Paul exhorts wives to submit to their husbands, husbands to love their wives, children to obey their parents, fathers not to embitter their children, slaves to obey their masters, and masters to be fair with their slaves (3:18–4:1).

Paul concludes by asking for prayer that he may preach this message effectively and clearly and that they would live wisely toward outsiders (4:2–6). He sends greetings from his co-workers in the gospel (vv. 7–15) and asks them to exchange letters with the Laodiceans and exhort Archippus to complete his ministry (4:16–18).

How to Respond to Critics

Colossians 1:18—*If Christ is only the firstborn in creation, how can he be God?*

Problem: John declared Christ to be eternal and equal with God (John 1:1; 8:58; 20:28), but here Paul seems to say that Christ was only a creature, the first one born (created) in the universe.

Solution: Clearly Paul declares Christ to be God in this very letter by saying he "created all things" (1:16) and has "the fullness of the Godhead" (2:9). The reference to "firstborn" does not mean he is the firstborn *in* creation but the firstborn *over* creation (v. 15), since "He is before all things" (v. 17). "Firstborn" in this context does not mean the first one to be born but the heir of all, the Creator and owner of all things. It refers to his priority over creation, not his temporality in it. As Creator of "all things," he could not have been a created thing.

Colossians 1:20—*Does this verse teach that all will be saved (universalism)?*

Problem: The apostle Paul wrote to the Colossians, "For it was the Father's good pleasure . . . *through Him [Christ] to reconcile all things to Himself,* having made peace through the blood of His cross; through Him, I say, whether things on earth or things in heaven" (Col. 1:19–20 NASB). If Paul says that all things are reconciled to Christ by his death and resurrection, this seems to imply that all people are saved. But other Scriptures declare that many will be lost (for example, Matt. 7:13–14; 25:41; Rev. 20:11–15).

Solution: First of all, Paul is not speaking about universal *salvation* here but simply the universal *sovereignty* of Jesus Christ. In other words, all authority has been given to Jesus Christ in heaven and on earth (Matt. 28:18). By virtue of his death and resurrection, Christ, as the last Adam, is Lord over all that was lost by the first Adam (see 1 Cor. 15:45–49).

Note the contrast between two crucial passages by Paul:

Ephesians/Colossians	Philippians
All are in Christ	All bow before Christ
All in:	All in:
heaven	heaven
earth	earth
–	under the earth
All in salvation	All in subjection

When Paul speaks in Colossians of being "in Christ" (being saved), he does not include "those under the earth" (the lost). However, all persons, saved and unsaved, will one day bow before Christ and acknowledge his universal lordship. But nowhere do the Scriptures teach that all people will be saved. Jesus will say to many, "Depart from Me, you cursed, into the everlasting fire prepared for the devil and his angels" (Matt. 25:41). John spoke of the devil, the beast, and the false prophet and all whose names are not written in the Book of Life being cast into the lake of fire forever (Rev. 20:10–15). Luke speaks of a great impassible gulf between heaven and hell in which those who have rejected God are living in torment (Luke 16:19–31). Paul speaks of punishment of the wicked as "everlasting destruction from the presence of the Lord" (2 Thess. 1:9). Jesus declared Judas was lost and called him "the son of perdition" (John 17:12). It is evident from all these passages that not everyone will be saved.

Colossians 1:24—*How can Christ's death on the cross be sufficient for salvation when Paul speaks of what is lacking in the sufferings of Christ?*

Problem: The Bible declares that Jesus's death on the cross was both sufficient and final for our salvation (John 19:30, Heb. 1:3). Yet Paul states that he is filling up "what is lacking in the afflictions of Christ." But if the cross is all-sufficient, how can anything be lacking in Christ's suffering for us?

Solution: Christ's death on the cross is sufficient for our salvation. The Bible makes this emphatically clear. Anticipating the cross, Jesus said to his Father, "I have finished the work which You have given Me to do" (John 17:4). On the cross he cried out, "It is finished!" (19:30). The book of Hebrews declares unequivocally that "by one offering [on the cross] He has perfected forever those who are being sanctified" (Heb. 10:14). And this he did "by Himself" (1:3) with no help from anyone else.

Nevertheless, there is a sense in which Christ still suffers after his death. Jesus said to Paul, "Why are you persecuting Me?" (Acts 9:4). In this sense, we too can suffer for him, since "it has been granted on behalf of Christ, not only to believe in Him, but also to suffer for His sake" (Phil. 1:29). But in no sense is our suffering for Christ a means of atoning for sin. Only Jesus suffered *for* sin. We suffer *because* of sin (ours and others), but never for sin. Each of us must bear the guilt of our own sin (Ezek. 18:20) and accept the fact that Christ suffered for our sin (2 Cor. 5:21; 1 Peter 2:21; 3:18). When we suffer for Christ, we are undergoing pain as part of his spiritual body, the church, but only what Christ suffered in his physical body on the cross is efficacious for our sins. Our suffering, then, is in *service* not for *salvation*.

Philemon

Who Wrote It?

Paul, the imprisoned apostle, wrote Philemon.

Internal Evidence
Several lines of evidence strongly support a Pauline authorship: (1) there are repeated claims in the book (vv. 1, 9, 19); (2) the doctrinal content of the book is Paul's; (3) the chronology of the book is Pauline; and (4) the companions are those of the apostle Paul (vv. 1, 10, 23).

External Evidence
The outside evidence for Pauline authorship of this tiny book is also strong: (1) it is cited by a very early Father (in Ignatius's Epistle to the Ephesians); (2) was accepted by the later great Fathers, like Cyril of Jerusalem, Eusebius, Augustine, and Jerome; (3) was accepted by the Gnostic heretic Marcion; (4) the lack of citations in other works is due to its size and personal nature.

When Was It Written?

Philemon was written about AD 60, during Paul's first imprisonment (see Col. 4:8–9).

To Whom Was It Written?

The letter was written to Philemon, Apphia, Archippus, and the church in their house (Philem. 1–2).

Where Were the Readers Located?

The recipients of the letter lived in Colosse (see Col. 4:9), in Asia Minor.

Why Was It Written?

The reasons for writing Philemon are evident in the text. (1) Paul wished to entreat Philemon to reinstate Onesimus (v. 12); (2) he wanted to suggest his possible release from prison (v. 22); (3) he sought to persuade Philemon to request the services of Onesimus in the gospel (vv. 10–13); (4) he wanted to state the Christian view on slavery.

What Is It About?

The Theme: Benefaction in Christ.

The Key Verse: "That the sharing of your faith may become effective by the acknowledgment of every good thing which is in you in Christ Jesus" (v. 6).

Key Words and Phrases: *accept, receive, have back* (3x), *appeal* (2x), *grace, joy* (3x), *joy, benefit* (1x), *pay* (1x), *love* (3x), *owe* (1x), *slave* (1x), *unprofitable* (1x), and *willing* (1x). See appendix 3 for a more complete word study.

Value: Although small, this book is significant in many ways:

Personally: It shows the character of Paul and names ten other people.

Ethically: It reveals his balanced sensitivity to rights.

Providentially: It manifests the providential hand of God behind events.

Evangelistically: It encourages winning the lost to Christ.

Socially: It shows the relation of Christianity to slavery.

Spiritually: It is a beautiful picture of the gospel—intercession (v. 10), substitution (vv. 18–19), restoration (v. 15), and elevation (v. 16).

THE OUTLINE:

    I. Paul's Preamble (vv. 1–3)
    II. Paul's Praise (vv. 4–7)
    III. Paul's Plea (vv. 8–20)
    IV. Paul's Purpose (vv. 21–25)

THE CONTENTS: Paul begins by greeting Philemon, Apphia, Archippus, and the church in his house (vv. 1–3). He then praises them because of their faith, and informs them that they have brought him much joy (vv. 4–7). In the next section he begins a plea on behalf of Onesimus to Philemon and his household (vv. 8–12). He says that he wishes Onesimus could remain with him while he is in prison but thought it better for Philemon to consent to Onesimus's service (vv. 13–14). Paul informs Philemon that Onesimus is no longer a slave but a fellow brother in Christ (vv. 15–16). He informs Philemon that he will settle any debt on Onesimus's behalf, reminding Philemon that he owes Paul his very self (vv. 17–20). Paul expresses his confidence that Philemon will carry out his wishes concerning Onesimus and also will prepare a place for him in preparation for his next visit (vv. 21–22). He ends his letter with a final greeting (vv. 23–25).

How to Respond to Critics

Philemon 16—*Does Paul approve of the institution of slavery?*

Problem: The apostle Paul seems to favor the institution of human slavery by sending a runaway slave, Onesimus, back to his owner. Paul makes no outright condemnation of slavery. But slavery is unethical, a violation of the principles of human freedom and dignity.

Solution: Slavery is unethical and unbiblical, and neither Paul's actions nor his writings approve of this debasing form of treatment. In fact it was the application of biblical principles that ultimately led to the overthrow of slavery. Here Paul neither commends nor condones it; rather he undermines it and condemns it implicitly. Several important facts should be noted in this connection.

1. From the very beginning, God declared that all humans bear the image of God (Gen. 1:27). The apostle reaffirmed this, declaring, "We are the offspring of God" (Acts 17:29), and "He has made from one blood every nation of men to dwell on all the face of the earth" (v. 26).

2. In spite of the fact that slavery was countenanced in the Semitic cultures of the day, the law demanded that slaves eventually be set free (Exod. 21:2; Lev. 25:40–41). Likewise, servants had to be treated with respect (Exod. 21:20, 26).

3. God reminded Israel constantly that they had been slaves in Egypt (Deut. 5:15), and their emancipation became the model for the liberation of all slaves (see Lev. 25:40–41).

4. In the New Testament Paul declared that in Christianity "there is neither Jew nor Greek, there is neither slave nor free, there is neither male nor female; for you are all one in Christ Jesus" (Gal. 3:28). All social classes are broken down in Christ; we are all equal before God.

5. The New Testament explicitly forbids the evil system of this world that traded the "bodies and souls of men" (see Rev. 18:9–13). Slave trade is so repugnant to God that he pronounces his final judgment on the evil system that perpetrated it (Revelation 17–18).

6. When Paul urges: "Servants, be obedient to those who are your masters" (Eph. 6:5; see Col. 3:22), he is not thereby approving of the institution of slavery, but simply alluding to the *de facto* situation in his day. His purpose is to instruct servants or slaves to be good employees, just as believers should be today, but he was not thereby commending slavery. Slaves were commanded to obey their masters (Eph. 6:5), but nowhere does the Bible command anyone to have slaves, nor does it even encourage us to do so.

7. A closer look at Philemon reveals that Paul did not perpetuate slavery but actually undermined it, for he urged Philemon, Onesimus's owner, to treat him as "a beloved brother" (v. 16). So by emphasizing the inherent equality of all human beings, both by creation and redemption, the Bible laid down the very moral principles that were used to overthrow slavery and help restore the dignity and freedom of all persons of whatever color or ethnic group.

8. It was futile in a monarchy to try to overthrow politically the institution of slavery (half the Roman Empire were slaves). It was better to undermine it spiritually, which eventually happened, by applying Christian principles.

STUDY QUESTIONS

1. Who wrote Colossians?
2. Why did he write Colossians?
3. What was the nature of the heresy Paul addressed in Colossians?
4. Respond to critics who claim Paul did not write Colossians.
5. Why did Paul write Philemon?
6. What do Philemon and the rest of the Bible tell us about slavery?
7. What are the many values of this tiny Epistle?

SELECTED SOURCES

Baxter, Sidlow. *Explore the Book*. Grand Rapids: Zondervan, 1987.

Bruce, F. F. *Epistles to the Colossians, to Philemon, and to the Ephesians*. New International Commentary on the New Testament. Grand Rapids: Eerdmans, 1988.

———. *Paul, Apostle of the Heart Set Free*. Grand Rapids: Eerdmans, 2000.

Carson, D. A., Douglas Moo, and Leon Morris. *An Introduction to the New Testament*. Grand Rapids: Zondervan, 1992.

Conybeare, William, and J. S. Howson. *The Life and Epistles of St. Paul*. Grand Rapids: Eerdmans, 1953.

Garland, David. *Colossians, Philemon*. NIV Application Commentary. Grand Rapids: Zondervan, 1997.

Geisler, Norman L., and Thomas Howe. *When Critics Ask: A Popular Handbook on Bible Difficulties*. Grand Rapids: Baker, 1997.

Guthrie, Donald. *New Testament Introduction*. Downers Grove, IL: InterVarsity, 1990.

Harrison, Everett F. *An Introduction to the New Testament*. Grand Rapids: Eerdmans, 1971.

Hawthorne, Gerald F., Ralph P. Martin, and Daniel G. Reid, eds. *Dictionary of Paul and His Letters*. Downers Grove, IL: InterVarsity, 1993.

Linnemann, Eta. *Historical Criticism of the Bible*. Translated by Robert Yarborough. Grand Rapids: Kregel, 2001.

Longenecker, Richard. *Paul: Apostle of Liberty*. New York: Harper & Row, 1964.

MacArthur, John. *Colossians and Philemon*. MacArthur New Testament Commentary. Chicago: Moody, 1992.

O'Brien, Peter T. *Colossians, Philemon*. Word Biblical Commentary. Nashville: Thomas Nelson, 1987.

Radmacher, Earl, Ronald Allen, and H. Wayne House, eds. *Nelson's New Illustrated Bible Commentary*. Nashville: Thomas Nelson, 1999.

Ramsay, Sir William. *St. Paul the Traveller and the Roman Citizen*. New York: G. P. Putnam's Sons, 1896.

Walvoord, John F., and Roy B. Zuck, eds. *The Bible Knowledge Commentary*. 2 vols. Wheaton: Victor, 1983.

Wright, N. T. *The Epistles of Paul to the Colossians and to Philemon: An Introduction and Commentary*. Tyndale New Testament Commentary. Grand Rapids: Eerdmans, 1987.

17

1 Thessalonians

Who Wrote It? Paul, the apostle, wrote 1 Thessalonians (see the information on Paul in chapter 10).

Internal Evidence
Paul's authorship of 1 Thessalonians is supported by the claim, companions, character, chronology, and contents of the book. The claim that Paul is the author is stated twice in the book (1:1; 2:18). Also the persons with Paul, such as Silvanus (Silas) (1:1) and Timothy (1:1; 3:2, 6), are known companions of Paul. The fatherly compassion expressed (2:11) is characteristic of Paul. Further, the chronology of the book fits in with the life of Paul, as narrated in Acts 17:1–9. Finally, the content (doctrine) is Pauline with his emphasis on the return of Christ mentioned in every chapter. Even the conclusion, charging that it be "read to all the holy brethren" (5:27) fits with Paul's apostolic and missionary style (see Col. 4:16; 1 Tim. 4:13).

External Evidence
The earliest known copies of 1 Thessalonians bear Paul's name in the first verse. What is more, the early Church Fathers cited it as Scripture with Paul's name on it. These include Ignatius, Polycarp, the *Shepherd of Hermas*, and the Didache, followed by Irenaeus, Justin Martyr, Clement of Alexandria, Tertullian, Origen, Cyril of Jerusalem, Eusebius, Jerome, and St. Augustine. Even many modern critics accept it as Pauline.

Answering the Critics
Some modern critics (like F. C. Baur) deny Paul's authorship because 1 Thessalonians lacks doctrinal emphasis, it is devoid of originality,

and it contains an uncharacteristic outburst against Jews, which is not Pauline (2:14–16). However, these are insufficient arguments. (1) It does have a doctrinal emphasis (eschatology) in every chapter (1:10; 2:19; 3:13; 4:16; 5:23). Also Philemon is not doctrinal, but most critics accept it. (2) It is original in its stress on the rapture (4:16–17), and a book does not have to have new truths to be authentic (indeed some critics deny Pauline authorship *even when* there is new doctrinal content, a fault they find with Colossians). (3) Paul criticizes the Judaizers in Galatians (3:1, 17; 5:2; 6:12), which virtually all critics, including Baur, accept as authentic. Hence, Baur's arguments for rejecting Pauline authorship fall flat.

When Was It Written?

Paul wrote 1 Thessalonians in AD 50 or 51, during his stay in Corinth (Acts 17:1–9; 18:1; 19:1). With the possible exception of Galatians (AD 48?), 1 Thessalonians is the earliest letter of Paul. Its date can be pinpointed by the following facts. (1) An inscription in Delphi, Greece, dates the beginning of Gallio's office at ca. AD 52. (2) Paul was at Corinth eighteen months before this (Acts 18:1–11). (3) Paul came before Gallio, but it was after he was in Corinth (v. 12). (4) 1 Thessalonians was written after Timothy returned to Corinth from visiting Thessalonica, a city in Macedonia (1:1; Acts 18:5), near the start of the eighteen months. This would place it at about AD 50–51.

To Whom Was It Written?

This letter was written to young Thessalonian converts. Paul was in Thessalonica for only three weeks (Acts 17:2). There was a Jewish synagogue there where he "reasoned with them from the Scriptures." His converts also included proselytes, "devout Greeks, and not a few of the leading women" (Acts 17:4; see 16:14). Pagan idolaters were also converted and became part of the church there (1 Thess. 1:9–10; see Acts 14).

Where Were the Readers Located?

The readers lived in Thessalonica in Macedonia (in Europe), a city that was called the Mother of all Macedon (1:8). It was the chief seaport of Macedonia, being located on the Egnatian Way, the main road between the Orient and Rome. Thessalonica was built by Cassander (315 BC), king of Macedonia, who named it after his wife, Thessalonica, who was a half sister of Alexander the Great. It was a strategic location, both commercially and militarily.

Why Was It Written?

Paul had many reasons for writing 1 Thessalonians. First of all, he wished to commend their faith and encourage their continuance in it (1:2–10). He wanted to encourage and exhort them in spite of bereavement and persecution in view of Christ's coming (4:18; 5:2–11). Likewise, he intended to warn against immorality (4:1–8).

and laziness (vv. 10–12) in view of Christ's coming. Then, too, Paul wanted to answer slurs against his character cast by opponents (2:1–20). Finally, he wished to encourage them in the exercise of their spiritual gifts (5:19).

What Is It About?
The Theme: Expectation in Christ.

The Key Verse: "Remembering without ceasing your . . . hope [expectation] in our Lord Jesus Christ" (1:3).

Key Words and Phrases: *coming* (4x), *day of the Lord* (2x), *faith* (8x), *gospel* (6x), *hope* (4x), *(to) love, love* (8x), *spirit* (5x), *suffer previously*, *affliction* (4x), and *word* (9x). See appendix 3 for a more thorough word study.

Emphasis on Christ's Coming: Each chapter has a verse on the return of Christ (1:10; 2:19; 3:13; 4:16; 5:23). It is the only book to use the word *rapture* (meaning "catching away") of Christ's coming for his saints (4:17), though numerous other texts refer to the same event (for example, John 14:3; 1 Cor. 15:52; Phil. 3:20–21; 4:5; 1 John 3:2).

Old Testament Citations: There are no direct quotations from the Old Testament. The audience was mainly Gentile converts.

Other Characteristics: This Epistle has a practical emphasis. It is rare in that it has commendations without much criticism. They were an exemplary young church, which Paul set forth as an example to others (1:6–8).

THE OUTLINE:

    I. **Personal Commendation** (chaps. 1–3)
        A. An edifying hope (chaps. 1–2)
            1. Works faithfully (1:1–9)
            2. Waits patiently (v. 10)
            3. Walks worthily (2:1–16)
            4. Waits expectantly (vv. 17–20)
        B. An enduring hope (chap. 3)
            1. Withstands temptation (vv. 1–5)
            2. Withholds consternation (vv. 6–13)
    II. **Practical Exhortation** (chaps. 4–5)
        A. An edifying hope (chap. 4)
            1. Walks purely (vv. 1–12)
            2. Waits patiently (vv. 13–18)
        B. An escaping hope (chap. 5)
            1. Watches soberly (vv. 1–11)
            2. Works conscientiously (vv. 12–28)

THE CONTENTS: Paul's epistle to the Thessalonians divides into two major sections: the personal (chaps. 1–3) and the practical (chaps. 4–5). In the first section he gives them a commendation for their edifying hope (chaps. 1–2) that maintains the balance between working faithfully (1:1–9) and waiting patiently (v. 10) and that walks worthily (2:1–16) and yet waits expectantly (vv. 17–20). Then he speaks of an enduring hope (chap. 3) that withstands temptation (vv. 1–5) and withholds consternation (vv. 6–13).

The second half of the book (chaps. 4–5) gives an exhortation to an edifying hope (chap. 4) that walks purely (vv. 1–12) and waits patiently for Christ's return (vv. 13–18), and an escaping hope (chap. 5) that watches soberly (vv. 1–11) and works conscientiously (vv. 12–28) until Christ returns. This hope, of course, is in the rapture (4:13–18), which will deliver believers from the wrath to come during the tribulation period (5:9; see Rev. 3:10).

How to Respond to Critics

1 Thessalonians 4:13—*Did Paul teach the doctrine of soul sleep?*
Problem: Several times the Bible refers to the dead as being asleep. Does this mean that the soul is not conscious between death and resurrection?
Solution: The souls of both believers and unbelievers are conscious between death and the resurrection. Unbelievers are in conscious woe (see Matt. 25:41; Mark 9:47–48; Luke 16:23), and believers are in conscious bliss. "Sleep" is a reference to the body not the soul. Sleep is an appropriate figure of speech for death of the body, since death is temporary until the resurrection when the body will "awake."

The evidence that the soul (spirit) is conscious between death and resurrection is very strong: (1) Enoch was taken to be with God (Gen. 5:24; Heb. 11:5). (2) David spoke of bliss in God's presence after death (Ps. 16:10–11). (3) Elijah was taken up into heaven (2 Kings 2:1). (4) Moses and Elijah were conscious on the mount of transfiguration long after their time on earth (Matt. 17:3). (5) Jesus said he was going to the Father the day he died (Luke 23:46). (6) Jesus promised the repentant thief that he would be with him in paradise the very day he died (Luke 23:43). (7) Paul said it was far better to die and be with Christ (Phil. 1:23). (8) Paul affirmed that when we are "absent from the body," we are "present with the Lord" (2 Cor. 5:8). (9) The writer of Hebrews refers to heaven as a place where "the spirits of just men [are] made perfect" (Heb. 12:23). (10) The "souls" of those martyred during the tribulation were conscious in heaven, singing and praying to God (Rev. 6:9).

STUDY QUESTIONS

1. What is the internal and external evidence that Paul wrote 1 Thessalonians?

2. How do we answer the critics who deny Paul wrote 1 Thessalonians?

3. Why was Thessalonica such an important city?

4. For what purposes did Paul write this Epistle?

5. How is Christ's coming a comfort to believers (see 4:17)?

6. What other effects should Christ's coming have on our lives (see Titus 2:13; 2 Peter 3:11–12; 1 John 3:2)?

SELECTED SOURCES

Baxter, Sidlow. *Explore the Book*. Grand Rapids: Zondervan, 1987.

Bruce, F. F. *Paul, Apostle of the Heart Set Free*. Grand Rapids: Eerdmans, 2000.

Carson, D.A., Douglas Moo, and Leon Morris. *An Introduction to the New Testament*. Grand Rapids: Zondervan, 1992.

Conybeare, William, and J. S. Howson. *The Life and Epistles of St. Paul*. Grand Rapids: Eerdmans, 1953.

Geisler, Norman L., and Thomas Howe. *When Critics Ask: A Popular Handbook on Bible Difficulties*. Grand Rapids: Baker, 1997.

Guthrie, Donald. *New Testament Introduction*. Downers Grove, IL: InterVarsity, 1990.

Harrison, Everett F. *An Introduction to the New Testament*. Grand Rapids: Eerdmans, 1971.

Hawthorne, Gerald F., Ralph P. Martin, and Daniel G. Reid, eds. *Dictionary of Paul and His Letters*. Downers Grove, IL: InterVarsity, 1993.

Holmes, Michael. *1 & 2 Thessalonians*. NIV Application Commentary. Grand Rapids: Zondervan, 1998.

Linnemann, Eta. *Historical Criticism of the Bible* Translated by Robert Yarborough. Grand Rapids: Kregel, 2001.

Longenecker, Richard. *Paul: Apostle of Liberty*. New York: Harper & Row, 1964.

Marshall, I. Howard. *1 and 2 Thessalonians*. New Century Bible Commentary. Grand Rapids: Eerdmans, 1983.

Morris, Leon. *The First and Second Epistle to the Thessalonians*. New International Commentary on the New Testament. Grand Rapids: Eerdmans, 1994.

Radmacher, Earl, Ronald Allen, and H. Wayne House, eds. *Nelson's New Illustrated Bible Commentary*. Nashville: Thomas Nelson, 1999.

Ramsay, Sir William. *St. Paul the Traveller and the Roman Citizen*. New York: G. P. Putnam's Sons, 1896.

Ryrie, Charles. *First and Second Thessalonians*. Everyman's Bible Commentary Series. Chicago: Moody, 2001.

Walvoord, John F., and Roy B. Zuck, eds. *The Bible Knowledge Commentary*. 2 vols. Wheaton: Victor, 1983.

18

2 Thessalonians

Paul the apostle wrote 2 Thessalonians.

Internal Evidence
This Epistle claims to be written by Paul along with Silvanus (Silas) and Timothy (1:1). Indeed, it ends with "the salutation of Paul" (3:17). The greeting of "grace to you and peace" is Pauline (1:2). Likewise, the character of the book is Pauline, with a typical commendation of the congregation at the beginning (v. 3). In addition, the contents reflect the thought of Paul with his emphasis on the coming of Christ (1:7–10; 2:1), as in his first epistle (see chapter 17), and the condition of the church to whom Paul is writing is like that of the recipient of his first epistle (see 2:1–17).

External Evidence
The earliest manuscripts of 2 Thessalonians bear the name of Paul. Indeed, they contain the apostle's "trademark" salutation: "The salutation of Paul with my own hand, which is a sign in every epistle; so I write" (3:17). It is inconceivable that the early church would have accepted such a book if it were not Pauline. Likewise, the early Fathers accepted it as from the hand of the apostle, including Polycarp, Irenaeus, Justin Martyr, Clement of Alexandria, Tertullian, Origen, Cyril of Jerusalem, Eusebius, and St. Augustine. In addition, both the Muratorian canon and even Marcion's truncated canon contain 2 Thessalonians.

Answering the Critics
Some modern critics argue for several reasons that Paul did not write 2 Thessalonians.

1. They insist that Paul would not have written two letters so similar in such a short time. But the parallels are only about a third of the book and are easily explained by the repetition made for the sake of emphasis in this new context.

2. Some critics claim also that there are two conflicting views of Christ's coming. In 2 Thessalonians it is with signs, while in 1 Thessalonians it is without signs. However, this is not a contradiction, since these describe two different aspects of his coming; first *for* his saints (which is without signs) and later *with* his saints (which has signs).

3. Nowhere else does Paul speak of "the lawless one" (2 Thess. 2:8), considered the Antichrist. But this only shows that Paul had no other occasion to speak of this evil personage of the last times. However, the apostle John did speak of him in 1 John 2:18 and Revelation 13:1–18.

4. Some critics claim that the tone of 1 Thessalonians and 2 Thessalonians is too different to have the same author. But conditions can change quickly. In 2 Corinthians Paul has two different tones in one book (chaps. 1–9 and chaps. 10–13).

When Was It Written?

Second Thessalonians was written in AD 50, shortly after 1 Thessalonians (see chapter 17). There is the following evidence that the two Thessalonian Epistles were written close together: (1) Silvanus (Silas) and Timothy were still with Paul when he wrote the second letter (1:1), (2) 2 Thessalonians actually refers to 1 Thessalonians (2:15); (3) the condition of the church is similar, only more intense, when the second epistle is written; (4) the change that occasioned the second letter was the intervening development of a heresy (2:1–2; 3:6–15).

To Whom Was It Written?

The letter was written to a young church that was already undergoing suffering (1:4), was shaken by false reports (2:1–2), and had some believers who were slack saints (3:10).

Where Were the Readers Located?

The readers were located in Thessalonica, a city of Macedonia in Europe.

Why Was It Written?

At least three reasons are evident for the writing of this epistle: (1) Paul desired to comfort the afflicted saints (1:4); (2) he wished to correct the "alarmist" misunderstanding of Christ's imminent coming (2:1–2); (3) he purposed to condemn the apathetic misapplication of Christ's imminence (3:14).

What Is It About? The Theme: Glorification in Christ.

The Key Verse: "That the name of our Lord Jesus Christ may be glorified in you, and you [glorified] in Him" (1:12).

Key Words and Phrases: *coming of Jesus Christ* (3x), *everlasting destruction* (1x), *faith* (5x), *flaming fire* (1x), *glorify, glory* (4x), *God* (19x), *(to) love, love* (7x), *man of lawlessness* (1x), *mystery of lawlessness/iniquity* (1x), *son of perdition/destruction* (1x), *spirit* (3x), *truth* (3x). See appendix 3 for a more complete word study.

A Contrast with 1 Thessalonians

1 Thessalonians	2 Thessalonians
coming *for* saints	coming *with* saints
rapture (in air)	revelation (on earth)
nature of Christ's coming	time of Christ's coming
nurse's tenderness	father's discipline
commendation	condemnation
coming of Christ	coming of Antichrist

Length of the Epistle: Of all Paul's epistles, only Titus and Philemon are shorter.

The Outline:

    I. **Expectation in Adversities**—Revelation of Christ (chap. 1)
        A. Of coming kingdom (vv. 4–6)
        B. Of coming King (vv. 7–9)
        C. Of coming King's court (vv. 10–12)
    II. **Explanation to the Alarmist**—Revelation of Antichrist (chap. 2)
        A. Apostasy from the truth (vv. 1–12)
            1. Sudden (vv. 1–3)
            2. Satanic (vv. 4–8)
            3. Subtle (vv. 9–12)
        B. Authority of the truth (vv. 13–14)
        C. Attitude toward the truth (vv. 15–17)
    III. **Exhortation to the Apathetic**—Revelation to Christ-ones (chap. 3)
        A. To supplication (vv. 1–5)
        B. To separation (vv. 6–7)
        C. To service (vv. 8–15)
        D. The salutation (vv. 16–18)

THE CONTENTS: The contents of the book fall neatly into three categories corresponding to the three chapters. First, Paul speaks of expectation in their adversities (chap. 1). Then he offers an explanation to the alarmist who believed the end had already come (chap. 2). Finally, he gives an exhortation to the apathetic (chap. 3). In his first section (chap. 1), he tells them of the coming kingdom (vv. 4–6), the coming King (vv. 7–9), and the coming King's court of believers (vv. 10–12). In the second section (chap. 2), Paul warns of apostasy from the truth, which will be sudden (vv. 1–3), satanic (vv. 4–8), and subtle (vv. 9–12). He then speaks of the authority of the truth (vv. 13–14) and their attitude toward the truth (vv. 15–17). In the last section (chap. 3), in view of Christ's coming, he exhorts the apathetic members who were idle to supplication to God (vv. 1–5), to separation from evil (vv. 6–7), and to service for Christ (vv. 8–15). He ends with his final salutation to believers (vv. 16–18).

How to Respond to Critics

2 Thessalonians 1:9—*Will the wicked be annihilated or suffer conscious punishment forever?*

Problem: In some passages of Scripture, like this one, we read of the wicked being destroyed by God, suffering "the second death" (Rev. 20:14), or going to "perdition" (2 Peter 3:7). Yet in other places, Scripture speaks of their suffering conscious torment (for example, Luke 16:22–28). Will unsaved persons be annihilated, or will they suffer consciously forever?

Solution: "Destruction" does not mean annihilation here, otherwise it would not be "everlasting" destruction. Annihilation takes only an instant, and it is over. If someone undergoes everlasting destruction, they have to have everlasting existence.

Furthermore, "death" does not mean annihilation, but separation. Adam and Eve died spiritually the moment they sinned, yet they still existed and could hear God's voice (Gen. 2:17; 3:10). Likewise, before a person is saved, he or she is "dead in trespasses and sins" (Eph. 2:1), and yet that person is still in God's image (Gen. 1:27; 9:6; James 3:9) and is called on to believe (Acts 16:31), to repent (17:30), and be saved.

Likewise, when the wicked are said to go into "perdition" (2 Peter 3:7), and Judas is called the "son of perdition" (John 17:12), it does not mean they will be annihilated. The word *perdition* (*apōleia*) simply means to perish or to come to ruin. But junk cars have perished in the sense of having been ruined, but they are still cars, ruined as they may be, and they are still in the junkyard. In this connection, Jesus spoke of hell as a junkyard or dump where the fire would not cease and where a person's resurrected body would not be consumed (see Mark 9:47–48).

Finally, there are several lines of evidence that support the everlasting consciousness of the lost:

1. The rich man who died and went to hell was in conscious torment (Luke 16:22–28), and there is absolutely no indication in the text that it was ever going to cease.

2. Jesus spoke repeatedly of hell as a place of "weeping and gnashing of teeth" (Matt. 8:12; 22:13; 24:51; 25:30), which indicates the persons were conscious.

3. Hell is said to be of the same duration as heaven, namely, everlasting (Matt. 25:41).

4. The fact that their punishment is everlasting indicates that they too must be everlasting. A person cannot suffer punishment, unless he or she exists.

5. The beast and the false prophet were thrown "alive" into the lake of fire at the beginning of the one thousand years (Rev. 19:20), and they were still there, conscious and alive, after the one thousand years (20:10).

6. The Scriptures affirm that the devil, the beast, and the false prophet "will be tormented day and night forever and ever" (Rev. 20:10). But there is no way to experience torment forever and ever without being conscious forever and ever.

7. Jesus repeatedly referred to hell as a place where "the fire is not quenched" (Mark 9:48), where the very bodies of the wicked will never die (see Luke 12:4–5). It would make no sense to have everlasting flames and bodies without any souls in them to experience the torment.

8. The same word used to describe the wicked perishing in the Old Testament (*abad*) is used to describe the righteous perishing (see Isa. 57:1; Mic. 7:2). The same word is used to describe things that are merely lost and then later found (Deut. 22:3), which proves that "lost" does not here mean to go out of existence. If *perish* means to be annihilated, the saved would have to be annihilated too. But we know they are not.

9. It would be contrary to the created nature of human beings to annihilate them, since they are made in God's image and likeness (Gen. 1:27), which is everlasting. For God to annihilate his image in man would be to attack the reflection of himself.

10. Annihilation would be demeaning both to the love of God and to the nature of human beings as free moral creatures.

It would be as if God said to them, "I will allow you to be free only if you do what I say! If you don't, then I will snuff out your very freedom and existence!" This would be like a father telling his son he wanted him to be a doctor, and, when the son chose instead to be a park ranger, the father shot him! Eternal suffering is an eternal testimony to the freedom and dignity of humans, even unrepentant humans.

2 Thessalonians 2:7—*How should we interpret the "restrainer"?*
Problem: Paul wrote: "For the mystery of lawlessness is already at work; only He who now restrains will do so until He is taken out of the way." Who is Paul talking about?
Solution: There are four views of who is restraining this Antichrist of the last days: the Roman Emperor, the principle of government (law and order), the Holy Spirit, or the Christian church indwelt by the Holy Spirit.

View 1 is eliminated because the Holy Spirit is the only person with sufficient power to restrain the ultimate embodiment of evil known as the Antichrist, who will perform lying signs so as to deceive many (2:9). The principle of government cannot be the restrainer, because "He" is used, and "He" is a person not a thing (or principle). Finally, the last two views are not mutually exclusive since the Spirit indwells the church (1 Cor. 3:16–17). Hence, whether indirectly (through the church) or directly, it would seem that in some sense the restraining influence of the Holy Spirit will be taken away to make possible the unrestrained evil of the Antichrist to come during the tribulation period.

STUDY QUESTIONS

1. What is the internal and external evidence that Paul wrote 2 Thessalonians?

2. What were the purposes for which he wrote it?

3. What response can be made to the critics who deny Paul's authorship?

4. Explain the difference between Christ coming *for* his saints and Christ coming *with* his saints as presented in 1 and 2 Thessalonians.

5. Who is the "restrainer" mentioned in 2 Thessalonians 2:7? Give reasons for your answer.

SELECTED SOURCES

Baxter, Sidlow. *Explore the Book*. Grand Rapids: Zondervan, 1987.

Bruce, F. F. *Paul, Apostle of the Heart Set Free*. Grand Rapids: Eerdmans, 2000.

Carson, D. A., Douglas Moo, and Leon Morris. *An Introduction to the New Testament*. Grand Rapids: Zondervan, 1992.

Conybeare, William, and J. S. Howson. *The Life and Epistles of St. Paul*. Grand Rapids: Eerdmans, 1953.

Geisler, Norman L., and Thomas Howe. *When Critics Ask: A Popular Handbook on Bible Difficulties*. Grand Rapids: Baker, 1997.

Guthrie, Donald. *New Testament Introduction*. Downers Grove, IL: InterVarsity, 1990.

Harrison, Everett F. *An Introduction to the New Testament*. Grand Rapids: Eerdmans, 1971.

Hawthorne, Gerald F., Ralph P. Martin, and Daniel G. Reid, eds. *Dictionary of Paul and His Letters*. Downers Grove, IL: InterVarsity, 1993.

Holmes, Michael. *1 & 2 Thessalonians*. NIV Application Commentary. Grand Rapids: Zondervan, 1998.

Linnemann, Eta. *Historical Criticism of the Bible*. Translated by Robert Yarborough. Grand Rapids: Kregel, 2001.

Longenecker, Richard. *Paul: Apostle of Liberty*. New York: Harper & Row, 1964.

Marshall, I. Howard. *1 and 2 Thessalonians*. New Century Bible Commentary. Grand Rapids: Eerdmans, 1983.

Morris, Leon. *The First and Second Epistle to the Thessalonians*. New International Commentary on the New Testament. Grand Rapids: Eerdmans, 1994.

Radmacher, Earl, Ronald Allen, and H. Wayne House, eds. *Nelson's New Illustrated Bible Commentary*. Nashville: Thomas Nelson, 1999.

Ramsay, Sir William. *St. Paul the Traveller and the Roman Citizen*. New York: G. P. Putnam's Sons, 1896.

Ryrie, Charles. *First and Second Thessalonians*. Everyman's Bible Commentary Series. Chicago: Moody, 2001.

Walvoord, John F., and Roy B. Zuck, eds. *The Bible Knowledge Commentary*. 2 vols. Wheaton: Victor, 1983.

19
1 Timothy

The letter of 1 Timothy was written by Paul, the aged apostle (see information about Paul in chapter 10).

Internal Evidence
This book claims to be written by Paul (1:1). Further, it mentions Paul's known companion twice (1:2; 6:20). What is more, the character of the polemical nature of the book is Pauline (compare Galatians and Colossians). Finally, the doctrinal content is Pauline, with its stress on sound doctrine (1:10).

External Evidence
This book was accepted in early biblical lists as Paul's (for example, in the Muratorian canon). Also, the earliest known manuscripts have Paul's name on them (1:1). What is more, it was cited by the earliest Fathers (for example, Clement of Rome, Ignatius, Polycarp, Irenaeus, Tertullian, Clement of Alexander). It is also cited by the *Shepherd of Hermas* and the Didache. Likewise, the great Fathers to follow accepted the book with Paul's name on it as genuine, including Origen, Cyril of Jerusalem, Eusebius, Jerome, and St. Augustine.

Answering the Critics
Some modern critics have rejected the Pauline authorship of 1 Timothy. Two main arguments are set forth.
Fragmentary view. Some suggest that parts of the letter are Paul's (for example, 1 Tim. 1:13–15,18; 2 Tim. 1:4–5; 3:14–15; 4:6–8). These fragments are said to have been incorporated by a later writer into his own material.

Response. In response, defenders of Pauline authorship have argued, first, that the claim of authorship in 1:1 stands for the whole book and would be false if the whole book were not from Paul. Further, the book forms a literary unity so that there is no need to attribute parts of it to others. In addition, if the fragments had been known to be Pauline, the writer could not have pawned them off as his own. And if they were not known as Pauline, there would have been no advantage in using them.

Fictional view. Other critics argue that a later writer used Paul's name to counter evils of his day and strengthen the Christian community. This is evidenced, they say, by a different (later) historical setting (2 Tim. 4:13, 20), different vocabulary from Paul's other writing (131 new words, one-third of the book), different church organization (with bishops and elders), lack of emphasis on gifts and working of the Spirit, no emphasis on Christ's return, and a doctrinal outlook that is different. These are serious charges and will be answered in order.

Response. None of these objections is telling and each is answerable. Hence, the internal and external evidence for the Pauline view stands.

1. The different (later) historical setting is explained by Paul's release from prison (Phil. 1:19; Philem. 22) and reimprisonment (2 Tim. 4:6–8). Paul had a desire to go to Spain, and Rome was on the way there (Rom. 15:28). Clement of Rome said he went to the "limits of the west" (1 Clement 5).

2. As for new vocabulary: (a) The vocabulary fits the new topic. (b) The sample is too limited to be determinative of authorship.[1] (c) It begs the question by assuming the other epistles are Paul's style. (d) It overlooks the fact that Paul had different secretaries over the years. For example, Tertius helped with Romans (16:22), and Luke was with Paul when he wrote 2 Timothy (4:11). (e) Living authors express different styles in different books, depending on the topic and audience. One need only compare this author's *Philosophy of Religion* written for scholars and *Living Loud* penned for teens. (f) Paul himself used different vocabulary in a book the critics accept. For example, Galatians, which critics accept, has thirty-five new words in it.

3. The church organization is not different. Elders (bishops) and deacons are found in early Acts (6:1–8; 14:23) and in an earlier epistle—Philippians (1:1), so there were bishops and elders at that time.

4. Gifts of the Spirit are mentioned (1 Tim. 1:18; 4:14). But sign

gifts (2 Cor. 12:12; see 1 Cor. 14:22) may have ceased by that time, since they were needed by the apostles only to lay the foundation of the church (Eph. 2:19–20; see Acts 2, 10) and would die out with the apostles (Acts 1:22; 1 Cor. 9:1).

5. While Christ's return is not emphasized in Paul's Pastoral Epistles, it is mentioned. Titus is told to look for it expectantly (2:13). Paul looks forward to it in 2 Timothy 4:8 (see 2:12, 18) and exhorts believers in view of it in 1 Timothy 6:14–15. There are other possible allusions to it in 1 Timothy as well: 1:17; 3:9; 5:24–25; 6:7. It is understandable that it is not the chief emphasis here since Paul is concerned with church organization.

6. Finally, the doctrinal outlook in the Pastoral Epistles is Pauline. He stresses sound doctrine over and over (1 Tim. 1:3, 10; 4:6, 16; 6:3–4; 2 Tim. 1:13; 2:15; 3:10, 15–17; 4:2; Titus 1:9; 2:1). He writes of God, election (2 Tim. 1:8–10), sin (5:24; 2 Tim. 3:1–17), grace (Titus 2:11–13; 3:5–7), Christ (1 Tim. 3:16; 6:14–15), resurrection (2 Tim. 1:10; 2:18), and the second coming—all Pauline emphases.

When Was It Written?

Paul wrote 1 Timothy from Macedonia between AD 64 and 66, during his release between the first and second imprisonments.

To Whom Was It Written?

Paul wrote the letter to Timothy (1:2), his "son" in the faith. Timothy was Paul's personal representative (3:14–15). He was often Paul's companion (2 Cor. 1:1; Phil. 1:1; Col. 1:1; 1 Thess. 1:1; 2 Thess. 1:1). He had a Greek father and Jewish mother (Acts 16:1). His grandmother was Lois and his mother, Eunice (2 Tim. 1:5). He was converted through Paul at Lystra (Acts 16:1; see 14:8–18). He was young and timid (1 Tim. 4:12; 2 Tim. 1:6–7) and was often sick (5:23), yet he was one of Paul's most trusted associates.

This epistle was written to Timothy but it was about how some false teachers believed in myths (1:4; see Titus 1:13–14; 2 Peter 1:16). They stressed genealogies (1:4, 6–7; see Titus 3:9). They were Jewish (Titus 1:10–11), and their ascetic tendencies were manifest in self-denial of food and marriage (1 Tim. 4:1–3). They denied a future resurrection (2 Tim. 2:18; see 1 Tim. 1:20), taught antitheses (contradictions) between the Jewish and Christian revelations (1 Tim. 6:20–21), and engaged in endless and aimless disputes about words (2 Tim. 2:14; 3:9). They also denied Christ's humanity (see 1 Tim. 2:5; 1 John 4:1d).

While this seems to be an early incipient form of Gnosticism, it is not to be identified with the second-century Marcion type of Gnosticism because of the following. (1) Paul wrote before his martyrdom ca. AD 67. (2) Marcion was anti-Jewish and Paul was not, constantly showing that his teaching was in accord with the Old Testament (see Acts 17:1–4). (3) Marcion was wealthy; these men were seeking wealth. (4) Marcion's followers were upright in life; these men were evil. (5) Paul's pastoral books were so inimical to Marcion's views that Marcion rejected them.

Where Was Timothy Located? Timothy served the church at Ephesus (1:3), where Paul had preached for three years (Acts 20:31).

Why Was It Written? There are a number of reasons for writing 1 Timothy that can be inferred from the text. (1) Paul wanted to encourage Timothy to oppose false teachers (1:3–20). (2) He desired to furnish Timothy with written apostolic credentials of his authority. (3) He wished to exhort Timothy to diligence in the ministry of Christ (1:18; 6:13–14). (4) Paul wanted to instruct him in church conduct (2:8–15; 3:15).

What Is It About? The Theme: Faithfulness in Christ (1:14).

The Key Verse: "For there is one God and one Mediator between God and men, the Man Christ Jesus" (2:5).

Key Words and Phrases: *be merciful, mercy* (3x), *be sound, well, good* (6x), *doctrine* (8x), *faith* (19x), *faithful* (not in connection with *saying* [*logos*]) (8x), *faithful saying* (3x), *godliness* (8x), *man of God* (1x, in 6:11; see 2 Tim. 3:17), and *Savior* (3x). See appendix 3 for a more complete word study.

Comparing the Recipients of New Testament Books:

1. Written to individuals for churches—Luke, Acts, 1 Timothy, 2 Timothy, Titus, Philemon, 2 John, 3 John

2. Written to individual churches—Romans, 1 Corinthians, 2 Corinthians, Galatians, Philippians, Colossians, 1 Thessalonians, 2 Thessalonians

3. Written to a group of churches:

   a. Primarily Jewish—Matthew, Hebrews, James, 1 Peter, 2 Peter

   b. Primarily Gentile—Mark, John, Ephesians, 1 John, Jude, Revelation

Pastoral Epistles: First Timothy is the first of the so-called Pastoral Epistles, since it was written to a church leader, about leadership in a church.

Discipleship: Timothy is to Paul what Elisha was to Elijah ("my son," disciple).

Early Hymns (Creeds): This book contains possible early creeds in hymn form: compare 3:16; 6:15–16.

Ancient Ephesus viewed from the theater.

THE OUTLINE:

II. **The Minister** (chaps. 4–6)
    A. Pattern for the minister (4:1–5:2)
        1. Good teaching (4:1–6)
        2. Good training (vv. 7–11)
        3. Good testimony (4:12–5:2)
    B. Principles for the minister (5:3–6:2)
        1. Provision for widows (5:3–16)
        2. Precepts for elders (vv. 17–25)
        3. Precautions for servants (6:1–2)
    C. Practices of ministry (6:3–21)
        1. Godly contentment (vv. 3–10)
        2. Godly confession (vv. 11–16)
        3. Godly contributions (vv. 17–19)
        4. Godly commitment (vv. 20–21)

THE CONTENTS: This epistle falls neatly into two sections: the ministry (chaps. 1–3) and the minister (chaps. 4–6). In the first part Paul speaks about the ministry of the Word (chap. 1), the ministry of worship (chap. 2), and the ministry of workers (or leaders) (chap. 3). In the first section he offers cautions about the ministry (1:3–11), gives his confession about the ministry (vv. 12–17), and offers a charge about the ministry (vv.18–20). Then he speaks of the ministry of worship (chap. 2) in both supplication for all men (vv. 1–8) and in the submission of women to men in the ministry (vv. 9–15). After this he turns to the ministry of workers—elders and deacons (chap. 3). In this chapter he lays down the requirements for elders or bishops (vv. 1–7), the requirements for deacons (vv. 8–13), and finally the requirements for members (vv. 14–16).

In the next major section of the book, Paul addresses the minister (chaps. 4–6), giving the pattern for the minister (4:1–5:2), the principles for the minister (5:3–25), and practices of the ministry (6:3–21). The pattern for the minister includes good teaching (4:1–6), good training (vv. 7–11), and having a good testimony (4:12–5:2). The principles of ministry (5:3–25) include provision for widows (vv. 3–16), precepts for elders (vv. 17–25), and precautions for all servants of Christ (6:1–2). Finally, Paul addresses the practices of the ministry (vv. 3–21), which include godly contentment (vv. 3–10), a godly confession (vv. 11–16), godly contributions (vv. 17–19), and a godly commitment (vv. 20–21).

How to Respond to Critics

1 **Timothy 5:8** (see Matt. 6:19)—*Does this contradict Jesus's instruction about not storing treasures on earth?*
Problem: Jesus exhorted his disciples: "Do not lay up for yourselves treasures on earth." Luke added, "Give to everyone who asks of

you" (Luke 6:30). By contrast Paul affirmed, "If anyone does not provide for his own . . . he has denied the faith and is worse than an unbeliever." And Proverbs 13:22 claims: "A good man leaves an inheritance to his children's children." But how can we give all our treasure to God and others and still have an inheritance left for our family?

Solution: The Bible does not command us to give away *all* our money to God and others. The Old Testament laid down the tithe as the minimum all should give (see Mal. 3:8) and said that those who brought more offerings would be blessed proportionally (v. 10) (compare 1 Cor. 16:2; 2 Cor. 8:14–15). In addition to this, we should help those in need, especially our own family and other believers (1 Tim. 5:8).

In no way did Jesus intend that we should give away all that we possess. His advice to the rich young ruler to do so was a special case, since money had become an idol to this man (see Luke 18:22). Jesus encouraged prudence and economy and forbade making "treasures" our chief good. He encouraged us not to be unduly "anxious" about our earthly provisions (Matt. 6:25) or to hoard treasures selfishly for ourselves on earth (vv. 19–20). But in no way did he say we should not invest our money or plan for the future. Indeed, he told parables about investing our treasures (25:14–30) and about counting the cost before building a tower (Luke 14:28).

Neither is there any indication that the early believers ever took Jesus's statement (to give to those who ask) to the extreme of giving away everything they possessed. In spite of some misunderstood verses to the contrary (see Acts 2.44–45), the early church did not practice any abiding form of communism or socialism. Most of them apparently owned their own homes and/or other property. Otherwise, how could they have fulfilled the command to provide for their own and to leave an inheritance to their families? The prudent believer gives of his or her possessions first to God (see Matt. 6:19, 33), then to family and other believers (1 Tim. 5:8), and then, as much as is possible, to help the poor (Gal. 2:10).

1 Timothy 6:17–18—*Should wealth be avoided or retained?*
Problem: Jesus urged the rich young ruler to "sell what you have and give to the poor" (Matt. 19:21). The early disciples sold their possessions and laid the money at the apostles' feet (Acts 4:34–35). And Paul warned that "the love of money is a root of all kinds of evil" (1 Tim. 6:10). However, God blessed Abraham and Job with riches, and Paul does not instruct the rich to give away all they have, but to use and richly enjoy all that God has given (1 Tim. 6:17–18).

Solution: It should be observed, as noted above, that Jesus's instruction to "sell what you have and give to the poor" (Matt. 19:21) was to a rich young man who had made money his god, not to those who are not rich. There is nothing wrong with *possessing riches*, but there is something wrong with *being possessed by riches*.

Further, there is no indication that the early disciples in Acts were urged to sell all that they had or that they actually did it. The land sold (Acts 4:34–35) may have been extra property. It is noteworthy that it does not say they sold their homes (see 2:44–45).

Finally, Paul does not say that money is evil, but only that the *love* of money is the root of all kinds of evil. Seeking riches for their own sake is wrong, but seeking to have something to share with others in need is not. Thus, while God's Word says he "gives us richly all things to enjoy" (1 Tim. 6:17), in the same breath he warns against trusting in "uncertain riches."

STUDY QUESTIONS

1. What is the internal and external evidence that Paul wrote I Timothy?

2. How can the arguments of the critics against Paul's authorship be answered?

3. For what purposes did Paul write I Timothy?

4. Describe the heresy that Paul was encountering. How did it differ from second-century Gnosticism?

5. Why is this book called a Pastoral Epistle?

6. What was Paul's relationship to Timothy? What ministry role to Timothy did he serve?

SELECTED SOURCES

Baxter, Sidlow. *Explore the Book*. Grand Rapids: Zondervan, 1987.

Bruce, F. F. *Paul, Apostle of the Heart Set Free*. Grand Rapids: Eerdmans, 2000.

Carson, D. A., Douglas Moo, and Leon Morris. *An Introduction to the New Testament*. Grand Rapids: Zondervan, 1992.

Conybeare, William, and J. S. Howson. *The Life and Epistles of St. Paul*. Grand Rapids: Eerdmans, 1953.

Geisler, Norman L., and Thomas Howe. *When Critics Ask: A Popular Handbook on Bible Difficulties*. Grand Rapids: Baker, 1997.

Guthrie, Donald. *New Testament Introduction*. Downers Grove, IL: InterVarsity, 1990.

Harrison, Everett F. *An Introduction to the New Testament*. Grand Rapids: Eerdmans, 1971.

Hawthorne, Gerald F., Ralph P. Martin, and Daniel G. Reid, eds. *Dictionary of Paul and His Letters*. Downers Grove, IL: InterVarsity, 1993.

Knight III, George W. *Pastoral Epistles*. New International Greek Testament Commentary. Grand Rapids: Eerdmans, 1992.

Liefeld, Walter. *1 & 2 Timothy, Titus*. NIV Application Commentary. Grand Rapids: Zondervan, 1999.

Linnemann, Eta. *Historical Criticism of the Bible*. Translated by Robert Yarborough. Grand Rapids: Kregel, 2001.

Longenecker, Richard. *Paul: Apostle of Liberty*. New York: Harper & Row, 1964.

MacArthur, John. *First Timothy*. MacArthur New Testament Commentary. Chicago: Moody, 1995.

Marshall, I. Howard. *The Pastoral Epistles: A Critical and Exegetical Commentary*. International Critical Commentary. New York: T & T Clark, 2004.

Oden, Thomas C. *First and Second Timothy and Titus*. Interpretation: A Bible Commentary for Preaching and Teaching. Lousville: John Knox, 1989.

Radmacher, Earl, Ronald Allen, and H. Wayne House, eds. *Nelson's New Illustrated Bible Commentary*. Nashville: Thomas Nelson, 1999.

Ramsay, Sir William. *St. Paul the Traveller and the Roman Citizen*. New York: G. P. Putnam's Sons, 1896.

Walvoord, John F., and Roy B. Zuck, eds. *The Bible Knowledge Commentary*. 2 vols. Wheaton: Victor, 1983.

20
Titus

Who Wrote It?	Paul, the apostle, wrote Titus (1:1) (see introduction to 1 Timothy in chapter 19).
When Was It Written?	Paul wrote Titus around AD 64–66, between his two imprisonments and between the writing of 1 and 2 Timothy.
To Whom Was It Written?	The letter was written to Titus, Paul's representative on the island of Crete. Paul had two young companions—Timothy and Titus. Timothy was a half Jew who was circumcised (2 Tim. 1:5; 3:15) and was physically weak (1 Tim. 5:23). Titus was Greek. He was not circumcised (Gal. 2:3), and he was physically strong. His home was in Antioch. He too was a convert of Paul's (Titus 1:4). He was in Jerusalem with Paul (Gal. 2:3) and accompanied Paul on his third missionary journey (2 Cor. 8:23). He was dispatched to Corinth to solve problems (2:12–13). In this epistle he is sent to solve a difficult situation in Crete (Titus 1:5). The Cretan church may have resulted from converts at Pentecost (Acts 2:11).
Where Was He Located?	Titus was on the island of Crete in the eastern Mediterranean, whose inhabitants were largely pagan.
Why Was It Written?	A number of reasons for the letter are evident in the book of Titus. First, Paul wanted to instruct and encourage Titus (1:4). Further, he wished to inform him how to amend a defective church (vv. 5–16). Finally, he asked for support in sending Zenas the lawyer and Apollos, an eloquent speaker, to aid him (3:13).

What Is It About?   The Theme: Soundness in Christ.

Key Verse: "Therefore rebuke them sharply, that they may be sound in the faith" (1:13).

Key Words and Phrases: *be sound* (4x), *deed/work* (8x), *doctrine* (4x), *faithful* (3x), *God* (13x), *good deeds/works* (4x), *grace* (4x), *Jesus Christ* (4x), *Savior* (6x), *sensible* (3x), *truth* (2x), and *word* (5x). See appendix 3 for a more complete word study.

Nonbiblical Quotation: One of Paul's three extra-biblical citations is found here when he refers to the heathen poet Epimenides: "The Cretans are always liars" (1:12; see also Acts 17:28 and 1 Cor. 15:33). None of these are cited as from inspired sources with any formulas like "Thus said the Lord" or "It is written" or "the Scripture says." Rather, they are cited as a truth contained in a book, not a verification that everything in the book is true or that it is an inspired source.

Two Great "Grace" Texts: Two of the important grace passages in the New Testament are found in this small book (2:11–13; 3:5–7).

Good Works: Good works are always connected to grace in the New Testament (see Eph. 2:8–10). Titus speaks of the pattern of good works (2:7), having zeal in good works (v. 14), being ready to do good works (3:1), being careful to maintain good works (v. 8), and the necessary uses of good works (v. 14).

THE OUTLINE:

      I. Rule of a Sound Church—Ecclesiastical (chap. 1)
          A. Nature of the rule (vv. 5–9)
          B. Necessity of the rule (vv. 10–16)
      II. Rules for a Sound Church —Domestic (chap. 2)
          A. Precepts for sound doctrine (vv. 1–10)
          B. Power for sound living (vv. 11–15)
      III. Responsibility of a Sound Church—Social (chap. 3)
          A. Outward responsibility (vv. 1–7)
          B. Inward responsibility (vv. 8–15)

THE CONTENTS: Titus is divided into three sections by chapters: the ecclesiastical (chap. 1), the domestic (chap. 2), and the social (chap. 3). In the first section Paul lays down the God-appointed rule for the sound church in the leadership of elders, giving both its nature (1:5–9) and its necessity (vv. 10–16). In the second section he speaks of the rules for the church in sound doctrine (2:1–10) and sound living (vv. 11–15), rooted in the grace of God. In the final section he discusses the believer's responsibility socially, giving first their outward responsibility to civil government

(3:1–7) and then their inward responsibility to each other (vv. 8–15), urging them to avoid disputes and divisions.

How to Respond to Critics

Titus 1:12—*Doesn't Paul involve himself in a paradox or contradiction here?*

Problem: Paul quoted a Cretan who said, "Cretans are always liars," but if this was said by a Cretan and Cretans always lie, then he too was lying. But if this Cretan was lying when he said Cretans always lie, then Cretans do not always lie and there is a lie in the Scripture. If on the other hand this Cretan was telling the truth about Cretans, then Cretans do not always lie, at least not the one who said this. In either event, by incorporating this statement in Scripture, the apostle seems to have included a falsehood.

Solution: Paul seemed to be aware of this dilemma and quickly added, "This testimony is true" (v. 13). In other words, the Cretans generally lie, but at least on this one occasion a Cretan uttered the truth when he characterized the Cretans as liars. In this way the paradox is broken, and no falsehood is thereby included in Scripture.

Titus 3:10 (see 2 Timothy 2:24–25)—*Should the wayward be instructed or expelled from the church?*

Problem: This verse says we should "reject" the wayward, and in 1 Corinthians 5:5 the adulterous member was excommunicated. But in 2 Timothy 2:24–25 leaders are exhorted to instruct the wayward: "In humility correcting those who are in opposition, if God perhaps will grant them repentance."

Solution: The severity of the action of the church will depend on the *seriousness of the sin* of the member being disciplined. Those who are living in immorality should, after being exhorted to change, be excommunicated, since their sin has a leavening or contagious effect on others (1 Cor. 5:5–7). Even so, if they repent, they should be reinstated in the church (see 2 Cor. 2:6–7), since the primary purpose of discipline is not to reject but to reform.

The main difference in the severity of the discipline was in the *penitence of the person* being disciplined. If the person repented, he or she was to be reinstated. If not, then "after the first and second admonition" (Titus 3:10), the person was to be rejected.

STUDY QUESTIONS

1. What evidence is there internally and externally that Paul is the author of this book?

2. What were the reasons Titus was written?

3. How does Paul's companion Titus differ from Timothy, another companion?

4. What is the relation of works to grace as reflected in the two great grace passages in Titus?

5. Does the citation of a pagan source indicate that the source is inspired?

SELECTED SOURCES

Baxter, Sidlow. *Explore the Book*. Grand Rapids: Zondervan, 1987.

Bruce, F. F. *Paul, Apostle of the Heart Set Free*. Grand Rapids: Eerdmans, 2000.

Carson, D. A., Douglas Moo, and Leon Morris. *An Introduction to the New Testament*. Grand Rapids: Zondervan, 1992.

Conybeare, William, and J. S. Howson. *The Life and Epistles of St. Paul*. Grand Rapids: Eerdmans, 1953.

Geisler, Norman L., and Thomas Howe. *When Critics Ask: A Popular Handbook on Bible Difficulties*. Grand Rapids: Baker, 1997.

Guthrie, Donald. *New Testament Introduction*. Downers Grove, IL: InterVarsity, 1990.

Harrison, Everett F. *An Introduction to the New Testament*. Grand Rapids: Eerdmans, 1971.

Hawthorne, Gerald F., Ralph P. Martin, and Daniel G. Reid, eds. *Dictionary of Paul and His Letters*. Downers Grove, IL: InterVarsity, 1993.

Knight III, George W. *Pastoral Epistles*. New International Greek Testament Commentary. Grand Rapids: Eerdmans, 1992.

Liefeld, Walter. *1 & 2 Timothy, Titus*. NIV Application Commentary. Grand Rapids: Zondervan, 1999.

Linnemann, Eta. *Historical Criticism of the Bible*. Translated by Robert Yarborough. Grand Rapids: Kregel, 2001.

Longenecker, Richard. *Paul: Apostle of Liberty*. New York: Harper & Row, 1964.

MacArthur, John. *Titus*. MacArthur New Testament Commentary. Chicago: Moody, 1996.

Marshall, I. Howard. *The Pastoral Epistles: A Critical and Exegetical Commentary*. International Critical Commentary. New York: T & T Clark, 2004.

Oden, Thomas C. *First and Second Timothy and Titus*. Interpretation: A Bible Commentary for Preaching and Teaching. Lousville: John Knox, 1989.

Radmacher, Earl, Ronald Allen, and H. Wayne House, eds. *Nelson's New Illustrated Bible Commentary*. Nashville: Thomas Nelson, 1999.

Ramsay, Sir William. *St. Paul the Traveller and the Roman Citizen*. New York: G. P. Putnam's Sons, 1896.

Walvoord, John F., and Roy B. Zuck, eds. *The Bible Knowledge Commentary*. 2 vols. Wheaton: Victor, 1983.

21
2 Timothy

Paul, the departing apostle (1:1; see 4:6), wrote the epistle to Timothy. Luke may have served as secretary (4:11; see Rom. 16:22).

Internal Evidence

Despite some modern criticism, the evidence for Paul's authorship is strong. First, there is the clear claim of the book (1:1). Likewise, the companions mentioned—Mark and Luke—are Paul's (4:11–21). Also the content is Pauline, with its stress on sound doctrine and the Word of God (1:13; 2:15; 3:15–17; 4:2). The circumstances are clearly those of Paul, speaking of his imprisonment and imminent death (4:6–8).

External Evidence

External support for Paul's authorship is early and strong. The earliest known manuscripts bear his name. In addition, the early Fathers attribute it to Paul (Barnabas, Ignatius, *Shepherd of Hermas*, and Irenaeus). Also the great later Fathers, like Tertullian, Origen, Jerome, and Augustine, supported Pauline authorship. And the early Muratorian canon contained it. Finally, the objections of modern critics are based on specious arguments concerning alleged Pauline vocabulary (see the discussion of Paul's vocabulary in chapter 19).

When Was It Written?

The letter was written ca. AD 67, just before Paul's martyrdom under Nero, during his second Roman imprisonment (2 Tim. 1:16–17).

To Whom Was It Written?

The letter was written to Timothy, his "beloved son" (1:2), who was encountering false teaching (see 1 Timothy, chapter 19).

Where Was He Located?

Timothy was probably in Macedonia at this time (see 2 Tim. 1:15).

Paul's First Imprisonment (Acts 28)	Paul's Second Imprisonment
accused of heresy	accused of a crime
held in a hired house	held in prison
expected acquittal	expected death
several friends	few friends left

Why Was It Written?

Several purposes for writing this letter stand out. (1) Paul desired to express his concern that Timothy preserve sound doctrine as he faced false teachers (1:13–14). (2) He wished to emphasize the importance of the Word of God in the ministry of Christ. (3) Paul needed his cloak for the cold prison and his books and parchments for study and writing (4:13). (4) He expressed his desire for fellowship in his lonesome condition (vv. 16–18).

What Is It About?

The Theme: Steadfastness in Christ.

Key Verse: "Hold fast the pattern of sound words which . . . are in Christ Jesus" (1:13).

Key Words and Phrases: *abide, continue in* (3x), *avoid, shun* (2x), *be ashamed, unashamed* (4x), *be diligent* (3x), *be ready* (2x), *be sober/watchful* (1x), *be sound* (2x), *doctrine, teaching* (4x), *endure* (5x), *faith* (8x), *gospel* (3x), *laden with sin* (1x), *lover of God* (1x), *lover of pleasure* (1x), *lover of self* (1x), *persecution* (2x), *retain, hold, have* (6x), and *word* (7x). See appendix 3 for a more complete word study.

The Style: The style of writing is personal, abrupt, and charged.

Personal Names: There are some twenty-three names mentioned in this short book.

Timothy's Relatives: Timothy's grandmother, Lois, and his mother, Eunice, are mentioned (1:5). They were Jewish but his father was Greek (Acts 16:1).

Objects of Love in Paul's Epistles to Timothy:

- love of money (1 Tim. 6:10)
- love of evil (2 Tim. 3:2–4)
- lovers of self (v. 2)
- lovers of pleasure (v. 4)
- love of the world (4.10)

The Cure for Worldly Objects of Love: Love his [Christ's] appearing (4:8).

Characters in Chapter 2: son (v. 1), soldier (vv. 3–4), athlete (v. 5), farmer (v. 6), worker (v. 15), vessel (vv. 20–21), servant (v. 24).

Emphasis on the Word of God: Each chapter has an emphasis on the Word of God (1:13; 2:15; 3:14–17; 4:2).

THE OUTLINE:

> **I. Affliction in Ministry**—Hold Fast to Sound Words (chap. 1)
> > A. Tears in the ministry (vv. 3–7)
> > B. Testimony in the ministry (vv. 8–14)
> > C. Traitors to the ministry (vv. 15–18)
>
> **II. Activity in Ministry**—Be Diligent in the True Word (chap. 2)
> > A. Training—son (vv. 1–2)
> > B. Triumph—soldier (vv. 3–4)
> > C. Testing—athlete (v. 5)
> > D. Toil—farmer (v. 6)
> > E. Traits—servant (vv. 20–26)
>
> **III. Apostasy in Ministry**—Continue in the Holy Word (chap. 3)
> > A. "Times" of apostasy (vv. 1–9)
> > B. Trials and apostasy (vv. 10–13)
> > C. Triumph over apostasy (vv. 14–17)
>
> **IV. Allegiance in Ministry**—Preach the Only Word (chap. 4)
> > A. The task of ministry (vv. 1–4)
> > B. The true Judge of ministry (vv. 5–8)
> > C. The tragedy of ministry (vv. 9–18)

THE CONTENTS: The last epistle of Paul is centered around the Word of God. In the first chapter, he exhorts Timothy to hold fast to sound words because of affliction in the ministry. In the next chapter he speaks of being diligent in the true Word. In chapter 3, Paul encourages Timothy to continue in the Holy Word, and in the last chapter he urges him to preach the only Word.

The need to hold on to sound words (chap. 1) is because of affliction in the ministry. Here, after the introduction (vv. 1–2), he speaks of tears in the ministry (vv. 3–7), he says we should maintain the testimony of the Lord in the ministry (vv. 8–14), and he warns of the traitors to the ministry we will encounter (vv. 15–18).

In chapter 2 he speaks of activity in the ministry, using several images: training of the son (vv. 1–2), triumph of the soldier (vv. 3–4), testing of the athlete (v. 5), toil of the farmer (v. 6), and the traits of the servant (vv. 20–26). Chapter 3 speaks of apostasy in the ministry: its times (vv. 1–9), its trials (vv. 10–13), and triumph over it (vv. 14–17) through God's holy and inspired Word.

Finally, Paul signs off urging Timothy to have allegiance to the Word of God in his ministry. He speaks of the task of ministry (vv. 1–4), the true Judge of ministry (vv. 5–8), and the tragedy faced in the ministry (vv. 9–18) as he faces his imminent death.

How to Respond to Critics

2 Timothy 1:10 (see Rom. 5:12; Heb. 9:27)—*If Jesus abolished death, why do we still die?*

Problem: Paul affirms in this text that Christ "has abolished death and brought life and immortality to light through the gospel." But death is not abolished, since "death spread to all men" (Rom. 5:12), and "it is appointed for men to die once" (Heb. 9:27).

Solution: First of all, Christ did not abolish physical death *immediately*, but by his death and resurrection, it will be abolished *eventually*. Christ is the first one to experience resurrection in an immortal body (1 Cor. 15:20)—the rest of the human race will experience this later, at his second coming (vv. 50–56). Second, Christ abolished death *officially* when he personally defeated it by his resurrection. However, physical death will not be completely destroyed *actually* until he returns again and "death is swallowed up in victory" (v. 54). For Paul tells us: "The last enemy that will be destroyed is death" (v. 26).

2 Timothy 2:14, 23—*Is it wrong for Christians to argue about theological matters?*

Problem: Paul seemed to forbid theological arguments when he instructed Timothy "not to strive about words to no profit" and to "avoid foolish and ignorant disputes." On the other hand, Paul himself argued with the Jews in their synagogues (Acts 17:2, 17) and disputed with the philosophers on Mars Hill (vv. 18–23). Indeed, Jude exhorts us "to contend earnestly for the faith which was once for all delivered to the saints" (Jude 3).

Solution: A distinction must be made between the two senses of what it means to argue or to contend. *Arguing* is not necessarily wrong, but being *argumentative* is. We should *contend* for the faith, but we should not be *contentious* in so doing. Making an *earnest effort* to defend the faith is good (see Phil. 1:16–17; 1 Peter 3:15), but engaging in *fruitless quarrels* is not. Likewise, Paul did not oppose disputing about what words really mean in a given context— he simply opposed *mere semantic wrangling*.

2 Timothy 2:24–25 (see Mark 1:15)—*Is repentance a gift of God or an act of man?*

Problem: Paul writes here: "if God perhaps will grant them repentance, so that they may know the truth" (see Acts 5:31). Yet in other places, repentance is considered a person's own act. For example in Mark 1:15, Jesus calls on people to "Repent, and believe in the gospel." Paul tells us that God "commands all men everywhere to repent" (Acts 17:30). But repentance cannot be both an act of God and an act of the individual believer, can it?

Solution: There are two possible answers here, neither of which negates a person's God-given responsibility to exercise free choice. First, repentance could be an actual gift of God, but like other gifts, we must receive it to enjoy it. On this view, God offers the gift of repentance to eternal life to all who are willing. Those who are not willing do not get repentance. In this way, God is impartial in his offer, but man is still responsible to accept or reject the gift of repentance necessary for salvation. This fits with God's call on all men to repent (Acts 17:30; 20:20–21; 2 Peter 3:9).

A second view simply notes the two different senses in which repentance is used in these seemingly opposed verses. One set of verses is speaking of repentance as an *opportunity* and the other as an *act*. The former is simply a *disposition* given by God, leaving the actual *action* of repenting to human beings. The former is a God-given *provision*, while the latter is a manmade *decision*. This view can be summarized as follows:

Two Different Senses of Repentance

as a God-given opportunity	as a free human act
as a disposition from God	as an action of man
as a provision of God	as a decision of man

So understood, there is no contradiction in the diverse texts on repentance. Whichever interpretation is taken, one thing is certain, there is no verse saying God repents for us. Each free moral creature is responsible to repent for himself or herself. God gives the power (grace) to repent, but each free creature must decide to do it (see Rom. 2:4). The same can be said about whether faith is a gift of God or not.

STUDY QUESTIONS

1. What is the internal and external evidence that Paul wrote 2 Timothy?

2. What purposes did Paul have in mind for writing 2 Timothy?

3. How do the key words support the overall theme of the book?

4. When did Paul write this epistle, and how were the conditions different than when he was in prison the first time?

5. How does Paul's emphasis on the Word of God fit in with the theme of the book?

6. How do the characters used in chapter 2 enhance Paul's emphasis in this epistle?

SELECTED SOURCES

Baxter, Sidlow. *Explore the Book*. Grand Rapids: Zondervan, 1987.

Bruce, F. F. *Paul, Apostle of the Heart Set Free*. Grand Rapids: Eerdmans, 2000.

Carson, D. A., Douglas Moo, and Leon Morris. *An Introduction to the New Testament*. Grand Rapids: Zondervan, 1992.

Conybeare, William, and J. S. Howson. *The Life and Epistles of St. Paul*. Grand Rapids: Eerdmans, 1953.

Geisler, Norman L., and Thomas Howe. *When Critics Ask: A Popular Handbook on Bible Difficulties*. Grand Rapids: Baker, 1997.

Guthrie, Donald. *New Testament Introduction*. Downers Grove, IL: InterVarsity, 1990.

Harrison, Everett F. *An Introduction to the New Testament*. Grand Rapids: Eerdmans, 1971.

Hawthorne, Gerald F., Ralph P. Martin, and Daniel G. Reid, eds. *Dictionary of Paul and His Letters*. Downers Grove, IL: InterVarsity, 1993.

Knight III, George W. *Pastoral Epistles*. New International Greek Testament Commentary. Grand Rapids: Eerdmans, 1992.

Liefeld, Walter. *1 & 2 Timothy, Titus*. NIV Application Commentary. Grand Rapids: Zondervan, 1999.

Linnemann, Eta. *Historical Criticism of the Bible*. Translated by Robert Yarborough. Grand Rapids: Kregel, 2001.

Longenecker, Richard. *Paul: Apostle of Liberty*. New York: Harper & Row, 1964.

Marshall, I. Howard. *The Pastoral Epistles: A Critical and Exegetical Commentary*. International Critical Commentary. New York: T & T Clark, 2004.

Oden, Thomas C. *First and Second Timothy and Titus*. Interpretation: A Bible Commentary for Preaching and Teaching. Lousville: John Knox, 1989.

Radmacher, Earl, Ronald Allen, and H. Wayne House, eds. *Nelson's New Illustrated Bible Commentary*. Nashville: Thomas Nelson, 1999.

Ramsay, Sir William. *St. Paul the Traveller and the Roman Citizen*. New York: G. P. Putnam's Sons, 1896.

Walvoord, John F., and Roy B. Zuck, eds. *The Bible Knowledge Commentary*. 2 vols. Wheaton: Victor, 1983.

22
Hebrews

Introduction to the General Epistles

Hebrews is the first of the General Epistles. In contrast to the Pauline Epistles, which stress exposition in Christ, the General Epistles emphasize exhortation for Christ. Most of Paul's letters are more doctrinal, while the General Epistles are more practical. Also Paul's letters are generally earlier and the General Epistles later (with the possible exception of James). They may be dated as follows:

Decade	Paul's Epistles	Date	General Epistles
AD 40s	Galatians	48 (or 55)	James 47–48 (or 60–62)
AD 50s	1 Thessalonians	50–51	
	2 Thessalonians	50–51	
	1 Corinthians	55–56	
	Galatians	55 (or 48)	
	2 Corinthians	55–56	
	Romans	57	
AD 60s	Ephesians	60	
	Colossians	60	
	Philemon	60	James 60–62 (or 47–48)
	Philippians	61–62	
	1 Timothy	64–66	1 and 2 Peter (64, 66)
	Titus	64–66	Hebrews (64–69)
	2 Timothy	67	
			Jude (68–69)
AD 90s			1, 2, 3 John (90–95)
			Revelation (90–95)

| **Who Wrote Hebrews?** | The author is unstated and unknown. There are several possibilities. |

Internal Evidence

There are several possibilities as to who wrote Hebrews:

1. *Luke.* The evidence is: the polished Greek, his association with Timothy who is mentioned in 13:23, and the similarities with Paul's doctrine.
2. *Paul.* The evidence is: the Pauline doctrine, the early Fathers in the East attributed it to Paul, and the reference to Timothy (13:23), his trusted companion.
3. *Barnabas.* The evidence is: he was an associate of Timothy, some Fathers (for example, Tertullian) held this view, and he was a Levite (Acts 4:36), which fits with the emphasis in Hebrews.
4. *Apollos.* The evidence is: the style of Greek fits his training, the Old Testament quotes fit his emphasis, and its eloquence matches his oratorical skills (see Acts 18:24).
5. *Priscilla and Aquila.* Adolph Harnack held this view, but it lacks both positive internal and external evidence.

What Is Known about the Author?

Many things are known about the author of Hebrews: (1) He was not one of the twelve apostles (2:3–4). (2) He wrote before the destruction of Jerusalem (chaps. 7–8). (3) He was well versed in the Old Testament (ninety-eight citations). (4) He wrote in a more technical Greek than the other New Testament writers. (5) He was familiar with Platonic thought. (6) He emphasized Jesus's earthly ministry and high priestly ministry (chaps. 2, 7–10). (7) He was associated with Timothy (13:23). (8) He was in Italy when he wrote (v. 24). (9) He was known well enough to be accepted by the readers without mentioning his name.

Note: Paul, Luke, Apollos, and Barnabas all fit these characteristics, but Paul fits them best. However, those who reject Paul's authorship point out that many things are unlike Paul's other letters: his name is not given; the style is different; there is the common use of the name Jesus, the emphasis on Jesus's earthly ministry, and the stress on Jesus's high priestly ministry; all but one citation is from LXX; and greater warnings are given than Paul gave elsewhere. Those who support the Pauline authorship attempt to explain these by the special nature of the book, its message, and audience. They further note that doubts about Hebrews' canonicity in the West were overcome when they were convinced that it was the work of the apostle Paul. Origen's comment that only God knows for sure is apt.

External Evidence

Whoever the author was, the book was considered authentic from the time it was received by its first audience, who knew Paul's companion Timothy (see 13:23). It was cited in the first century by Clement of Rome. It is alluded to in *Shepherd of Hermas*. It was accepted by Irenaeus, Clement, Tertullian, Cyril of Jerusalem, Eusebius, Jerome, and Augustine. The West was slower to accept it because the author is not named and because the Montanist sect used chapter 6 to support their aberrant view that no second repentance is possible for those who slip away from the faith. But once the West was convinced of Hebrews' apostolic source, it was universally accepted. The many personal references (5:11–12; 6:10; 10:32–34; 12:4; 13:23–24) show the readers knew and accepted the author.

When Was It Written?

Hebrews was written between AD 64 and 69. There are several indicators in the book for its date. (1) It was in the "earlier days" of Christianity (10:32–34). (2) It was before AD 70 while the temple still stood (8:4; 9:9; 10:1). (3) It was while Timothy was still alive (13:23). (4) It was just before a time of impending doom for Judaism (8:13). This would place it before AD 70 and probably after Nero had ascended the throne and the persecution of Jews and Christians had begun.

To Whom Was It Written?

As the title indicates, the book is addressed to Hebrew Christians. Many were immature (5:12–14) and were encouraged to move on to maturity (6:1). Since they had given generously to others, they probably were not poor, as were the Jerusalem saints (v. 10). They had undoubtedly gone through persecution (10:32–34), and some were slipping back into Judaism (chaps. 7–10) and spiritual immaturity (6:11–12), particularly into the ritual of Judaism in place of the reality of Christ who fulfilled them.

Where Were They Located?

The recipients of the letter were probably Jewish Christians in the churches in the East, though there are several different views as to their geographical location. Some claim the letter was written to the churches in Jerusalem and the surrounding region because of references to the temple, priests, and Judaism and the extensive use of the Old Testament. However, the Jerusalem saints were poor, and these brethren were not, since they gave to others (6:10).

Others say it focuses on the converted priests (see Acts 6:7), but a broader group of "brethren" seem to be in view (3:1, 12; 10:19).

Still others have claimed they were really Gentiles, but this overlooks the title "Hebrews," the numerous Old Testament quotes, and the emphasis on Jewish ritual.

Inscription from Herod's Temple warning Gentiles not to enter the courts reserved for the Jews.

It is more likely that the letter was written from Rome to Jewish Christians in the churches in the East, as is indicated by the greetings sent from Italy (13:24), the reference to Timothy (v. 23), and its similarities to Colossians (see 2:11–19) in its references to circumcision, Sabbaths, new moons, shadow, Jewish ritual, and perfection in Christ (chaps. 6–10).

Why Was It Written?

Hebrews was written by a Hebrew Christian to Hebrew Christians to show the superiority of Christianity over Judaism. It was written to show how the Old Testament Levitical system was fulfilled in Christ, who is a priest forever after the order of Melchizedek (7:20–21). It was designed as a strong warning against the dangers of falling away from Christian perfection (5:12–6:1) back into Jewish legalism. Also the author wished to encourage the readers who had undergone persecution and suffering for their faith (10:32–34; 12:3–4).

What Is It About?

The Theme: Perfection (maturity) in Christ.

The Key Verse: "Therefore, leaving the discussion of the elementary principles of Christ, let us go on to perfection" (6:1).

Key Words and Phrases: *age, world, eternal, forever* (21x), *angels* (13x), *better* (13x), *covenant* (17x), *faith, faithful* (37x), *God* (68x), *great (greater)* (6x), *high priest, priest, priesthood* (34x), *Jesus* (13x), *many, all the more* (7x), *once, once for all* (11x), *perfect* (9x), *salvation* (7x), *sin* (25x), and *son* (24x). These key words summarize the message of the book, namely, since Christ is better than the Old

Testament, having offered a once-for-all sacrifice, let us move on to perfection in him. See appendix 3 for a more complete word study.

Three Key Word Studies:

Better—Christ is better than the angels (1:4), has given us better things (6:9; 11:40), is symbolized by a better person (7:7), offers a better hope (v. 19), has a better covenant (v. 22; 8:6a), with better promises (v. 6b), offered a better sacrifice (9:23), gives us a better possession (10:34), a better country (11:16), a better resurrection (v. 35), based on the shedding of better blood (12:24)—the blood of the spotless Lamb of God.

Eternal—Christianity also provides an eternal salvation (5:9); warns of eternal judgment (6:2) for those who reject it; gives eternal redemption (9:12) to those who accept it, which is applied by his eternal Spirit (v. 14); gives to us an eternal inheritance (v. 15), which comes through an eternal covenant (13:20).

Once (for all)—The finality of Christianity is summed up in one phrase: "once for all." Regarding "once (for all)" salvation, Hebrews says: We were, once for all, enlightened to it (6:4). Jesus entered, once for all, into the holy place to obtain it (9:12). He, once for all, put away our sins (v. 26). We will face, once for all, judgment without it (v. 27). He offered himself, once for all, to bear our sins (v. 28). He purged our sins, once for all, by it (10:2). He offered his body, once for all, for our sins (v. 10).

The Finality of Christianity: No book in the New Testament, including Romans, stresses the superiority and finality of Christianity better than Hebrews.

Use of the Old Testament: There are some ninety-eight–plus Old Testament citations (all from the Septuagint or Greek translation of the Old Testament, except 10:30).

Names for Christ: Jesus, Christ, and Lord are used sixty-eight times, as opposed to Lord Jesus Christ, which is used often in the Pauline Epistles.

The Outline:

    I. Doctrinal—Christ is better than anything else
      (chaps. 1–10)
        A. Prophets (1:1–3)
        B. Angels (1:4–2:18)—peril of drifting (2:1–4)
        C. Moses (chap. 3)—peril of doubting (3:7–19)
        D. Joshua (4:1–13)
        E. Levitical priests (4:14–7:28)—peril of dullness
          (5:11–14); peril of departing (6:1–20)

THE CONTENTS: Hebrews is divided into two sections: the doctrinal (chaps. 1–10) and the practical (chaps. 11–13). In the first section Christ is demonstrated to be better than the prophets (1:1–3), angels (1:4–2:18), Moses (chap. 3), Joshua (4:1–13), Levitical priests (4:14–7:28), the tabernacle (8:1–5), the Old Covenant (8:6–9:22), and Levitical sacrifices (9:23–10:39).

As the superiority and finality of Christ is progressively presented, the readers are warned with increasing intensity about the perils of drifting (2:1–4), doubting (3:7–19), dullness (5:11–14), departing (6:1–20), despising (10:26–39), and denying (12:18–29). Each passage comes after a new revelation and each becomes more intense as the revelations about the superiority of Christ progress.

The final section is practical (chaps. 11–13). It stresses the three great Christian virtues: faith (chap. 11), hope (chap. 12), and love (13:1–17). Faith is the soul looking upward to God, hope is looking forward to the future, and love is looking outward to others.

Before signing off with grace to them all, he gives instructions to remember (13:7), obey (v. 17), pray for (v. 18), and greet their leaders (v. 24).

How to Respond to Critics

Hebrews 2:10—*If Jesus was already perfect, how could he be made perfect through suffering?*

Problem: The Bible declares that Jesus was absolutely perfect and without sin, even in his human nature (2 Cor. 5:21; Heb. 4:15; 1 Peter 2:21–22; 3:18; 1 John 3:3). But according to this verse, Jesus was made "perfect through sufferings." And to be made perfect implies that he was not perfect to begin with, which is a contradiction.

Solution: Jesus was absolutely and unchangeably perfect in his divine nature. God is perfect (Matt. 5:48), and he cannot change (Mal. 3:6; Heb. 6:17–18). But Jesus was also human, and as such was subject to change, though without sin. For example, "Jesus increased in wisdom and stature" (Luke 2:52). If his knowledge as a man increased, then his experience also did. Thus "He learned obedience by the things which He suffered" (Heb. 5:8). In this sense he was "made perfect" in that he experienced the perfecting work of suffering in his own sinless life (see Job 23:10; Heb. 12:11; James 1:2–4). That is, he gained all the experiential benefits of suffering without sinning (Heb. 4:15). In this way he can be of real comfort and encouragement to those who suffer.

Hebrews 6:4–6 (see 10:26–31)—*Does this passage teach that it is possible for Christians to lose their salvation?*
Problem: Hebrews 6:4–6 seems to be written for Christians because it contains certain characteristics that would be true only of them, such as "partakers of the Holy Spirit" (v. 4). But it declares that if they fall away, it is impossible "to renew them again to repentance, since they crucify again for themselves the Son of God, and put Him to an open shame" (v. 6). Does this mean that Christians can lose their salvation?
Solution: There are two basic interpretations of this passage. Some take it to refer to believers and others to unbelievers.

Those who say this refers to unbelievers argue that all of these characteristics could belong to those who merely *profess* Christianity but who do not really *possess* the Holy Spirit. They note that they are not depicted in the normal ways of describing a true Christian, such as being "born again" (John 3:3), being "in Christ" (Eph. 1:3), or being "sealed" by the Holy Spirit (4:30). They point to Judas Iscariot as a classic example. He walked with the Lord, was sent out and commissioned by Jesus on missions having "power over unclean spirits, to cast them out, and to heal all kinds of sickness and all kinds of disease" (Matt. 10:1). However, Jesus, in his prayer in John's Gospel, spoke of Judas as "the son of perdition" (John 17:12).

There are several problems with taking this to refer to unbelievers, even for those who hold that a believer can lose his or her salvation (i.e., Wesleyan Arminians). First, the passage declares emphatically that "it is impossible . . . to renew them again to repentance" (Heb. 6:4–6), but no Wesleyans believe that, once a person has backslidden, it is impossible for him to be saved again. Further, while the description of their spiritual status differs from other ways of expressing it in the New Testament, some of the phrases are very difficult to take any other way than that the person was saved. For example: (1) those spoken of had experienced "repentance" (v. 6), which is the condition of salvation (Acts 17:30); (2) they were "enlightened, and have tasted the heavenly gift" (Heb. 6:4); (3) they were "partakers of the Holy Spirit" (v. 4); (4) they had "tasted the good word of God" (v. 5); and (5) they have tasted the "powers of the age to come" (v. 5).

Of course, if they were believers, then the question arises as to

Artist's impression of Jewish high priest.

their status after they had "fallen away" (v. 6). Here interpretations differ along theological lines. Classical Arminians argue that these people actually lose their salvation, but only for the sin of apostasy. However, the text indicates that they cannot be saved again, something even Wesleyan Arminians reject.

On the other hand, those who hold a Calvinistic point of view (such as the author) point to several facts. (1) The word for "fall away" (*parapiptō*) does not indicate a one-way action. Rather, it is the word for "drift," indicating that the status of the individuals is not hopeless. (2) The fact that it is "impossible" for them to repent again indicates the once-for-all nature of repentance. In other words, they don't need to repent again since they did it once and that is all

259

that is necessary for "eternal redemption" (9:12). (3) The text seems to indicate that there is no more need for "drifters" (backsliders) to repent again and get saved all over any more than there is for Christ to die again on the cross (6:6). (4) The writer of Hebrews calls those he is warning "beloved," a term hardly appropriate for unbelievers.[1]

Hebrews 8:1—*Is Jesus our priest or our sacrifice?*
Problem: Christ is presented here as the "High Priest" of believers (see 7:21). However, later Jesus is depicted as the "sacrifice" for our sins (9:26, 28; 10:10). Which is he?
Solution: Jesus is represented correctly by both figures. He is our priest in that he speaks to God on behalf of man. Yet he is our sacrifice, since he offered himself on the cross for our sins. He is the offerer and the offered, both sacrificer and sacrificed. "He offered up Himself" (7:27).

Hebrews 12:17—*Why couldn't Esau repent if he sought it with tears?*
Problem: The Bible informs us here that Esau "was rejected, for he found no place for repentance, though he sought it diligently with tears." But why wouldn't God accept his sincere repentance, when he commands all men everywhere to repent (Acts 17:30) and is patiently waiting for people to repent (2 Peter 3:9)?
Solution: There are two important things to observe about this passage. First, the statement "no place for repentance" may refer to his father's inability to change his mind about giving the inheritance to Jacob, and not to Esau's change of mind. At any rate, the circumstances did not afford Esau the opportunity to reverse the situation and get the blessing.

Second, tears are not a sure sign that a person has genuinely repented. One can have tears of regret and remorse that fall short of true repentance or change of mind (for example, Judas in Matt. 27:3).

Finally, this text is not talking about *spiritual blessing* (salvation), but *earthly blessing* (inheritance). God always honors the sincere repentance of sinners and grants them salvation (Acts 10:35; Heb. 11:6).

STUDY QUESTIONS

1. Who was the author of Hebrews?
2. What is the evidence for the dating of Hebrews?
3. To whom did the author write? Give reasons.
4. To whom are all the warnings given? What are the warnings about?
5. How do the warnings fit with the theme of the epistle?
6. In how many ways is Christ superior to the Old Testament?

SELECTED SOURCES

Baxter, Sidlow. *Explore the Book.* Grand Rapids: Zondervan, 1987.

Bruce, F. F. *Epistle to the Hebrews.* New International Commentary on the New Testament. Grand Rapids: Eerdmans, 1995.

Carson, D. A., Douglas Moo, and Leon Morris. *An Introduction to the New Testament.* Grand Rapids: Zondervan, 1992.

Ellingworth, Paul. *The Epistle to the Hebrews.* New International Greek Testament Commentary. Grand Rapids: Eerdmans, 1993.

Geisler, Norman L., and Thomas Howe. *When Critics Ask: A Popular Handbook on Bible Difficulties.* Grand Rapids: Baker, 1997.

Guthrie, Donald. *New Testament Introduction.* Downers Grove, IL: InterVarsity, 1990.

Guthrie, George. *Hebrews.* NIV Application Commentary. Grand Rapids: Zondervan, 1998.

Harrison, Everett F. *An Introduction to the New Testament.* Grand Rapids: Eerdmans, 1971.

Hughes, Philip. *A Commentary on the Epistle to the Hebrews.* Grand Rapids: Eerdmans, 1988.

Linnemann, Eta. *Historical Criticism of the Bible.* Translated by Robert Yarborough. Grand Rapids: Kregel, 2001.

MacArthur, John. *Hebrews.* MacArthur New Testament Commentary. Chicago: Moody, 1984.

Radmacher, Earl, Ronald Allen, and H. Wayne House, eds. *New Illustrated Bible Commentary.* Nashville: Thomas Nelson, 1999.

Walvoord, John F., and Roy B. Zuck, eds. *The Bible Knowledge Commentary.* 2 vols. Wheaton: Victor, 1983.

23
James

James, the brother of Jesus, an elder and pillar in the Jerusalem church, is the author of this letter.

Several persons are called James in the New Testament:

1. James the son of Zebedee (Mark 1:19), brother of John the apostle (4:21), who was martyred about AD 44 (Acts 12:2), before the book of James was written.

2. James the son of Alphaeus (Mark 3:18), who was not prominent enough to write an encyclical letter.

3. James the Less (Mark 15:40), who was well-known enough to write an encyclical letter.

4. James the father of Judas (Thaddaeus), an apostle (Luke 6:16; see Matt.10:3; John 14:22), but he was not prominent enough to write this General Epistle.

5. James, the (half-) brother of Jesus (Mark 6:3; Gal. 1:19) and brother of Jude (Jude 1). (a) James was an unbeliever before Jesus's resurrection (John 7:5). (b) Christ appeared to him after his resurrection, and James was converted (1 Cor. 15:7). (c) Later he received a visit from Paul (Gal. 1:18–19). (d) He was called "the Lord's brother" (v. 19). (e) He was a "pillar" in the Jerusalem church (2:9). (f) He presided at the Jerusalem council in Acts 15:13–19. (g) He agreed with Paul on justification (Acts 15) but urged him to respect the Jewish law (21:17–21). (h) Peter referred to him with deference (12:17). Hence, he is the only James in the New Testament who was prominent enough to write a General Epistle.

Internal Evidence

There is strong internal evidence that James the brother of Jesus is the author of the book of James. (1) He was commonly referred to in the New Testament as simply "James" (Gal. 2:9, 12; Acts 12:17; 15:13; 21:18). (2) He was the only one by that name with the authority to write the letter. (3) His style was very much like that of Jesus (for example, his figures of speech). (4) His content was like that of his brother Jesus (see below). (5) The letter has strong similarities to James's speech in Acts 15.[1] For example, the greeting in James 1:1 is similar to that in Acts 15:23 and is used nowhere else by a New Testament author; the word meaning "to visit" (1:27) appears in Acts 15:14; the word for "turning" sinners to God (5:20) appears in James's address in Acts 15:19; and a similar use of the "name" of the Lord is in James 2:7 and Acts 15:17.

External Evidence

There is good external support in the early church that James the brother of Jesus was the author of this book. The early church accepted it as coming from James. This included Clement of Rome, Ignatius, and the *Shepherd of Hermas*. Also the early Syrian Bible (*The Peshitta*) contained James, and later Fathers accepted it, including Origen, Eusebius, Cyril of Jerusalem, Athanasius, Jerome, and Augustine.

When Was It Written?

The book of James was written either in AD 47 to 48 or in AD 60 to 62.

The Early View

The early view (that James was written before Acts 15, between AD 47 and 48) argues that:

1. It is highly Jewish in nature (with references to the Old Testament, law, and synagogue [assembly]—2:2)

2. It reflects Christ's oral teachings before the Gospels were written.

3. The form of church government was not highly developed (5:14) as it was later.

4. James shows no awareness of the Acts 15 council (AD 49), which would have been relevant to his theme had it already occurred.

5. The book is totally silent on the non-Jewish church, which came later.

6. The author seems to be unaware of Paul's writings, and this implies a date before Paul wrote (see 2 Peter 3:15–16).

7. The economic conditions of the poor reflect an early date (5:1–6).

8. The stress on the freshness of Christ's coming (5:7–9) supports an early date.

The Late View

The late view (that James was written after Acts 15, between AD 60 and 62) argues that:

1. It was not written until after the Jewish dispersion (1:1; see Acts 18:2), which occurred after AD 50.

2. It was after Paul's teaching on justification (see 1:25; 2:21–22) with which James agreed (Acts 15) and as a possible correction to misinterpretation of it (AD 57+).

3. The ethical and exhortational emphasis fits a later date.

4. The other General Epistles were written later.

5. There is no mention of Christ's resurrection, which was an early emphasis (in Acts 2–13).

6. It was before AD 62 when James was martyred (see Josephus, Antiquities, 9.1).

7. Hence, it was written about AD 60 to 62.

To Whom Was It Written?

The letter is addressed to "the twelve tribes scattered abroad" (1:1). There are three views as to the identity of these twelve tribes:

1. **Unbelieving Jews.** *Response:* The recipients are believers (2:1). If it had been written to unbelievers, it would not have been accepted into the Christian canon, which it was.

2. **All Christians.** *Response:* "Tribe" and "Israel" are never used spiritually in the New Testament (see Matt. 19:28; Rom. 9:3–4), and in the Old Testament the terms are always used of the literal children of Abraham.

3. **Jews of the western dispersion** (Peter wrote to those of the eastern dispersion—1 Peter 1:1). This view fits with the literal meaning of the term *tribes*, with Peter's primary mission to Jewish believers (Gal. 2:7), and with the content of the book of James.

Where Were They Located?

The recipients of the letter were in Israel and perhaps the surrounding areas.

Why Was It Written?

Several reasons for writing James can be derived from the text. (1) He desired to comfort persecuted believers (1:5); (2) he wished to commend "pure religion" (v. 27); (3) he wanted to convict the mere "professors" of the faith who were not "doers" of the faith (2:14–26).

What Is It About? The Theme: Wisdom in Christ.
The Key Verse: "If any of you lacks wisdom, let him ask of God, who gives to all liberally and without reproach" (1:5).
Key Words and Phrases: *brethren* (19x), *deed/work* (15x), *doer* (4x), *faith* (15x), *judge, judgment* (8x), *law* (10x), (*to*) *perfect*, *perfect* (5x), *sin* (6x), and *wisdom* (4x). See appendix 3 for a more complete word study.
Similarity to Proverbs: James has been called the "Proverbs of the New Testament" (see, for example, 1:5; 3:13–14, 15, 17).
Poverty: Like Amos in the Old Testament, James has a deep concern for the poor.
Good Works: James places a strong emphasis on "good works" (2:14–26) as a manifestation of our faith. Luther wrongly called it "a right strawy epistle." Calvin rightly saw: "We are justified by faith alone, but the faith that justifies is not alone."

A Comparison of Paul and James on Justification and Works

Paul	James
justification before God	justification before man
not by works	by good works
root of justification	fruit of justification
against dead works	against dead faith

It is not faith + works = justification. It is faith → works = justification.
Style: The style is Jewish in illustrations, emphasis, figures of speech, and appeal. It is written in a high-quality Greek (favorable to Hebrews). But the syntax is Semitic. It abounds in metaphors, similes, and figures of speech (for example, 1:6; 3:6).
Encyclical Nature: In addition to being written to a wide audience of Jewish believers, it is notably impersonal. Unlike Paul's writings, there are no personal references in the entire book.
Moral Emphasis: The book of James is very practical and moral, not doctrinal and theological. It is against social injustice. The author stressed orthopraxy (sound deeds) and not just orthodoxy (sound doctrine). James's moral emphasis is similar to that of Jesus. James says less about the Master and is more like him in

teaching, expressions, and figures of speech than any other New Testament book.

Sermon on the Mount: James's writing is like Jesus's Sermon on the Mount. He speaks about being humble (James 4:10; see Matt. 5:5; see also 23:12), judging (4:11–12; see Matt. 7:1), and swearing (James 5:12; see Matt. 5:34–37).

Love of Nature: James reflects a love for nature in his numerous references to it. He mentions waves of the sea tossed by the wind (1:6); flowers of the field (v. 10), where the sun withers the grass and causes plants to perish (v. 11). He speaks of the heavenly lights (v. 17), in contrast to shadows (v. 17) and firstfruits (v. 18). He talks of horses' mouths (3:3), ships driven by strong winds (v. 4), great forests (v. 5), fire (v. 6), different kinds of animals and birds (v. 7), deadly poisons (v. 8), fresh and salt water (v. 11), grapevines, olives, and figs (v. 12), sowing (v. 18), and reaping (3:18). He also mentions a vapor or mist (4:14), moths (5:2), gold and silver (v. 3), fields and harvesters (v. 4), fattened hearts (v. 5), crops (v. 7), fall and spring rain (v. 7), oil (v. 14), rain (v. 17), drought (v. 17), heavens giving rain (v. 18), and the earth's crops (v. 18).

A Comparison of the General Epistles:

> James is *ethical* (stressing prayer and practice).
>
> Peter is *experiential* (emphasizing hope and knowledge).
>
> John is *edificational* (focusing on love and truth).
>
> Jude is *exhortational* (highlighting faith and conflict).

The Outline:

> I. **Patience in Trials Rewarded** (1:1–15)
> A. Purpose of trials (vv. 1–12)
> B. Principles of temptation (vv. 13–15)
> II. **Practice of Truth Required** (1:16–27)
> A. Truth is the instrument of life (vv. 16–18)
> B. Truth is the mirror of life (vv. 19–27)
> III. **Partiality in Thoughts Rebuked** (2:1–13)
> A. Respect of others (vv. 1–9)
> B. Requirement of the law (vv. 10–13)
> IV. **Productivity of Trust Revealed** (2:14–26)
> A. Profit of good works (vv. 14–20)
> B. Picture of good works (vv. 21–26)
> V. **Perfection of Tongue Related** (chap. 3)
> A. Need of perfection (vv. 1–6)

THE CONTENTS: James is a practical book. He speaks of patience in trials (1:1–5), the practice of truth telling (vv. 16–27), the wrongness of partiality in our thoughts (2:1–13), the profitability of trust manifested in good works (vv. 14–26), the perfection of the tongue (chap. 3), the principles of transgression (chap. 4), the perversion of treasures (5:1–6), and perseverance in testing (vv. 7–20).

In the first section on patience in trials, he speaks of the purpose of trials (1:1–12) and the principles of temptation (vv. 13–15). Then he addresses the practice of truth as the instrument of life (vv. 16–18) and the mirror of life (vv. 19–27). This leads him to rebuke partiality in thoughts toward others, urging respect of persons (2:1–9) and the requirement of the law (vv. 10–13). Thus it is necessary for us to have productivity in our trust (faith), for faith without works is dead (2:14–26). He states the profit of good works (vv. 14–20) and offers a picture of good works in Abraham, whose faith led to good works (vv. 21–26).

Then James focuses on an area where many believers are lacking—the perfection of the tongue (chap. 3), stating the need for perfection (vv. 1–6), lack of perfection (vv. 7–12), and means of perfection of the tongue (vv. 13–18). In chapter 4 James presents the principles of transgression, speaking of their root in lust (vv. 1–3), their fruit in licentious living (vv. 4–6), and their cure in submission to God (vv. 7–14). Then he warns against the perversion of treasures (wealth) (5:1–6), the love of which is at the root of all evil. Finally, James speaks of perseverance in testing (vv. 7–20), recommending patience (vv. 7–11), propriety (v. 12), and prayer (vv. 13–18), concluding with an exhortation for sinners to turn from the error of their ways (vv. 19–20).

How to Respond to Critics

James 1:13 (see Gen. 22:1)—*If God doesn't tempt anyone, why did he tempt Abraham?*

Problem: The Bible says that God tempted Abraham (Gen. 22:1 KJV), and Jesus taught his disciples to pray to God: "Do not lead us into temptation" (Matt. 6:13). How then can James say of God: "nor does He Himself tempt anyone" (1:13)?

Solution: God did not *tempt* Abraham (nor anyone) to sin. Rather, he *tested* Abraham to see if he would sin or be faithful to him. God allows Satan to tempt us (see Matt 4:1–10; James 4:7; 1 Peter 5:8–9), but James is correct in saying, never does God "Himself tempt anyone." God cannot be tempted by sin, since he is absolutely and unchangeably perfect (Matt 5:48; Heb. 6:18), nor can he tempt anyone else to sin (James 1:13). When we sinful human beings are tempted, it is because we allow ourselves to be drawn away by our own lustful desires (vv. 14–15). The source of temptation comes from within not from without. It comes from sinful man not from a sinless God.

While God does not and cannot actually tempt anyone to sin, he can and does allow us to be tempted by Satan and our own lustful desires. Of course his purpose in permitting (but not producing or promoting) evil is to make us more perfect. God allowed Satan to tempt Job so that Job could say, "When He has tested me, I shall come forth as gold" (Job 23:10). God allowed evil to befall Joseph at the hands of his brothers, but in the end Joseph was able to say to them: "You meant evil against me; but God meant it for good" (Gen. 50:20).

James 2:21—*If Abraham was saved by works, why does the Bible say he was justified by faith?*

Problem: Paul clearly teaches that we are justified by faith and not by works (Rom. 1:17). He declared, "But to him who does not work but believes on Him who justifies the ungodly, his faith is accounted for righteousness" (4:5). It is "not by works of righteousness which we have done, but according to His mercy He saved us" (Titus 3:5). "For by grace you have been saved through faith, and that not of yourselves; it is the gift of God, not of works, lest anyone should boast" (Eph. 2:8–9).

But James seems to flatly contradict this by declaring, "A man is justified by works, and not by faith only" (2:24), for "faith without works is dead" (v. 26). Indeed, while Paul said Abraham was justified by faith (Rom. 4:1–4), James declares, "Was not Abraham our father justified by works?" (2:21). Are these not flatly contradictory?

Solution: James and Paul would be contradicting each other if they were speaking about the same thing, but there are many indications in the text that they are not. Paul is speaking about justification *before God*, while James is talking about justification *before humans*. This is indicated by the fact that James stressed that we should "show" (2:18) our faith. It must be something that can be seen by others in "works" (vv. 18–20). Further, James acknowledged that Abraham was justified before God by faith, not works, when he said, "Abraham believed God, and it was accounted to him for righteousness" (v. 23). When he says that Abraham was "justified by works" (v. 21), he is speaking of what Abraham *did that could be seen by people*, namely, offering his son Isaac on the altar (vv. 21–22).

Further, while Paul is stressing the *root* of justification (faith), James is stressing the *fruit* of justification (works). But each man acknowledges both. Immediately after affirming that we are saved by grace through faith (Eph. 2:8–9), Paul quickly adds, "We are His workmanship, created in Christ Jesus for good works, which God prepared beforehand that we should walk in them" (v. 10). Likewise, right after declaring that it is "not by works of righteousness which we have done, but according to His mercy He saved us" (Titus 3:5), Paul urges that "those who have believed in God should be careful to maintain good works" (v. 8). The relation between Paul and James can be summarized this way:

Paul	James
justification *before* God	justification *before humans*
the *root* of justification	the *fruit* of justification
justification *by* faith	justification *for* works
faith as *producer of works*	works as *the proof of faith*

James 5:17—*Was the drought three years or three-and-a-half years?*
Problem: Both here and in Luke 4:25 it speaks of a three-and-one-half-year drought in the days of Elijah. But in 1 Kings 17:1 and 18:1 it refers to the drought lasting three years.
Solution: There are three possible solutions here. (1) The three years may be a round number. (2) The third year in 1 Kings may be reckoned from the time of Elijah's stay with the widow of Zarephath, not the full time of the *drought*. (3) It is possible that the drought began six months before the *famine* did, making both passages precise but referring to different things.

STUDY QUESTIONS

1. What is the evidence that James, the brother of Jesus, is the author of this book?

2. Which date is most likely, the early or late one, and why?

3. Why was the book written?

4. To whom was it written? Give reasons.

5. How can Paul and James be reconciled on faith and works?

6. In what ways is James's teaching similar to that of Jesus?

SELECTED SOURCES

Baxter, Sidlow. *Explore the Book.* Grand Rapids: Zondervan, 1987.

Carson, D.A., Douglas Moo, and Leon Morris. *An Introduction to the New Testament.* Grand Rapids: Zondervan, 1992.

Geisler, Norman L., and Thomas Howe. *When Critics Ask: A Popular Handbook on Bible Difficulties.* Grand Rapids: Baker, 1997.

Guthrie, Donald. *New Testament Introduction.* Downers Grove, IL: InterVarsity, 1990.

Harrison, Everett F. *An Introduction to the New Testament.* Grand Rapids: Eerdmans, 1971.

Linnemann, Eta. *Historical Criticism of the Bible.* Translated by Robert Yarborough. Grand Rapids: Kregel, 2001.

MacArthur, John. *James.* MacArthur New Testament Commentary. Chicago: Moody, 1998.

Martin, Ralph P. *James.* Word Biblical Commentary. Nashville: Thomas Nelson, 1988.

Moo, Douglas J. *Letters of James.* Pillar New Testament Commentary. Grand Rapids: Eerdmans, 2000.

Nystrom, David. *James.* NIV Application Commentary. Grand Rapids: Zondervan, 1997.

Radmacher, Earl, Ronald Allen, and H. Wayne House, eds. *Nelson's New Illustrated Bible Commentary.* Nashville: Thomas Nelson, 1999.

Walvoord, John F., and Roy B. Zuck, eds. *The Bible Knowledge Commentary.* 2 vols. Wheaton: Victor, 1983.

24

1 Peter

Who Wrote It? Peter, the apostle of the circumcision, wrote the letter.

Internal Evidence

Although some modern critics deny Peter's authorship, the internal evidence is strongly in favor of it, and the early external evidence is also good. (1) The claim of the book is that it comes from "Peter, an apostle of Jesus Christ" (1:1). (2) He also claims to be an eyewitness of Christ's sufferings (5:1)—as Peter was. (3) In addition, the character and content of the book is similar to Peter's speeches in Acts 2, 4, and 10. (4) The speeches in Acts are similar to the vocabulary, diction, and thought in 1 Peter (see Acts 2, 4, 10).[1] (5) The authoritative tone and command in 5:2, telling elders to be "shepherds," fits Peter who was given the same charge by Jesus the Great Shepherd (see John 21:16). (6) Any differences in style can be accounted for by the fact that, although Peter was an untrained fisherman (Acts 4:13), he had had some thirty years of learning since then, and he used Silvanus (Silas) as his scribe (5:12). (7) As for the critics' charge of pseudonymity (someone else assuming Peter's name), it would be a denial of its authenticity—a deliberate forgery. Such a practice did not exist in the first-century Christian context.[2]

External Evidence

(1) Often overlooked is the fact that the first mention of 1 Peter is in another first-century book—the book of 2 Peter (3:1). Also Jude 17 cites 2 Peter 3:2, confirming its late first-century existence. Few New Testament books have this kind of first-century confirmation (see Acts 1:1 and Luke 1:1). (2) Peter's name was on the earliest

manuscripts found of this book, and the early church, which was in the best position to know who wrote it, would not have accepted it, if it had not been Peter's. (3) It was cited by some of the earliest Fathers as from Peter, including Polycarp, a disciple of the apostle John, Pseudo-Barnabas, Clement of Rome, Irenaeus, Cyril of Jerusalem, Eusebius, and Augustine.[3] (4) Those who later questioned it simply lacked the evidence available to others who accepted it.

When Was It Written?

First Peter was written about AD 64. It was written before Peter's death under Nero's persecution, which began in AD 64. Further, it was written after many of Paul's epistles were written, since Peter refers to "his [Paul's] epistles" (2 Peter 3:15–16). Finally, the declining conditions described in the book depict a period later than that of Ephesians, Philippians, and Colossians, which were written about AD 60–62. Thus a date of about AD 64 fits well.

To Whom Was It Written?

It was written to "the pilgrims of the Dispersion in Pontus, Galatia, Cappadocia, Asia, and Bithynia" (1:1). This was a major part of Asia Minor.

The Jewish view. Some say the recipients were Hebrew Christians of the eastern dispersion because: (1) Peter was an "apostle to the circumcision" (Gal. 2:7), but just as Paul the apostle to the Gentiles did not limit his ministry to Gentiles (see Acts 17:1–3), Peter the apostle to the Jews did not limit his ministry to Jews (see Acts 10). (2) Also he references "pilgrims" and "dispersion," terms that are appropriate for Jewish pilgrims or the Jewish Diaspora. (3) Further, Peter's readers were asked to do praiseworthy acts among the Gentiles (2:12), which seems to imply that the readers were Jews.

The Gentile view. Others claim this epistle was aimed at Gentile readers. (1) They understand "Gentile" not in an ethnic sense but in the spiritual sense of "pagan." (2) Also they note that the text does not claim the readers were part of a Jewish dispersion. (3) Furthermore, the readers were formerly involved in typical Gentile sins (like idolatry) (4:3). (4) They once lived in "ignorance" of God's truth (1:14), which was not true of Jews. (5) What is more, the reference to belief of their fathers in salvation "by silver and gold" (v. 18) indicates they were Gentiles. (6) Finally, Peter says they were once not "the people of God" (as the Jews were) (2:10). Of course there could have been both Jews and Gentiles in these churches.

Where Were They Located?

According to 1:1 the recipients were in Asia Minor, particularly the areas of "Pontus, Galatia, Cappadocia, Asia, and Bithynia." *Note*: Peter said he wrote from "Babylon" (5:13), which has been

A cave church in
Cappadocia.

taken literally, as a city in Mesopotamia or Egypt, or symbolically, as Rome (see Rev. 17:5–6, 18). Given the dangers of persecution of Peter's time, he could have been concealing his location to outsiders by the use of this symbolic term. It is widely agreed by historians that Peter eventually went to Rome.

Why Was It Written?

Peter manifests several reasons for writing this epistle. (1) He wanted to encourage believers in their suffering (5:10–12; see 1:6). (2) He wished to show them how to live out their salvation (2:2, 12), even in difficult circumstances. (3) He desired to exhort them to submission for Christ's sake (2:13; see v. 18; 5:5), with the hope that it would mitigate governmental oppression.

What Is It About?   The Theme: Submission to Christ in suffering for him.

Key Verse: "Elect . . . for obedience and sprinkling of the blood of Jesus Christ" (1:2; see 2:18, 23; 3:1, 5).

Key Words and Phrases: *be submissive* (7x), *call* (6x), *chosen* (one who is chosen) (5x), *end* (4x), *flesh* (7x), *glorify, glory* (16x), *grace* (10x), *holy* (8x), *hope* (3x), *live, life* (9x), (*to*) *love, love* (6x), *obey, obedience* (4x), *precious* (5x), *revelation* (3x), *salvation* (3x), *spirit* (9x), *suffer, suffering, trial* (18x), and *time* (8x). See appendix 3 for a more complete word study.

Influences: Peter shows the influence of the theology of Paul and the ethics of James.

Contrasts:

>   Paul—apostle of faith
>
>   John—apostle of love
>
>   Peter—apostle of hope

Motif: First Peter has a servant motif (2:22–24; see John 13) as does the writing of Mark (10:45), whom Peter mentored.

THE OUTLINE:

>   I. **Explanation of Suffering**—It Is from God (1:1–12)
>   II. **Exemplification of Suffering**—It Is in Christ (1:13–3:12)
>   III. **Exhortation to Suffer**—It Is for Christians (3:13–4:11)
>   IV. **Expectation for the Sufferer**—It Is for Glory (4:12–19)
>   V. **Encouragement in Suffering** (5:1–14)

THE CONTENTS: Peter begins by offering an explanation of suffering (1:1–12) by pointing out that it is from God. This exemplification of suffering (1:13–3:12) is found in Christ, our model for suffering. The readers are then given an exhortation to suffer (3:13–4:11) because it is of the essence of being a Christian (Christ-one). Ultimately, however, the expectation for the sufferer (4:12–19) is to know it is for the glory of God. Peter ends his letter with encouragement in suffering (5:1–11) and final greetings (vv. 12–14).

How to Respond to Critics   1 Peter 1:2—*Are we sanctified by God's truth or by God's Spirit?*

Problem: Peter speaks in this text about "sanctification of the Spirit," but Jesus prayed, "Sanctify them by Your truth" (John 17:17). How are we set apart to God—by his Spirit or by his truth?

Solution: We are sanctified *through* God's truth, which is *from* God's Spirit. The Spirit of God is the *efficient* cause (that by which God works in our hearts), and the truth of God is the *instrumental* cause (that through which God works in our hearts). In short, God is the *source*, and God's truth is the *means* of our *sanctification*.

1 Peter 3:15—*Why does Peter command believers to reason about their faith when the Bible says elsewhere to simply believe?*

Problem: Over and over again the Scriptures insist that one should simply believe in God (see John 3:16; Acts 16:31). Hebrews declares: "Without faith it is impossible to please [God]" (Heb. 11:6). Paul contended: "The world through wisdom did not know God" (1 Cor. 1:21). Yet Peter here instructs believers to "defend" and give a "reason" for their faith. Aren't faith and reason opposed?

Solution: Faith and reason are not mutually exclusive. A person should not believe in something without first inquiring whether it is a worthy object of belief. For example, few people would undergo a serious medical operation by a totally unknown person whom they had no reason to believe was anything but a quack. Likewise, God does not call on us to exercise blind faith.

Since God is a God of reason (Isa. 1:18), and since he has made us rational creatures in his image (Gen. 1:27; Col. 3:10), he wants us to look before we leap. No rational person should step into an elevator without first looking to see if there is a floor. Likewise, God wants us to take a step of faith in the light of the evidence, but not a leap of faith into the dark.

The Bible is filled with exhortations to use our reason. Jesus commanded, "You shall love the Lord . . . with all your *mind*" (Matt. 22:37). Paul wrote: "Whatsoever things are true . . . *think* on these things" (Phil. 4:8 KJV). Paul also "reasoned" with the Jews (Acts 17:17) and with the philosophers on Mars Hill (vv. 22–31), winning many to Christ (v. 34). Bishops were instructed to be able "to *refute* those who contradict" (Titus 1:9 NASB). Paul declares that he was "appointed for the *defense* of the gospel" (Phil. 1:17). Jude urged us to "*contend* earnestly for the faith which was once for all delivered to the saints" (Jude 3). And Peter commanded, "Be ready to give a *defense* to everyone who asks you a *reason* for the hope that is in you" (1 Peter 3:15).

There are two kinds of belief. Understanding the relationship between them is a key to discerning the relationship between faith and reason.

Faith

Believing That	Believing In
prior	subsequent
evidence	no evidence
mind	will
proof	persuasion
human reason	Holy Spirit

The devil believes *that* God exists, but he does not believe *in* God. Belief *that* is a matter of the mind knowing something based on the evidence that human reason can see. Belief *in* God (or Christ), however, is a choice of the human will under the persuasion of the Holy Spirit. So belief *that* will never save anyone (see James 2:14–20)—only belief *in* Christ can do that. However, no rational person should ever believe *in* something, unless he or she first has evidence to believe *that* it is true. No sensible traveler gets into an airplane that is missing a wing. So reason is valid as a basis for belief *that*, but is wrong to demand as a basis for belief *in* (see John 20:27–29).

1 Peter 3:18—*Was Jesus raised in the Spirit or in a physical body?*
Problem: Peter declares that Christ was "put to death in the flesh, but made alive in the spirit" (NASB). This seems to imply that Jesus did not rise in the flesh but only in his spirit, which conflicts with Jesus's statement that his resurrection body was "flesh and bones" (Luke 24:39).
Solution: To interpret this as proof of a spiritual, rather than a physical, resurrection is neither necessary nor consistent with the context of this passage and the rest of Scripture. Several reasons support this conclusion.

1. The passage can be translated, "He was put to death in the body but made alive by the [Holy] Spirit" (NIV). The passage is translated with this same understanding by the NKJV and others.

2. In the New Testament the parallel between death and being made alive refers normally to the resurrection of the body. For example, Paul declared: "Christ died and rose and lived again" (Rom. 14:9), and "He was crucified in weakness, yet He lives by the power of God" (2 Cor. 13:4).

3. The context refers to the event as "the resurrection of Jesus Christ" (1 Peter 3:21), and this is everywhere understood as

a bodily resurrection in the New Testament (see Acts 4:33; Rom 1:4; 1 Cor. 15:21; 1 Peter 1:3; Rev. 20:5).

4. Even if "spirit" refers to Jesus's human spirit (not to the Holy Spirit), it cannot mean he had no resurrection body. Otherwise, the reference to his "body" (flesh) before the resurrection would mean he had no human spirit then. It seems better to take "flesh" in this context as a reference to his whole condition of humiliation before the resurrection and "spirit" to refer to his unlimited power and imperishable life after the resurrection.

1 Peter 3:19—*Can we be saved after we die?*
Problem: First Peter 3:19 declares: Christ "preached to the spirits in prison." Some take this to mean that there is a second chance after death for salvation, but this would be contrary to many other Scriptures (Luke 16:25–26; John 8:24; Heb. 9:27).
Solution: There are at least three other views that avoid this serious theological deviation.
View one—Christ preaching through Noah. According to this view, Christ preached by the Spirit through Noah to human spirits imprisoned in bodies who were living in Noah's day.
  Response. This is a platonic view of human beings not a biblical one. Humans are not spirits imprisoned in human bodies. They are soul-body unities (Gen. 2:7) who are created in God's image (1:27).
View two—Christ announced his victory to spirits in Hades. This position claims that Jesus went to Hades to announce the doom of demons and/or his victory over them (see Col. 2:14–15; Heb. 2:14).
  Response. This view seems more likely. However, it leaves a couple of problems open that are addressed by the next view.
View three—Christ announced his victory to spirits by the Holy Spirit. This position holds that Christ announced his victory to the spirit world but notes that the text says several things. (1) He did this after his resurrection. (2) He "preached" to the spirits indirectly through the Holy Spirit not directly himself. (3) It does not appear to be all fallen spirits but only those who were "disobedient" in "the days of Noah" (1 Peter 3:20). If so, this would seem to be a reference to the "sons of God" (Gen. 6:1–4), a reference that always means angels in the Old Testament (see Job 1:6; 2:1; 38:7). Indeed, the Greek translation of the Old Testament (the Septuagint) translates the phrase "angels of God" in Genesis 6:2. Also 2 Peter 2:4 speaks of angels sinning and being judged by God in connection with Noah's flood (vv. 4–5) in the same sentence.
  Response. It is correctly noted that angels, as such, do not marry (Matt. 22:30). Hence, if the reference is to angels, they would

have to be fallen angels who enticed humans to sin, perhaps by possessing them and producing the "giants" (*Nephilim*: fallen ones) of Genesis 6:4. Also it should be noted that the announcement of Christ's victory happened after his resurrection, not between death and resurrection. Indeed, it was his resurrection that made the victory possible (see Rom. 4:25; 1 Cor. 15:12–28).

1 Peter 3:21—*Does one have to be baptized to be saved?*
Problem: First Peter 3:21 says that baptism "now saves us." But Paul says that it is faith that saves us. This is contradictory. Hence, some take this to be proof that water baptism is necessary for salvation.
Solution: (1) The Bible declares that God saves us from the penalty of sin actually by grace through faith. This occurs at Spirit baptism (1 Cor. 12:13) when we are placed in the body of Christ. (2) We are saved from the power of sin (from a bad conscience) by water baptism (1 Peter 3:21), since it is a command of Christ (Matt. 28:18–20), and the unbaptized are living in disobedience to Christ's command. (3) Baptism also saves in a symbolic way in water baptism, since Peter says it is like the water of Noah's flood that "symbolizes baptism" (1 Peter 3:21 NIV). But we know that Noah was saved by faith (Heb. 11:7). Going through the water of the flood was only an outward manifestation of his inward faith.

1 Peter 4:6 (see Hebrews 9:27)—*Is the gospel preached to people after they die?*
Problem: Peter says, "the gospel was preached also to those who are dead." This appears to claim that people have a chance to be saved after they die. But this runs into conflict with Hebrews 9:27, which insists: "It is appointed for men to die once, but after this the judgment."
Solution: In response, the following should be noted.

1. There is no hope held out anywhere in Scripture for salvation after death. Death is final, and there are only two destinies—heaven and hell, between which there is a great gulf that no one can pass over. So whatever preaching to the "dead" may mean, it does not imply that a person can be saved after he or she dies.

2. This is an unclear passage, subject to many interpretations, and no doctrine should be based on an ambiguous passage like this. The difficult texts should be interpreted in the light of the clear ones and not the reverse.

3. There are other possible interpretations of this passage that do not conflict with the teaching of the rest of Scripture. For

example, it is possible that it refers to those who are now dead who heard the gospel while they were alive. In favor of this is cited the fact that the gospel "was preached" (in the past) to those who "are dead" (now, in the present). Or some believe this might not be a reference to human beings but to the "spirits in prison" (angels) of 1 Peter 3:19 (see the earlier discussion of this verse; see also 2 Peter 2:4; Gen. 6:1–3). (3) Still others claim that, although the dead suffer the destruction of their flesh (1 Peter 4:6), yet they still live with God by virtue of what Christ did through the gospel (namely, his death and resurrection). This victorious message was announced by Christ himself to the spirit world after his resurrection (see 3:19).

STUDY QUESTIONS

1. What is the internal and external evidence that the apostle Peter wrote this book?

2. To whom did Peter write: Jews or Gentiles? Give reasons.

3. What is the evidence that this book was written in the mid-60s AD?

4. Why did Peter write this book?

5. Give reasons why Peter is not teaching baptismal regeneration in 3:21.

6. Were the "spirits in prison" (3:19–20) humans who were given a second chance after death?

SELECTED SOURCES

Barbieri, Louis. *First & Second Peter*. Everyman's Bible Commentary Series. Chicago: Moody, 2003.

Baxter, Sidlow. *Explore the Book*. Grand Rapids: Zondervan, 1987.

Carson, D.A., Douglas Moo, and Leon Morris. *An Introduction to the New Testament*. Grand Rapids: Zondervan, 1992.

Davids, Peter. *1 Peter*. New International Commentary on the New Testament. Grand Rapids: Eerdmans, 1995.

Geisler, Norman L., and Thomas Howe. *When Critics Ask: A Popular Handbook on Bible Difficulties*. Grand Rapids: Baker, 1997.

Guthrie, Donald. *New Testament Introduction*. Downers Grove, IL: InterVarsity, 1990.

Harrison, Everett F. *An Introduction to the New Testament*. Grand Rapids: Eerdmans, 1971.

Linnemann, Eta. *Historical Criticism of the Bible*. Translated by Robert Yarborough. Grand Rapids: Kregel, 2001.

MacArthur, John. *First Peter*. MacArthur New Testament Commentary. Chicago: Moody, 2004.

Marshall, I. Howard. *1 Peter*. NIV Application Commentary. Grand Rapids: Zondervan, 1996.

Radmacher, Earl, Ronald Allen, and H. Wayne House, eds. *Nelson's New Illustrated Bible Commentary*. Nashville: Thomas Nelson, 1999.

Walvoord, John F., and Roy B. Zuck, eds. *The Bible Knowledge Commentary*. 2 vols. Wheaton: Victor, 1983.

25
2 Peter

"Simon Peter, . . . apostle of Jesus Christ" (1:1) is the author.

Internal Evidence

The internal evidence for Peter's authorship is strong. (1) The repeated claim of the book supports Peter the apostle as the author (1:1; 3:1–2). (2) This claim is confirmed by the fact that it is sent to the same group as 1 Peter (2 Peter 3:1). (3) The character of the book is similar to that of 1 Peter in vocabulary, diction, and thought. Second Peter and Peter's speeches in Acts 2, 4, and 10 use similar words and phrases that either appear nowhere else in the New Testament or very rarely. These include *obtained* (1:1; Acts 1:17), *godliness* (1:3, 6–7; 3:11; see Acts 1:17), *lawless* (2:8; see Acts 2:23), *wages of unrighteousness* or *iniquity* (2:13, 15; Acts 1:18), *the day of the Lord* (3:10; see Acts 2:20).[1] (4) Peter mentions a colleague, the apostle Paul, and his "letters" (3:15). (5) The contents confirm it is from Peter by telling the manner of his death and saying that he was an eyewitness of the transfiguration of Christ (1:14–18). (6) The date of the book is about AD 66 (see below), which supports Peter as author, since the "letters" of Paul were in circulation by then (3:15–16). (7) The citation by Jude (Jude 6–7 of 2 Peter 2:5–7) verifies that 2 Peter was from a late first-century writer. (8) Pseudonymity (writing under another's name) denies authenticity. It would have been considered a deliberate forgery.[2]

External Evidence

Despite critics, ancient and modern, the evidence that Peter wrote this epistle is good. (1) The citation of 2 Peter from Jude 6–7 verifies it was from the first century (see also Jude 8 and 2 Peter 2:10). (2) The earliest manuscripts accepted it with Peter's name on it. This is something they would not have done if they had believed Peter did not write it. (3) There are allusions to 2 Peter in some of the earliest writers, such as the *Shepherd of Hermas* and the Didache. (4) Many early Fathers cited it, including Origen, Rufinus, Clement of Rome, Irenaeus, Clement of Alexandria, Cyril of Jerusalem, Athanasius, Jerome, and Augustine. (5) There is more evidence for 2 Peter's genuineness than for the Greek classics, such as Herodotus and Thucydides. (6) While some have doubted it, it was never rejected by the Christian church. In fact the church has recognized it as authentic and accepted it into the canon of Scripture. (7) As B. B. Warfield pointed out, there is more evidence for 2 Peter's genuineness than for other books from antiquity; it only seems weak when compared to the overwhelmingly strong evidence for some other New Testament books.

Answering the Critics

1. The difference in vocabulary from 1 Peter (230 words are not used in 1 Peter) is due to a difference in topic and secretary. Further, the difference in vocabulary is similar to the difference between 1 Timothy and Titus, which has only 161 words in common with the 537 words of 1 Timothy. Yet both are from the same author.

2. Some have doubted Peter's authorship because the grammar is better in 1 Peter, but this can be explained by several factors. His use of Silvanus as a secretary for 1 Peter could account for that (5:12). The differences are not great. There are strong similarities in content with Peter's known speeches in Acts. The different topic, time, and conditions of the recipients can account for variations in style by the same author.

3. Others have argued that the Old Testament is quoted more in 1 Peter (31x) than 2 Peter (only 5x), but this can be explained by the fact that 2 Peter is shorter, the conditions in 1 Peter called for more quotations, other known authors do the same thing, and it overlooks the fact that both books tend to use the same Old Testament books (Psalms, Proverbs, and Isaiah).

4. Some critics sense a greater warmth and intensity in 1 Peter, but this does not prove there were two authors. The same is true between 1 and 2 Thessalonians, which come from the same author. In 2 Corinthians there is even a different intensity in the two parts of the same book (compare chaps. 1–9 with 10–13).

5. Others insist that second-century Gnostic thought is reflected in 2 Peter. However, similar language does not need

to mean similar thought. There are no distinctly second-century Gnostic beliefs here, such as a demiurgic creator, angelic emanations from God, evil nature of matter, or salvation by mystical knowledge. An incipient kind of first-century Gnosticism (which combines legalism, mysticism, and asceticism) found and criticized in the writings of Paul (Colossians and 1 Timothy) comes from the first century but is not reflected in this book.

6. Still others claim that Peter would not commend Paul, as he did here (in 3:15–16) after Paul rebuked him (Gal. 2:11–21). But this fails to disprove Peter's authorship because there is no evidence Peter held a grudge, Paul made a favorable reference to Peter in 1 Corinthians 9:5, and second-century references to apostles are more venerational than personal, as they are in the New Testament.

7. Other critics claim that 2 Peter is citing Jude who wrote in AD 68–69, and this places 2 Peter after Peter's death (around AD 66–67). However, it is more likely that Jude is citing Peter, since Peter predicts the apostasy (chap. 3) and it is present in Jude; Jude is in a habit of using sources, more than the apostles did; and Jude refers to apostles as if many were gone (Jude 17).

8. Critics stress the differences between the Epistles but ignore the likenesses. Both place emphasis on Christ, 1 Peter on his suffering and 2 Peter on his glory. And in both Epistles Peter refers to Noah and the flood (1 Peter 3:20; 2 Peter 2:5; 3:5–6).

In summation, there is strong internal and good external evidence that the apostle Peter wrote this epistle, and all of the arguments to the contrary are answerable.[3]

When Was It Written?

Peter wrote the letter about AD 66, just before his martyrdom. The evidence points to a date in the mid-60s because: (1) It was written before the destruction of Jerusalem (AD 70), since this momentous event is not mentioned as being in the recent past. (2) Paul's "letters," which extend into the AD 60s, are cited as in existence when Peter wrote (3:15–16). (3) Yet Peter wrote before Jude (who wrote in AD 68–69), since Jude 6–7 cites 2 Peter 2:5–7. (4) And it must have been written before Peter's martyrdom (AD 67–68). Thus AD 66 is the most likely date.

To Whom Was It Written?

The recipients are the same as for 1 Peter (see 2 Peter 3:1), who were described as "the pilgrims of the Dispersion in Pontus, Galatia, Cappadocia, Asia, and Bithynia" (1 Peter 1:1). This was a major part of Asia Minor.

Where Were They Located?

The recipients of the letter were located in the churches of Asia Minor.

Why Was It Written?

There are several purposes for the writing of 2 Peter. (1) Peter wished to warn the readers against impurity (1:4, 9; 2:6–7, 18) and apostasy (2:20–22). (2) He wanted to encourage Christian growth in grace and knowledge (3:18). (3) He desired to warn them against antinomianism and incipient Gnosticism (1:16; 2:10). (4) He exhorted them to godly living in view of Christ's return (3:11).

What Is It About?

The Theme: Purification by Christ.

Key Verse: "For he who lacks these things is shortsighted, even to blindness, and has forgotten that he was purged from his old sins" (1:9).

Key Words and Phrases: *be diligent* (3x), *corruption*, *destroyed* (4x), *destroy* (5x), *know*, *knowledge* (8x), *promise* (4x), *prophecy* (2x), *prophet* (2x), and *reminder* (2x). See appendix 3 for a more complete word study.

Comparison to Jude: It is much like Jude, though scoffers are present in Jude and yet future in 2 Peter.

Similarity to 2 Timothy: The books are alike in that they are against heresy, express joy in death, emphasize the Scriptures, and are the last book each apostle wrote.

A Comparison of 1 and 2 Peter

1 Peter	2 Peter
tribulation	truth
consolation	exhortation
hope	knowledge
suffering	error
external dangers	internal dangers

Dominant Doctrines: knowledge, ethics, and last things (eschatology).

THE OUTLINE:

I. **Knowledge and Its Principles** (chap. 1)
   A. Provisions (vv. 2–4)
   B. Progress (vv. 5–11)
   C. Pledge (vv. 12–21)

Opposite: Hierapolis at sunset.

THE CONTENTS: The message of the book falls neatly into the three chapter divisions: the principles of knowledge (chap. 1), the perils of knowledge (chap. 2), and the promise of knowledge (chap. 3). In the first section, dealing with the principles of knowledge, Peter deals with the provisions of knowledge by God (1:2–4), its progress in the man of God (vv. 5–11), and its pledge for the future in the Word of God (vv. 12–21). In the second section, treating the perils to true knowledge, he speaks of facing the perils of false teachers, their doctrine (2:1–3a), their destruction (1:3b–9), and the deeds of false teachers (vv. 10–22). Finally, Peter discusses the promise of true knowledge, that even though truth is assailed (3:1–4), it will be attested (vv. 5–10), and should be applied to our lives (vv. 11–18), so we can "grow in the grace and knowledge of our Lord and Savior Jesus Christ" (v. 18). Only in this way can we be purified from our sins (1:9).

How to Respond to Critics

2 Peter 2:4—*Are fallen angels bound or are they free to tempt human beings?*

Problem: Peter affirms in this passage that God cast the fallen angels "down to hell and delivered them into chains of darkness, to be reserved for judgment" (see Jude 6). However, it is evident from the New Testament that demons roam freely over the earth, oppressing and even possessing people (see Matt. 12:22; 17:14–18; Acts 16:16–18; Rev. 16:14).

Solution: There are two basic explanations of this apparent contradiction. First, it is possible that Peter is speaking of the *official* and *ultimate* destiny of fallen angels (demons), not their *actual* and *immediate* status. That is, while they are already sentenced by God to eternal damnation, they have not yet actually started serving their term. Nonetheless, they know their time is coming (Matt. 8:29; Rev. 12:12).

Second, these passages may be speaking of two different classes of fallen angels, some already in chains (2 Peter 2:4) and the rest yet loose. Some believe Peter is referring to the "sons of God" (angels) of Genesis 6:4, who instigated intermarriage with women just before the flood, since the very next verse refers to Noah (v. 5). If so, this may account for why these particular angels are already in chains (so they cannot repeat their feat), as opposed to other demons who are loose.

STUDY QUESTIONS

1. What is the internal and external evidence that the apostle Peter wrote this book?

2. What were his purposes for writing this Epistle?

3. Respond to the arguments critics give for rejecting 2 Peter.

4. What evidence is there that Jude cited 2 Peter and not the reverse?

5. What evidence is there for dating 2 Peter around AD 66?

6. How are the last letters of Peter and Paul similar?

SELECTED SOURCES

Barbieri, Louis. *First & Second Peter*. Everyman's Bible Commentary Series. Chicago: Moody, 2003.

Bauckham, Richard J. *Jude, 2 Peter*. Word Biblical Commentary. Nashville: Thomas Nelson, 1983.

Baxter, Sidlow. *Explore the Book*. Grand Rapids: Zondervan, 1987.

Carson, D.A., Douglas Moo, and Leon Morris. *An Introduction to the New Testament*. Grand Rapids: Zondervan, 1992.

Geisler, Norman L., and Thomas Howe. *When Critics Ask: A Popular Handbook on Bible Difficulties*. Grand Rapids: Baker, 1997.

Guthrie, Donald. *New Testament Introduction*. Downers Grove, IL: InterVarsity, 1990.

Harrison, Everett F. *An Introduction to the New Testament*. Grand Rapids: Eerdmans, 1971.

Linnemann, Eta. *Historical Criticism of the Bible*. Translated by Robert Yarborough. Grand Rapids: Kregel, 2001.

Moo, Douglas J. *2 Peter, Jude*. NIV Application Commentary. Grand Rapids: Zondervan, 1996.

Radmacher, Earl, Ronald Allen, and H. Wayne House, eds. *Nelson's New Illustrated Bible Commentary*. Nashville: Thomas Nelson, 1999.

Walvoord, John F., and Roy B. Zuck, eds. *The Bible Knowledge Commentary*. 2 vols. Wheaton: Victor, 1983.

Warfield, B. B. *Syllabus on the Special Introduction to the Catholic Epistles*. Pittsburgh: W. W. Waters, 1883.

26
1 John

The author of the letter is John, the apostle.

Two Views

John "the Elder." Some believe that John "the Elder" wrote the letter (2 John 1:1; 3 John 1:1). He was not an apostle but may have been a follower of the apostle. He may have been the writer since he does not use the term *apostle* of himself. The letter is written later than John the apostle's time, and, according to Irenaeus, Papias named another John, who was not an apostle, in chapter 39 of *The Writings of Papias.*[1]

Response. (1) John was the youngest apostle and lived to near the end of the first century. (2) Apostles were elders (or bishops) by office (Acts 1:20; 1 Tim. 3:1) and apostles by gift (1 Cor. 12:4, 28; Eph. 4:11). (3) Peter also called himself an elder (1 Peter 5:1). (4) The existence of another New Testament author named John is doubtful, being based on a questionable statement by Papias.

John the Apostle. Some believe the author is John the apostle, who also wrote the Gospel of John (see chapter 7) and the book of Revelation (see chapter 28). Both the internal and external evidence is good for John the apostle.

Internal Evidence for John the Apostle

There is very good evidence from the text that John the apostle was the writer. (1) He was an eyewitness of Christ's life and teachings (1:1–3), which was one of the characteristics of an apostle (Acts 1:21–25; 1 Cor. 9:1). (2) He spoke with the authority of an apostle (4:6). (3) He wrote with the same style (using, for example, "this is . . .", "by this . . ."), the same basic vocabulary (*Father, Son, Spirit, beginning, Word* [*logos*], *Paraclete, believe, life, eternal, love, remain/abide, keep, commandment, true, know, beget, witness, light, darkness, world, sin,* and *devil*), and the same doctrine as the author of the fourth Gospel.[2] (4) He wrote in the same style as "John" who wrote "the [book of] Revelation" (Rev. 1:1), which is known to be John the apostle. (5) Who else could write at this time, with this authority, with the same style, the same doctrine, and have his book accepted without ever placing his name on it?

External Evidence for John the Apostle

The evidence from outside the Epistle of 1 John that the apostle John wrote it is more than substantial. (1) It was called an epistle of "John" from the earliest times by persons who would be in the best position to know who wrote it. (2) It was accepted by a disciple of John named Polycarp, and it was accepted by the early Fathers as a work of John. (3) Other early writings claim it as a work of John, including the *Shepherd of Hermas* and Irenaeus. (4) Later Fathers accepted it too, such as Clement of Alexandria, Tertullian, Cyril of Jerusalem, Eusebius, Jerome, and Augustine.

When Was It Written?

The Epistle was written between AD 90 and 95. (1) It was written before AD 100, since an early manuscript of this book was found all the way across the Mediterranean in a small town in Egypt and dated about AD 115 to 125. (2) It must have been written before John died, which, according to Irenaeus, was about AD 98. (3) The conditions prevailing at the time indicate it was written during the reign of Domitian, which was AD 81–96 (see the introduction to the book of Revelation). (4) It also gives evidence of being written after the Gospel of John, which was composed about AD 85 to 90, since it builds on the teachings of the Gospel (1 John 2:7–8 with John 13:34; 1 John 3:8–18 with John 8:41–47; 1 John 5:9–10 with John 5:19–47; and 1 John 1:1–4 is a summary of John's message [1:1, 14] in his Gospel). This would place it about AD 90 to 95.

To Whom Was It Written?

The recipients of the letter were a group of mostly Greek-speaking Jewish churches with Gentiles as well. (1) They were John's disciples ("little children"—2:18). (2) He knew them well (2:19). (3) They knew him well since they accepted his book without even his name on it. (4) They were warned about idols (5:21), which was not a Jewish problem but was often a part of Greek culture. (4) They were being influenced by the heresy of Docetism, which denied the humanity of Christ (4:1–3).

Where Were They Located? The readers were located in Asia Minor (modern Turkey), probably the same general area as the seven churches of Revelation (1:11).

Why Was It Written? There are at least four reasons for John's writing the book that can be seen in the text. (1) He wanted to urge them to continue in their fellowship with God and other believers (1:3). (2) He desired to warn them against denial of Christ's humanity, a heresy called Docetism (4:2–3). (3) He wished to exhort them not to sin and to remind them of the provision for sin made by Christ (2:1; 5:21). (4) He aimed to provide assurance of salvation for all believers (5:13–20).

What Is It About? The Theme: Communion with Christ.
Key Verse: "But if we walk in the light as He is in the light, we have fellowship with one another, and the blood of Jesus Christ His Son cleanses us from all sin" (1:7).
Key Words and Phrases: *abide* (23x), *born of God* (8x), *darkness* (7x), *evil* (6x), *fellowship* (3x), *know* (39x), *life* (17x), *light* (6x), *(to) love, love* (45x), *(to) sin, sin* (27x), *truth, true,* (15x), *(to) witness, testify, witness* (13x), *world* (23x), and *write* (13x). See appendix 3 for a more complete word study.

A Comparison of John's Epistles:
> 1 John—Christ is the *life.*
> 2 John—Christ is the *truth.*
> 3 John—Christ is the *way.*

Jesus said . . . , "I am the way, the truth, and the life" (John 14:6).

Styles of Writings Compared:
> Peter is realistic.
> Paul is syllogistic.
> James is graphic.
> John is symphonic and antithetic.

A Comparison of John's Writings: He wrote five New Testament books.
> *Gospel*—Christian theology—veracity of Christianity (past)
> *Epistles*—Christian ethics—virtue of Christianity (present)
> *Revelation*—Christian politics—vision of Christianity (future)

A Comparison of John's Gospel and Epistles

Gospel	Epistle
theological	ethical
didactical	polemical
objective	subjective
arouses faith	establishes faith

An Apostolic Comparison:

Peter—*founded* the church

Paul—*liberated* the church

John—*established* the church

THE OUTLINE:

I. **Advance in Divine Light**—Walk in Him (chaps. 1–2)
   A. Conditions of (chap. 1)
   B. Command about (2:1–17)
   C. Continuance in (vv. 18–29)
II. **Attitude toward Divine Love**—Dwell in Him (chaps. 3–4)
   A. Salvation received through divine love (3:1–9)
   B. Service rendered through divine love (vv. 10–24)
   C. Steadfastness realized through divine love (4:1–21)
III. **Affinity with Divine Love**—Live in Him (chap. 5)
   A. Possession of divine life (vv. 1–13)
   B. Prayer in divine life (vv. 14–17)
   C. Product of divine life (vv. 18–21)

THE CONTENTS: The message of John's epistle—fellowship with Christ—is centered around light and love. First, believers are asked to advance in the divine light by walking in it (chaps. 1–2); then they are asked to have the right attitude toward divine love by dwelling in it (chaps. 3–4). Finally, John speaks about our affinity with the divine life by our dwelling in it. In the first section John gives the conditions of advancing in the light (chap. 1), details the commands about it (2:1–17), and urges continuance in it (vv. 18–29). In the sections where he focuses on the proper attitude toward divine love, he speaks of our salvation received through it (3:1–9), our service rendered through it (vv. 10–24), and our steadfastness realized through it (4:1–21). Finally, John returns to the theme of love—our affinity with it and urges believers to live in it. First, he addresses our possession of it (5:1–13), our prayers in it (vv. 14–17), and the product of this love in our lives (vv. 18–21).

1 John 3:9 (see 1:8)—*Doesn't John contradict himself when he
asserts that Christians are without sin?*

Problem: John affirms here: "Whoever has been born of God does
not sin." But in the first chapter he insisted: "If we say that we
have no sin, we deceive ourselves, and the truth is not in us"
(1:8).

Solution: Nowhere does John claim that believers are without sin
or never commit a sin. First John 3:9 is in the present continuous
tense and should be translated "Whoever is born of God does
not continually practice sin." Conversely, if a person habitually
practices sin, he is not born of God. As James argued, true faith
will produce good works (James 2:14–18). If a pig and a lamb fall
into the mud, the pig wants to stay there, but the lamb wants to
get out. Both a believer and an unbeliever can *fall* into the same
sin, but a believer cannot *stay* in it and feel comfortable. To say
one "cannot sin" can also be understood in various ways:

1. One cannot sin mortally (lose life): possible—1 Cor. 11:30;
   1 John 5:16.

2. One cannot sin absolutely (lose salvation): impossible—
   John 10:28–29; Rom. 8:36–37; Phil. 1:6; 2 Tim. 2:13.

3. One cannot sin deliberately (Heb. 10:26): improbable—
   most (if not all) sin is willful (2 Peter 3:5), and Christians
   sin (1 John 1:8).

4. One cannot sin habitually—(present progressive): probable,
   since it is in the present tense, meaning continually.

1 John 5:7—*Why is this verse on the Trinity missing in many modern
translations?*

Problem: John declares that "there are three who bear witness in
heaven: the Father, the Word, and the Holy Spirit; and these three
are one." This is the clearest statement on the Trinity in the Bible.
However, most modern translations omit this verse. Why?

Solution: The reason is very simple. This verse has virtually no
support among the early Greek manuscripts, though it is found
in Latin manuscripts. Its appearance in late Greek manuscripts
is based on the fact that Erasmus was placed under ecclesiastical
pressure to include it in his Greek New Testament of 1522, having
omitted it in his two earlier editions of 1516 and 1519 because he
could not find any Greek manuscripts that contained it.

Probably its inclusion in the Latin Bible results from a scribe
incorporating a marginal comment (gloss) into the text as he
copied the manuscript of 1 John. But including it in the text

violates almost every rule of textual criticism. Even the New King James Version, which generally retains the longer readings and disputed passages (see Mark 16:9–20 and John 7:53–8:11), comments in the margin that this is "a passage found in only four or five very late *Greek* mss."

1 John 5:16—*What is a sin leading to death? Is it forgivable?*
Problem: On the one hand, the Scriptures speak of God's free and unconditional forgiveness to all who want it (see Acts 13:38–39; Rom. 5:20–21; 1 John 2:1). On the other hand, Jesus spoke of an unpardonable sin that can never be forgiven (Matt. 12:32). And John declares here that there is a "sin leading to death."
Solution: Bible commentators differ on just what John had in mind here. Some say he was referring to *repeated* sin (see comments on 1 John 3:9). Others believe he was speaking of a *grave* sin. Still others believe he had *apostasy* in mind (see 2 Peter 2).

Whatever John envisioned, there is no reason that it could not refer to a sin so serious that it would eventuate in physical death. Paul mentioned that the Corinthians had so participated in the Lord's Supper in an unworthy manner that some were sick and others were dead as a result (1 Cor. 11:29–30). In fact the priests Nadab and Abihu were killed for their disobedience to the Lord (Num. 3:4), as were Ananias and Sapphira for their sin (Acts 5:1–10). So it is entirely possible that John has some such serious sin in mind here whereby the believer is turned over to Satan for "the destruction of the flesh, that his spirit may be saved in the day of the Lord Jesus" (1 Cor. 5:5). Further, there are various ways "sin leading to death" can be understood:

1. Spiritual death (Eph. 2:1): not possible—spiritual death is an unregenerate state into which we are all born (John 3:3–7), not one we acquire by sin after we are regenerated.

2. Moral death (dead conscience—1 Tim. 4:2): possible but not probable in this context because it speaks of a particular sin, not a gradual process leading to a deadening of our moral nerves.

3. Physical death: probable since, elsewhere in the Bible, physical death results from serious sin (Acts 5:1–10; 1 Cor. 11:30).

STUDY QUESTIONS

1. What is the evidence, internal and external, that John the apostle wrote this Epistle?

2. How are the style and vocabulary similar?

3. Why was this letter written?

4. Compare the Gospel of John with his epistles.

5. What does John mean when he says believers "cannot sin" (1 John 3:9)?

6. What is a "sin leading to death" (5:16)?

SELECTED SOURCES

Baxter, Sidlow. *Explore the Book*. Grand Rapids: Zondervan, 1987.

Burge, Gary. *The Letters of John*. NIV Application Commentary. Grand Rapids: Zondervan, 1996.

Carson, D.A., Douglas Moo, and Leon Morris. *An Introduction to the New Testament*. Grand Rapids: Zondervan, 1992.

Geisler, Norman L., and Thomas Howe. *When Critics Ask: A Popular Handbook on Bible Difficulties*. Grand Rapids: Baker, 1997.

Guthrie, Donald. *New Testament Introduction*. Downers Grove, IL: InterVarsity, 1990.

Harrison, Everett F. *An Introduction to the New Testament*. Grand Rapids: Eerdmans, 1971.

Linnemann, Eta. *Historical Criticism of the Bible*. Translated by Robert Yarborough. Grand Rapids: Kregel, 2001.

Marshall, I. Howard. *The Epistles of John*. New International Commentary on the New Testament. Grand Rapids: Eerdmans, 1995.

Radmacher, Earl, Ronald Allen, and H. Wayne House, eds. *Nelson's New Illustrated Bible Commentary*. Nashville: Thomas Nelson, 1999.

Stott, John R.W. *The Letters of John: An Introduction and Commentary*. Tyndale New Testament Commentary. Grand Rapids: Eerdmans, 1988.

Walvoord, John F., and Roy B. Zuck, eds. *The Bible Knowledge Commentary*. 2 vols. Wheaton: Victor, 1983.

27

2 John, 3 John, and Jude

2 John

John the apostle, author of the Gospel of John, wrote this letter.

Internal Evidence
First, the book claims to come from "the Elder" (1:1). Given the time and nature of the book, there is no person alive other than John whose writing would be recognized as authoritative by a general audience. John was an apostle who, like other apostles (see 1 Peter 5:1), was an elder (bishop) by office (1 Tim. 3:1) and an apostle by gift (Eph. 4:11; 1 Cor. 12:4, 28). Further, the author spoke with the authority of an apostle, giving a commandment (v. 4) and a warning (v. 8) on how to live. Also the style and vocabulary of the book are like those of the apostle John (see Key Words below). Likewise, the heresy being addressed is the same as that attacked by the apostle John in his first epistle (see chap. 26), namely, those "who do not confess Jesus Christ as coming in the flesh" (2 John 7; see 1 John 4:2). Finally, both epistles refer to Antichrist as behind the denial of Christian truth (1 John 4:3; 2 John 7).

External Evidence
The external evidence for John the apostle is sufficient but less than for many other New Testament books, since 2 John is brief and personal in nature. Nonetheless, there is some early and good testimony for the beloved apostle being the author. First of all, the early Father Irenaeus, who knew John's disciple Polycarp, attributes it to John the apostle. Further, the Muratorian canon accepts it into the canon with John's name on it. Also other Fathers cited it as authentic, such as Clement of Alexandria, Origen, Cyril

of Jerusalem, Jerome, and Augustine. The fact that the author did not call himself an apostle is not problematic. "The Elder" is a term of respect and authority appropriate to John. In fact, at this late date (see below), no apostle was alive who commanded this much respect other than John the apostle.

When Was It Written?	The letter was written in AD 90–95. (1) According to Irenaeus, John died in AD 98, so the book must have been written before then. (2) He also said it was written during the reign of Domitian, which was AD 81–96. Thus this would place it before AD 96. (3) It was written after the Gospel of John (AD 85–90), which it presupposes. (4) Its similarity with 1 John reflects a similar time, namely, about AD 90 to 95.
To Whom Was It Written?	The letter was written to "the elect lady and her children" (1:1). John does not specify just who this is and, hence, it can be interpreted in more than one way. *An individual named "Eklekte" (chosen one) or "Kyria" (lady).* This woman may have had a church in her house (see Philem. 2). But nothing is known of any such lady, and this does not account for the plurals used in reference to the church (vv. 8, 10, 12). *Personification of a church.* Others believe "elect lady" may have been a reference to a church and not an individual because there are no personal names mentioned in the book, as there are in 3 John, which is also only one short chapter; the reference to a "sister" may be another church (v. 13); on this view, "children" would be members, just as Paul referred to a disciple as a "son" (2 Tim. 1:2); and the recipients of this epistle are referred to several times in the plural (vv. 8, 10, 12).
Where Were They Located?	The recipients were probably located in the same general area to which 1 John was written, Asia Minor (modern Turkey).
Why Was It Written?	Three reasons can be discovered from the test for writing this book. (1) He wanted to warn them against the heresy of denying the humanity of Christ (v. 7). (2) He wished to exhort them to Christian charity or love (v. 5). (3) He desired to encourage them to live a life of fidelity in the faith (vv. 4, 6).
What Is It About?	The Theme: Continuation with Christ (v. 4). Key Verse: "This is love, that we walk according to His commandments" (v. 6). Key Words and Phrases: *abide* (3x), *antichrist* (1x), *beginning* (2x), *children* (3x), *commandment* (4x), *deceiver* (2x), *elect, chosen* (2x),

Father (4x), flesh (1x), (to) love, love (4x), teaching, doctrine (3x), truth (4x), and walk (3x). See appendix 3 for a more complete word study.

Uses of "Truth": body of Christian teaching (v. 1)—substantive (noun); of Christ (v. 2)—personal (pronoun); for "truly" (v. 4)—(adverb).

The Heresy: He warns against denying the humanity of Christ (v. 7), which is known as Docetism, in contrast to Colossians where they were denying the deity of Christ (2:8–9).

THE OUTLINE:

> I. **Path of Truth—Love** (vv. 1–6)
>   A. Introduction—Grace and peace in truth and love (vv. 1–3)
>   B. Walking in truth (v. 4)
>   C. The command of truth (vv. 5–6)
> II. **Peril of Truth—Laxity** (vv. 7–13)
>   A. Exhorting believers about deceivers who deny the truth (v. 7)
>   B. Rewarding believers for keeping the truth (v. 8)
>   C. Warning about transgressors of the truth (v. 9)
>   D. No hospitality for deniers of the truth (vv. 10–11)
>   E. Conclusion (vv. 12–13)

THE CONTENTS: After the introduction (vv. 1–3), John speaks of the path of truth (vv. 4–6) and warns against the peril of truth (vv. 7–13), which arises out of laxity. In the first section he speaks of the path of truth, rejoicing that they were walking in it (v. 4) and exhorting them to continue to walk in love (vv. 5–6). In the second part, he warns against the peril of becoming lax in the truth and drifting from it (vv. 7–13), exhorting believers about deceivers who deny the truth (v. 7), rewarding believers for keeping the truth (v. 8), warning about transgressors of the truth (v 9), and urging them to show no hospitality for those who deny the truth (vv. 10–11). He concludes with the hope he will visit them (v. 12) and greetings from a sister church (v. 13).

How to Respond to Critics

2 John 1—Who was the "elect lady"?

Problem: John addresses his second letter to "the elect lady." Some have argued that because this was strictly a personal letter addressed to a particular lady, that it does not belong in the canon of Scripture. Was the "elect lady" a person or not?

Solution: First of all, if the "elect lady" were a particular person, this would not exclude it from the canon of Scripture. Several of the epistles of Paul were personal letters to particular individuals (for example, Timothy, Titus, Philemon).

Second, it is possible that the elect lady was not a particular person. The proposals of commentators basically fall into two categories, the literal and the figurative. Those who understand this address to be *literal* hold that this was indeed a certain individual whom John knew. The following points are offered in favor of this view. (1) It seems to be more natural to take the words as an address to an actual lady and her children. (2) This view fits with the references to the children of the elect lady, her sister and her sister's children (v. 13). (3) The basic structure of the greeting in verse 1 fits with the basic structure of the greeting of 3 John 1 ("To the . . . whom I love in truth"), which was an address to a certain individual. (4) If the term *lady* refers to the church, then to whom does the word children refer? Are the "*children*" not included in the church? Are they somehow different from the church?

Third, those who hold the view that this is a *figure of speech* maintain that this is a reference to the church as a whole or to a particular local church. The following points are made in support of this view. (1) John states that the lady is loved not only by him but by "all those who have known the truth" (v. 1). This would mean that everyone knew her. However, this kind of observation would fit better when referring to a local church than to an individual. (2) Although John uses the singular pronoun *you*, he does switch to the plural in verse 8 where he seems to be warning the lady: "Look to yourselves." But if this were a literal woman, why would he use a plural at all? (3) The appeal to "love one another" (v. 5) makes more sense when directed to a community of believers than to a woman and her children. (4) The personification of the church in feminine terms is common in the Bible (for example, Eph. 5:30–33 where Paul develops the idea that the church is the bride of Christ; 1 Peter 5:13 where Peter uses the feminine expression of the church).

Although we may not be able to decide the issue definitively on the basis of our current information, it is clear that, if this was a personal letter to a literal woman, this fact would not exclude it from the canon of Scripture. And it is not at all clear that it is a reference to an individual lady.

2 John 10 (see Matt. 5:44)—*Why does this verse tell us not to receive certain people when Jesus told us to love our enemies?*
Problem: According to Jesus, we are supposed to love our enemies, bless those who curse us, and do good to those who hate us.

The theater, Aspendos, Pamphylia.

However, according to John, we are not to receive into our house or even greet anyone who comes to us and does not believe that Christ has come in the flesh. Which are we supposed to do?

Solution: We are supposed to follow both instructions. The apparent discrepancy between these directives arises from the fact that they are talking about two totally different situations.

In the passage in Matthew, Jesus is contrasting his own teaching to that of the Pharisees. The divine principle of love should be the guiding principle of one's life. Even though some people are the enemies of God, he still allows the rain to fall on their crops and causes the sun to shine on them. God treats the wicked with lovingkindness. However, he never condones their wickedness. As Paul points out in Romans, the goodness of God is not a sign of his approval of their actions. Rather, the goodness of God is designed to lead to repentance (Rom. 2:4).

The passage in 2 John is not talking about someone who simply comes to visit. Rather, John is talking about false teachers who are deceivers (v. 7) and who come to present their doctrines.

First, John is instructing the local church, and the individuals of the local church, not to extend hospitality to these persons, because that would imply that the church accepted or approved of their teaching. The people of the local church were directed not even to give a Christian greeting to them, lest this be misconstrued as an attitude of tolerance of their false doctrines. This was by no means a command not to love one's enemy. In fact following John's directives would be the supreme act of love for one's enemy. By clearly demonstrating an intolerance for false doctrine, it would be possible to communicate to false teachers that they needed to repent. On the contrary, if the church or individual were to extend hospitality to a false teacher, he would be encouraged in his position and take this action as an acceptance of his doctrine or as a covering of his unrighteousness.

Second, it must be remembered that, in the early church, the evangelistic and pastoral ministry of the church was conducted primarily by individuals who traveled from location to location. These itinerant pastors depended on the hospitality of the people of a local congregation. John is directing the church not to extend this kind of hospitality to teachers of false doctrine. This is not contradictory to Jesus's teaching. We are to love our enemies, but not encourage them in their evil deeds. We are to do good to them that hate us, but not condone their wickedness. As Jesus said, we are to show ourselves to be children of our Father. In the very same Sermon on the Mount, Jesus went on to warn his disciples to beware of false prophets "who *come* . . . in sheep's clothing" (Matt. 7:15). John gave practical application to this warning, and thereby encouraged the local church to maintain its purity and devotion to Christ.

STUDY QUESTIONS

1. What is the internal and external evidence that John the apostle wrote this Epistle?

2. What were his purposes in writing?

3. To whom was the book written?

4. What was the heresy held by this church?

5. Comment on the many ways the word *truth* is used in 2 John.

3 John

Who Wrote It? John the apostle, author of the Gospel of John, wrote this letter.

Internal Evidence
(1) "The Elder" (v. 1) is a title of seniority and authority, characteristics known to be true of the apostle John. Apostles were elders by office (see 1 Tim. 3:1) and apostles by gift (Eph. 4:11; 1 Cor. 12:4, 28). (2) The apostle Peter also spoke of himself as an elder (1 Peter 5:1). (3) The author of 3 John spoke with the authority of an apostle (vv. 5–12). (4) John the apostle was the only well-known apostle alive at this time whose letter would have been recognized and accepted from one who simply used the title "the elder." (5) He wrote in the same style as the author of 1 and 2 John (see chapter 26), who was the apostle John (see Who Wrote It? in chapter 26 and under 2 John in this chapter).

External Evidence
The outside evidence for this book is small but sufficient, considering its size and contents. First of all, some early Fathers cite it, such as Cyril of Jerusalem, Jerome, and Augustine. Further, the Muratorian canon has 3 John in it. Indeed, Jerome put it in the Latin Vulgate Bible, which became the standard Bible of Christendom for a thousand years. Finally, the title "The Third Epistle of John" is on Greek manuscripts of it from the earliest times.

When Was It Written? The letter was written in AD 90 to 95, about the same time as John's two other epistles. (1) It was written before AD 98, because this is when John died. (2) He probably also wrote it during the reign of Domitian, which was AD 81–96. Thus it was before AD 96. (3) It assumes the Gospel of John (AD 85–90), so it must have been written after it. (4) Its similarity with 1 and 2 John reflect a similar time, namely, about AD 90 to 95.

To Whom Was It Written? The letter was written to Gaius and his house church (v. 1).

Where Were They Located?

They were located somewhere in Asia Minor (modern Turkey), the same general location of the recipients of 1 and 2 John.

Why Was It Written?

The reasons for which John wrote are made clear in several places. (1) John desired to praise Gaius for his fidelity to the truth (v. 1); (2) he wished to commend the congregation for their hospitality and support for those in the ministry (vv. 3–8); (3) he wanted to condemn Diotrephes for his lack of humility (vv. 9–11); (4) John desired to commend Demetrius for his testimony (v. 12).

What Is It About?

The Theme: Contribution for Christ.

Key Verses: "Beloved, you do faithfully whatever you do for the brethren and for strangers. . . . We therefore ought to receive such, that we may become fellow workers for the truth" (vv. 5, 8).

Key Words and Phrases: *beloved* (4x), *do evil, evil* (2x), *do good, be in good health, be well* (3x), *truth* (6x), *walk* (2x), and (*to*) *witness, testify, witness* (5x). See appendix 3 for a more complete word study.

Significant Persons: John wrote it (v. 1), Gaius received it (v. 1), Diotrephes occasioned it (v. 9), and Demetrius carried it (v. 12).

Missions: It manifests concern and care for missionaries.

Truth: It is used as a sphere of compassion (v. 1), a sphere of conduct (v. 4), a source of power (v. 3), a standard of practice (v. 12b), and a savior of participants (v. 12a).

The Friends: The special name for Christians used is "friends" (v. 14; see John 15:15). In Acts 9:2 believers were called "of the Way." The term *Christian* was first applied to Christ's followers in Antioch (11:26). Elsewhere they are called "the sect of the Nazarenes" (24:5).

A Comparison of 2 and 3 John:

> 2 John—Truth is worth *standing* for.
>
> 3 John—Truth is worth *working* for.

THE OUTLINE:

   I. **Confirmation of Gaius**—Loved in the Truth (vv. 1–8)
  II. **Condemnation of Diotrephes**—Who Loved Not the Truth (vv. 9–10)
 III. **Commendation of Demetrius**—Who Was Loved by the Truth (vv. 11–12)
 IV. **Conclusion** (vv. 13–14)

Temple of Artemis, Sardis, Asia.

THE CONTENTS: John wrote in confirmation of Gaius who was loved in the truth (vv. 1–8); in condemnation of Diotrephes, who loved not the truth (vv. 9–10); and in commendation of Demetrius, who was loved by the truth (vv. 11–12). His greatest joy was to see his disciples faithful to the truth (v. 4) and then to be supportive of those who proclaimed the truth (v. 8). Unlike 1 and 2 John, no specific heresy is attacked, simply those who do not walk in the truth and who desire a dominant position in the church. Indeed, Diotrephes appears to be the beginning of the drift away from an autonomous local church with a plurality of elders (see Acts 14:23; Phil. 1:1) and no single bishop over them or a group of churches.

How to Respond to Critics

3 John 7—*Should money be taken from unbelievers to do God's work?*
Problem: John claims here that the brethren took no support for their ministry from unbelievers. Yet when Solomon built the temple he accepted gifts from Gentiles (1 Kings 5:10; 2 Chron. 2:13–16). Is it always wrong to take money from unbelievers for God's work?

Solution: As a rule, God's work should be supported by God's people, for those who benefit spiritually should share materially with their teachers (1 Cor. 9:1–14). On the other hand, it may offend an unbeliever to have his or her gift turned down and could place an obstacle in the way of the person's becoming a believer. Moses did not reject gifts from Egypt (Exod. 12:25–36), nor did Solomon reject the gifts and help of the Gentile King Hiram (2 Chron. 2:13–16) or from the Queen of Sheba (1 Kings 10:10). So while money should not be sought from unbelievers, neither should it be rejected, unless of course there are strings attached. Under no conditions should spiritual or other favors be bought by anyone.

Furthermore, it should be noted that this passage in 3 John is descriptive not prescriptive. It does not say, "Never take money from unbelievers." It simply notes that these believers on this journey did not accept help from unbelievers. No doubt they wanted to refrain from any appearance of selling the truth (see 2 Cor. 11:7; 1 Thess. 2:9). Rather, as it should have been, they depended on other believers to "send them forward on their journey in a manner worthy of God" (v. 6). We should not expect unbelievers to support the cause of faith.

STUDY QUESTIONS

1. What is the evidence inside and outside of the book that John the apostle wrote it?

2. Why did John write this Epistle?

3. Discuss the various ways the word *truth* is used in 3 John.

4. What evidence is there even in this early time of a single individual assuming authority in a church (vv. 9–10)?

Jude

Who Wrote It?

The author is Jude, "the brother of James" (Matt. 13:55), both of whom were (half-) brothers of Jesus (see Acts 1:14).[1]

Internal Evidence

(1) The author claims to be "Jude, . . . brother of James" (v. 1). (2) Jude was not an apostle. He refers to the apostles in the third person (vv. 17–18). (3) Nevertheless, he spoke with authority (vv. 3–23), as someone closely associated with the apostles. (4) When the name James is used alone in the New Testament, it usually means James, the brother of Jesus (see Who Wrote It in chapter 23). (5) Since Matthew puts his name last in the list of Jesus's brothers, he was probably the younger brother (see Matt. 13:55; see Mark 6:3). (6) Along with his brothers, he was an unbeliever before Jesus's resurrection (John 7:5). (7) But since he was in the upper room at Pentecost (Acts 1:14), we can assume he, like James, became a believer after the appearances of Jesus (1 Cor. 15:7). (8) Likewise, he became an itinerant missionary after Pentecost with the other "brothers of the Lord" (9:5).

External Evidence

There is a significant amount of evidence that this Epistle is genuine. (1) Many of the earliest Fathers allude to it, including the Didache (2.7); Barnabas (2.10); the *Shepherd of Hermas* (*Similitude* 5.7 2); and Polycarp (*Epistle to Philippians* 3). (2) Other early Fathers accepted it as canonical with Jude's name on it, such as Athenagoras, Clement of Alexandria, Origen, Didymus of Alexandria, Tertullian, Athanasius, Augustine, and Jerome. (3) Some of the earliest New Testament Greek manuscripts have Jude in them (for example, Bodmer Papyri, AD 200). (4) The early Muratorian canon contains the book of Jude.

When Was It Written?

Jude was written between AD 67 and 69. It was written after 2 Peter (AD 64), since scoffers are referred to as future in 2 Peter 3:3 and they are present in Jude 18. It must have been composed before AD 70, since the temple was not yet destroyed. If it had been destroyed, surely he would have mentioned it because it would have supported the central point he was making in the book, namely, that apostasy brings the judgment of God.

To Whom Was It Written?

Some say it was written to Gentile believers because of the reference to "our common salvation" (see v. 3). Others say it was to Jewish believers because of Old Testament references, references to other Jewish literature, and no mention of idolatry. Maybe there were both Jews and Gentiles among them.

Where Were They Located?

The recipients of the letter may have been in Antioch where there were both Jewish and Gentile Christians in large numbers and where they could be susceptible to apostate influences.

Why Was It Written?

Four basic reasons for writing are evident. (1) Jude wanted them to be steadfast in the faith (v. 3). (2) He hoped to explain the apostasy from the faith to them (vv. 4–16). (3) He wished to inform them of how to avoid the coming catastrophe (vv. 17–19). (4) He wanted to encourage them to mature in the faith (vv. 20–24).

What Is It About?

The Theme: Contention for Christ.
Key Verse: "I found it necessary to write to you exhorting you to contend earnestly for the faith which was once for all delivered to the saints" (v. 3).
Key Words and Phrases: *act in an ungodly way, ungodliness, ungodly* (6x), *beloved* (3x), *condemnation* (1x), *contend* (1x), *everlasting, eternal* (3x), *faith* (2x), *judgment* (3x), and *save* (2x). See appendix 3 for a more complete word study.
Use of Old Testament: The vocabulary reveals a strong use of the Greek Old Testament (see vv. 5–7).
Nonbiblical Citations: There are two allusions to noncanonical or pseudepigraphal books: *The Book of Enoch* (vv. 14–15) and *The Assumption of Moses* (v. 9). Neither of these is cited as Scripture. Jude uses them simply for a truth recorded in them, the way Paul cited three pagan writers: Aritas (Acts 17:28), Meander (1 Cor. 15:33), and Epimenides (Titus 1:12).
Note: None of these citations approve of everything in its source but merely the truth of the particular citation made. Ultimately, all truth is God's truth no matter where it is found.
Use of Nature: Jude, like his brother James (and Jesus), uses many illustrations from nature (vv. 12–13).
Style: The literary style is direct and vigorous. Like his brother James and their "brother" Jesus, there are lively figures of speech drawn from nature.

THE OUTLINE:

I. Salutation—Preservation from Apostasy (vv. 1–2)
II. Exhortation—Warning about Apostasy (vv. 3–23)
    A. Contending against apostates (vv. 3–4)
    B. Conduct of apostates (vv. 5–16)
        1. Examples in the past—Egypt, angels, Sodom (vv. 5–7)
        2. Actions in the present (vv. 8–16)
            a. Rejecting authority (vv. 8–10)
            b. Walking in error (v. 11)
            c. Leading falsely (vv. 12–13)
            d. Pleasing self (vv. 14–16)
    C. Consequences of apostasy (vv. 17–23)
        1. Warning about it (vv. 17–18)
        2. Divisions from it (v. 19)
        3. Separation from apostasy (vv. 20–23)
III. Benediction—Victory over Apostasy (vv. 24–25)

THE CONTENTS: Jude is about contending for the faith against apostasy from the faith. In the salutation (vv. 1–2) he speaks about God's preservation of the faithful from apostasy and then gives a warning about apostasy (vv. 3–23), concluding with a promise of victory over apostasy (vv. 24–25). In the major section in which he gives an exhortation against apostasy or falling away from the faith, he urges contending against apostates (vv. 3–4), and he describes the conduct of the apostates (vv. 5–16), both from the past in Israel (vv. 5–7) and the present in the church (vv. 8–16). Jude reminds his readers of the characteristics of apostates: rejecting authority (vv. 8–10), walking in error (v. 11), leading falsely (vv. 12–13), and pleasing themselves (vv. 14–16). Then he shows the consequences of apostasy (vv. 17–23) based in the apostles' warning about it (vv. 17–18) and resulting in divisions (v. 19). He urges believers to separate from it (vv. 20–23). The author concludes his exhortation with a benediction that promises ultimate victory over apostasy at the coming again of our Lord (vv. 24–25).

How to Respond to Critics

Jude 9—*Isn't the dispute between Michael the archangel and the devil based on an apocryphal story?*

Problem: Jude records an account in which Michael the archangel and the devil have a dispute over the body of Moses, saying, "Yet Michael the archangel, in contending with the devil, when he disputed about the body of Moses, dared not bring against him a reviling accusation, but said, 'The Lord rebuke you!'" This account is not found in the Old Testament and is also considered to be found in a pseudepigraphal book (false writing) titled *The Assumption of Moses*.

Solution: Just because the account is not found in any Old Testament passages of Scripture doesn't mean that the event did not occur. The Bible often cites truths from books that are not inspired, but which contain, nevertheless, some true statements. A biblical author is not limited to citing only Scripture. All truth is God's truth, wherever it is found.

Jude 14—*Doesn't Jude cite the uninspired* Book of Enoch *as divinely authoritative?*

Problem: Jude quotes the *Book of Enoch*, saying, "Now Enoch, the seventh from Adam, prophesied about these men also, saying, 'Behold, the Lord comes with ten thousands of His saints.'" However, *Enoch* is not an inspired book but is considered pseudepigraphal (a false writing) by the Christian church.

Solution: First, it is not certain that Jude is actually citing the *Book of Enoch*. He may simply be mentioning an event that is *also* found in this uninspired book. It is noteworthy that Jude does not affirm that Enoch wrote this statement. He simply records what Enoch *said*. Jude may have been using a valid oral tradition and not the *Book of Enoch*.

Furthermore, even if Jude took this statement from the *Book of Enoch*, it is still true. As I have already stated, many true statements can be found outside of Scripture. Just because Jude quoted from a noncanonical (extrabiblical) source does not mean that what he says is necessarily wrong. Not everything in the *Book of Enoch* is correct, but this does not warrant the conclusion that everything in it is wrong.

Remember that the apostle Paul cited truths from pagan poets (Acts 17:28; 1 Cor. 15:33; Titus 1:12) without implying that these books are inspired. Indeed, even Balaam's donkey uttered a truth (Num. 22:30). The inspiration of the book of Jude guarantees that all it cites is true.

Finally, the external evidence for Jude is extensive from the time of Irenaeus (ca. AD 170) onward. It is in the Bodmer Papyri ($\mathfrak{P}^{72}$) of AD 250, and traces of it are found even earlier in the Didache (2:7), which probably dates from the second century. So there is evidence for the authenticity of the book of Jude, which is not diminished by this allusion to what Enoch said. The existence of Enoch and his communication with God is a fact established elsewhere, both in the Old Testament (Gen. 5:24) and New Testament (Heb. 11:5).

STUDY QUESTIONS

1. What is the internal and external evidence that the author is Jude the (half-) brother of Jesus?

2. Why did Jude write this book?

3. What evidence is there that it was written in the late 60s?

4. Do the nonbiblical citations in Jude prove that he thought these sources were divinely inspired?

SELECTED SOURCES

Baxter, Sidlow. *Explore the Book*. Grand Rapids: Zondervan, 1987.

Burge, Gary. *The Letters of John*. NIV Application Commentary. Grand Rapids: Zondervan, 1996.

Carson, D.A., Douglas Moo, and Leon Morris. *An Introduction to the New Testament*. Grand Rapids: Zondervan, 1992.

Geisler, Norman L., and Thomas Howe. *When Critics Ask: A Popular Handbook on Bible Difficulties*. Grand Rapids: Baker, 1997.

Guthrie, Donald. *New Testament Introduction*. Downers Grove, IL: InterVarsity, 1990.

Harrison, Everett F. *An Introduction to the New Testament*. Grand Rapids: Eerdmans, 1971.

Linnemann, Eta. *Historical Criticism of the Bible*. Translated by Robert Yarborough. Grand Rapids: Kregel, 2001.

MacArthur, John. *2 Peter & Jude*. MacArthur New Testament Commentary. Chicago: Moody, 2005.

Moo, Douglas J. *2 Peter, Jude*. NIV Application Commentary. Grand Rapids: Zondervan, 1996.

Radmacher, Earl, Ronald Allen, and H. Wayne House, eds. *Nelson's New Illustrated Bible Commentary*. Nashville: Thomas Nelson, 1999.

Walvoord, John F., and Roy B. Zuck, eds. *The Bible Knowledge Commentary*. 2 vols. Wheaton: Victor, 1983.

28
Revelation

John the apostle, author of the Gospel of John (see chapter 7) and the three Epistles of John (see chapters 26 and 27), is the author of Revelation.

Internal Evidence
(1) The author calls himself "John" five times (1:1, 4, 9; 21:2; 22:8). (2) No one else but the apostle John could use just his name, John, and have his book accepted. (3) It is the only book, other than the Gospel of John (also written by the apostle John), to refer to Christ as the Word (*Logos*) in the personal sense (John 1:1; Rev. 19:13). (4) The basic style and content use of the Greek fit the apostle John.[1] (5) The vocabulary has a strong overlap, with 416 words in the Gospel the same as 913 separate words in Revelation. (6) The author's detailed knowledge of the land and events fits the apostle John (chaps. 1–3). (7) The late date (AD 95—see below) fits John who alone among the apostles lived to this date.

External Evidence
(1) Justin Martyr called the author "A certain man among us, whose name was John, one of the apostles of Christ . . ." (Justin, *Against Heresies*). (2) Irenaeus, an early resident of Asia, cited it as John's writing. (3) The *Shepherd of Hermas* refers to it. (4) The early Muratorian canon includes it in the Bible. (5) Other early Fathers cited it as coming from John the apostle, including Tertullian, Hippolytus, Clement of Alexandria, Origen, Athanasius, and Augustine. (6) Later voices to reject John's authorship did so on dogmatic grounds, largely because they opposed John's millennialism

The Seven Churches
of Asia Minor.

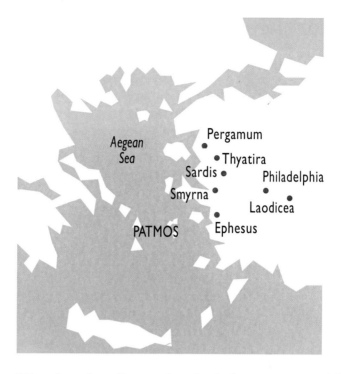

(chap. 20) and used an allegorical method of interpretation. (7) The alleged assertion by Papias that John was martyred before AD 70 is contradicted by many other sources (see points 1–6) and is subject to other interpretations.

When Was It Written?

The book of Revelation was probably written in AD 95, but there are two views as to when it was written—the early view and the late view.

The Early View
Those who hold the early view believe the book was written in the late 60s, after Nero's reign ended in AD 68–69.
Argument One: John reflects a time of persecution of Christians, which fits Nero's time (see 1:9; 2:13; 3:10; 6:9; 17:6; 18:24; 19:2; 20:4).

Response: Intense persecution also occurred under Domitian in AD 96. There is no evidence that Nero's persecution occurred beyond Rome as Domitian's probably did, but John is speaking about such a persecution in the churches in Asia Minor (2:13; 3:10).
Argument Two: John's allusions to emperor worship reflect a time just after Nero (13:4, 15–16; 14:9–11; 15:2; 16:2; 19:20; 20:4).
Response: There is no solid evidence that Nero made worshiping him a requirement. It is known that Domitian stressed his deity, ordering that he be addressed as "lord and god." In the futurists' interpretation (see below) the texts cited above are not references

to first-century Roman emperors but to the Antichrist of the future tribulation period.

Argument Three: Revelation speaks of the beast recovering from a mortal wound (Rev. 13:3–4), and a legend holds that Nero came back to life from a mortal wound. The existence of this "Nero myth" is said to be more compatible with the earlier date, shortly after Nero's time.

Response: It takes longer than a few years (Nero died in AD 68 or 69) for a myth like this to grow; it takes decades, if not generations. There are some significant dissimilarities with Nero since there is no evidence that he demanded worship of all or used a mark of the beast on all citizens. In the futurists' interpretation this refers to the future Antichrist.

Argument Four: The numerical value of the letters in Nero's name equal 666, the very number of the Antichrist (Rev. 13:18). This too argues for an early date just after Nero.

Response: First of all, this same argument has been used for Popes, Hitler, and many others (including Ronald Reagan) being the Antichrist—none of them were. It may apply to one who is yet future, namely the Antichrist of the tribulation period to come. There is a way to interpret the 666 other than adding the numerical value of the letters in a name. Three is the number of Divine perfection for God, and six is the number of man or human imperfection. Thus the Antichrist is merely an imperfect man who claims to be God.[2]

Argument Five: The book of Revelation refers to the Jerusalem temple as still standing (11:1–2, and it was destroyed in AD 70). Hence, the book must have been written before AD 70.

Response: John may be referring to a rebuilt temple of the future tribulation period (see below) and not to any temple standing in his day.

Argument Six: John refers to seven kings, five of whom are fallen, and the sixth who is alive when he was writing (17:9–11). This would take us to Galba who reigned shortly after Nero.

Response: The text is not clear. Where does the counting begin, with Augustus or from Caesar, who first claimed imperial rights? Or from Caligula who was the first to persecute Christians? Should the three minor ones be included who reigned only for a short time in AD 68 to 69? Is this a reference to the emperors in John's day or to future kings, as some futurists claim?

Argument Seven: John used terms like *near* (1:3) and *quickly* (3:11; 22:12), indicating that he anticipated an immediate fulfillment. But the only near event that occurred when these things could have been fulfilled was the destruction of Jerusalem in AD 70.

The amphitheater, Pergamum.

Response: *Quickly* can mean "suddenly" or "not soon." *Near* is a relative term that can be used of events thousands of years in the future. The question is, near for whom, God or for us (see 2 Peter 3:10)? Hebrews refers to the second coming of Christ as "a little while" (Heb. 10:37), and it has been almost two thousand years since, and it still has not happened.

The Later View
The later view, that Revelation was written in the AD 90s, is supported by good evidence.

1. Early Father Irenaeus (second century) said of John: ". . . who beheld the apocalyptic vision" that he received "almost in our day, toward the end of Domitian's reign" (*Against Heresies* 5.30.3).

2. Victorinus (third century) wrote: "When John said these things, he was on the Island of Patmos, condemned to the mines by Caesar Domitian" (*Commentary of Revelation* 10:11).

3. Eusebius (fourth century) confirmed the Domitian date (*Ecclesiastical History* 3.18).

4. Other early Fathers after AD 70 refer to the tribulation or Antichrist spoken of in Revelation as yet future (see Commondianus [third century], *Instructions* 44, and Ephraem of Syria [fourth century], *On the Last Times*, 2).

5. John's exile on the island of Patmos implies a later date when persecution was more rampant (1:9).

6. References to persecution and martyrdom in the churches reflect a later date (see Rev. 2:10, 13).

7. Polycarp's reference to the church at Smyrna (*Epistle to the Philippians* 11.3) reveals that it did not exist in Paul's day (by AD 64) as it did in Revelation 2:8.

8. The conditions of the seven churches (chaps. 2–3) fit this later period rather than that reflected in Paul's epistles written in the 60s.

9. Emperor worship reflected in Revelation did not exist in Nero's day, so he could not have been a fulfillment of it.

10. Laodicea was a prosperous city in Revelation 3:17, yet it was destroyed by an earthquake ca. AD 61 and is unlikely to have been rebuilt into such a prosperous city so fast in only a few years.

11. The Nicolaitans referred to in Revelation 2:6 were not firmly established until nearer the end of the century.

12. For the early date there is not enough time for John to replace Paul as the main leader of the Asian church.[3]

To Whom Was It Written?

The book of Revelation was written "to the seven churches which are in Asia: to Ephesus, to Symrna, to Pergamos, to Thyatira, to Sardis, to Philadelphia, and to Laodicea" (1:11; see v. 4).

Where Were They Located?

The readers were located in Asia Minor (1:4), which is modern Turkey. They were strategically located on circular roads that bound populous, wealthy, and influential sections of the province.

Why Was It Written?

There are many reasons for the writing of the book of Revelation: (1) to communicate the person, power, and program of the Savior (1:1); (2) to comfort the persecuted saints (v. 9); (3) to condemn the princes of sin (chaps. 17–20); (4) to complete the plan of

The gymnasium, Sardis, Asia Minor.

Scripture (22:18–19); and (5) to convey the promise of Christ's second coming (v. 12).

What Is It About? The Theme. The consummation of all things in Christ (11:15).

Key Verse: "Write the things which you have seen [chap. 1], and the things which are [chaps. 2–3], and the things which will take place after this [chaps. 4–22]" (Rev. 1:19).

Key Words and Phrases: *after* (*these things*) (47x), *angel* (75x), *Babylon* (6x), *beast* (38x), *bowl* (12x), *Christ* (11x), *church* (20x), *devil, Satan* (13x), *dragon* (13x), *earthquake* (7x), *God* (98x), *Jesus* (14x), *judge, judgment* (16x), *know* (11x), *lamb* (29x), *mystery* (4x), *nations* (22x), *overcome* (17x), *plague* (15x), *repent* (12x), *(to) seal, seal* (31x), *see, behold* (62x), *seven* (54x), *spirit* (23x), *throne* (46x), *thunder* (10x), *trumpet* (6x), *twelve* (22x), *voice, sound* (55x), *woe* (14x), and *wrath* (16x). See appendix 3 for a more complete word study.

Use of the Old Testament: The language of Revelation is heavily dependent on the Old Testament. The most used books are Psalms, Isaiah, Ezekiel, and Daniel.

The Nature of Revelation: It is a book with:

1. a prophetic program (1:19)
2. enigmatic proclamations (having mysterious meaning; see 13:18)
3. a dramatic plot and climactic plan (see 11:15)
4. cataclysmic pronouncements (judgments) (chaps. 6–18)
5. an apocalyptic presentation (revelations)
6. a polemic purpose (anti-"Babylon")
7. numeric proliferation (many numbers: 7s and 12s)
8. rhythmic (and parenthetic) progression
9. symbolic pictures (see 1:1—sign-ified)
10. Hebraic phraseology (278 of 404 verses are from the Old Testament)

Prophecy: It is the most prophetic of all New Testament books. John classed himself as a prophet (22:9) and refers to his book as a prophecy five times (1:3; 22:7, 10, 18, 19).

Heaven and Earth: It is characterized by its notable interplay between heaven and earth.

Worship: It stresses worship more than any book in the New Testament (see 3:9; 4:10; 5:14; 7:11; 9:20; 11:1, 16; 14:7; 15:4; 19:4, 10, 20; 22:9).

THE OUTLINE:

I. The Person of Christ—His Character (chap. 1)
- A. His prophet (vv. 1–2)
- B. His promise (v. 3)
- C. His priests (vv. 4–6)
- D. His parousia (coming) (v. 7)
- E. His pedigree (v. 8)
- F. His proclamation (vv. 9–11)
- G. His pictorial presentation (vv. 12–18)
- H. His prophetic program (vv. 19–20)

II. The Possession of Christ—His Church (chaps. 2–3)
- A. His preserving of a patient church—Ephesus (2:1–7)
- B. His priority in a persecuted church—Smyrna (vv. 8–11)
- C. His power in a polluted church—Pergamos (vv. 12–17)
- D. His purity in a paganized church—Thyatira (vv. 18–29)

Zeus, from Antalya
Museum.

E. His providence in a professing church—Sardis
(3:1–6)

F. His protection of a pure church—Philadelphia
(vv. 7–13)

G. His primacy in a passive church—Laodicea
(vv. 14–22)

III. The Program of Christ—His Coming (chaps. 4–22)

A. In heaven (chaps. 4–5)

1. Praise God for creation (chap. 4)

2. Praise God for redemption (chap. 5)

B. On earth (chaps. 6–22)

1. During tribulation—for seven years
(chaps. 6–18)

a. Seven seals (6:1–8:5)

b. Seven trumpets (8:6–15:8)

c. Seven bowls (chaps. 16–18)

2. At second coming (chap. 19)

3. During the millennium—one thousand
years (chap. 20)

4. In the new heaven and new earth—forever
(chaps. 21–22)

THE CONTENTS: Taking a literal futurist interpretation of the text of Revelation (see below) yields the following message: It is the *revelations* of Jesus Christ. First, there is the revelation of his person (chap. 1), setting forth his prophet (vv. 1–2), his promise (v. 3), his priests (vv. 4–6), his parousia or coming (v. 7), his pedigree as the Alpha and Omega (v. 8), his proclamation to write this book (vv. 9–11), his pictorial presentation as the Head of his church (vv. 12–18), and his prophetic program (vv. 19–20).

Having spoken of the person of Christ, the book turns to the possession of Christ—his church (chaps. 2–3). In this section his character is shown to be sufficient for the varied conditions in his church. In 2:1–7 he is preserving a patient church (Ephesus); in verses 8–11 he has priority in a persecuted church (Smyrna); in verses 12–17 his power is manifest in a polluted church (Pergamos); in verses 18–29 his purity is sufficient for a paganized church (Thyatira); in 3:1–6 his providence is evident in a professing church (Sardis); in verses 7–13 his protection is provided for a pure church (Philadelphia); and in verses 14–22 his primacy is projected in a passive church (Laodicea).

In the final section, we turn from the person and possession of Christ to the program of Christ (chaps. 4–22). First, we see his program in heaven (chaps. 4–5), which is to praise God for creation (chap. 4) and to praise him for his redemption (chap. 5). Then we see his program on earth unfolded with the seven-sealed book (chaps. 6–22). His program during the tribulation (chaps. 6–18) is unfolded by the seven seals (6:1–8:5), the seven trumpets (8:6–15:8), and the seven bowls (chaps. 16–18). Then we see his program at the second coming (chap. 19), during the millennium (chap. 20), and in the new heaven and new earth (chaps. 21–22) when paradise lost becomes paradise regained, the devil is finally defeated, and righteousness will reign in a world of no sorrow, crying, disease, or death—forever.

How Should Revelation Be Interpreted?

There are several ways the book of Revelation has been understood:

Idealist or Spiritual View: According to this view, the predictions in Revelation are allegorical, symbolizing the ageless struggle between good and evil.

Response: If this view is correct, the second coming and the resurrection must also be allegorical, which is heresy. If other sections of the Bible (like Christ's death and resurrection) are allegorized, it undermines our salvation (see Rom. 10:9; 1 Cor. 15:17).[4]

The Historicist View: Revelation is a symbolic picture of the total history of the church, age by age, from apostolic to modern times. *Response*: This view simply does not fit the historical events, as is evident from the fact that there are many different interpretations. It is a serious stretch of the imagination to see in John's visions the Islamic invasion, the rise of the Papacy, and the great modern European wars. This view is also a form of allegorical interpretation, which suffers from the same criticism just given.

The Preterist View: There are full preterists and partial preterists. The full preterists take all the predictions in Revelation as referring to the past, having been fulfilled between AD 64 and 70 under Nero's reign, including the resurrection of believers and the second coming of Christ (chaps. 19–20). Partial preterists believe that only the predictions about the tribulation (chaps. 6–18) have been fulfilled, not the resurrection of believers and the second coming of Christ.

Response to Full Preterism: (1) This view is heretical, since it affirms that the resurrection is past (2 Tim. 2:18). (2) It is opposed to the early creeds and councils of the church, which are the test for orthodoxy and affirm that Christ's coming was still future after AD 70. (3) It allegorizes away much of the literal truth of Revelation (see next section), which method, if used consistently, would undermine other fundamentals of the faith, such as creation and the life, death, and resurrection of Christ.

Response to Partial Preterism: First of all, it is inconsistent since the same terms (for example, *near* and *quickly* used to prove it was fulfilled by AD 70) are used in the whole book (see 1:3; 3:11; 22:12), including the resurrection of believers and the second coming. But this is a heresy. There are many things mentioned in Revelation 6–18 (and other parallel passages) that did not in fact happen between 64 and 70 AD, as partial preterists claim. For example: (1) the moon did not turn to blood (Acts 2:20); (2) the stars did not fall from the sky (Matt. 24:29); (3) one-third of human beings were not killed (Rev. 9:15, 18); (4) all life in the sea did not die (Rev. 16:3); (5) Christ did not come visibly (Matt. 24:30; Rev. 1:7); (6) he is not literally reigning on a throne on earth right now (Matt. 19:28; see Acts 1:10–11); (7) he did not distribute the final rewards in AD 70 (Rev. 22:12); and (8) Israel was not yet converted (Matt. 23:37–39). To allegorize all of this away is to undercut the very foundation of orthodox Christianity, which is based on a literal understanding of the biblical text.[5]

The Futurist View: According to this position, the prophecies of John are future (1:19) and literal, though the book uses symbols and figures of speech to convey this literal meaning. For example, "keys" to the bottomless pit are figurative but Satan, the pit, and the millennium are all literal (20:1–6). "Stars" are symbols of literal angels (1:20). Indeed, the various symbols used in Revelation are invariably interpreted there (see Rev. 1:20; 17:15) or elsewhere in Scripture (see Dan. 2:32–40).

Several things demonstrate that these predictions are for the future. (1) John was told that they were for things that would be after his time (1:19). (2) The book of Revelation was written after AD 70 (see above) and, hence, could not have been fulfilled in the first century as preterists claim. (3) The events that must happen before the end comes have never happened, including stars falling from the sky (Matt. 24:29), one-third of human beings being killed (Rev. 9:15, 18), all life in the sea dying (16:3), Christ coming back visibly (1:7; 19:11–21), and Christ reigning on earth for one thousand years (20:1–6). The first and second resurrections have not yet occurred, one before and one after the thousand-year reign of Christ (vv. 4–6), and Jesus has not yet distributed our final rewards. To claim all of this is merely allegorical is to deny the literal sense of Scripture and undermine many of the great fundamentals of the faith.

How to Respond to Critics

Revelation 1:4—*How can the Holy Spirit be seven spirits if he is one person?*

Problem: According to the orthodox doctrine of the Trinity, the Holy Spirit is one person, the third person of the triune Godhead. Jesus referred to the Holy Spirit as "he" (singular), but John referred to "the seven Spirits who are before His [God's] throne," which many commentators see as a reference to the Holy Spirit. But how can the Holy Spirit be seven spirits?

Solution: The book of Revelation contains a good bit of symbolism, and this is only one example. There is similar symbolism in other portions of this book. For instance, most agree that Revelation 12:3 speaks about Satan, but he is called a "great, fiery red dragon" with "seven heads and ten horns." Here, the seven heads and ten horns are attributed to one individual, Satan. Also, speaking of the beast from the sea, Revelation 13:1 says that he has "seven heads and ten horns." The number seven symbolizes completeness, as there are seven days in a complete week.

Other symbols are used of the Holy Spirit in Scripture. For instance, he is spoken of as a dove in Mark 1:10 and is likened to the wind in John 3:8 and water in John 4:14. He is also portrayed as "tongues, as of fire," in Acts 2:3. And Ephesians 1:13 says we are "sealed" by the Holy Spirit, signifying God's ownership of us and the security of our salvation.

Temple of the Emperor Trajan, Pergamum.

Many Bible students believe the sevenfold nature of the Holy Spirit may derive from the reference in Isaiah 11:2, where he is called the Spirit of the LORD, the Spirit of *wisdom*, of *understanding*, of *counsel*, of *might*, of *knowledge*, and of the *fear of the LORD*—seven different characteristics of one and the same Spirit.

Revelation 7:1—*Does the Bible teach that the world is square?*

Problem: John speaks here of the "four corners of the earth," which implies that the earth is square. But modern science teaches that it is round. Isn't this a mistake in the Bible?

Solution: The Bible does not teach that the world is square. This is a figure of speech meaning "from every section of the globe," or as Jeremiah put it, "from the four quarters of heaven" (Jer. 49:36). It is a succinct way of referring to the four directions: north, south, east, and west. In this sense it is akin to the phrase "the four winds . . . of heaven" (v. 36).

In the Bible the only references to the shape of the earth speak of it as round. Isaiah spoke of God "who sits above the circle of the earth" (Isa. 40:22). Job, referring to the world as hanging in space, asserted that God "stretches out the north over empty space; He hangs the earth on nothing" (Job 26:7). There is certainly nothing unscientific about these statements.

Revelation 14:13 (see Revelation 4–5)—*Is heaven a place of rest and quiet or of incessant praise and singing?*
Problem: According to this verse, heaven is a place in which the saints "rest from their labors." However, earlier in the book of Revelation, heaven is described as a place of constant praise and singing. Which is it?
Solution: Heaven is both. There is no contradiction between resting from labor and singing praises to God. It is exactly what God's people do today on their day of rest and worship. Heaven is just an extension of what we do on the Lord's Day now. "Labor" implies what is wearisome and painful. Resting from this and praising God forever are not mutually exclusive. In fact they go hand in hand.

Revelation 16:14—*Can demons perform miracles?*
Problem: Sometimes the Bible uses the same words (*sign, wonders, power*) to describe the power of demons and to describe the miracles of God (see 2 Thess. 2:9). However, a miracle is a supernatural act of God, and only God can perform such acts. The devil is a created being and has only limited power.
Solution: Although Satan has great spiritual powers, there is a gigantic difference between the power of the devil and the power of God. First, God is infinite in power (omnipotent); the devil (and demons) is only finite and limited. Only God can create life (Gen. 1:1, 21; Deut. 32:39); the devil cannot (see Exod. 8:18–19). Only God can raise the dead (John 5:28–29; 10:17–18; Rev. 1:18); the devil cannot raise the dead, though he gave "breath" (animation) to the idolatrous *image* of the Antichrist (Rev. 13:15).

The devil has great power to deceive people (12:9), to oppress those who yield to him, and even to possess them (Acts 16:16). He is a master magician and a super scientist. And with his vast knowledge of God, man, and the universe, he is able to perform "lying wonders" (2 Thess. 2:9; see Rev. 13:13–14). But only God can perform true miracles. The devil can do the supernormal but not the supernatural. Only God can control the natural laws he has established, though on one occasion he granted Satan the power to bring a whirlwind on Job's family (Job 6–19). Further, God gives the devil any power the devil has, and God limits and carefully monitors him (see Job 1:10–12). Christ defeated the devil and triumphed over him and all his host (Col. 2:15; Heb. 2:14–15), thus giving power to his people to be victorious over demonic forces (Eph. 4:4–11). Thus John informed believers: "He who is in you is greater than he who is in the world" (1 John 4:4).

STUDY QUESTIONS

1. What is the internal and external evidence that John wrote Revelation?

2. When do you think Revelation was written? Give reasons.

3. What is the theme of Revelation? How is this evident in the content?

4. How should Revelation be interpreted? List your reasons for the view chosen.

5. Why did John write Revelation?

SELECTED SOURCES

Baxter, Sidlow. *Explore the Book*. Grand Rapids: Zondervan, 1987.

Carson, D.A., Douglas Moo, and Leon Morris. *An Introduction to the New Testament*. Grand Rapids: Zondervan, 1992.

Geisler, Norman L., and Thomas Howe. *When Critics Ask: A Popular Handbook on Bible Difficulties*. Grand Rapids: Baker, 1997.

Guthrie, Donald. *New Testament Introduction*. Downers Grove, IL: InterVarsity, 1990.

Harrison, Everett F. *An Introduction to the New Testament*. Grand Rapids: Eerdmans, 1971.

Linnemann, Eta. *Historical Criticism of the Bible*. Translated by Robert Yarborough. Grand Rapids: Kregel, 2001.

Radmacher, Earl, Ronald Allen, and H. Wayne House, eds. *Nelson's New Illustrated Bible Commentary*. Nashville: Thomas Nelson, 1999.

Ryrie, Charles. *Revelation*. Everyman's Bible Commentary Series. Chicago: Moody, 1996.

Seiss, J.A. *The Apocalypse*. Grand Rapids: Zondervan, 2000.

Thomas, Robert L. *Revelation*. Wycliffe Exegetical Commentary. 2 vols. Chicago: Moody, 1992, 1995.

Walvoord, John F. *The Revelation of Jesus Christ*. Chicago: Moody, 1995.

Walvoord, John F., and Roy B. Zuck, eds. *The Bible Knowledge Commentary*. 2 vols. Wheaton: Victor, 1983.

Acknowledgments

I wish to express my appreciation for the able assistance
of Lanny Wilson, Christina Woodside, Joel Paulus,
and my dear wife, Barbara.
This book is greatly improved because of their efforts.

Appendix 1
Early Church Fathers and Sources

Ignatius (70–115): Antioch, wrote seven epistles, cited by Polycarp

Polycarp (AD 70–155): Smyrna, disciple of John, wrote several epistles

First Clement (AD 95–97): Rome, wrote an *Epistle to Corinthians*

Shepherd of Hermas (AD 115–40): Early second-century Christian allegory with New Testament citations

Didache (AD 120–50): Early church manual, also known as *The Teaching of the Twelve*

Muratorian Canon (AD 170): An incomplete but the oldest and most valuable listing of New Testament writings

Papias (AD 60–140): Hierapolis, wrote *Exposition on Oracles of the Lord*

Marcion (AD 140): Gnostic heretic, rejected all but Luke and ten of Paul's writings

Irenaeus (AD 120–200): Lyons, France; pupil of Polycarp; wrote *Against Heresies* and *Proof of Apostolic Teaching*

Justin Martyr (AD 100–65): Samaritan philosopher, wrote *Apology* and *Dialogue with Trypho*

Tatian (AD 110–72): Assyrian rhetorician, wrote *Diatessaron* (earliest harmony of the Gospels)

Tertullian (AD 160–222): African lawyer, Latin Father, wrote many books

Origen (AD 185–254): Alexandria, great scholar, wrote numerous books, unorthodox on some doctrines

Clement of Alexandria (AD 155–220): Athenian theologian, wrote many books

Cyprian (AD 200–58): Tertullian's pupil, taught rhetoric, wrote many books

Eusebius (AD 260–340): Caesarea, greatest early church historian

Athanasius (AD 296–373): Alexandria, defender of orthodoxy (versus Arius)

Cyril of Jerusalem (AD 315–86): Bishop, defender of orthodoxy

Gregory of Nasianzus (AD 325–90*): Bishop of Constantinople, ordained by Athanasius, friend of Basil, discipled Jerome

Gregory of Nyssa (AD 336–95*): Bishop at Nyssa, brother of Basil

Basil the Great (AD 330–79*): Educated in Caesarea, monk in Egypt, one of our great orthodox Fathers in the East

Ambrose (AD 340–97): Bishop of Milan, helped convert St. Augustine

Chrysostom (AD 347–407): Bishop of Constantinople, wrote many books

Jerome (AD 342–420): Lived in Bethlehem, great Bible translator of *The Latin Vulgate*

Augustine (AD 354–430): Bishop of Hippo, Africa; great teacher; writer of *City of God*, *Confessions*, and numerous other books

*Most dates are taken from William Graham Scroggie, *A Guide to the Gospels* (1952; repr., Grand Rapids: Kregel, 1995), 39–43.

Appendix 2

Early Citations of the New Testament

Books	Mt	Mk	Lk	Jn	Ac	Ro	1C	2C	Ga	Ep	Ph	Co	1Th	2Th	1T	2Ti	Ti	Phe	Hb	Js	1P	2P	1J	2J	3J	Jd	Re
Pseudo-Barnabas (ca. 70–130)	•	•	•														•		•		•	•					
First Clement (ca. 95–97)	•	•	•		•	•	•										•		•	•	•	•					•
Ignatius (ca. 110)	•			•	•	•	•					•	•				•										
Polycarp (ca. 110–50)	•	•	•		•	•	•	•	•	•	•			•	•	•					•		•				
Hermas (ca. 115–40)	•	•								•										•	•		•				
Didache (ca. 120–50)	•		•		•																•						
Papias (ca. 130–40)	•	•																									
Marcion (ca. 140)			•			•	•	•	•	•	•	•	•	•				•									
Irenaeus (ca. 130–202)	•	•	•	•	•	•	•	•	•	•	•	•	•	•	•	•	•			•	•		•	•		•	•
Justin Martyr (ca. 150–55)	•	•	•	•		•	•	•					•	•													•
Muratorian Canon (ca. 170)	•	•	•	•	•	•	•	•	•	•	•	•	•	•	•	•	•	•					•	•		•	•
Clement of Alexandria (ca. 150–215)	•	•	•	•	•	•	•	•	•	•	•	•	•	•	•	•	•		•	•	•		•	•		•	•
Tertullian (ca. 150–220)	•	•	•	•	•	•	•	•	•	•	•	•	•	•	•	•	•	•	•	•	•		•			•	•
Origen (ca. 185–254)	•	•	•	•	•	•	•	•	•	•	•	•	•	•	•	•	•	•	•	•	•	•	•	•	•	•	•
Old Latin (ca. 200)	•	•	•	•	•	•	•	•	•	•	•	•	•	•	•	•	•	•	•		•		•	•	•	•	•
Cyprian (d. 258)	•		•	•	•	•	•	•	•	•	•	•	•	•	•	•	•				•		•				•
Apostolic Constitutions (ca. 300)	•	•	•	•	•	•	•	•	•	•	•	•	•	•	•	•	•	•	•	•	•	•	•	•	•	•	
Cyril of Jerusalem (ca. 315–86)	•	•	•	•	•	•	•	•	•	•	•	•	•	•	•	•	•	•	•	•	•	•	•	•	•	•	
Eusebius (ca. 325–40)	•	•	•	•	•	•	•	•	•	•	•	•	•	•	•	•	•	•	•	○	•	○	•	○	○	○	
Athanasius (367)	•	•	•	•	•	•	•	•	•	•	•	•	•	•	•	•	•	•	•	•	•	•	•	•	•	•	•
Jerome (ca. 349–420)	•	•	•	•	•	•	•	•	•	•	•	•	•	•	•	•	•	•	•	•	•	•	•	•	•	•	•
Council of Hippo (393)	•	•	•	•	•	•	•	•	•	•	•	•	•	•	•	•	•	•	•	•	•	•	•	•	•	•	•
Council of Carthage (397)	•	•	•	•	•	•	•	•	•	•	•	•	•	•	•	•	•	•	•	•	•	•	•	•	•	•	•
Augustine (ca. 400)	•	•	•	•	•	•	•	•	•	•	•	•	•	•	•	•	•	•	•	•	•	•	•	•	•	•	•

• = Citation or allusion   o = Citation disputed

Appendix 3
Key Words and Phrases
in the New Testament

Compiled by Lanny Wilson

This appendix provides an alphabetical list of key English words or phrases within each book of the New Testament. Transliterations of the corresponding lexical or inflected Greek forms (for phrases) are provided in parentheses along with the number of times each of these words or phrases occur within a given book. Verb forms are usually listed before other forms (e.g., noun, adjective) and when the English verb and noun are identical in form, word entries are preceded by *do* or (*to*) to indicate both (e.g., *do evil, evil*; (*to*) *love, love*).

Matthew

end of the age (*synteleia aiōnos*; 5x): 13:39, 40, 49; 24:3; 28:20

Father (of God) (*patēr*; 44x): 5:16, 45, 48; 6:1, 4, 6 (2x), 8, 9, 14, 15, 18 (2x), 26, 32; 7:11, 21; 10:20, 29, 32, 33; 11:25, 26, 27 (3x); 12:50; 13:43; 15:13; 16:17, 27; 18:10, 14, 19, 35; 20:23; 23:9; 24:36; 25:34; 26:29, 39, 42, 53; 28:19

kingdom (*basileia*; 23x): 4:23; 6:10, 13, 33; 8:12; 9:35; 12:25, 26, 28; 13:19, 38, 41, 43; 16:28; 19:24; 20:21; 21:31, 43; 24:7 (2x), 14; 25:34; 26:29

kingdom of heaven (*basileia tōn ouranōn*; 32x): 3:2; 4:17; 5:3, 10, 19 (2x), 20; 7:21; 8:11; 10:7; 11:11, 12; 13:11, 24, 31, 33, 44, 45, 47, 52; 16:19; 18:1, 3, 4, 23; 19:12, 14, 23; 20:1; 22:2; 23:13; 25:1

righteous (*dikaios*; 17x): 1:19; 5:45; 9:13; 10:41 (3x); 13:17, 43, 49; 20:4; 23:28, 29, 35 (2x); 25:37, 46; 27:19

righteousness (*dikaiosynē*; 7x): 3:15; 5:6, 10, 20; 6:1, 33; 21:32

Son of David (*huios Dauid*; 10x): 1:1; 1:20; 9:27; 12:23; 15:22; 20:30, 31; 21:9, 15; 22:42

that it might be fulfilled (*plēroō, anaplēroō*; 15x): 1:22; 2:15, 17, 23; 3:15; 4:14; 5:17; 8:17; 12:17; 13:14, 35; 21:4; 26:54, 56; 27:9

which was spoken (in the Old Testament) (*rheō*; 20x): 1:22; 2:15, 17, 23; 3:3; 4:14; 5:21, 27, 31, 33, 38, 43; 8:17; 12:17; 13:35; 21:4; 22:31; 24:15; 27:29, 35

worship (*proskyneō, sebomai*; 14x): 2:2, 8, 11; 4:9, 10; 8:2; 9:18; 14:33; 15:9, 25; 18:26; 20:20; 28:9, 17

Mark

authority (*exousia*; 10x): 1:22, 27; 2:10; 3:15; 6:7; 11:28 (2x), 29, 33; 13:34

immediately, straightway (*eutheōs*; 40x): 1:10, 18, 20, 21, 29, 30, 31, 42, 43; 2:2, 8, 12; 3:6; 4:5, 15, 16, 17, 29; 5:2, 13, 29, 30, 36, 42; 6:25, 27, 45, 50, 54; 7:35; 8:10; 9:15, 20, 24; 10:52; 11:2, 3; 14:43, 45; 15:1

spirit (*pneuma*; 23x): 1:8, 10, 12, 23, 26, 27; 2:8; 3:11, 29, 30; 5:2, 8, 13; 6:7; 7:25; 8:12; 9:17, 20, 25 (2x); 12:36; 13:11; 14:38

Luke

announce glad tidings, preach good news (*euangelizō*; 10x): 1:19; 2:10; 3:18; 4:18, 43; 7:22; 8:1; 9:6; 16:16; 20:1

grace (*charis*; 8x): 1:30; 2:40, 52; 4:22; 6:32, 33, 34; 17:9

salvation (*sōtēria, sōtērion*; 6x): 1:69, 71, 77; 2:30; 3:6; 19:9

save (*sōzō*; 19x): 6:9; 7:50; 8:12, 36, 48, 50; 9:24 (2x), 56; 13:23; 17:19, 33; 18:26, 42; 19:10; 23:35 (2x), 37, 39

Savior (*sōtēr*; 2x): 1:47; 2:11

(to) sin, sin, sinner, sinful (*hamartanō, hamartia, hamartōlos*; 33x): 1:77; 3:3; 5:8, 20, 21, 23, 24, 30, 32; 6:32, 33, 34 (2x); 7:34, 37, 39, 47, 48, 49; 11:4; 13:2; 15:1, 2, 7, 10, 18, 21; 17:3, 4; 18:13; 19:7; 24:7, 47

John

abide (*menō*; 41x): 1:32, 33, 38, 39 (2x); 2:12; 3:36; 4:40 (2x); 5:38; 6:27, 56; 7:9; 8:31, 35 (2x); 9:41; 10:40; 11:6; 12:24, 34, 46; 14:10, 16, 17, 25; 15:4 (3x), 5, 6, 7 (2x), 9, 10 (2x), 11, 16; 19:31; 21:22, 23

ask (*aiteō, erōtaō*; 38x): 1:19, 21, 25; 4:9, 10, 31, 40, 47; 5:12; 8:7; 9:2, 15, 19, 21, 23; 11:22; 12:21; 14:13, 14, 16; 15:7, 16; 16:5, 19, 23 (2x), 24 (2x), 26 (2x), 30; 17:9 (2x), 15, 20; 18:19; 19:31, 38

believe (*pisteuō*; 100x): 1:7, 12, 50; 2:11, 22, 23, 24; 3:12 (2x), 15, 16, 18 (3x), 36; 4:21, 39, 41, 42, 48, 50, 53; 5:24, 38, 44, 46 (2x), 47 (2x); 6:29, 30, 35, 36, 40, 47, 64 (2x), 69; 7:5, 31, 38, 39, 48; 8:24, 30, 31, 45, 46; 9:18, 35, 36, 38; 10:25, 26, 37, 38 (3x), 42; 11:15, 25, 26 (2x), 27, 40, 42, 45, 48; 12:11, 36, 37, 38, 39, 42, 44 (2x), 46, 47; 13:19; 14:1 (2x), 10, 11 (2x), 12, 29; 16:9, 27, 30, 31; 17:8, 20, 21; 19:35; 20:8, 25, 29 (2x), 31 (2x)

eternal, eternity (*aiōn, aiōnios*; 29x): 3:15, 16, 36; 4:14 (2x), 36; 5:24, 39; 6:27, 40, 47, 51, 54, 58, 68; 8:35 (2x), 51, 52; 9:32; 10:28 (2x); 11:26; 12:25, 34, 50; 13:8; 14:16; 17:2

Father (of God) (*patēr*; 122x): 1:14, 18; 2:16; 3:35; 4:21, 23 (2x); 5:17, 18, 19, 20, 21, 22, 23 (2x), 26, 30, 36 (2x), 37, 43, 45; 6:27, 32, 37, 39, 44, 45, 46 (2x), 57 (2x); 6:65; 8:16, 18, 19 (3x), 27, 28, 29, 38, 41, 42, 49, 54; 10:15 (2x), 17, 18, 25, 29 (2x), 30, 32, 36, 37, 38; 11:41; 12:26, 27, 28, 49, 50; 13:1, 3; 14:2, 6, 7, 8, 9 (2x), 10 (3x), 11 (2x), 12, 13, 16, 20, 21, 23, 24, 26, 28 (2x), 31 (2x); 15:1, 8, 9, 10, 15, 16, 23, 24, 26 (2x); 16:3, 10, 15, 16, 17, 23, 25, 26, 27, 28 (2x), 32; 17:1, 5, 11, 21, 24, 25; 18:11; 20:17 (3x), 21

glorify, glory (*doxazō, doxa*; 42x): 1:14 (2x); 2:11; 5:41, 44 (2x); 7:18 (2x), 39; 8:50, 54 (3x); 9:24; 11:4 (2x), 40; 12:16, 23, 28 (3x), 41, 43 (2x); 13:31 (2x), 32 (3x); 14:13; 15:8; 16:14; 17:1 (2x), 4, 5 (2x), 10, 22, 24; 21:19

heaven (*ouranos*; 19x): 1:32, 51; 3:13 (3x), 27, 31; 6:31, 32 (2x), 33, 38, 41, 42, 50, 51, 58; 12:28; 17:1

hour (*hōra*; 26x): 1:39; 2:4; 4:6, 21, 23, 52 (2x), 53; 5:25, 28, 35; 7:30; 8:20; 11:9; 12:23, 27 (2x); 13:1; 16:2, 4, 21, 25, 32; 17:1; 19:14, 27

the Jews (*Ioudaios* [singular form]; 71x): 1:19; 2:6, 13, 18, 20; 3:1, 22, 25; 4:9 (2x), 22; 5:1, 10, 15, 16, 18; 6:4, 41, 52; 7:1, 2, 11, 13, 15, 35; 8:22, 31, 48, 52, 57; 9:18, 22 (2x); 10:19, 24, 31, 33; 11:8, 19, 31, 33, 36, 45, 54, 55; 12:9, 11; 13:33; 18:12, 14, 20, 31, 33, 35, 36, 38, 39; 19:3, 7, 12, 14, 19, 20, 21 (3x), 31, 38, 40, 42; 20:19

judge, judgment (*krisis, krinō*; 30x): 3:17, 18 (2x), 19; 5:22 (2x), 24, 27, 29, 30 (2x); 7:24 (3x), 51; 8:15 (2x), 16 (2x), 26, 50; 12:31, 47 (2x), 48 (2x); 16:8, 11 (2x); 18:31

know (*ginōskō*; 54x): 1:10, 48; 2:24, 25; 3:10; 4:1, 53; 5:6, 42; 6:15, 69; 7:17, 26, 27, 49, 51; 8:27, 28, 32, 43, 52, 55; 10:6, 14, 15 (2x), 27, 38; 11:57; 12:9, 16; 13:7, 12, 28, 35; 14:7 (3x), 9, 17, 20, 31; 15:18; 16:3, 19; 17:3, 7, 8, 23, 25 (3x); 19:4; 21:17

know (*oida*; 83x): 1:26, 31, 33; 2:9 (2x); 3:2, 8, 11; 4:10, 22 (2x), 25, 32, 42; 5:13, 32; 6:6, 42, 61, 64; 7:15, 27, 28 (3x), 29; 8:14 (2x), 19 (3x), 37, 55 (3x); 9:12, 20, 21 (2x), 24, 25 (2x), 29 (2x), 30, 31; 10:4, 5; 11:22, 24, 42, 49; 12:50; 13:1, 3, 7, 11, 17, 18; 14:4 (2x), 5 (2x); 15:15, 21; 16:18, 30 (2x); 18:2, 4, 21; 19:10, 35; 20:2, 9, 13, 14; 21:4, 12, 15, 16, 17, 24

life (*zōē*; 36x): 1:4 (2x); 3:15, 16, 36 (2x); 4:14, 36; 5:24 (2x), 26 (2x), 29, 39, 40; 6:27, 33, 35, 40, 47, 48, 51, 53, 54, 63, 68; 8:12; 10:10, 28; 11:25; 12:25, 50; 14:6; 17:2, 3; 20:31

light (*phōs*; 23x): 1:4, 5, 7, 8 (2x), 9; 3:19 (2x), 20 (2x), 21; 5:35; 8:12 (2x); 9:5; 11:9, 10; 12:35 (2x), 36 (3x), 46

(to) love, love (*agapaō, agapē*; 44x): 3:16, 19, 35; 5:42; 8:42; 10:17; 11:5; 12:43; 13:1 (2x), 23; 13:34 (3x), 35; 14:15, 21 (4x), 23 (2x), 24, 28, 31; 15:9 (3x), 10 (2x),12 (2x), 13, 17; 17:23 (2x), 24, 26 (2x); 19:26; 21:7, 15, 16, 20

receive, take (*lambanō, paralambanō*; 48x): 1:11, 12, 16; 3:11, 27, 32, 33; 4:36; 5:34, 41, 43 (2x), 44; 6:7, 11, 21; 7:23, 39; 10:17, 18 (2x); 12:3, 13, 48; 13:4, 12, 20 (4x), 30; 14:3, 17; 16:14, 15, 24; 17:8; 18:3, 31; 19:1, 6, 16, 23, 27, 30, 40; 20:22; 21:13

see, behold (*horaō*; 61x): 1:18, 33, 34, 39 (2x), 46, 47 (2x), 48, 50 (2x); 3:3, 11, 32; 4:29, 45, 48; 5:6, 37; 6:2, 36, 46 (2x); 6:14, 22, 24, 26, 30; 8:38 (2x), 56 (2x), 57; 9:1, 37; 11:31, 32, 33, 34; 12:9, 21, 40, 41; 14:7, 9 (2x); 15:24; 18:26; 19:6, 26, 28, 33, 35; 20:8, 18, 20, 25, 27, 29 (2x), 21:21

send (*apostellō*; 28x): 1:6, 19, 24; 3:17, 28, 34; 4:38; 5:33, 36, 38; 6:29, 57; 7:29, 32; 8:42; 9:7; 10:36; 11:3, 42; 17:3, 8, 18 (2x), 21, 23, 25; 18:24; 20:21

sign, miracle (*sēmeion*; 17x): 2:11, 18, 23; 3:2; 4:48, 54; 6:2, 14, 26, 30; 7:31; 9:16; 10:41; 11:47; 12:18, 37; 20:30

sin, sinner (*hamartanō, hamartia, hamartolos*; 25x): 1:29; 5:14; 8:11, 21, 24 (2x), 34 (2x), 46; 9:2, 3, 16, 24, 25, 31, 34, 41 (2x); 15:22 (2x), 24; 16:8, 9; 19:11; 20:23

truth, truly, true (*alētheia, alēthēs, alēthinos*; 46x): 1:9, 14, 17; 3:21, 33; 4:18, 23 (2x), 24, 37; 5:31, 32, 33; 6:32; 7:18, 28; 8:13, 14, 16, 17, 26, 32 (2x), 40, 44 (2x), 45, 46; 10:41; 14:6, 17; 15:1, 26; 16:7, 13 (2x); 17:3, 17 (2x), 19; 18:37 (2x), 38; 19:35 (2x); 21:24

verily (truly) (*amēn*; 50x): 1:21 (2x); 3:3 (2x), 5 (2x), 11 (2x); 5:19 (2x), 24 (2x), 25 (2x); 6:26 (2x), 32 (2x),

47 (2x), 53 (2x); 8:34 (2x), 51 (2x), 58 (2x); 10:1
(2x), 7 (2x); 12:24 (2x); 13:16 (2x), 20 (2x), 21 (2x),
38 (2x); 14:12 (2x); 16:20 (2x), 23 (2x); 21:18 (2x)

testify, testimony (*martyreō, martyria*; 47x): 1:7 (2x),
8, 15, 19, 32, 34; 2:25; 3:11 (2x), 26, 28, 32 (2x),
33; 4:39, 44; 5:31 (2x), 32 (3x), 33, 34, 36 (2x),
37, 39; 7:7; 8:13 (2x), 14 (2x), 17, 18 (2x); 10:25;
12:17; 13:21; 15:26, 27; 18:23, 37; 19:35 (2x);
21:24 (2x)

world (*kosmos*; 78x): 1:9, 10 (3x), 29; 3:16, 17 (3x),
19; 4:42; 6:14, 33, 51; 7:4, 7; 8:12, 23 (2x), 26;
9:5 (2x), 39; 10:36; 11:9, 27; 12:19, 25, 31 (2x),
46, 47 (2x); 13:1 (2x); 14:17, 19, 22, 27, 30, 31;
15:18, 19 (5x); 16:8, 11, 20, 21, 28 (2x), 33 (2x);
17:5, 6, 9, 11 (2x), 12, 13, 14 (3x), 15, 16 (2x), 18
(2x), 21, 23, 24, 25; 18:20, 36 (2x), 37; 21:25

Acts

announce good news, bring good news, gospel
(*euangelizō, euangelion*; 17x): 5:42; 8:4, 12, 25,
35, 40; 10:36; 11:20; 13:32; 14:7, 15, 21; 15:7,
35; 16:10; 17:18; 20:24

apostle (*apostolos*; 30x): 1:2, 26; 2:37, 42, 43; 4:33,
35, 36, 37; 5:2, 12, 18, 29, 34, 40; 6:6; 8:1, 14,
18; 9:27; 11:1; 14:4, 14; 15:2, 4, 6, 22, 23, 33;
16:4

baptize, baptism (*baptizō, baptisma*; 27x): 1:5 (2x),
22; 2:38, 41; 8:12, 13, 16, 36, 38; 9:18; 10:37, 47,
48; 11:16 (2x); 13:24; 16:15, 33; 18:8, 25; 19:3
(2x), 4 (2x), 5; 22:16

be written, scriptures, (*graphō, graphē* [singular
form]; 19x): 1:16, 20; 7:42; 8:32, 35; 13:29,
33; 15:15, 23; 17:2, 11; 18:24, 27, 28; 23:5, 25;
24:14; 25:26 (2x)

believe (*pisteuō*; 38x): 2:44; 4:4, 32; 5:14; 8:12, 13,
37 (2x); 9:26, 42; 10:43; 11:17, 21; 13:12, 39,
41, 48; 14:1, 23; 15:5, 7, 11; 16:31, 34; 17:12,
34; 18:8 (2x), 27; 19:2, 4, 18; 21:20, 25; 22:19;
24:14; 26:27; 27:25

church (*ekklēsia*; 24x): 2:47; 5:11; 7:38; 8:1, 3; 9:31;
11:22, 26; 12:1, 5; 13:1; 14:23, 27; 15:3, 4, 22,
41; 16:5; 18:22; 19:32, 39, 41; 20:17, 28

grow, increase (*auxanō*; 4x): 6:7; 7:17; 12:24; 19:20

Holy Spirit (*pneuma hagion, pneuma*; 42x): 1:2, 5,
8, 16; 2:4 (2x), 17, 18, 33, 38; 4:8, 31; 5:3, 9, 32;
6:3, 5; 7:51, 55; 8:15, 17, 18, 19, 29, 39; 9:17, 31;
10:19, 38, 44, 45, 47; 11:12, 15, 16, 24, 28; 13:2,
4, 9, 52; 15:8, 28; 16:6, 7; 18:5, 25; 19:2 (2x), 6,
21; 20:23, 28; 21:4, 11; 28:25

name (in reference to Jesus) (*onoma*; 33x): 2:21, 38;
3:6, 16 (2x); 4:7, 10, 12, 17, 18, 30; 5:28, 40, 41;
8:12, 16; 9:14, 15, 16, 21, 27, 29; 10:43, 48; 15:14,
17, 26; 16:18; 19:5, 13, 17; 21:13; 22:16; 26:9

people (*ochlos* [singular form]; 22x): 1:15; 6:7; 8:6;
11:24, 26; 13:45; 14:11, 13, 14, 18, 19; 16:22;
17:8, 13; 19:26, 33, 35; 21:27, 34, 35; 24:12, 18

persecute, suffer, persecution, affliction (*diōkō, paschō,
diōgmos, thlipsis*; 21x): 1:3; 3:18; 7:10, 11, 52;
8:1; 9:4, 5, 16; 11:19; 13:50; 14:22; 17:3; 20:23;
22:4, 7, 8; 26:11, 14, 15; 28:5

pray (beseech), prayer (*deomai, proseuchomai,
proseuchē*; 32x): 1:14, 24; 2:42; 3:1; 4:31; 6:4, 6;
8:15, 22, 24, 34; 9:11, 40; 10:2, 4, 9, 30, 31; 11:5;
12:5, 12; 13:3; 14:23; 16:13, 16, 25; 20:36; 21:5,
39; 22:17; 26:3; 28:8

raise, raise up (*egeirō, epairō*; 19x): 1:9; 2:14; 3:6, 7,
15; 4:10; 5:30; 9:8; 10:26, 40; 12:7; 13:22, 23,
30, 37; 14:11; 22:22; 26:8; 27:40

raise, stand up (*anistēmi*; 44x): 1:15; 2:24, 30, 32;
3:22, 26; 5:6, 17, 34, 36, 37; 6:9; 7:18, 37; 8:26,
27; 9:6, 11, 18, 34, 39, 40, 41; 10:13, 20, 26, 41;
11:7, 28; 12:7; 13:16, 33, 34; 14:10, 20; 15:7;
17:3, 31; 20:30; 22:10, 16; 23:9; 26:16, 30

repent, repentance (*metanoeō, metanoia*; 11x): 2:38;
3:19; 5:31; 8:22; 11:18; 13:24; 17:30; 19:4;
20:21; 26:20 (2x)

resurrection (*anastasis*; 11x): 1:22; 2:31; 4:2, 33;
17:18, 32; 23:6, 8; 24:15, 21; 26:23

save (*sōzō*; 13x): 2:21, 40, 47; 4:9, 12; 11:14; 14:9;
15:1, 11; 16:30, 31; 27:20, 31

spirit (in reference to things other than the Holy
Spirit) (*pneuma*; 19x): 5:16; 6:10; 7:59; 8:7;
11:12, 28; 16:16, 18; 17:16; 18:5, 25; 19:12, 13,
15, 16, 21; 20:22; 23:8, 9

(to) witness, witness (*martyreō, martyrion, martys*;
27x): 1:8, 22; 2:32; 3:15; 4:33; 5:32; 6:3, 13;
7:44, 58; 10:22, 39, 41, 43; 13:22, 31; 14:3; 15:8;
16:2; 22:5, 12, 15, 20; 23:11; 26:5, 16, 22

word (*logos*; 32x): 1:1; 2:22, 40, 41; 4:4; 5:5, 24;
6:5; 7:22, 29; 8:21; 10:29, 36, 44; 11:22; 13:15;
14:12; 15:6, 15, 24, 27, 32; 16:36; 18:14, 15;
19:38, 40; 20:2, 7, 24, 38; 22:22

word (in connection with the Lord) (*logos*; 20x):
4:29; 6:4; 8:4, 25; 11:19; 13:26, 48, 49; 14:3, 25;
15:7, 35, 36; 16:6, 32; 17:11; 19:10, 20; 20:32,
35

word of God (*logos tou theou*; 12x): 4:31; 6:2, 7; 8:14;
11:1; 12:24; 13:5, 46, 7, 44; 17:13; 18:11

Romans

all (*pas*; 71x): 1:5, 7, 8, 16, 18, 29; 2:1, 9, 10; 3:2, 4, 9,
12, 19 (2x), 20, 22, 23; 4:11, 16 (2x); 5:12 (2x), 18
(2x); 7:8; 8:22, 28, 32 (2x), 37; 9:5, 6, 7, 17, 33;
10:4, 11, 12 (2x), 13, 16, 18; 11:26, 32 (2x), 36;
12:3, 4, 17, 18; 13:1, 7; 14:2, 5, 10, 11 (2x), 20, 23;
15:11 (2x), 13, 14, 33; 16:4, 15, 16, 19, 24, 26

all (whole, quantity) (*holos, hosos*; 12x): 1:8; 2:12
(2x); 3:19; 6:3; 7:1; 8:14, 36; 10:21; 11:13; 15:4;
16:23

announce good news, gospel (*euangelizō, euangelion*;
10x): 1:1, 9, 15, 16; 2:16; 10:15, 16; 11:28;
15:16, 19, 20, 29, 16:25

believe (*pisteuō*; 21x): 1:16; 3:2, 22; 4:3, 5, 11, 17, 18, 24; 6:8; 9:33; 10:4, 9, 10, 11, 14 (2x), 16; 13:11; 14:2; 15:13

brethren (*adelphos* [singular form]; 19x): 1:13; 7:1, 4; 8:12, 29; 9:3; 10:1; 11:25; 12:1; 14:10 (2x), 13, 15, 21; 15:15, 30; 16:14, 17, 23

certainly not, may it never be, God forbid (*mē genoito*; 10x): 3:4, 6, 31; 6:2, 15; 7:7, 13; 9:14; 11:1, 11

counted, impute, imputed, reckon (*logizomai, ellogeō*; 21x): 2:3, 26 (2x); 3:28; 4:3, 4, 5, 6, 8, 9, 10, 11, 15, 22, 23, 24; 6:11; 8:18, 36; 9:8; 14:14

die, put to death, death (*apothnēskō, thanatoō, thanatos*; 45x): 1:32; 5:6, 7 (2x), 8, 10, 12, 14, 15, 17, 21; 6:2, 3, 4, 5, 7, 8, 9 (2x), 10, 16, 21, 23; 7:2, 3, 4, 5, 6, 9, 10, 13 (2x), 24; 8:2, 6, 13 (2x), 34, 36, 38; 14:7, 8 (2x), 9, 15

faith (*pistis*; 40x): 1:5, 8, 12, 17 (3x); 3:3, 22, 25, 26, 27, 28, 30 (2x), 31; 4:5, 9, 11, 12, 13, 14, 16 (2x), 19, 20; 5:1, 2; 9:30, 32; 10:6, 8, 17; 11:20; 12:3, 6; 14:1, 22, 23 (2x); 16:26

flesh (*sarx*; 27x): 1:3; 2:28; 3:20; 4:1; 6:19; 7:5, 18, 25; 8:1, 3 (3x), 4, 5 (2x), 6, 7, 8, 9, 12 (2x), 13; 9:3, 5, 8; 11:14; 13:14

Gentiles (*ethnos* [singular form]; 28x): 1:5, 13; 2:14, 24; 3:29 (2x); 4:17, 18; 9:24, 30; 10:19; 11:11, 12, 13 (2x), 25; 15:9 (2x), 10, 11, 12 (2x), 16 (2x), 18, 27; 16:4, 26

God (*theos*; 71x): 1:1, 4, 7, 10, 16, 17, 18, 19, 25, 32; 2:2, 3, 4, 5, 17, 24, 29; 3:2, 3, 5, 7, 18, 21, 22, 23, 26; 4:20; 5:2, 5, 15; 6:23; 7:22, 25; 8:7, 9, 14 (2x), 16, 17, 19, 21, 27, 33, 34, 39; 9:6, 8, 11, 16; 10:2, 3 (2x), 17; 11:22, 29, 33; 12:1, 2; 13:1 (2x), 2, 4 (2x); 14:17, 20; 15:7, 8, 15, 16, 19, 32

grace (*charis*; 25x): 1:5, 7; 3:24; 4:4, 16; 5:2, 15 (2x), 17, 20, 21; 6:1, 14, 15, 17; 11:5, 6 (4x); 12:3, 6; 15:15; 16:20, 24

in Christ (*en Christō*; 11x): 3:24; 6:11; 8:1, 2, 39; 9:1; 12:5; 16:3, 7, 9, 10

Israel, Israelite (*Israēl, Israēlitēs*; 13x): 9:4, 6, 27 (2x), 31; 10:1, 19, 21; 11:1, 2, 7, 25, 26

Jesus Christ (*Iēsous Christos*; 39x): 1:1, 3, 4, 6, 7, 8; 2:16; 3:22, 24, 26; 4:24; 5:1, 11, 15, 17, 21; 6:3, 11, 23; 7:25; 8:1, 2, 11, 39; 10:9; 13:14; 14:14; 15:5, 6, 8, 16, 17, 30; 16:3, 18, 20, 24, 25, 27

judge, judgment (*krinō, krima*; 22x): 2:1, 2, 3 (2x), 12, 16, 27; 3:4, 6, 7, 8; 5:16; 11:33; 13:2; 14:3, 4, 5 (2x), 10, 13 (2x), 22

justify, righteous deed, righteous (*dikaioō, dikaiōma, dikaios, dikaiosynē*; 57x): 1:17 (2x), 32; 2:13 (2x), 26; 3:4, 5, 10, 20, 21, 22, 24, 25, 26 (3x), 28, 30; 4:2, 3, 5 (2x), 6, 9, 11 (2x), 13, 22; 5:1, 7, 9, 16, 17, 18, 19, 21; 6:7, 13, 16, 18, 19, 20; 7:12; 8:4, 10, 30, 33; 9:28, 30, 31; 10:3, 4, 5, 6, 10; 14:17

law (*nomos*; 75x): 2:12 (2x), 13 (2x), 14 (4x), 15, 17, 18, 20, 23 (2x), 25 (2x), 26, 27 (2x); 3:19 (2x), 20 (2x), 21 (2x), 27 (2x), 28, 31 (2x); 4:13, 14, 15 (2x), 16;

5:13 (2x), 20; 6:14, 15; 7:1 (2x), 2 (2x), 3, 4, 5, 6, 7 (3x), 8, 9, 12, 14, 16, 21, 22, 23 (3x), 25 (2x); 8:2 (2x), 3, 4, 7; 9:31 (2x), 32; 10:4, 5; 13:8, 10

be lord of, rule, Lord (*kyrieuō, kyrios*; 49x): 1:3, 7; 4:8, 24; 5:1, 11, 21; 6:9, 11, 14, 23; 7:1, 25; 8:39; 9:28, 29; 10:9, 12, 13, 16; 11:3, 34; 12:11, 19; 13:14; 14:4, 6 (4x), 8, 9, 11, 14; 15:6, 11, 30; 16:2, 8 (3x), 11, 12 (2x), 13, 18, 20, 22, 24

love, brotherly love (*agapaō, agapē, philadelphia*; 18x): 5:5, 8; 8:28, 35, 37, 39; 9:13, 25 (2x); 12:9; 10; 13:8 (2x), 9, 10 (2x); 14:15; 15:30

make alive, life (*zōopoieō, zōē*; 14x): 2:7; 4:17; 5:10, 17, 18, 21; 6:4, 22, 23; 7:10; 8:2, 6, 10, 11, 38; 11:15

save, salvation (*sōzō, sōtēria*; 13x): 1:16; 5:9, 10; 8:24; 9:27; 10:1, 9, 13; 11:11, 14, 26; 13:11

sin (*hamartia*; 48x): 3:9, 20; 4:7, 8; 5:12 (2x), 13 (2x), 20, 21; 6:1, 2, 6 (2x), 7, 10, 11, 12, 13, 14, 16, 17, 18, 20, 22, 23; 7:5, 7 (2x), 8 (2x), 9, 11, 13 (3x), 14, 17, 20, 23, 25; 8:2, 3 (3x), 10; 11:27; 14:23

Spirit (*pneuma*; 35x): 1:4, 9; 2:29; 5:5; 7:6; 8:1, 2, 4, 5 (2x), 6, 9 (3x), 10, 11 (2x), 13, 14, 15 (2x), 16 (2x), 23, 26 (2x), 27; 9:1; 11:8; 12:11; 14:17; 15:13, 16, 19, 30

1 Corinthians

body (*sōma*; 44x): 5:3; 6:13 (2x), 15, 16, 18 (2x), 19, 20; 7:4 (2x), 34; 9:27; 10:16, 17; 11:24, 27, 29; 12:12 (3x), 13, 14, 15 (2x), 16 (2x), 17, 18, 19, 20, 22, 23, 24, 25, 27; 13:3; 15:35, 37, 38 (2x), 40 (2x), 44

brethren (*adelphos* [singular form]; 38x): 1:1, 10, 11, 26; 2:1; 3:1; 4:6; 5:11; 6:5, 6 (2x), 8; 7:12, 15, 24, 29; 8:11, 12, 13 (2x); 9:5; 10:1; 11:2, 33; 12:1; 14:6, 20, 26, 39; 15:1, 6, 50, 58; 16:11, 12 (2x), 15, 20

church (*ekklēsia*; 22x): 1:2; 4:17; 6:4; 7:17; 10:32; 11:16, 18, 22; 12:28; 14:4, 5, 12, 19, 23, 28, 33, 34, 35; 15:9; 16:1, 19 (2x)

cross (*stauros*; 2x): 1:17, 18

crucify (*stauroō*; 4x): 1:13, 23; 2:2, 8

discern, examine, judge (*anakrinō*; 10x): 2:14, 15 (2x); 4:3 (2x), 4; 9:3; 10:25, 27; 14:24

exercise authority, authority (*exousiazō, exousia*; 13x): 6:12; 7:4 (2x), 37; 8:9; 9:4, 5, 6, 12 (2x), 18; 11:10; 15:24

holy, saints (*hagios* [singular form]; 13x): 1:2; 2:13; 3:17; 6:1, 2, 19; 7:14, 34; 12:3; 14:33; 16:1, 15, 20

know (*eideō, oida, ginōskō, epiginōskō*; 48x): 1:16, 21; 2:2, 8 (2x), 9, 11 (2x), 12, 14, 16; 3:16, 20; 4:19; 5:6; 6:2, 3, 9, 15, 16, 19; 7:16 (2x); 8:1, 2 (3x), 3, 4, 10; 9:13, 24; 11:3; 12:2; 13:2, 9, 12 (3x); 14:7, 9, 11, 16, 37; 15:58; 16:7, 15, 18

power (*dynamis*; 15x): 1:18, 24; 2:4, 5; 4:19, 20; 5:4; 6:14; 12:10, 28, 29; 14:11; 15:24, 43, 56 raise, raise up, resurrection (*egeirō, anastasis*; 20x): 6:14; 15:4, 12 (2x), 13 (2x), 14, 15, 16, 17, 20, 21, 29, 32, 35, 42 (2x), 43, 44, 52

sanctify (*hagiazō*; 4x): 1:2; 6:11; 7:14 (2x)

Spirit (*pneuma*; 41x): 2:4, 10 (2x), 11 (2x), 12 (2x), 13, 14; 3:16; 4:21; 5:3, 4, 5; 6:11, 17, 19, 20; 7:34, 40; 12:3 (2x), 4, 7, 8 (2x), 9 (2x), 10, 11, 13 (2x); 14:2, 12, 14, 15 (2x), 16, 32; 15:45; 16:18

spiritual, spiritually (*pneumatikos, pneumatikōs*; 15x): 2:13, 14, 15; 3:1; 9:11; 10:3, 4 (2x); 12:1; 14:1, 37; 15:44 (2x), 46 (2x)

unbelievers (*apistos* [singular form]; 11x): 6:6; 7:12, 13, 14 (2x), 15; 10:27; 14:22 (2x), 23, 24

wisdom, wise (*sophia, sophos*; 26x): 1:17, 19 (2x), 20 (2x), 21 (2x), 22, 24, 25, 26, 27, 30; 2:1, 4, 5, 6 (2x), 7, 13; 3:10, 18, 19 (2x); 6:5; 12:8

world (*kosmos*; 21x): 1:20, 21, 27 (2x), 28; 2:12; 3:19, 22; 4:9, 13; 5:10 (2x); 6:2 (2x); 7:31 (2x), 33, 34; 8:4; 11:32; 14:10

you, your (*hymeis*; 150x): 1:3, 4 (2x), 6, 7, 8, 10 (2x), 11 (2x), 12, 13, 14, 26, 30; 2:1 (2x), 2, 3, 5; 3:1, 2, 3, 16, 17, 18, 21, 22, 23; 4:3, 6, 8, 10 (3x), 14, 15, 16, 17 (2x), 18, 19, 21; 5:1, 2, 4, 6, 9, 11, 12, 13; 6:1, 2, 5 (2x), 7, 8, 15, 19 (2x), 20 (2x); 7:5 (2x), 14, 28, 32, 35 (2x); 8:9; 9:1, 2 (2x), 11 (2x), 12; 10:1, 13 (3x), 15, 20, 27 (2x), 28; 11:2 (2x), 3, 13, 14, 18 (2x), 19 (2x), 20, 22 (2x), 23, 24, 30; 12:1, 3, 21, 27, 31; 14:5, 6 (3x), 9, 12, 18, 25, 26, 34, 36 (2x), 37; 15:1 (2x), 2, 3, 12, 14, 17 (2x), 34, 51, 58; 16:1, 2, 3, 5, 6 (2x), 7 (2x), 10, 12, 14, 15, 16, 17, 18, 19 (2x), 20, 23, 24

2 Corinthians

afflict, affliction suffering (*thlibō, thlipsis, pathēma*; 15x): 1:4 (2x), 5, 6 (2x), 7, 8; 2:4; 4:8, 17; 6:4; 7:4, 5; 8:2, 13

be weak, weakness (*astheneō, astheneia*; 12x): 11:21, 29 (2x), 30; 12:5, 9 (2x), 10 (2x); 13:3, 4, 9

boast, boasting, act boldly (*kauchaomai, kauchēma, kauchēsis, tharreō*; 35x): 1:12, 14; 5:6, 8, 12; 7:4, 14 (2x); 7:16; 8:24; 9:2, 3, 4; 10:1, 2, 8, 13, 15, 16, 17 (2x); 11:10, 12, 16, 17, 18 (2x), 30 (2x); 12:1, 5 (2x), 6, 9, 11

(to) comfort, comfort (*parakaleo, paraklēsis*; 27x): 1:3, 4 (3x), 5, 6 (3x), 7; 2:7, 8; 5:20; 6:1; 7:4, 6, 7 (2x), 13 (2x); 8:4, 6, 17; 9:5; 10:1; 12:8, 18; 13:11

death (*thanatos*; 9x): 1:9, 10; 2:16 (2x); 3:7; 4:11, 12; 7:10; 11:23

forgive (*charizomai*; 5x): 2:7, 10 (3x); 12:13

glory (*doxa*; 19x): 1:20; 3:7 (2x), 8, 9 (2x), 10, 11 (2x), 18 (3x); 4:4, 6, 15, 17; 6:8; 8:19, 23

grace (*charis*; 18x): 1:2, 12, 15; 2:14; 4:15; 6:1; 8:1, 4, 6, 7, 9, 16, 19; 9:8, 14, 15; 12:9; 13:14

heart (*kardia*; 11x): 1:22; 2:4; 3:2, 3, 15; 4:6; 5:12; 6:11; 7:3; 8:16; 9:7

know (*eideō, oida, ginōskō, epiginōskō*; 29x): 1:7, 13 (2x), 14; 2:4, 9; 3:2; 4:14; 5:1, 6, 11, 16 (3x), 21; 6:9; 8:9; 9:2; 11:11, 31; 12:2 (4x), 3 (3x); 13:5, 6

(to) love, love (*agapaō, agapē*; 13x): 2:4, 8; 5:14; 6:6; 8:7, 8, 24; 9:7; 11:11; 12:15 (2x); 13:11, 14

manifest (*phaneroō*; 9x): 2:14; 3:3; 4:10, 11; 5:10, 11 (2x); 7:12; 11:6

one another, other, another (*allēlōn, allos, heteros*; 8x): 1:13; 8:8, 13; 11:4 (3x), 8; 13:12

rejoice, joy (*chairō, chara*; 13x): 1:24; 2:3 (2x); 6:10; 7:4, 7, 9, 13 (2x), 16; 8:2; 13:9, 11

service (*diakonia, leitourgia*; 13x): 3:7, 8, 9 (2x); 4:1; 5:18; 6:3; 8:4; 9:1, 12 (2x), 13; 11:8

(to) sorrow, sorrow (*lypeō, lypē*; 18x): 2:1, 2 (2x), 3, 4, 5 (2x), 7; 6:10; 7:8 (2x), 9 (3x), 10 (2x), 11; 9:7

sufficient, adequate (*hikanos, hikanotēs, autarkeia*; 5x): 2:6, 16; 3:5 (2x); 9:8

veil (*kalymma*; 4x): 3:13, 14, 15, 16

Galatians

believe, faith (*pisteuō, pistis*; 26x): 1:23; 2:7, 16 (3x), 20; 3:2, 5, 6, 7, 8, 9, 11, 12, 14, 22 (2x), 23 (2x), 24, 25, 26; 5:5, 6, 22, 6:10

Christ (*Christos*; 41x): 1:1, 3, 6, 7, 10, 12, 22; 2:4, 16 (3x), 17 (2x), 20 (2x), 21; 3:1, 13, 14, 16, 17, 22, 24, 26, 27 (2x), 28, 29; 4:7, 14, 19; 5:1, 2, 4, 6, 24; 6:2, 12, 14, 15, 18

circumcise, circumcision (*peritemnō, peritomē*; 13x): 2:3, 7, 8, 9, 12; 5:2, 3, 6, 11; 6:12, 13 (2x), 15

grace (*charis*; 7x): 1:3, 6, 15; 2:9, 21; 5:4; 6:18

freedom, free (*eleutheria, eleutheros*; 9x): 2:4; 3:28; 4:22, 23, 26, 30, 31; 5:1, 13

Jesus (*Iesous*; 17x): 1:1, 3, 12; 2:4, 16 (2x); 3:1, 14, 22, 26, 28; 4:14; 5:6; 6:14, 15, 17, 18

law (*nomos*; 33x): 2:16 (3x), 19 (2x), 21; 3:2, 5, 10 (2x), 11, 12, 13, 17, 18, 19, 21 (3x), 23, 24; 4:4, 5, 21 (2x); 5:3, 4, 14, 18 (2x), 23, 6:2, 13

preach good news, gospel (*euangelizō, euangelion*; 13x): 1:6, 7, 8, 9, 11 (2x), 16, 23; 2:2, 5, 7, 14; 4:13

promise (*epangelia*; 9x): 3:14, 16, 17, 18, 21, 22, 29; 4:23, 28

spirit (*pneuma*; 18x): 3:2, 3, 5, 14; 4:6, 29; 5:5, 16, 17 (2x), 18, 22, 25 (2x); 6:1, 8 (2x), 18

uncircumcision (*akrobustia*; 3x): 2:7; 5:6; 6:15

Ephesians

body, same body (*sōma, syssōmos*; 9x): 1:23; 2:16; 3:6; 4:4, 12, 16 (2x); 5:23, 28, 30

church (*ekklēsia*; 9x): 1:22; 3:10, 21; 5:23, 24, 25, 27, 29, 32

formerly (*pote*; 6x): 2:2, 3, 11, 13; 5:8, 29

grace (*charis*; 12x): 1:2, 6, 7; 2:5, 7, 8; 3:2, 7, 8; 4:7, 29; 6:24

heavenly places (*epouranioi*; 5x): 1:3, 20; 2:6; 3:10; 6:12

in Christ, in him, in whom (*en Christos, en autos*; 32x): 1:1, 3, 4, 7, 9, 10, 11, 12, 13 (2x), 15, 20; 2:6, 7 (2x), 10, 13, 15 (2x), 21 (2x), 22; 3:6, 11, 12, 21; 4:21, 32; 5:8; 6:1, 10, 21

(to) love, love (*agapaō, agapē*; 20x): 1:4, 6, 15; 2:4 (2x); 3:17, 19; 4:2, 15, 16; 5:2 (2x), 25 (2x), 28 (3x), 33; 6:23, 24

make alive together, join together, build together, bring together (*syzōopoieō, synarmologeō, synoikodomeō, symbibazō*; 5x): 2:5, 21, 22; 4:16 (2x)

one (*heis*; 12x): 2:14, 15, 16, 18; 4:4 (2x), 5 (2x), 6, 7, 16; 5:33

power (*dynamis*; 5x): 1:19, 21; 3:7, 16, 20

spirit (*pneuma*; 15x): 1:13, 17; 2:2, 18, 22; 3:5, 16; 4:3, 4, 23, 30; 5:9, 18; 6:17, 18

walk (*peripateō*; 8x): 2:2, 10; 4:1, 17 (2x); 5:2, 8, 15

Philippians

abound (*perisseuō*; 5x): 1:9, 26; 4:12 (2x), 18

affection (*splanchnon*; 2x): 1:8; 2:1

think, adopt an attitude, have a mind (*phroneō*; 11x): 1:7; 2:2 (2x), 5; 3:15 (2x), 16, 19; 4:2, 10 (2x)

Christ (*Christos*; 38x): 1:1 (2x), 2, 6, 8, 10, 11, 13, 15, 16, 18, 19, 20, 21, 23, 26, 27, 29; 2:1, 5, 11, 16, 21, 30; 3:3, 7, 8 (2x), 9, 12, 14, 18, 20; 4:7, 13, 19, 21, 23

fellowship (*koinōnia*; 3x): 1:5; 2:1; 3:10

gospel (*euangelion*; 9x): 1:5, 7, 12, 17, 27 (2x); 2:22; 4:3, 15

imprisonment (*desmos*; 4x): 1:7, 13, 14, 16

know, knowledge (*eideō, oida, ginōskō, epiginōsis, gnōrizō*; 18x): 1:9, 12, 17, 19, 22, 25, 27, 30; 2:19, 22, 28; 3:10; 4:5, 6, 9, 12 (2x), 15

rejoice, joy (*chairō, chara, synchairō*; 14x): 1:4, 18, 25; 2:2, 17 (2x), 18 (2x), 28, 29; 3:1; 4:1, 4, 10

Colossians

all (*pas*; 40x): 1:4, 6, 9, 10 (2x), 11 (2x), 15, 16 (2x), 17 (2x), 18, 19, 20, 23, 28 (4x); 2:2, 3, 9, 10, 13, 19, 22; 3:8, 11 (2x), 14, 16, 17 (2x), 20, 22, 23; 4:7, 9, 12

complete, fill (*plēroō*; 5x): 1:9, 25; 2:10; 4:12, 17

elements (*stoicheia* [singular form]; 2x): 2:8, 20

faith, faithful (*pistis, pistos*; 9x): 1:2, 4, 7, 23; 2:5, 7, 12; 4:7, 9

knowledge (*epignōsis*; 4x): 1:9, 10; 2:2; 3:10

mystery (*mystērion*; 4x): 1:26, 27; 2:2; 4:3

through, on account of (*dia*; 14x): 1:1, 5, 9, 16, 20 (3x), 22; 2:8, 12, 19; 3:6, 17; 4:3

wisdom (*sophia*; 6x): 1:9, 28; 2:3, 23; 3:16; 4:5

1 Thessalonians

coming (*parousia*; 4x): 2:19; 3:13; 4:15; 5:23

day of the Lord (*hēmera kyriou*; 2x): 5:2, 4

faith (*pistis*; 8x): 1:3, 8; 3:2, 5, 6, 7, 10; 5:8

gospel (*euangelion*; 6x): 1:5; 2:2, 4, 8, 9; 3:2

hope (*elpis*; 4x): 1:3; 2:19; 4:13; 5:8

(to) love, love (*agapaō, agapē*; 8x): 1:3, 4; 2:10; 3:6, 12; 4:9; 5:8, 13

spirit (*pneuma*; 5x): 1:5, 6; 4:8; 5:19, 23

suffer previously, affliction (*propaschō, thlipsis*; 4x): 1:6; 2:2; 3:3, 7

word (*logos*; 9x): 1:5, 6, 8; 2:5, 13 (3x); 4:15, 18

2 Thessalonians

coming of Jesus Christ (*parousia Iēsou Christou*; 3x): 2:1, 8, 9

everlasting destruction (*aiōnios olethros*; 1x): 1:9

faith (*pistis*; 5x): 1:3, 4, 11; 2:13; 3:2

flaming fire (*phlox pyr*; 1x): 1:8

glorify, glory (*endoxazō, doxa*; 4x): 1:9, 10, 12; 2:14

God (*theos*; 19x): 1:1, 2, 3, 4, 5 (2x), 6, 8, 11, 12; 2:4 (4x), 11, 13 (2x), 16; 3:5

(to) love, love (*agapaō, agapē*; 7x):1:3; 2:10, 13, 16; 3:5; 4:8, 10

man of lawlessness (*anthrōpos anomia*; 1x): 2:3

mystery of lawlessnes/iniquity (*mystērion anomias*; 1x): 2:7

son of perdition/destruction (*huios apōleias*; 1x): 2:3

spirit (*pneuma*; 3x): 2:2, 8, 13

truth (*alētheia*; 3x): 2:10, 12, 13

1 Timothy

be merciful, mercy (*eleeō, eleos*; 3x): 1:2, 13, 16

be sound, well, good (*hygiainō, kalos*; 6x): 1:10; 3:4, 12, 13; 5:17; 6:3

doctrine (*didaskalia*; 8x): 1:10; 4:1, 6, 13, 16; 5:17; 6:1, 3

faith (*pistis*; 19x): 1:2, 4, 5, 14, 19 (2x); 2:7, 15; 3:9, 13; 4:1, 6, 12; 5:8, 12; 6:10, 11, 12, 21

faithful (not in connection with saying [*logos*]) (*pistos*; 8x): 1:12; 3:11; 4:3, 10, 12; 5:16; 6:2 (2x)

faithful saying (*pistos logos*; 3x): 1:15; 3:1; 4:9

godliness (*eusebeia*; 8x): 2:2; 3:16; 4:7, 8; 6:3, 5, 6, 11

man of God (*anthrōpos theou*; 1x): 6:11

Savior (*sōtēr*; 3x): 1:1; 2:3; 4:10

2 Timothy

abide, continue in (*menō*; 3x): 2:13; 3:14; 4:20

avoid, shun (*periistēmi, apotrepomai*; 2x): 2:16; 3:5

be ashamed, unashamed (*epaischynomai, anepaischyntos*; 4x): 1:8, 12, 16; 2:15

be diligent (*spoudazō*; 3x): 2:15; 4:9, 21

be ready (*ephistēmi*; 2x): 4:2, 6

be sober/watchful (*nēphō*; 1x): 4:5
be sound (*hygiainō*, 2x): 1:13; 4:3
doctrine, teaching (*didaskalia, didakē*; 4x): 3:10, 16;
  4:2, 3
endure (*hypomenō, kakopatheō*; 5x): 2:3, 9, 10, 12; 4:5
faith (*pistis*; 8x): 1:5, 13; 2:18, 22; 3:8, 10, 15; 4:7
gospel (*euangelion*; 3x): 1:8, 10; 2:8
laden with sin (*sesōreumenos hamartias*; 1x): 3:6
lover of God (*philotheos*; 1x): 3:4
lover of pleasure (*philēdonos*; 1x): 3:4
lover of self (*philautos*; 1x): 3:2
persecution (*diōgmos*; 2x): 3:11 (2x)
retain, hold, have (*echō*; 6x): 1:3 (2x), 13; 2:17, 19; 3:5
word (*logos*; 7x): 1:13; 2:9, 11, 15, 17; 4:2, 15

Titus

be sound (*hygiainō*; 4x): 1:9, 13; 2:1, 2
deed/work (*ergon*; 8x): 1:16 (2x); 2:7, 14; 3:1, 5, 8,
  14
doctrine (*didaskalia*; 4x): 1:9; 2:1, 7, 10
faithful (*pistos*; 3x): 1:6, 9; 3:8
God (*theos*; 13x): 1:1 (2x), 2, 3, 4, 7, 16; 2:5, 10, 11,
  13; 3:4, 8
good deeds/works (*kalōn ergōn*; 4x): 2:7, 14; 3:8, 14
grace (*charis*; 4x): 1:4; 2:11; 3:7, 15
Jesus Christ (*Iēsous Christos*; 4x): 1:1, 4; 2:13; 3:6
Savior (*sōtēr*; 6x): 1:3, 4; 2:10, 13; 3:4, 6
sensible (*sōphrōn*; 3x): 1:8; 2:2, 5
truth (*alētheia*; 2x): 1:1, 14
word (*logos*; 5x): 1:3, 9; 2:5, 8; 3:8

Philemon

accept, receive, have back (*proslambanomai, apechō*;
  3x): 12, 15, 17
appeal (*parakaleō*; 2x): 9, 10
grace, joy (*charis*; 3x): 3, 7, 25
joy, benefit (*oninamai*; 1x): 20
pay (*apotinō*; 1x): 19
love (*agapē*; 3x): 5, 7, 9
owe (*prosopheilō*; 1x): 19
slave (*doulos*; 1x): 16
unprofitable (*achrēstos*; 1x): 11
willing (*hekousios*; 1x): 14

Hebrews

age, world, eternal, forever (*aiōn, aiōnios*; 21x): 1:2, 8
  (2x); 5:6, 9; 6:2, 5, 20; 7:17, 21, 24, 28; 9:12, 14,
  15, 26; 11:3; 13:8, 20, 21 (2x)
angels (*angelos* [singular form]; 13x): 1:4, 5, 6, 7
  (2x), 13; 2:2, 5, 7, 9, 16; 12:22; 13:2
better (*kreisson*; 13x): 1:4; 6:9; 7:7, 19, 22; 8:6 (2x);
  9:23; 10:34; 11:16, 35, 40; 12:24
covenant (*diathēkē*; 17x): 7:22; 8:6, 8, 9 (2x), 10; 9:4
  (2x), 15 (2x), 16, 17, 20; 10:16, 29; 12:24; 13:20

faith, faithful (*pistis, pistos*; 37x): 2:17; 3:2, 5; 4:2;
  6:1, 12; 10:22, 23, 38, 39; 11:1, 3, 4, 5, 6, 7 (2x),
  8, 9, 11 (2x), 13, 17, 20, 21, 22, 23, 24, 27, 28,
  29, 30, 31, 33, 39; 12:2; 13:7
God (*theos*; 68x): 1:1, 6, 8, 9; 2:4, 9, 13, 17; 3:4, 12;
  4:4, 9, 10, 12, 14; 5:1, 4, 10, 12; 6:1, 3, 5, 6, 7, 10,
  13, 17, 18; 7:1, 3, 19, 25; 8:10; 9:14 (2x), 20, 24;
  10:7, 9, 12, 21, 29, 31, 36; 11:3, 4 (2x), 5 (2x), 6,
  10, 16 (2x), 19, 25, 40; 12:2, 7, 15, 22, 23, 28, 29;
  13:4, 7, 15, 16, 20
great (greater) (*megas*; 6x): 4:14; 8:11; 10:21, 35;
  11:24; 13:20
high priest, priest, priesthood (*archiereus, hiereus,
  hierōsynē*; 34x): 2:17; 3:1; 4:14, 15; 5:1, 5, 6, 10;
  6:20; 7:1, 3, 11, 15, 17, 21 (2x), 23, 26, 27, 28;
  8:1, 3, 4 (2x); 9:6, 7, 11, 12, 14, 24, 25; 10:11,
  21; 13:11
Jesus (*Iēsous*; 13x): 2:9; 3:1; 4:14; 6:20; 7:22; 10:10,
  19; 12:2, 24; 13:8, 12, 20, 21
many, all the more (*polys*; 7x): 2:10; 5:11; 9:28;
  10:32; 12:9, 15, 25
once, once for all (*ephapax, hapax*; 11x): 6:4; 7:27;
  9:7, 12, 26, 27, 28; 10:2, 10; 12:26, 27
perfect (*teleioō*; 9x): 2:10; 5:9; 7:19, 28; 9:9; 10:1, 14;
  11:40; 12:23
salvation (*sōtēria*; 7x): 1:14; 2:3, 10; 5:9; 6:9; 9:28;
  11:7
sin (*hamartia*; 25x): 1:3; 2:17; 3:13; 4:15; 5:1, 3;
  7:27; 8:12; 9:26, 28 (2x); 10:2, 3, 4, 6, 8, 11, 12,
  17, 18, 26; 11:25; 12:1, 4; 13:11
son (*huios*; 24x): 1:2, 5 (2x), 8; 2:6, 10; 3:6; 4:14; 5:5,
  8; 6:6; 7:3, 5, 28; 10:29; 11:21, 22, 24; 12:5 (2x),
  6, 7 (2x), 8

James

brethren (*adelphos* [singular form]; 19x): 1:2, 9, 16,
  19; 2:1, 5, 14, 15; 3:1, 10, 12; 4:11 (3x); 5:7, 9,
  10, 12, 19
deed/work (*ergon*; 15x): 1:4, 25; 2:14, 17, 18 (3x),
  20, 21, 22 (2x), 24, 25, 26; 3:13
doer (*poiētēs*; 4x): 1:22, 23, 25; 4:11
faith (*pistis*; 15x): 1:3, 6; 2:1, 5, 14 (2x), 17, 18 (2x),
  20, 22 (2x), 24, 26; 5:15
judge, judgment (*krinō, krisis, kritēs*; 8x): 2:4, 12, 13
  (2x); 4:11 (2x), 12; 5:9
law (*nomos*; 10x): 1:25; 2:8, 9, 10, 11, 12; 4:11 (4x)
(to) perfect, perfect (*teleioō, teleios*; 5x): 1:4, 17, 25;
  2:22; 3:2
sin (*hamartia*; 6x): 1:15 (2x); 2:9; 4:17; 5:15, 20
wisdom (*sophia*; 4x): 1:5; 3:13, 15, 17

1 Peter

be submissive (*hypotassō*; 7x): 2:13, 18; 3:1, 5, 22;
  5:5 (2x)
call (*kaleo*; 6x): 1:15; 2:9, 21; 3:6, 9; 5:10

chosen (one who is chosen) (*eklektos, syneklektos*; 5x): 1:1; 2:4, 6, 9; 5:13

end (*telos*; 4x): 1:9; 3:8; 4:7, 17

flesh (*sarx*; 7x): 1:24; 3:18, 21; 4:1 (2x), 2, 6

glorify, glory (*doxazō, doxa*; 16x): 1:7, 8, 11, 21, 24; 2:12; 4:11 (2x), 13, 14 (2x), 16; 5:1, 4, 10, 11

grace (*charis*; 10x): 1:2, 10, 13; 2:19, 20; 3:7; 4:10; 5:5, 10, 12

holy (*hagios*; 8x): 1:12, 15 (2x), 16 (2x); 2:5, 9; 3:5

hope (*elpis*; 3x): 1:3, 21; 3:15

live, life (*zaō, zōē*; 9x): 1:3, 23; 2:4, 5, 24; 4:5, 6; 3:7, 10

(to) love, love (*agapaō, agapē*; 6x): 1:8, 22; 2:17; 3:10; 4:8; 5:14

obey, obedience (*hypakouō, hypakoē*; 4x): 1:2, 14, 22; 3:6

precious (*timē, timios*; 5x): 1:7 (2x), 19; 2:7; 3:7

revelation (*apokalypsis*; 3x): 1:7, 13; 4:13

salvation (*sōtēria*; 3x): 1:5, 9, 10

spirit (*pneuma*; 9x): 1:2, 11, 12, 22; 3:4, 18, 19; 4:6, 14

suffer, suffering, trial (*paschō, pathēma, peirasmos*; 18x): 1:6, 11; 2:19, 20, 21, 23; 3:14, 17, 18; 4:1 (2x), 12, 13, 15, 19; 5:1, 9, 10

time (*kairos, chronos*; 8x): 1:5, 11, 17, 20; 4:2, 3, 17; 5:6

2 Peter

be diligent (*spoudazō*; 3x): 1:10, 15; 3:14

corruption, destroyed (*phthora*; 4x): 1:4; 2:12 (2x), 19

destroy (*apollymi, luō*; 5x): 3:6, 9, 10, 11, 12

know, knowledge (*epiginōskō, epignōsis, ginōskō*; 8x): 1:2, 3, 8, 20; 2:20, 21 (2x); 3:3

promise (*epangelia, epangelma*; 4x): 1:4; 3:4, 9, 13

prophecy (*prophēteia*; 2x): 1:20, 21

prophet (*prophētēs*; 2x): 2:16; 3:2

reminder (*hypomnēsis*; 2x): 1:13; 3:1

1 John

abide (*menō*; 23x): 2:6, 10, 14, 17, 19, 24 (2x), 27 (2x), 28; 3:6, 9, 14, 15, 17, 24 (2x); 4:12, 13, 15, 16 (3x)

born of God (*gegennēmenos theou*; 8x): 2:29; 3:9 (2x); 4:7; 5:1, 4, 18 (2x)

darkness (*skotia, skotos*; 7x): 1:5, 6; 2:8, 9, 11 (3x)

evil (*ponēros*; 6x): 2:13, 14; 3:12 (2x); 5:18, 19

fellowship (*koinōnia*; 3x): 1:3, 6, 7

know (*ginōskō, oida*; 39x): 2:3, 4, 5, 11, 13 (2x), 14, 18, 20, 21, 29 (2x); 3:1 (2x), 2, 5, 6, 14, 15, 16, 19, 20, 24; 4:2, 6 (2x), 7, 8, 13, 16; 5:2, 13, 15 (2x), 16, 18, 19, 20 (2x)

life (*zōē, psychē, bios*; 17x): 1:1, 2 (2x); 2:16, 25; 3:14, 15, 16 (2x), 17; 5:11 (2x), 12 (2x), 13, 16, 20

light (*phōs*; 6x): 1:5, 7 (2x); 2:8, 9, 10

(to) love, love (*agapaō, agapē*; 45x): 2:5, 10, 15 (3x); 3:1, 10, 11, 14 (2x), 16, 17, 18, 23; 4:7 (3x), 8 (2x), 9, 10 (3x), 11, 12, 16 (3x), 17, 18 (3x), 19 (2x), 20 (3x), 21 (2x); 5:1 (2x), 2 (2x), 3

(to) sin, sin (*hamartanō, hamartia*; 27x): 1:7, 8, 9 (2x), 10; 2:1 (2x), 2, 12; 3:4 (2x), 5 (2x), 6 (2x), 8 (2x), 9 (2x); 4:10; 5:16 (4x), 17 (2x), 18

truth, true (*alētheia, alēthēs, alēthinos*; 15x): 1:6, 8; 2:4, 8 (2x), 21 (2x), 27; 3:18, 19; 4:6; 5:6, 20 (3x)

(to) witness, testify, witness (*martyreō, martyria*; 13x): 1:2; 4:14; 5:6, 7, 8, 9 (4x), 10 (3x), 11

world (*kosmos*; 23x): 2:2, 15 (3x), 16 (2x), 17; 3:1, 13, 17; 4:1, 3, 4, 5 (3x), 9, 14, 17; 5:4 (2x), 5, 19

write (*graphō*; 13x): 1:4; 2:1, 7, 8, 12, 13 (3x), 14 (2x), 21, 26; 5:13

2 John

abide (*menō*; 3x): 2, 9 (2x)

antichrist (*antichristos*; 1x): 7

beginning (*archē*; 2x): 5, 6

children (*teknon* [singular]; 3x): 1, 4, 13

commandment (*entolē*; 4x): 4, 5, 6 (2x)

deceiver (*planos*; 2x): 7 (2x)

elect, chosen (*eklektos*; 2x): 1, 13

Father (*patēr*; 4x): 3 (2x), 4, 9

flesh (*sarx*; 1x): 7

(to) love, love (*agapaō, agapē*; 4x): 1, 3, 5, 6

teaching, doctrine (*didachē*; 3x): 9 (2x), 10

truth (*alētheia*; 4x): 1 (2x), 2, 3, 4

walk (*peripateō*; 3x): 4, 6 (2x)

3 John

beloved (*agapētos*; 4x): 1, 2, 5, 11

do evil, evil (*kakopoieō, kakos*; 2x): 11 (2x)

do good, be in good health, be well (*agathopoieō, agathos, hygiainō*; 3x): 2, 11 (2x)

truth (*alētheia*; 6x): 1, 3 (2x), 4, 8, 12

walk (*peripateō*; 2x): 3, 4

(to) witness, testify, witness (*martyreō, martyria*; 5x): 3, 6, 12 (3x)

Jude

act in an ungodly way, ungodliness, ungodly (*asebeō, asebeia, asebes*; 6x): 4, 15 (4x), 18

beloved (*agapētos*; 3x): 3, 17, 20

condemnation (*krima*; 1x): 4

contend (*epagōnizomai*; 1x): 3

everlasting, eternal (*aidios, aiōnos*; 3x): 6, 13, 25

faith (*pistis*; 2x): 3, 20

judgment (*krisis*; 3x): 6, 9, 15

save (*sōzō*; 2x): 5, 23

Revelation

after (these things) (*meta*; 47x): 1:7, 12, 19; 2:16, 22; 3:4, 20, 21 (2x); 4:1 (3x); 6:8; 7:1, 9; 9:12; 10:8; 11:7, 11; 12:9, 17; 13:4, 7; 14:1, 4, 13; 15:5; 17:1, 2, 12, 14 (2x); 18:1, 3, 9; 19:1, 19, 20; 20:3, 4, 6; 21:3 (2x), 9, 15; 22:12, 21

angel (*angelos*; 75x): 1:1, 20; 2:1, 8, 12, 18; 3:1, 5, 7, 14; 5:2, 11; 7:1, 2 (2x), 11; 8:2, 3, 4, 5, 6, 7, 8, 10, 12, 13 (2x); 9:1, 11, 13, 14, 15; 10:1, 5, 7, 8, 9, 10; 11:1, 15; 12:7 (2x), 9; 14:6, 8, 9, 10, 15, 17, 18, 19; 15:1, 6, 7, 8; 16:1, 3, 4, 5, 8, 10, 12, 17; 17:1, 7; 18:1, 21; 19:17; 20:1; 21:9, 12, 17; 22:6, 8, 16

Babylon (*Babylōn*; 6x): 14:8; 16:19; 17:5; 18:2, 10, 21

beast (*thērion*; 38x): 6:8; 11:7; 13:1, 2, 3, 4 (3x), 11, 12 (2x), 14 (3x), 15 (2x), 17, 18; 14:9, 11; 15:2; 16:2, 10, 13; 17:3, 7, 8 (2x), 11, 12, 13, 16, 17; 19:19, 20 (2x); 20:4, 10

bowl (*phialē*; 12x): 5:8; 15:7; 16:1, 2, 3, 4, 8, 10, 12, 17; 17:1; 21:9

Christ (*Christos*; 11x): 1:1, 2, 5, 9 (2x); 11:15; 12:10, 17; 20:4, 6; 22:21

church (*ekklēsia*; 20x): 1:4, 11, 20 (2x); 2:1, 7, 8, 11, 12, 17, 18, 23, 29; 3:1, 6, 7, 13, 14, 22; 22:16

devil, Satan (*diabolos, Satanas*; 13x): 2:9, 10, 13 (2x), 24; 3:9; 12:9 (2x), 12; 20:2 (2x), 7, 10

dragon (*drakōn*; 13x): 12:3, 4, 7 (2x), 9, 13, 16, 17; 13:2, 4, 11; 16:13; 20:2

earthquake (*seismos*; 7x): 6:12; 8:5; 11:13 (2x), 19; 16:18 (2x)

God (*theos*; 98x): 1:1, 2, 6, 9; 2:7, 18; 3:1, 2, 12 (4x), 14; 4:5, 8; 5:6, 9, 10; 6:9; 7:2, 3, 10, 11, 12, 15, 17; 8:2, 4; 9:4, 13; 10:7; 11:1, 4, 11, 13, 16 (2x), 17, 19; 12:5, 6, 10 (2x), 17; 13:6; 14:4, 5, 7, 10, 12, 19; 15:1, 2, 3 (2x), 7, 8; 16:1, 7, 9, 11, 14, 19, 21; 17:17 (2x); 18:5, 8, 20; 19:1, 4, 5, 6, 9, 10, 13, 15, 17; 20:4, 6, 9, 12; 21:2, 3 (2x), 4, 7, 10, 11, 22, 23; 22:1, 3, 5, 6, 9, 18, 19

Jesus (*Iēsous*; 14x): 1:1, 2, 5, 9 (2x); 12:17; 14:12; 17:6; 19:10 (2x); 20:4; 22:16, 20, 21

judge, judgment (*krinō, krima, krisis*; 16x): 6:10; 11:18; 14:7; 16:5, 7; 17:1; 18:8, 10, 20 (2x); 19:2 (2x), 11; 20:4, 12, 13

know (*oida*; 11x): 2:2, 9, 13, 19; 3:1, 8, 15, 17; 7:14; 12:12; 19:12

lamb (*arnion*; 29x): 5:6, 8, 12, 13; 6:1, 16; 7:9, 10, 14, 17; 12:11; 13:8, 11; 14:1, 4 (2x), 10; 15:3; 17:14 (2x); 19:7, 9; 21:9, 14, 22, 23, 27; 22:1, 3

mystery (*mystērion*; 4x): 1:20; 10:7; 17:5, 7

nations (*ethnos* [singular form]; 22x): 2:26; 5:9; 7:9; 10:11; 11:2, 9, 18; 12:5; 13:7; 14:6, 8; 15:4; 16:19; 17:15; 18:3, 23; 19:15; 20:3, 8; 21:24, 26; 22:2

overcome (*nikaō*; 17x): 2:7, 11, 17, 26; 3:5, 12, 21 (2x); 5:5; 6:2 (2x); 11:7; 12:11; 13:7; 15:2; 17:14; 21:7

plague (*plēgē*; 15x): 9:20; 11:6; 13:3, 12, 14; 15:1, 6, 8; 16:9, 21 (2x); 18:4, 8; 21:9; 22:18

repent (*metanoeō*; 12x): 2:5 (2x), 16, 21 (2x), 22; 3:3, 19; 9:20, 21; 16:9, 11

(to) seal, seal (*sphragizō, sphragis*; 31x): 5:1, 2, 5, 9; 6:1, 3, 5, 7, 9, 12; 7:2, 3, 4 (2x), 5 (3x), 6 (3x), 7 (3x), 8 (3x); 8:1; 9:4; 10:4; 20:3; 22:10

see, behold (*horaō*; 62x): 1:2, 12, 17, 19, 20; 4:1 (2x); 5:1, 2, 6, 11; 6:1 (2x), 2, 5 (2x), 8, 9, 12; 7:1, 2, 9 (2x); 8:2, 13; 9:1, 17; 10:1, 5; 12:13; 13:1, 2, 11; 14:1 (2x), 6, 14 (2x); 15:1, 2, 5; 16:13; 17:3, 6, 8, 12, 15, 16, 18; 18:1, 7; 19:10, 11 (2x), 17, 19; 20:1, 4, 11, 12; 21:1, 2, 22; 22:9

seven (*hepta*; 54x): 1:4 (2x), 11, 12, 13, 16, 20 (6x); 2:1 (2x); 3:1 (2x); 4:5 (2x); 5:1, 5, 6 (3x); 8:2 (2x), 6 (2x); 10:3, 4 (2x); 11:13; 12:3 (2x); 13:1; 15:1 (2x), 6 (2x), 7 (2x), 8 (2x); 16:1; 17:1 (2x), 3, 7, 9 (2x), 10, 11; 21:9 (3x)

spirit (*pneuma*; 23x): 1:4, 10; 2:7, 11, 17, 29; 3:1, 6, 13, 22; 4:2, 5; 5:6; 11:11; 13:15; 14:13; 16:13, 14; 17:3; 18:2; 19:10; 21:10; 22:17

throne (*thronos*; 46x): 1:4; 2:13; 3:21 (2x); 4:2 (2x), 3, 4 (3x), 5 (2x), 6 (3x), 9, 10 (2x); 5:1, 6, 7, 11, 13; 6:16; 7:9, 10, 11 (2x), 15 (2x), 17; 8:3; 11:16; 12:5; 13:2; 14:3, 5; 16:10, 17; 19:4, 5; 20:4, 11; 21:5, 22:1, 3

thunder (*brontē*; 10x): 4:5; 6:1; 8:5; 10:3, 4 (2x); 11:19; 14:2; 16:18; 19:6

trumpet (*salpinx*; 6x): 1:10; 4:1; 8:2, 6, 13; 9:14

twelve (*dōdeka*; 22x): 7:5 (3x), 6 (3x), 7 (3x), 8 (3x); 12:1; 21:12 (3x), 14 (2x), 16, 21 (2x), 22:2

voice, sound (*phōnē*; 55x): 1:10, 12, 15 (2x); 3:20; 4:1, 5; 5:2, 11, 12; 6:1, 6, 7, 10; 7:2, 10; 8:5, 13 (2x); 9:9 (2x), 13; 10:3 (2x), 4 (2x), 7, 8; 11:12, 15, 19; 12:10; 14:2 (4x), 7, 9, 13, 15; 16:1, 17, 18; 18:2, 4, 22 (2x), 23; 19:1, 5, 6 (3x), 17; 21:3

woe (*ouai*; 14x): 8:13 (3x); 9:12 (2x); 11:14 (2x); 12:12; 18:10 (2x), 16 (2x), 19 (2x)

wrath (*orgē, thymos*; 16x): 6:16, 17; 11:18; 12:12; 14:8, 10 (2x), 19; 15:1, 7; 16:1, 19 (2x); 18:3; 19:15 (2x)

Appendix 4
Miracles in the Gospels

Description	Matthew	Mark	Luke	John
Angel appears to Zacharias			1:11–19	
Zacharias struck dumb			1:20–22	
Angel appears to Mary			1:26–38	
Zacharias healed of dumbness			1:64	
Angels appear to shepherds			2:9–15	
Holy Spirit descends, and voice from Heaven spoke	3:16–17	1:9–11	3:21–23	
Angels minister to Jesus	4:11	1:13		
Jesus sees Nathanael under fig tree				1:42–48
Water turned to wine				2:1–11
Jesus performs signs				2:23
Nobleman's son healed				4:46–53
Jesus escapes hostile crowd			4:30	
Catching draught of fish			5:6	
Casting out an unclean spirit		1:23–25	4:33–35	
Healing Peter's mother-in-law	8:14–15	1:30–31	4:38–39	
Healing many sick people	8:16	1:32–34	4:40	
Heals all manners of sickness and casts out many demons	4:23	1:39		
Cleansing a leper	8:2–3	1:40–42	5:12–13	
Healing a paralytic	9:2	2:3–5	5:18–20	
Healing man at Bethesda				5:6–9
Healing man's withered hand	12:9–13	3:1–5	6:6–10	
Healing many people	12:15	3:10		
Healing a centurion's servant	8:5–13		7:1–10	
Raising a widow's son at Nain			7:11–15	
Cast demon from blind mute	12:22			
Stilling the storm on Sea of Galilee	8:23–26	4:35–39	8:22–24	
Exorcised demons allowed to enter swine	8:28–32	5:6–13	8:28–33	
Raising the ruler's daughter	9:23–25	5:35–42	8:49–55	
Healing the woman with an issue of blood	9:20–22	5:25–34	8:43–48	

Description	Matthew	Mark	Luke	John
Healing two blind men	9:27–30			
Jesus heals a few sick people in Nazareth		6:5		
Cast out demon from deaf mute	9:32–33			
Jesus heals the sick in many cities	9:35			
Jesus heals sick among great multitude	14:14			
Feeding the five thousand	14:15–21	6:35–44	9:10–17	6:5–13
Walking on the sea	14:25	6:48		6:19
Healing of many at Gennesaret	14:35–36	6:55–56		
Healing the Canaanite woman's daughter	15:21–28	7:24–30		
Healing a deaf mute		7:31–35		
Jesus heals many among a great multitude	15:30–31			
Feeding the four thousand	15:32–38	8:1–8		
Healing a blind man at Bethsaida		8:22–25		
Jesus's transfiguration	17:1–8	9:2–8	9:28–36	
Healing the epileptic boy	17:14–18	9:17–27	9:38–42	
Temple tax in fish's mouth	17:24–27			
Healing a man born blind				9:1–7
Curing a demon-possessed, blind mute			11:14	
Healing an infirmed woman			13:11–13	
Healing a man with dropsy			14:2–4	
Raising Lazarus				11:43–44
Cleansing ten lepers			17:12–14	
Jesus heals many at the borders of Judea	19:1–2			
Healing the two blind men	20:30–34			
Jesus heals the blind and the lame man in the temple	21:14		18:35	
Withering the fig tree	21:18–19	11:12–14, 20		
A voice from heaven				12:28–29
Restoring a servant's ear			22:51	
Temple veil torn top to bottom	27:51	15:38	23:45	
A great earthquake, and the rocks broken	27:51			
Tombs opened and many of the dead are raised	27:52–53			

Description	Matthew	Mark	Luke	John
The resurrection of Jesus	28:1–10	16:1–8	24:1–12	20:1–9
An angel rolls the stone from the tomb and speaks to the women	28:1–7			
Angelic appearance at the sepulcher	28:5–8	16:5–7	24:4–8	
Two angels appear to Mary				20:11–13
Jesus appears to Mary Magdalene		16:9		20:14–17
Jesus appears to the women	28:9–10			
Jesus appears to the two on the road to Emmaus		16:12	24:13–35	
Jesus appears to ten apostles				20:19–23
Jesus appears to eleven apostles	28:16–20	16:14–18	24:36–49	20:26–31
Jesus appears to seven apostles				21:1–25
Miraculous catch of fish				21:6

Bibliography

Books

Baxter, Sidlow. *Explore the Book*. Grand Rapids: Zondervan, 1987.

Blomberg, Craig. *The Historical Reliability of John's Gospel*. Downers Grove, IL: InterVarsity, 1998.

———. *The Historical Reliability of the Gospels*. Downers Grove, IL: InterVarsity, 1987.

Bruce, F. F. *Jesus and Christian Origins Outside the New Testament*. Grand Rapids: Eerdmans, 1974.

———. *The New Testament Documents: Are They Reliable?* Grand Rapids: Eerdmans, 2003.

———. *Paul, Apostle of the Heart Set Free*. Grand Rapids: Eerdmans, 2000.

Carson, D. A., Douglas Moo, and Leon Morris. *An Introduction to the New Testament*. Grand Rapids: Zondervan, 1992.

Conybeare, William, and J. S. Howson. *The Life and Epistles of St. Paul*. Grand Rapids: Eerdmans, 1953.

Craig, William Lane. *The Son Rises*. Eugene, OR: Wipf & Stock, 2001.

Forster, Roger, and Paul Marston. *God's Strategy in Human History*. Wheaton: Tyndale, 1974.

Geisler, Norman. *Chosen But Free*. Minneapolis: Bethany House, 1999.

———. *A Popular Survey of the Old Testament*. 1977. Grand Rapids: Baker, 2007.

———. *To Understand the Bible, Look for Jesus*. Eugene, OR: Wipf and Stock, 2005.

Geisler, Norman L., and Thomas Howe. *When Critics Ask: A Popular Handbook on Bible Difficulties*. Grand Rapids: Baker, 1997. Reprint, Grand Rapids: Baker, 1997.

Geisler, Norman L., and William E. Nix. *A General Introduction to the Bible*. 1968. Rev. ed. Chicago: Moody, 1986.

Geisler, Norman L., and Frank Turek. *I Don't Have Enough Faith to Be an Atheist*. Wheaton: Crossway, 2004.

Glueck, Nelson. *Rivers in the Desert*. New York: Farrar, Straus and Cudahy, 1959.

Greenleaf, Simon. *The Testimony of the Evangelist*. Grand Rapids: Kregel, 1995.

Gromacki, Robert G. *New Testament Survey*. Grand Rapids: Baker, 1974.

Guthrie, Donald. *New Testament Introduction*. Downers Grove, IL: InterVarsity, 1990.

Habermas, Gary. *The Historical Jesus: Ancient Evidence for the Life of Christ*. Joplin, MO: College Press, 1996.

Harrison, Everett F. *An Introduction to the New Testament*. Grand Rapids: Eerdmans, 1971.

Hawthorne, Gerald F., Ralph P. Martin, and Daniel G. Reid, eds. *Dictionary of Paul and His Letters*. Downers Grove, IL: InterVarsity, 1993.

Hemer, Colin. *The Book of Acts in the Setting of Hellenic History.* Winona Lake, MN: Eisenbrauns, 1990.

Hodgkin, A. M. *Christ in All the Scripture.* London: Pickering & Inglis, 1922.

Hoehner, Harold. *Chronological Aspects of the Life of Christ.* Grand Rapids: Zondervan, 1977.

Kenyon, Frederic. *The Bible and Archaeology.* New York: Harper & Brothers, 1940.

———. *Our Bible and the Ancient Manuscripts.* London: Eyre & Spottiswoode, 1958.

Lewis, C. S. *Christian Reflections.* Grand Rapids: Eerdmans, 1967.

Linnemann, Eta. *Historical Criticism of the Bible.* Translated by Robert Yarborough. Grand Rapids: Kregel, 2001.

———. *Is There a Synoptic Problem?* Grand Rapids: Baker, 1992.

Longenecker, Richard. *Paul: Apostle of Liberty.* New York: Harper & Row, 1964.

Metzger, Bruce. *The Text of the New Testament.* New York: Oxford University Press, 1990.

Payne, J. Barton. *Encyclopedia of Biblical Prophecy.* Grand Rapids: Baker, 1980.

Ramsay, Sir William. *Luke the Physician and Other Stories.* Grand Rapids: Baker, 1979.

———. *St. Paul the Traveller and the Roman Citizen.* New York: G. P. Putnam's Sons, 1896.

Robertson, A. T. *A Harmony of the Gospels.* New York: HarperCollins, 1922.

———. *Introduction to the Textual Criticism of the New Testament.* Nashville: Broadman, 1925.

Robinson, John A. T. *Redating the New Testament.* Eugene, OR: Wipf & Stock, 2000.

Scroggie, William Graham. *Christ the Key to Scripture.* Chicago: Bible Institute Colportage Association, 1924.

———. *A Guide to the Gospels.* London: Pickering & Inglis, 1948. Reprint, Grand Rapids: Kregel, 1995.

Sherwin-White, A. N. *Roman Society and Roman Law in the New Testament.* Oxford: Clarendon Press, 1963.

Thomas, Robert, and Stan Gundry. *The New Harmony of the Gospels.* New York: HarperSanFrancisco, 1991.

Wiseman, Donald J. "Archaeological Confirmation of the Old Testament." Quoted in Carl F. H. Henry, *Revelation and the Bible* (Grand Rapids: Baker, 1958), 301–16.

Commentaries

Barbieri, Louis. *First & Second Peter.* Everyman's Bible Commentary Series. Chicago: Moody, 2003.

Barrett, C. K. *1 Corinthians.* Black's New Testament Commentary. 2nd ed. Peabody, MA: Hendrickson, 1993.

Bauckham, Richard J. *Jude, 2 Peter.* Word Biblical Commentary. Nashville: Thomas Nelson, 1983.

Belleville, Linda L. *2 Corinthians.* IVP New Testament Commentary. Downers Grove, IL: InterVarsity, 1996.

Blomberg, Craig. *1 Corinthians.* NIV Application Commentary. Grand Rapids: Zondervan, 1995.

———. *Matthew.* New American Commentary. Nashville: Broadman, 1992.

Bock, Darrell L. *Luke.* Baker Exegetical Commentary on the New Testament. 2 vols. Grand Rapids: Baker, 1994, 1996.

Brooks, James. *Mark.* New American Commentary. Nashville: Broadman & Holman, 1991.

Bruce, F. F. *Acts.* New International Commentary on the New Testament. Grand Rapids: Eerdmans, 1968.

———. *Epistles to the Colossians, to Philemon, and to the Ephesians.* New International Commentary on the New Testament. Grand Rapids: Eerdmans, 1988.

———. *Epistle to the Galatians.* New International Greek Testament Commentary. Grand Rapids: Eerdmans, 1982.

———. *Epistle to the Hebrews.* New International Commentary on the New Testament. Grand Rapids: Eerdmans, 1995.

————. *The Gospel According to John*. New International Commentary on the New Testament. Grand Rapids: Eerdmans, 1994.

————. *Romans*. Tyndale New Testament Commentary. Grand Rapids: Eerdmans, 1989.

Burge, Gary. *John*. NIV Application Commentary. Grand Rapids: Zondervan, 2000.

————. *The Letters of John*. NIV Application Commentary. Grand Rapids: Zondervan, 1996.

Carson, D.A. *The Gospel According to John*. Pillar New Testament Commentary. Grand Rapids: Eerdmans, 1992.

————. *Matthew*. Expositor's Bible Commentary. 2 vols. Grand Rapids: Zondervan, 1984.

Cranfield, C. E. B. *Romans: Critical and Exegetical Commentary*. 2 vols. New York: T & T Clark, 1975, 1979.

Davids, Peter. *1 Peter*. New International Commentary on the New Testament. Grand Rapids: Eerdmans, 1995.

Dunn, James D. G. *Romans*. Word Biblical Commentary. Nashville: Thomas Nelson, 1988.

Earle, Ralph. *Mark: Gospel of Action*. Everyman's Bible Commentary Series. Chicago: Moody, 1987.

Ellingworth, Paul. *The Epistle to the Hebrews*. New International Greek Testament Commentary. Grand Rapids: Eerdmans, 1993.

Fernando, Ajith. *Acts*. NIV Application Commentary. Grand Rapids: Zondervan, 1998.

Garland, David. *Colossians, Philemon*. NIV Application Commentary. Grand Rapids: Zondervan, 1997.

————. *Mark*. NIV Application Commentary. Grand Rapids: Zondervan, 1996.

Glasscock, Lawrence E. *Matthew*. Moody Gospel Commentary. Chicago: Moody, 1997.

Guthrie, Donald. *Galatians*. New Century Bible Commentary. Grand Rapids: Eerdmans, 1989.

Guthrie, George. *Hebrews*. NIV Application Commentary. Grand Rapids: Zondervan, 1998.

Hafemann, Scot. *2 Corinthians*. NIV Application Commentary. Grand Rapids: Zondervan, 2000.

Harrison, Everett F. *Romans*. Expositor's Bible Commentary. Grand Rapids: Zondervan, 1995.

Holmes, Michael. *1 & 2 Thessalonians*. NIV Application Commentary. Grand Rapids: Zondervan, 1998.

Hughes, Philip. *A Commentary on the Epistle to the Hebrews*. Grand Rapids: Eerdmans, 1988.

————. *2 Corinthians*. New International Commentary on the New Testament. Grand Rapids: Eerdmans, 1992.

Hughes, R. Kent. *Ephesians: The Mystery of the Body of Christ*. Preaching the Word. Wheaton: Crossway, 1990.

————. *Mark: Jesus, Servant and Savior*. Preaching the Word. 2 vols. Wheaton: Crossway, 1989.

Johnson, Alan. *Romans*. Everyman's Bible Commentary Series. Chicago: Moody, 2000.

Knight III, George W. *Pastoral Epistles*. New International Greek Testament Commentary. Grand Rapids: Eerdmans, 1992.

Lane, William. *The Gospel of Mark*. New International Commentary on the New Testament. Grand Rapids: Eerdmans, 1993.

Liefeld, Walter. *Ephesians*. IVP New Testament Commentary. Downers Grove, IL: InterVarsity, 1997.

————. *1 & 2 Timothy, Titus*. NIV Application Commentary. Grand Rapids: Zondervan, 1999.

————. *Luke*. Expositor's Bible Commentary. Grand Rapids: Zondervan, 1995.

Longenecker, Richard N. *Acts*. Expositor's Bible Commentary. Grand Rapids: Zondervan, 1996.

MacArthur, John. *Acts*. MacArthur New Testament Commentary. 2 vols. Chicago: Moody, 1994, 1996.

————. *Colossians and Philemon*. MacArthur New Testament Commentary. Chicago: Moody, 1992.

————. *Ephesians*. MacArthur New Testament Commentary. Chicago: Moody, 1986.

————. *First Corinthians*. MacArthur New Testament Commentary. Chicago: Moody, 1984.

————. *First Peter*. MacArthur New Testament Commentary. Chicago: Moody, 2004.

————. *First Timothy*. MacArthur New Testament Commentary. Chicago: Moody, 1995.

————. *Galatians*. MacArthur New Testament Commentary. Chicago: Moody, 1987.

————. *Hebrews*. MacArthur New Testament Commentary. Chicago: Moody, 1984.

————. *James*. MacArthur New Testament Commentary. Chicago: Moody, 1998.

————. *John 1–11*. MacArthur New Testament Commentary. Chicago: Moody, 2006.

————. *Matthew*. MacArthur New Testament Commentary. 4 vols. Chicago: Moody, 1985–89.

————. *Philippians*. MacArthur New Testament Commentary. Chicago: Moody, 2001.

————. *Romans*. MacArthur New Testament Commentary. 2 vols. Chicago: Moody, 1991, 1994.

————. *Second Corinthians*. MacArthur New Testament Commentary. Chicago: Moody, 2003.

————. *2 Peter & Jude*. MacArthur New Testament Commentary. Chicago: Moody, 2005.

————. *Titus*. MacArthur New Testament Commentary. Chicago: Moody, 1996.

Marshall, I. Howard. *Acts*. Tyndale New Testament Commentary. Grand Rapids: Eerdmans, 1980.

————. *The Epistles of John*. New International Commentary on the New Testament. Grand Rapids: Eerdmans, 1995.

————. *Epistle to the Philippians*. Norwich, UK: Epworth, 1997.

————. *1 and 2 Thessalonians*. New Century Bible Commentary. Grand Rapids: Eerdmans, 1983.

————. *1 Peter*. NIV Application Commentary. Grand Rapids: Zondervan, 1996.

————. *The Gospel of Luke*. New International Greek Testament Commentary. Grand Rapids: Eerdmans, 1983.

————. *The Pastoral Epistles: A Critical and Exegetical Commentary*. International Critical Commentary. New York: T & T Clark, 2004.

Martin, Ralph P. *James*. Word Biblical Commentary. Nashville: Thomas Nelson, 1988.

McKnight, Scot. *Galatians*. NIV Application Commentary. Grand Rapids: Zondervan, 1995.

Moo, Douglas J. *The Epistle to the Romans*. New International Commentary on the New Testament. Grand Rapids: Eerdmans, 1996.

————. *Letters of James*. Pillar New Testament Commentary. Grand Rapids: Eerdmans, 2000.

————. *Romans*. NIV Application Commentary. Grand Rapids: Zondervan, 2000.

————. *2 Peter, Jude*. NIV Application Commentary. Grand Rapids: Zondervan, 1996.

Morris, Leon. *1 Corinthians*. Tyndale New Testament Commentary. Grand Rapids: Eerdmans, 1988.

————. *The First and Second Epistle to the Thessalonians*. New International Commentary on the New Testament. Grand Rapids: Eerdmans, 1994.

————. *Galatians*. Downers Grove, IL: InterVarsity, 1996.

————. *The Gospel According to John*. New International Commentary on the New Testament. Rev. ed. Grand Rapids: Eerdmans, 1995.

————. *The Gospel According to St. Luke*. Tyndale New Testament Commentary. Rev. ed. Grand Rapids: Eerdmans, 1988.

————. *Matthew*. Pillar New Testament Commentary. Grand Rapids: Eerdmans, 1992.

Mounce, Robert. *Luke–Acts*. Grand Rapids: Zondervan, 2007.

Murray, John. *Epistle to the Romans*. New International Commentary on the New Testament. Grand Rapids: Eerdmans, 1960.

Nystrom, David. *James*. NIV Application Commentary. Grand Rapids: Zondervan, 1997.

O'Brien, Peter T. *Colossians, Philemon*. Word Biblical Commentary. Nashville: Thomas Nelson, 1987.

Oden, Thomas C. *First and Second Timothy and Titus*. Interpretation: A Bible Commentary for Preaching and Teaching. Lousville: John Knox, 1989.

Radmacher, Earl, Ronald Allen, and H. Wayne House, eds. *Nelson's New Illustrated Bible Commentary*. Nashville: Thomas Nelson, 1999.

Ryrie, Charles. *Acts of the Apostles*. Everyman's Bible Commentary Series. Chicago: Moody, 1961.

————. *First and Second Thessalonians*. Everyman's Bible Commentary Series. Chicago: Moody, 2001.

————. *Revelation*. Everyman's Bible Commentary Series. Chicago: Moody, 1996.

Seiss, J.A. *The Apocalypse*. Grand Rapids: Zondervan, 2000.

Silva, Moisés. *Philippians*. Baker Exegetical Commentary on the New Testament. 2nd ed. Grand Rapids: Baker, 2005.

Snodgrass, Klyne. *Ephesians*. NIV Application Commentary. Grand Rapids: Zondervan, 1996.

Stott, John R.W. *The Letters of John: An Introduction and Commentary*. Tyndale New Testament Commentary. Grand Rapids: Eerdmans, 1988.

Thielman, Frank. *Philippians*. NIV Application Commentary. Grand Rapids: Zondervan, 1995.

Thomas, Robert L. *Revelation*. Wycliffe Exegetical Commentary. 2 vols. Chicago: Moody, 1992, 1995.

Walvoord, John F. *The Revelation of Jesus Christ*. Chicago: Moody, 1995.

Walvoord, John F., and Roy B. Zuck, eds. *The Bible Knowledge Commentary*. 2 vols. Wheaton: Victor, 1983.

Wright, N.T. *The Epistles of Paul to the Colossians and to Philemon: An Introduction and Commentary*. Tyndale New Testament Commentary. Grand Rapids: Eerdmans, 1987.

Articles

Albright, William F. "Toward a More Conservative View." *Christianity Today*, January 18, 1963, 3–5.

Linnemann, Eta. "Is There a Q?" *Biblical Review*, October 1995, 42–43.

Sheler, Jeffrey. "Is the Bible True?" *US News and World Report*, October 25, 1999, 50.

Yamauchi, Edwin. "The Word from Nag Hammadi." *Christianity Today*, January 13, 1978, 19–22.

Notes

Chapter 1 A Christ-Centered Introduction to the Bible

[1] Augustine, *City of God in Nicene and Post-Nicene Fathers*, vol. 2, ed. Philip Schaff (repr., Peabody, MA: Hendrickson, 1999), 326.

Chapter 2 The Gospel Record—History or Mythology?

[1] Frederic Kenyon, *The Bible and Archaeology* (New York: Harper, 1940), 288.

[2] A. T. Robertson estimated that we are in doubt about only one-tenth of 1 percent. See his *Introduction to the Textual Criticism of the New Testament* (Nashville: Broadman, 1925), 22.

[3] Frederic Kenyon, *Our Bible and the Ancient Manuscripts* (London: Eyre and Spottiswoode, 1958), 55 (emphasis added).

[4] If Paul wrote Hebrews, as many believe, then there were only eight New Testament writers.

[5] See Norman L. Geisler and William Nix, *A General Introduction to the Bible*, rev. ed. (Chicago: Moody, 1986), chap. 22.

[6] For the evidence of authorship of the following books see the corresponding chapters on them below.

[7] Josephus, *Antiquities*, 20.9.1.200.

[8] See chapter 6.

[9] William Lane Craig, *The Son Rises* (Eugene, OR: Wipf and Stock, 2001), 101.

[10] Edwin Yamauchi, "The Word from Nag Hammadi," *Christianity Today* 13 (January 1978), 22.

[11] C. S. Lewis, *Christian Reflections* (Grand Rapids: Eerdmans, 1967), 209.

[12] W. F. Albright, "Toward a More Conservative View," *Christianity Today* (January 18, 1963). Many conservative scholars believe that John wrote after this time. See chapters 7 and 26–28.

[13] John A. T. Robinson, *Redating the New Testament* (Eugene, OR: Wipf and Stock, 2000), 352–54.

[14] See Craig Blomberg, *The Historical Reliability of the Gospels* (Downers Grove, IL: InterVarsity, 1987); see also Norman Geisler, *Systematic Theology*, vol. 1 of *Introduction and Bible* (Minneapolis: Bethany, 2002), 479.

[15] See Norman Geisler and Thomas Howe, *When Critics Ask: A Popular Handbook of Bible Difficulties* (Grand Rapids: Baker, 1997), for general principles (chap. 1), and for specific details on how to harmonize difficult passages, see the rest of the book.

[16] For elaboration of these points, see Norman L. Geisler and Frank Turek, *I Don't Have Enough Faith to Be an Atheist* (Wheaton, IL: Crossway, 2004), chap. 11.

[17] A. N. Sherwin-White, *Roman Society and Roman Law in the New Testament* (Oxford: Clarendon Press, 1963), 187, 189.

[18] See Colin Hemer, *The Book of Acts in the Setting of Hellenic History* (Winona Lake, MN: Eisenbrauns, 1990).

[19] Simon Greenleaf, *The Testimony of the Evangelist* (Grand Rapids: Kregel, 1995), 53–54.

[20] Ibid., 46.

21 Nelson Glueck, *Rivers in the Desert* (New York: Farrar, Straus and Cudahy, 1959), 31.

22 Donald J. Wiseman, "Archaeological Confirmation of the Old Testament," in Carl F. H. Henry, *Revelation and the Bible* (Grand Rapids: Baker, 1958), 301–2.

23 Jeffrey Sheler, "Is the Bible True?" *US News and World Report* (October 25, 1999), 52.

24 Of course this does not always mean we have the exact words Jesus spoke (*ipsissima verba*), but we do have an accurate reproduction of their meaning (*ipsissima vox*). After all, Jesus probably spoke in Aramaic and the New Testament is written in Greek. So even in the original, the New Testament authors were translating what Jesus said. Also, a comparison of parallel passages in the Gospels reveals that the words Jesus spoke on the same occasion are not always exactly the same. Sometimes one Gospel gives only part of what he said, and other times the wording is different, though the meaning is the same.

Chapter 3 Introduction to the Gospels

1 See F. F. Bruce, *Jesus and Christian Origins outside the New Testament* (Grand Rapids: Eerdmans, 1974), 193.

2 According to Professor Harold Hoehner in *Chronological Aspects of the Life of Christ* (Grand Rapids: Zondervan, 1977), 115–38, there are exactly 483 lunar years from 444 BC to AD 33. This is calculated as follows: 444 BC to AD 33 is 477 lunar years, but lunar years equal only 360 days a year (12 months of 30 days each). Hence, the 5 extra days for each of the 477 years equal 61 more years. And 477 plus 6 equals 483 years.

3 This information is based on Hoehner, *Chronological Aspects of the Life of Christ*, 143.

4 *Synoptic* means to view with or together (*syn* = with; *optic* = view), and *autoptic* means a view of its own.

5 It is important to note that the overlap in the Synoptic Gospels is only in content, not in word-for-word identity. There is little of that, as I detail below.

6 See Eta Linnemann, *Is There a Synoptic Problem?* (Grand Rapids: Baker, 1992).

7 See Hemer, *Acts in the Setting of Hellenic History*.

Chapter 4 The Gospel of Matthew

1 See appendix 1 for dates and description of the early Church Fathers.

2 The term *Logia*, however, is vague and it is uncertain to what it refers.

3 Eusebius, *Ecclesiastical History*, 6.25.4.

4 William Graham Scroggie, *A Guide to the Gospels* (Grand Rapids: Kregel, 1995), 270.

5 Ibid., 549–51.

6 "How to Respond to Critics" sections are taken largely from Geisler and Howe, *When Critics Ask*.

7 *Greek New Testament* (Stuttgart, Germany: Nestle-Aland/United Bible Societies, 1994).

Chapter 5 The Gospel of Mark

1 See comments on Acts 12:12 in John F. Walvoord and Roy B. Zuck, eds., "Acts" in *The Bible Knowledge Commentary* (Colorado Springs: Victor, 1983), 385.

2 Papias, quoted in Eusebius, *Ecclesiastical History*, trans. Kirsopp Lake; Loeb Classical Library (Cambridge: Harvard University Press, 1926), 3.39.15.

3 Verses 9–14 are not in many of the earliest manuscripts. See discussion in Geisler and Nix, *General Introduction to the Bible*, 486–88.

4 These sections (vv. 9–20) are not in many of the earliest manuscripts of Mark (see note 3 above). Nonetheless, from parallel accounts we know the events recorded are accurate and no truth is lost either way. The debate is strictly an intramural textual one, as to which textual tradition represents the original text of Mark. See below under section titled "How to Respond to Critics."

Chapter 6 The Gospel of Luke

1 See Scroggie, *Guide to the Gospels*, 361.

2 Ibid.

3 Ibid., 277–79.

4 See Adolph Harnack, *Luke the Physician: The Author of the Third Gospel and the Acts of the Apostles* (New York: G. P. Putnam's Sons, 1907).

5 See Sir William Ramsay, *St. Paul: The Traveler and the Roman Citizen* (Grand Rapids: Kregel, 2001), chap. 17.

6 Hemer, *Acts in the Setting of Hellenic History*, 308–35.

7 Luke has 39 Old Testament citations in Acts. This means Luke has 71 total citations. However, if one counts individual verses instead of whole sections, then Luke cites the Old Testament 90 to 100x between his two books.

8 The longer ending of Mark (16:9–20) has the ascension as well (v. 19).

9 See Sir William M. Ramsay, *Was Christ Born in Bethlehem?* (1898; repr., Grand Rapids: Baker, 1989), 46–47, 117–30, 149–73.

10 See Ramsay, *St. Paul*, chap. 17.

11 Sir William Ramsay, *Luke the Physician and Other Stories* (Grand Rapids: Baker, 1979); see also Hemer, *Acts in the Setting of Hellenic History*.

12 John A. Martin, "Luke" in *Bible Knowledge Commentary*, ed. Walvoord and Zuck, 213.

Chapter 7 The Gospel of John

1 See Scroggie, *Guide to the Gospels*, 426.

2 See Ibid., 431–32.

3 This is modified from Sidlow Baxter's suggestion in *Explore the Book* (Grand Rapids: Zondervan, 1987), 5.312.

Chapter 8 The Book of Acts

1 See Ramsay, *Luke the Physician*, chap. 1; and Hemer, *Acts in the Setting of Hellenic History*, 310–12.

2 This same saying of Jesus is also recorded in Matthew 10:10.

3 Ramsay, *Luke the Physician*, 26; Hemer, *Acts in the Setting of Hellenic History*, 312–21.

4 See Hemer, *Acts in the Setting of Hellenic History*, 101–243.

5 This has been documented by Ramsay, *St. Paul*, 1–10.

6 First Timothy and Titus were written between Paul's first and second imprisonment, and 2 Timothy was written during his second imprisonment.

Chapter 9 Introduction to the Epistles

1 Revelation is also a General Epistle written to seven churches in Asia Minor (see Rev. 1:4, 20).

2 In 2 Timothy it is the second use of "in Christ" (1:13) that has the theme, since the first use is in the salutation (v. 1). In Titus the phrase "in Christ" is not used, but the equivalent phrase "in the faith" does occur (1:13).

3 If Galatians is early (AD 48), it would fit in a category of its own (see chapter 13).

Chapter 10 Romans

1 However, the book of Hebrews is for many a close second. Indeed, Hebrews demonstrates the superiority and finality of Christ more than any book in the New Testament.

Chapter 12 2 Corinthians

1 See comments on this in chapter 11.

Chapter 13 Galatians

1 Ramsay, *St. Paul*, 140–41.

2 Ramsay attributes this view to Lightfoot in *St. Paul*, 141; see J. B. Lightfoot, *St. Paul's Epistle to the Galatians* (repr.; Peabody, MA: Hendrickson, 1999), 19–20.

3 It is also possible that Jesus was crucified in AD 29, which would give almost four more years before Paul was saved, but Harold Hoehner in *Chronological Aspects of the Life of Christ* (Grand Rapids: Zondervan, 1977) makes a good case for an AD 33 crucifixion for Jesus.

Chapter 14 Ephesians

1 See chapter 16 for a discussion of this point.

2 See Merrill Tenney, *Gospel of John* (Grand Rapids: Eerdmans, 1957), 148.

Chapter 19 1 Timothy

1 Everett F. Harrison, *Introduction to the New Testament* (Grand Rapids: Eerdmans, 1964), 338.

Chapter 22 Hebrews

1 For further discussion of the various views, see J. M. Pinson, ed., *Four Views on Eternal Security* (Grand Rapids: Zondervan, 2002).

Chapter 23 James

1 Harrison, *Introduction to the New Testament*, 365.

Chapter 24 1 Peter

1 Harrison, *Introduction to the New Testament*, 399.

2 Ibid., 400.

3 Harrison comments that in Clement's letter to the Corinthians "Lightfoot found twelve parallels. Harnack extended the list to twenty. . . . The evidence is hardly conclusive, although Clement's allusion to the blood of Christ as 'precious' is strikingly like Peter's statement in 1:19." Harrison, *Introduction to the New Testament*, 372.

Chapter 25 2 Peter

1 See Harrison, *Introduction to the New Testament*, 399.

2 Ibid., 400.

3 See Donald Guthrie, *New Testament Introduction*, vol. 3 (Downers Grove, IL: InterVarsity, 1990).

Chapter 26 1 John

1 Eusebius, *Church History*, *Life of Constantine the*

Great, and *Oration in Praise of Constantine,* vol. 1, *Nicene and Post-Nicene Fathers,* ed. Phillip Schaff, (repr., Peabody, MA: Hendrickson, 1995), 170.

[2] See Harrison, *Introduction to the New Testament,* 416.

Chapter 27 2 John, 3 John, and Jude

[1] James is called "the Lord's brother" (Gal. 1:19). Mark referred to Jesus's "brothers and His mother" (Mark 3:31). He also spoke of Jesus as "the carpenter, the Son of Mary, and brother of James, Joses, Judas [Jude], and Simon" (Mark 6:3). John refers to "His [Jesus's] brothers" (John 7:5). Since literal brother (not cousin) is the normal meaning of the Greek word *adelphos* ("brother"), and since it is used in direct connection with His mother and other siblings who were her children, then it is most reasonable to take both James and Jude as the half brothers of Jesus, having the same mother (Mary), but not the same father.

Chapter 28 Revelation

[1] Other similarities include: (1) use of *lamb* (in John 1:29, 36, and used 28x in Revelation); (2) tendency to use the name Jesus without the definite article; (3) use of the word *witness* as a verb or noun frequently in both; (4) *true* found 13x in John and 10x in Revelation; (5) *overcome* (John 16:33) used 16x in Revelation; (6) *dwell* or *dwelt* (John 1:14) used 4x in Revelation; (7) *fountain of living water* or its equivalent (Rev. 7:17; 21:6) used 2x in John's Gospel (4:14; 7:38); (8) the prophecy of Zechariah (Zech. 12:10) cited only in John 19:37 and Rev. 1:7); (9) both present the supreme conflict between good and evil; and (10) in both the author has intimate knowledge and concern about the churches in Asia Minor. Harrison, *Introduction to the New Testament,* 441–42.

[2] See Erich Sauer, *The Triumph of the Crucified: A Survey of Historical Revelation in the New Testament,* trans. G. H. Lang (London: Paternoster, 1951), 129.

[3] See Guthrie, *New Testament Introduction,* vol. 2, chap. 7.

[4] For a critique of the allegorical method of interpretation, see Norman Geisler, *Systematic Theology,* vol. 4 (Minneapolis: Bethany, 2005), chap. 13.

[5] Of course, the literal method of interpretation allows for figures of speech (see Geisler, *Systematic Theology,* chap. 13), but they are expressions of a literal truth. For example, Peter used the "keys" Jesus gave him (Matt. 16:16–18) to literally open the way to the gospel to Jews (Acts 2) and Gentiles (Acts 10).

Norman L. Geisler is cofounder and former dean of Southern Evangelical Seminary and one of the world's leading Christian apologists. He has produced nearly seventy books and defended the cause of Christ throughout the United States and abroad for over fifty years. For more information about Dr. Geisler or Southern Evangelical Seminary, visit the websites www.normgeisler.com or www.ses.edu.